Counseling and Mental Health

in the Church

Counseling and Mental Health
in the Church

THE ROLE OF PASTORS AND THE MINISTRY

Kevin Van Lant, Ph.D.

&

Robyn Bettenhausen Geis, Psy.D.

Biola University

cognella®

SAN DIEGO

Bassim Hamadeh, CEO and Publisher
Laura Pasquale, Specialist Acquisitions Editor
Amy Smith, Project Editor
Casey Hands, Associate Production Editor
Emely Villavicencio, Senior Graphic Designer
Sara Schennum, Licensing Associate
Natalie Piccotti, Senior Marketing Manager
Kassie Graves, Vice President of Editorial
Jamie Giganti, Director of Academic Publishing

Cover image: Copyright © 2018 iStockphoto LP/Mihailomilovanovic.

Printed in the United States of America.

ISBN: 978-1-5165-2825-7 (pbk) / 978-1-5165-2826-4 (br)

3970 Sorrento Valley Blvd., Ste. 500, San Diego, CA 92121

Brief Contents

Detailed Contents

2   Depression

Jaclyn Yorkey, LMFT

12   Understanding Psychopharmacology   301

Thomas Okamoto, MD

13   Personality Disorders   329
Robyn Bettenhausen Geis, PsyD

     Learning Objectives   329
     Introduction to Personality Disorders   329
         Screening Test   330
         Hallmarks of Personality Disorders   331
         Causes of Personality Disorders   332
         Personality Disorder Facts   334
         Treatment   334
         Key Terms   335
         Discussion Questions   335
     The *Diagnostic and Statistical Manual, 5th Edition*
         Personality Disorders: Cluster A: The Odd, Bizarre, and
         Eccentric Category, Which Includes Paranoid, Schizoid,
         and Schizotypal Personality Disorders   335
         Paranoid Personality Disorder   336
         Schizoid Personality Disorder   337
         Schizotypal Personality Disorder   339
         Key Terms   340
         Discussion Questions   341
     The Diagnostic and Statistical Manual of Mental Disorders, 5th
         Edition Personality Disorders: Cluster B: Dramatic, Emotional,
         and Overly Unpredictable Behavior, Which Includes Antisocial,
         Borderline, Histrionic, and Narcissistic Personality Disorders   341
         Antisocial Personality Disorder   341
         Borderline Personality Disorder   343
         Histrionic Personality Disorder   345
         Narcissistic Personality Disorder   346
         Key Terms   347
         Discussion Questions   348
     The Diagnostic and Statistical Manual of Mental Disorders,
         5th Edition Personality Disorders: Cluster C: "Anxious
         and Fearful," Which Include Avoidant, Dependent, and
         Obsessive-Compulsive Personality Disorders   349
         Avoidant Personality Disorder   349
         Dependent Personality Disorder   350
         Obsessive-Compulsive Personality Disorder   352
         Key Terms   353
         Discussion Questions   353
     Reviewing the Concepts   354
         Learning Objectives   354
         Chapter Review Questions   355
     Resources   358
     References   359

Preface

THE RATIONALE BEHIND this textbook was born out of a tragic reality: The population of America, and much of the world, is suffering from a mental health crisis. At the time of this writing, the United States and many other high-income nations have seen a multi-year decrease in average life expectancy due in large part to deaths of despair: suicide, drug overdose, and alcoholism. Many of these deaths are invariably linked to significant national increases in the rates of clinical depression and anxiety. As one would imagine, the church has not been immune to this crisis, leaving many ministry leaders confused and overwhelmed by the mental health needs of their congregations and the shortage of adequate resources for those serving in ministry. This reality takes on even more importance when one considers the fact that the majority of church attenders seek guidance and counsel from a pastor prior to seeking help from a mental health professional. This places considerable weight on ministry leaders to have a basic understanding of common mental health issues, the typical approach to treating such issues, and guidance on how to walk alongside someone who is suffering from a mental health concern.

The inspiration for this book comes from a recognition that there are few academic resources addressing the broad scope of congregant mental health for those training to enter the ministry in all its permutations. Although those in professional or lay ministry are often expected to counsel or triage those in their care who may be suffering with some type of mental health concern, few receive adequate training or resources to attend to this population meaningfully. This text attempts to bridge the knowledge gap between foundational mental health constructs and their application to practical ministry by providing pragmatic and vital information to those serving in both pastoral ministry and various types of parachurch environments. Our goal is to provide significant, yet concise, depth on a number of critical topics to equip pastoral leaders to provide insightful, practical care within their scope of ministry.

Each chapter is written by a mental health professional who possesses advanced expertise and training relevant to the chapter content. In addition, each author is a seasoned Christian practitioner and has spent years working with Christian patients and training those who work in professional ministry. A number of the authors have also served in pastoral or professional ministry prior to transitioning to careers in mental health and medicine. This diversity of experience and training is instrumental in bringing appropriate depth and accessibility to each chapter. Realistic case studies are used throughout the text to make the content practical and accessible to non-psychologically trained readers.

An "applied narrative" structure is used throughout this text giving readers the opportunity to explore how a specific form of psychopathology may manifest, how one should respond to that form of psychopathology, known etiologies and treatments, and potential resources that may be available to a parishioner suffering with that type of mental health issue. In addition, a significant chapter distilling down the complexity of psychopharmacology and its role in treatment is necessary and unusual both for its concise treatment of the topic and in addressing psychotropic medication in a manner that is sensitive to the unique concerns of Christian patients. Each chapter contains true/false, multiple choice, and essay questions for student review and classroom discussion. In addition, classroom exercises are provided within each chapter to facilitate better learning and increase the retention of content. Each chapter also contains additional resources to provide practical support for those in professional and lay ministry, as well as video and Internet links to broaden readers' knowledge base.

And, finally, this text concludes with a chapter on pastoral health, responding to the emotional demands of ministry. Professional and lay ministries are emotionally demanding endeavors that are often fraught with compassion fatigue, isolation, vicarious trauma, and burnout. It is our hope that the concluding chapter will encourage, empower, and reorient those in ministry to pursue spiritual and emotional health in a biblically and psychologically sound manner that will invigorate both their hearts and their ministries.

Acknowledgments

I (KEVIN) WOULD like to acknowledge the invaluable contribution and expertise of each contributing author as well as their willingness to share the depth of their hard-earned knowledge with current and future ministry leaders. Their enthusiastic support for this project was evident from its inception, and it could not have happened without them. I would also like to thank the leadership of the Center for Individual and Family Therapy for supporting this project with prayer, wisdom, and ongoing encouragement. In addition, I wish to express my heartfelt gratitude for what I have learned from my students and patients over the past 25 years. They have taught me much and deepened my heart and soul in innumerable ways. I would also like to thank my wonderful wife, Kimberly, for her steadfast love and support as I stole many days and hours away to see this project through to completion—you are my rock. Lastly, I wish to express gratitude to Laura Pasquale and the wonderful staff at Cognella for enthusiastically supporting this project from concept to completion.

I (Robyn) would first of all like to thank Dr. Kevin Van Lant for sharing his vision and giving me the opportunity to partner with him on this meaningful project. Working with all the contributors for this book has been a privilege and blessing. Learning from colleagues and my clients over the years is one of my greatest joys. The Center for Individual and Family Therapy is a unique place to be inspired, to grow professionally and to learn to identify where God is working in people's lives. I am very thankful for all the people there who contribute to that environment. Lastly, thanks to my husband, Brian, and my children Macey, Owenn, and Ellis for loving, supporting, and encouraging me in my endeavors.

CHAPTER 1

Working with Mental Health Issues from a Christian Perspective

Kevin Van Lant, PhD and Robyn Bettenhausen Geis, PsyD

LEARNING OBJECTIVES

Upon completion of this chapter, readers will be able to

1. describe the foundational aspects of being a good listener;

2. articulate a biblically constructed view of attachment;

3. conceptualize ministry to those suffering with mental health issues as a fundamental care ministry within the church; and

4. define a spiritually integrated approach to care.

"The purposes of a person's heart are deep waters,
but one who has insight draws them out."
—Proverbs 20:5 (New International Version [NIV])

THE CONCEPTS PRESENTED in this chapter are a brief overview to prepare the reader conceptually to explore the mental health topics covered in the following chapters. We begin by describing the status of mental health and treatment in the United States and the church's capacity to care for parishioners who may struggle with mental health issues better. Next, we address how people develop attachments to significant figures in their lives and what potential problems one may encounter from congregants who had poor early relational experiences. Following that, we discuss the skill of listening and how developing this ability is key to pastoral ministry. Last, we explore an integrated perspective on Christianity, pastoral counseling, and psychotherapy. The reader will notice that each of these ideas are addressed throughout the text. Although the topics discussed in this chapter are quite complex in their own rite, the brief presentation in this chapter is primarily meant to provide a framework with which to understand the scope of the information that follows better.

FIGURE 1.1   Considering how Jesus cares for people

THE CASE OF JENNIFER

Many years ago, I (Kevin) received a somewhat urgent call from a local pastor whom I had met only briefly several weeks prior. Pastor Jim asked me if I could meet with one of his parishioners, Jennifer, who had a long-term history of depression and anxiety but also appeared to have a complex history of mental health struggles that he was only remotely aware of. Jennifer's inner struggles had been growing for a number of months, and Pastor Jim felt that she definitely needed a professional referral. Upon meeting with her, it quickly became apparent that Jennifer, an educated professional, wife, and mother of three, was struggling with a long-term history of psychological trauma, depression, dissociation, and suicidal ideation. In fact, it was quite surprising that Jennifer had been able to function at such a high level for so many years. Jennifer reported feeling safe and supported by her church and by her pastor; therefore, she requested that I regularly interact with Pastor Jim regarding her ongoing care. We discussed the nature of confidentiality with regard to her therapy and how it would be necessary for her to sign a release allowing me to speak with her pastor about her care. This was acceptable to Jennifer, and I gave her my assurance that I would share with her whenever I spoke to Pastor Jim as well as the general nature of the conversation.

This arrangement was ultimately very helpful for Jennifer. My interactions with Pastor Jim were always very professional, and he did not probe for deeper or more nuanced information about Jennifer's treatment or process. He typically asked how he could support and pray for her. Pastor Jim continued to meet with Jennifer on occasion for spiritual counseling and discipleship. In due time, our interactions gave Pastor Jim a context with which to understand Jennifer's emotional struggles and to help guide her into a Celebrate Recovery care ministry which became an important source of support through some of the worst parts of her journey. Because of the complexity of Jennifer's presenting problems, as well as her desire for personal growth, her therapy lasted for several years. In the early stage of her treatment, Pastor Jim and I would interact by phone every month or two. The frequency of these conversations slowly decreased as Jennifer's symptoms subsided. During this time, my relationship with Pastor Jim developed into a collegial friendship, which reflected my respect for him as a pastor who cared deeply for his flock. His willingness to participate in Jennifer's mental health journey was a significant factor in her road to recovery and could serve as a model for how ministry leaders can participate in the recovery of their congregants who are receiving psychotherapy.

A CHRISTIAN RESPONSE TO THE GROWING MENTAL HEALTH CRISIS

In 2016, nearly **1 in 5** U.S. adults lived with some form of mental illness (NIMH, 2017). This number represents 44,700,000 people. Younger adults ages 18–25 show the highest incidence rates of mental illness (22.1%), and females appear to struggle with higher rates of mental illness than males (21.7% and 14.5%, respectively). Among those who struggle with any form of mental illness, fewer than half (43.1%) receive treatment (NIMH, 2016). The numbers of those receiving treatment vary greatly by ethnicity and gender, with Caucasians reporting the highest rates of treatment at 48.7% and Asian Americans receiving the lowest (21.6%). Although specific mental illness rates among professing Christians is unknown, one can assume that they are similar to the population at large. We see that mental illness does affect the Christian community through the rate of reported mental illness among pastors. Lifeway Research (2014) reports that 23% of pastors have personally struggled with some form of mental illness, and this is indicative of the reality that no group of people is immune from its impact. Although the pastoral rate of mental illness is higher than the general population, this should generally be expected given the stressful nature of being a member of the clergy (Proeschold-Bell, et al., 2015).

The rate of suicide in America is a particular tragedy. Although suicide is not considered a mental illness per se, it is inextricably linked to a number of psychiatric disorders, such as depression, bipolar disorder, and addiction (Slavich & Auerbach, 2018). **Suicide** is the second leading cause of death among 10- to 34-year-olds, the fourth leading cause of death among 35- to 54-year-olds, and ranked the 10th leading cause of death overall (NIMH, 2018). In addition, overall rates of suicide have increased by 28% from the years 1999 to 2016. Although people of faith at times commit suicide, Protestants and Catholics (as well as those of other religious faiths) have historically demonstrated a lower rate of suicide than the secular community (Wang, Wong, Nyutu, Spears & Nichols 2016). However, there is no evidence to suggest that Christians entertain fewer suicidal ideations or experience less emotional pain related to depressive symptoms (Hall, Webb, & Hirsch, 2018). A deeper discussion on suicide and suicide prevention can be found in Chapter 2 of this text.

The data on mental illness and suicide are significantly affected by substance abuse, which itself is considered a type of mental illness. The NIMH (2014) reports that 20,200,000 American adults have a substance use disorder. In addition, 7,900,000 American adults have both a substance use disorder and another type of mental illness. Having two types of illnesses is also referred to as **comorbidity**, which significantly exacerbates the complexity of treatment for either disorder. Although we know that religious commitment is inversely correlated to the development of substance use disorders (Gmel et al., 2013), it is also abundantly clear that substance use disorders among Christians is significant and needs to be better understood by most clergy (CASA, 2001).

Few congregational concerns will affect the life of a ministry leader more than the issues of mental health. Although none of the mental health issues and diagnoses described in this text are new, they are being experienced and treated in a contemporary manner that is influenced by the expectations of the culture and the growing knowledge and research base available to both mental health professionals and laypersons who interact with those suffering with mental illness. We now have a profound opportunity to minister to those with mental illness in a compassionate manner that reflects the tradition of Christian charity and care, as well as current medical and psychological research.

How Pastors and the Church Can Respond: In the Congregation

Nearly 1 in 5 parishioners attending any given church service in America are struggling with some form of mental illness (NIMH, 2016). It's also quite likely that fewer than half of these individuals are receiving any form of care for their symptoms. In addition, research suggests that many Christians who are suffering from mental health concerns will seek out care from clergy prior to, or instead of, consulting with a mental health professional. It is encouraging to note that nearly 67% of Christians describe their church as supportive relative to their mental health issues (Lifeway Research, 2014). These data suggest that pastors and churches need to be equipped to assess and triage common mental health scenarios, counsel when appropriate, and refer to mental health professionals when needed. This component of church ministry and pastoral care may require significant formal and informal training to equip oneself, church lay leadership, and congregational volunteers for this component of church ministry and pastoral care.

The Unintentional Therapist

Pastoral ministry, particularly in a small- to mid-size church, requires a diverse skill set. Pastors and ministry leaders are frequently expected to preach sermons, run a staff, lead ministries, visit the sick and infirm, manage a budget, and attend to unexpected crises that arise on many days. In addition, pastors are expected to counsel parishioners who are in need, and some are quite likely to be suffering from some type of mental illness. I commonly hear of a pastor counseling an individual or couple for many months or even years—well beyond the typical pastor's level of expertise and training. For these reasons, it is important to define the number of counseling sessions you will facilitate prior to or at the beginning of the first session, lest you become an *unintentional therapist*. Although there are many schools of thought on this topic, I commonly recommend that pastors and lay leaders without professional, clinical training limit the number of counseling sessions to no more than five appointments. A maximum of five counseling sessions will meet the needs of at least 87% of your counselees and minimize your potential of becoming an unintentional therapist or seeing someone with significant mental health concerns that are beyond the scope of your expertise (Benner, 2003). How to facilitate a professional referral will be addressed later in this chapter.

Avoiding Counselor Burnout and Unhealthy Attachments

Adhering to a maximum counseling session limit also minimizes the potential for counselor burnout. Congregational needs are complex, and at any given time, your parishioners may be experiencing a variety of emotional and mental health crises. Maintaining reasonable, yet compassionate, boundaries relative to your time and expertise may limit the potential to develop counselor burnout as well as leave you more margin to care for a broader segment of your church community. Being a wise steward of your time is an important aspect of pastoral longevity and job satisfaction (please see Chapter 15 of this text for a longer treatment of pastoral health). Although the communication of session limits may be an uncomfortable necessity for you, and at times result in resentment among certain parishioners, it is a vital aspect of acknowledging your own counseling limitations and normalizing the need for professional help among a certain percentage of your congregation.

In addition, counselor boundaries and session limits are a necessary prophylactic against unhealthy and even pathological counselee attachments. Unhealthy and chaotic attachments are a defining characteristic of some mental health disorders. Parishioners with these types of disorders are often approached naively by the pastoral counselor with a minimal understanding of the nature or dynamics of their mental illness. This can result in a tremendous amount of frustration or unhealthy emotional vulnerability for the pastor, as well as an unnecessary continuation of destructive relationship patterns for the counselee. Counseling limits are protective for both the counselor and the counselee. Counselors must maintain these limits and boundaries, as they are the individuals who hold the "power" in the counseling relationship. For example, some pastors limit their counseling meetings to somewhere between 3–5 "sessions."

Approaches to Mental Health Ministry

Ministering to the needs of those who are suffering, including those who suffer with mental health issues, has been a part of church ministry since the foundations of the church were laid (II Cor. 1:3–7, Matt. 25:34–40). The biblical and historical conceptualization of Christian charity is to help those in need, and certainly a practical Christian theology would suggest that ministering to those who suffer with mental illness is a form of redemptive Christian care. Unfortunately, the church's 2,000-year history of ministering to the mentally ill has been mixed, ranging from compassion and love to denial and barbarism (Vacek, 2015). To be sure, much of the mistreatment resulted from ignorance, cultural stigma, and unbiblical spiritual attributions. Similar to the culture at large, the church has evolved in its understanding of mental illness and mental health. In fact, historical movements toward compassionate and moral care for the mentally ill have generally been championed by Christian physicians and activists, such as Cotton Mather, Benjamin Rush, Dorthea Dix, and Karl Menninger (Vacek, 2015).

Fortunately, the church in America appears to be experiencing a renewed desire to minister proactively to those in their congregations who suffer with mental illness (Lifeway Research, 2014). Many denominations, churches, pastors, and parachurch leaders are taking a contemporary, yet thoroughly biblical, look at how mental illness is affecting those in their ministries and developing programs to meet some of the needs. Churches such as Saddleback Church in Orange County California (http://hope4mentalhealth.com/), Woodlands Church in Texas (https://www.wc.org/care-prayer/), and Grace Baptist Church in Santa Clarita California (http://www.gracebaptist.org/careresources) are just a few examples of church communities that have invested significant resources to develop effective and sophisticated care ministries that are oriented toward the mental and spiritual health of their congregations. Although programs such as these can require significant financial and human resources, they are also scalable and can be modified to fit the realities of nearly any size church or parachurch organization.

Types of Mental Health Care Ministries

Many types of mental health–oriented care ministries are simply a deliberate integration of a more modern understanding of mental illness and mental health with what the church has historically referred to as pastoral care or care ministry. Clergy, deacons, elders, and lay ministers have responded to the emotional needs of the church body throughout history. This is a beautiful example of God's call to "love one another" (John 13:34). The following care ministries are simply examples of how this integration has been applied in a practical and effective manner.

Celebrate Recovery

Celebrate Recovery is a Christ-centered 12-step-type recovery program oriented toward those who are struggling with various addictions and compulsive behaviors. Celebrate Recovery (https://www.celebraterecovery.com) was founded by Pastor John Baker of Saddleback Church in 1990 and typically includes a time of both teaching and instruction, as well as a small-group support component made up of individuals experiencing similar forms of addiction or emotional distress. Although Celebrate Recovery is typically thought of as a church-based addiction recovery program, the model has been applied to various types of mental health issues, including anxiety, depression, anger management, disordered eating, abuse recovery, etc. Celebrate Recovery can play an important role in people's emotional and spiritual healing, and for many, it is an important adjunctive component of their ongoing work in Alcoholics Anonymous, psychotherapy, and pastoral counseling.

Grief Recovery Ministries

Ministering to those who are grieving is an important, and frequent, part of ministering to a congregation. Pastors are commonly called to care for those who are grieving the loss of a loved one. Typically, however, the grieving individual needs care and follow-up long after the pastor or ministry leader has moved on to more urgent issues. Church-based grief recovery ministries, such as GriefShare, (https://www.griefshare.org) can be an effective way to minister to the emotional and mental health needs of those who are grieving. GriefShare can be a staff or lay-led program that includes a weekly video-based instructional time followed by a small-group discussion. Programs such as these can be vital to the grieving individual and family, are often low in cost, and require very little training or time commitment from pastoral staff.

Divorce Care Ministries

Regardless of fault, the process of going through a divorce is considered the second highest life stressor, ranked just behind the death of a spouse (Lester, Leitner, & Posner, 1983). Divorce can carry a unique set of emotional concerns for Christians in particular who may have been taught a variety of messages about how God feels about divorcing one's spouse. These uniquely Christian perspectives on divorce, accompanied by frequent feelings of guilt, anxiety, depression, and even suicidal feelings, make divorce care ministries a vital ministry to any congregation. Divorce care ministries, such as DivorceCare, (https://www.divorcecare.org) follow a recovery type model that includes readings, instruction, and support group components. Some, such as DivorceCare for Kids (https://www.dc4k.org), provide extended care and support to the entire family system. Given the profoundly disruptive nature of divorce, ministries such as these can provide a safe, constructive, and accepting environment that facilitates healing and growth.

Marriage Mentoring

An approach to decreasing the likelihood of divorce among congregants might begin with a well-developed marriage mentoring ministry. Beyond the church and professional marriage counselors, there are very few institutions or individuals prepared to encourage, support, educate, and walk alongside those who may be struggling in their marital relationship. Marriage mentoring ministries, such as the Center for Marriage and Relationships (http://cmr.biola.edu/resources/mentors/) or Marriage Mentoring (https://www.marriagementoring.com) provide structured, effective content and mentoring relationship models to pastoral or lay ministers in a church ministry context. These programs are typically workbook based and combined with an ongoing mentoring relationship with a mature couple in your congregation. The mentoring couple is not expected to provide all the answers to the mentee couple, but simply to walk alongside and share from what they have learned about marriage and relationships. Marriage mentoring can be a tremendous blessing to young or struggling couples in your church context and indirectly strengthen the marriages of mentoring couples as well.

Short-Term Counseling

There is a broad continuum on how counseling is approached within a church environment. As described earlier in the chapter, formal pastoral counseling should generally be short-term in nature. I typically suggest five sessions or fewer. Pastoral counseling, however, is only one form of church-based counseling. Some churches offer more comprehensive lay counseling ministries, such as a Stephen Ministries type program (https://www.stephenministries.org/default.cfm). Others develop a church-housed professional counseling ministry staffed with licensed therapists. How church or parachurch-based counseling is approached will depend greatly on church resources and counseling philosophy. Resources for consideration will be provided at the end of the chapter.

Alzheimer's Dementia Support

Alzheimer's dementia affects 17% of persons between 75 and 84 years of age, and 32% of those 85 and over (Taylor, Bouldin, & McGuire, 2018). The numbers are rising as populations in industrialized nations begin to age. Family members of those afflicted with various forms of dementia also represent a large and growing number of those effected by this disease. Packaged care ministries oriented toward Alzheimer's support do not appear to exist at the time of this writing. Saddleback Church in Orange County California, for example, hosts an Alzheimer's support group for caregivers and the United Methodist denomination provides an outline of what a "dementia friendly church" might look like (https://www.umcdiscipleship.org/resources/the-dementia-friendly-church). Support ministries for the caregivers of those afflicted with dementia can be a godsend to those whose lives are consumed with the daily needs of those in their care as well as an opportunity to learn about these illnesses and the need for self-care.

The type of mental health ministries listed earlier are not meant to be exhaustive, but to simply highlight the ways in which the church can provide practical forms of care to those who are either struggling with mental health issues or emotionally demanding life situations, or to support those who are providing care. Churches are asked to do a lot of things, and at times, the needs appear endless. However, with varying degrees of pastoral oversight, each of the ministries listed in this section can be led by a lay leader or ministry team. The great benefit of this is clear: ministries that directly attend to practical congregational needs without overstretching a pastoral staff that is already working at its margins.

Knowing When and How to Refer to Mental Health Professionals

This text will expose you to a broad range of mental health issues that are generally treated by professional clinicians, such as psychiatrists, psychologists, marriage and family therapists, and social workers. Knowing when a parishioner needs professional help is a crucial part of your work. Knowing who to send a parishioner to for help can be a daunting task and one that you will rarely be prepared for when first entering church or parachurch ministry.

When Should a Pastor or Clergy Member Refer to a Mental Health Professional?

After determining that the individual's needs cannot be met through one of your care ministries, the possibility of referral should be considered. The potential for referral can be part of a broader conversation about the limit of the number of pastoral counseling sessions you will facilitate as well as any other limitations you may place on counseling (e.g., same gender counseling, conflicts of interest, lack of time). The necessity of a professional referral should be discussed when

- significant clinical symptoms become evident;
- thoughts of self-harm are shared;
- your involvement becomes emotionally inappropriate, and you are no longer able to remain objective;

- you clearly know that you are beyond your level of competency;
- you're reaching your session limit and have begun to feel "tapped out";
- your instinct tells you that something "more" is taking place or you feel uneasy, but you can't articulate what or why; or
- the Lord's Spirit is encouraging you to refer this person for professional help.

Making a referral can be difficult and sometimes experienced by the parishioner as a form of rejection. The potential to feel rejected can be moderated by referencing the conversation from the first session and having a willingness to shepherd the person through the therapeutic or psychiatric process when appropriate.

What Types of Professionals' Work With Those Suffering With Mental Health Issues

In most states, professionals who work with those suffering from mental illness are required to be licensed in a specific area of mental health treatment. **Psychiatrists** are medical doctors who specialize in the diagnosis, treatment, and prevention of mental disorders. Psychiatrists often choose not to offer psychotherapy but rather refer psychotherapy clients to other providers. Psychiatrists commonly treat symptoms of mental illness through medical treatments, such as psychopharmacological intervention, neuromodulation procedures, and interventions involving overall medical health. Psychologists have typically received a doctorate in psychology and specialize in the assessment and psychotherapeutic treatment of mental illness, and often have research interests in specific areas of mental health and mental illness. Psychologists commonly facilitate marriage and family therapy as well. Marriage and family therapists and licensed clinical social workers are master's level clinicians who provide mental health treatment ranging from psychotherapy and marriage counseling to providing assistance and access to available social resources for those who are mentally ill or underserved.

Must the Referred Individual Be a Christian?

Nuances of one's faith experience are often better understood by someone who shares that same faith tradition. That being said, many practitioners are trained to respect diverse faiths. Also, competency must be the primary consideration, even more so than a shared faith tradition, when the seriousness of the clinical situation requires such a choice (e.g., eating disorders, addiction, trauma work). When a competent Christian therapist is not available, treatment is better than no treatment. Therapists are ethically bound to be respectful of the faith traditions of their patients and, in my experience, I have found that most therapists are quite respectful of the patient's faith, seeing it as a resource to the patient rather than a hindrance. In addition, the lack of resources and insurance restrictions may make a referral to a Christian therapist quite difficult. In these situations, it will be immensely valuable to have you as their pastor continue to walk alongside to help them assess their experience with the therapist or psychiatrist, particularly when they are older adults or younger people without family support and guidance.

What Is the Pastor's Role After a Referral?

The pastoral counselor's role changes once a referral to a professional takes place. The pastor's involvement might change to being more of spiritual guide, offering support and wisdom while attempting to honor the clinical process that is developing. In addition, the parishioner now **holds the privilege** of confidentiality and must sign a release to allow the therapist to speak with you about his or her care. For various reasons, patients are often reluctant to sign broad releases of confidentiality—even when they trust the good intentions of the pastor. In these circumstances, it is typically best to honor their boundaries and simply come alongside in whatever way feels appropriate. Lastly, the clinical process can be confusing and at times may even exacerbate some types of symptomatology. This is something that you may attempt to normalize with your parishioner while also monitoring his or her emotional experiences. When something is out of the ordinary, your observations may be helpful to the clinician. With the parishioner's permission, it may be beneficial to contact the therapist to share your observations. Remember, however, that without a signed release, the therapist will not be able to share anything in return.

KEY TERMS

One in 5: the number of U.S. adults who live with some form of mental illness

Suicide: the 10th leading cause of death in the United States

Celebrate Recovery: a Christ-centered, 12 step–type recovery program oriented toward those who are struggling with various addictions and compulsive behaviors

Comorbidity: having two types of co-occurring illnesses

Psychiatrist: medical doctor who specializes in the treatment of mental illness

Privilege: legal term meaning that patient or client communication with his or her therapist cannot be disclosed without expressed permission

Discussion Questions

1   What are three types of mental health ministries that can be implemented in nearly any church?

2   How might a pastor avoid becoming an "unintentional therapist"?

3   List seven guidelines for knowing when to consider a professional referral for a counselee.

4   How might a pastor or ministry leader develop a mental health referral network?

HOW PEOPLE ATTACH TO OTHERS

Now that you have a broad understanding of how the church at large is affected by mental health issues and how to respond, we turn our attention to the specifics of individual relationships. In the next two sections, we will discuss how to better understand the congregant(s) you are trying to help by exploring their internal paradigms. A pastor need not become an expert theorist to better identify how attachments occur in their own work within the church family.

Overview of Attachment Theory

Being familiar with a person's attachment style is important because there are many different ways people can experience relationships. **Attachment theory** focuses on the quality of the bond between a child and their primary caregiver, and how that relationship affects interactions with others into adulthood (Mooney, 2010). Although its beginnings go back to the late 1940s, attachment theory has stimulated much research and is one of the more popular and intensely researched areas of study in the field of psychology today. Attachment theory is helpful because it provides us with some clues into people's internal experiences. This awareness significantly facilitates our ability to help others with intra- and interpersonal issues.

There was a time when leading psychologists did not emphasize the quality of the parent-child relationship. For example, in the1920s, Freud focused more on a person's internal drive to determine what motivates a person (De Lauretis, 2008). Later, some significant pioneers, such as John Bowlby and Mary Ainsworth, did see value in observing the interactions between primary caregivers and their children. They discovered the significance of parenting and its effects on children's ability to develop future healthy relationships. Attachment theory was first developed when Bowlby and Ainsworth observed the "aspect of the relationship between a child and caregiver that is involved with making the child safe, secure and protected" (Benoit, 2004).

It is of great benefit to understand a person's attachment style in order to effectively help them. Successful interventions are dependent on determining how well an individual is able to connect with and be understood by others. This capacity informs us as to what they need and how to help.

In the 1940s, John Bowlby began taking an interest in studying childhood development and the family patterns that promoted future healthy or unhealthy relationships. His curiosity was raised after seeing some of the damaging effects of the war on children who were either separated from parents and/or institutionalized. His studies began to put the spotlight on the importance of early parent-child interactions (Mooney, 2010). Bowlby's work inspired Mary Ainsworth to join him in his research and to create the famous "strange situation" (Crittendon, 2017). This lab experiment included a room with toys, a stranger, and a parent-child dyad. The purpose was to observe the child's reactions in a number of scenarios, which included having the stranger enter the room, leaving the stranger alone with the child, and, finally, having the caregiver reenter the room. After analyzing the variety of observations in the children, the experimenters proposed that people experience one or more of three attachment styles: secure, anxious, and/or avoidant/ambivalent (Mooney, 2010). Later, Mary Main's research with the Adult Attachment Interview discovered a fourth attachment experience: disorganized (Steele & Steele, 2008).

Secure Attachment

We begin with **secure attachment**. People typically experience a secure attachment when they receive "good enough" parenting so that when they experience distress, they are able to self-soothe. Since there are no perfect parents, this means the parents were emotionally attentive and available *enough* to meet the physical and relational needs of their child. Ainsworth says that with secure attachment, we develop an affectional bond, which is "a relatively enduring tie in which the partner is important as a unique individual and is interchangeable with none other" (Ainsworth, 1989). She states that this positive primary experience has an effect on the entire life span.

Case Example of a Secure Attachment

Both of Adrian's parents worked hard to provide for their family. After Adrian was born, her mother had to go back to work within three months to help pay the bills. She was left with her aunt, who provided her childcare along with her two cousins. Her aunt was attentive to all the children's needs and was able to console Adrian when she was dropped off in the morning and cried for her parents. When Adrian's parents returned at the end of the workday, they took great joy in the reunion with their daughter. They made sure the time they did get with Adrian was focused and purposeful. Sometimes mom would be fatigued from work and get grumpy or yell. She usually noticed Adrian's sad or scared response and would help her identify her feelings. Her mom would then apologize, comfort, and repair with Adrian.

Anxious attachment

Anxious attachment happens when an individual experiences some good connection with his or her caretaker; however, the positive interactions are too inconsistent to be reliable for the child. This creates anxiety in a person because he or she cannot be sure when his or her needs will next be met. This type of parent often experiences his or her own anxiety as well, which limits the parent's ability to calm or soothe his or her child consistently (Ainsworth, 1989).

Case Example of Anxious Attachment

Brianne's father had always been high-strung. It was very important for her dad to always feel some sense of control most of the day. For example, when Brianne sat at the table for family meals there were a lot of rules regarding cleanliness and order of eating. If anyone failed to follow these expectations, her dad would get very nervous and angry. If Brianna was upset about anything, she did not feel comfortable talking with her father because she knew even little things made him anxious, and it was not worth bothering him.

Avoidant/Detached Attachment

The **avoidant/detached attachment** style results when the primary caretaker has a more detached relational pattern and does not emotionally connect with his or her child. This means the parent was mostly emotionally unavailable (Ainsworth, 1989). Unfortunately, because of the parent's neglect, the child learns to also ignore his or her own emotional needs. The pain of not being known or seen causes the child to cut off feelings so as to not feel hurt. This parent is likely very disconnected from his or her own emotions, which usually leads to not being able to teach the child how to identify and respond to needs. Ainsworth described observing this as "some infants who were clearly insecure at home ... were apparently indifferent to their mothers' departure in the strange situation and avoided them upon reunion" (Ainsworth & Bowlby, 1991).

Case Example of Avoidant/Detached Attachment

Clark's home could be described as very sterile. There was nothing extra, like decorations, that did not need to be there. This created a cold and uncomfortable atmosphere in the house that was noticeable to anyone who visited. This minimalist environment was also a reflection his mother's personality. She was a no-nonsense type of person who did not show much emotion. It never would have occurred to Clark that some mothers hug and kiss their children until one day he visited a friend's house. He observed his friend's mother physically affirming and demonstrating kindness to her children.

Disorganized Attachment

Lastly, there is the **disorganized attachment** style. This occurs when a parent demonstrates both anxiousness and avoidance, and may also be abusive in some form, thus leaving the child almost no choice but to emotionally shut down (Reisz, Duschinsky, & Siegel, 2017). The emotional connection from the parent is either nonexistent, or if it is present, it may even be experienced as startling, feeling incongruent to the situation, or an overreaction to the need. The disorganized parenting style often leads to **dissociative** experiences. This is when a person shuts off emotionally and sometimes does not feel physically present to avoid being overwhelmed. One study by Bohlin, Eninger, Brocki, and Thorell demonstrated that an individual with a disorganized attachment style could be predicted to be callous and unemotional in his or her relational patterns (2012). As you may conclude, this is the most difficult type of attachment experience to have and to work through.

Case Example of Disorganized Attachment

Denzel was so embarrassed of his mother. The doctor's diagnosed his mom with schizophrenia, but she usually was very belligerent and would not take her medication. His dad had no control over her behavior, and he seemed to work a lot to avoid dealing with her. There were very brief moments of normalcy, like when his mom made him an occasional breakfast. Most of the time, she seemed angry, hated being around people, and would yell at imaginary enemies. Denzel had no one to turn to for help or comfort.

(If you are curious about what attachment style you might have, please visit the following website, which offers a brief screening test: https://dianepooleheller.com/attachment-test/.)

Knowing a parishioner's attachment style can assist us in choosing the right resources for the person seeking help. Sometimes what looks reasonably good might not be the best recommendation based on a person's attachment experience. We can actually facilitate doing more damage when we do not understand a person's relational background. For example, two people may come to your office, both presenting with depressed symptoms. Very anxious parents may have raised the first person. This person might need support in learning how to self-regulate to decrease his or her anxiety before he or she can go to any kind of support group. Being around others may seem like an obviously good thing to do, but in this case, it could cause this individual more sadness by being reminded that he or she feels too anxious to connect with others. Avoidant parents may have raised the second person. In that case, this person may need to be encouraged to attend a group in spite of his or her shy presentation. Without having more contact with others, it could contribute to more loneliness and depression. We want to avoid creating more discouragement by being aware of their attachment style and planning accordingly.

The Neurobiology of Attachment

Being familiar with attachment theory is important because of its relationship to brain development. Neuropsychological research is demonstrating that our early bonding experiences actually have an effect on the neurons in our brain and our subsequent relationship quality (Schore & Schore, 2008). Infancy is a crucial time for brain development. It is vital that babies and their parents are supported during this time to promote attachment. Without a good initial bond, children are less likely to grow up to become happy, independent, and resilient adults (Winston & Chicot, 2016). Schore and Schore further state, "We understand any individual's personal trajectory of emotional growth, including the development of his/her unconscious, to be facilitated or inhibited by the context of his/her family and culture" (2008, p. 1).

Here are the neuropsychological basics of how our brain works in relationships. Generally speaking, there are two main areas of our brain, the amygdala and prefrontal cortex (see Figure 1.2). Both of these areas are involved in our experiences of others. The amygdala is known to be the center of emotion and emotional memory. It is the first part to receive information from the external world and first to react before the information travels to the rest of the brain. When we experience a strong emotional reaction to any stimulus, this part of our brain is activated. The second brain area involved in nearly all aspects of relationships is the prefrontal cortex. This section is defined as the logical, practical, and problem-solving part of our brain. When we are trying to determine how to respond to stress, this is the part of our brain we want activated (Ghashghaei, Hilgetag, & Barbas, 2007).

The prefrontal cortex and amygdala are meant to cooperate with each other through strong neural networking and communication. God gave us each of these parts for a purpose. One is to detect danger, and the other is to identify as well as respond to our needs. Unfortunately, along with other complex factors, poor attachment experiences have been linked to inadequate neural networking between these two parts of the brain (Arden & Linford, 2009). On the one hand, this means that some people may experience strong feeling reactions to a stimulus and significantly struggle to regulate or relax themselves emotionally. Even if they wanted to calm themselves, they are at a disadvantage to

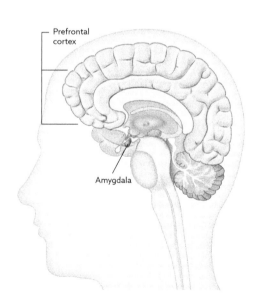

Prefrontal cortex

Amygdala

FIGURE 1.2 **Amygdala and Prefrontal Cortex**

make that happen. This lack of communication in the brain between emotional reactions and problem-solving capacities may result from poor neural connections, along with other factors, such as temperament and personality (Arden & Linford, 2009). Our brain can feel hijacked by an activated amygdala, and then we feel unable to recover very quickly. This is very painful and frustrating for the person experiencing this. On the other hand, other people may demonstrate a severe disconnection from emotions because of a lack of neural connectedness. This type of person may be activated in the prefrontal cortex and not able to access any emotional content to inform them. The result is this person can get stuck mostly thinking logically and appear to have little or no feelings (Ghashghaei et al., 2007). Trying to be in a relationship with someone who cannot emotionally connect with others can also cause significant distress. An individual's inability to access feelings creates a situation where it is difficult to identify emotional or relational needs in oneself. Both of these predicaments can be painful to experience and may lead to a problematic relationship history and/or poor coping symptoms, such as addictions.

Fortunately, there is some good news when it comes to repairing poor neural connections. God does provide a way out, and we are not determined by our pasts (1 Cor. 10:13). We already learned that there are three possible problematic attachment experiences. Research also demonstrates that we can actually strengthen our neural connections to create more secure attachment paradigms.

This is where we really see God's general grace on all mankind. In other words, when people choose to make sense of their histories by bringing the truth to the light, this frees them up to create new connected neural structures. All people have a choice to look at their pain, engage in grieving, and receive from others what might be missing (Siegel, 2007). It is encouraging to see how a pastor can listen patiently and be empathic with peoples' experiences, and, therefore, change parishioner's paradigms of themselves for the better.

KEY TERMS

Attachment theory: the study of the quality of the bond in childhood between a person and his or her primary caregiver and how that relationship affects a person's interactions with others into adulthood

Secure attachment: when an individual received "good enough" parenting so that when he or she experiences distress, he or she is able to self-soothe

Anxious attachment: when an individual does experience a good connection with the caretaker, but it is too inconsistent, therefore creating anxiety in the child

regarding when his or her needs will next be met

Avoidant attachment: the parent was mostly emotionally unavailable; therefore, the child learned to ignore his or her own emotional needs

Disorganized attachment: results when a parent demonstrates both anxiousness and avoidance, and may also be abusive in some form, leaving the child almost no choice but to emotionally shut down

Dissociation: when a person shuts off emotionally and does not feel present relationally

Discussion Questions

1   Name the four attachment styles and provide a definition for each.

2   Pick one of the attachment styles and write an example of how that style may affect a person in adulthood.

3   Describe the two main parts of the brain used and their functions when it comes to relating to oneself and others.

4   Either think of a time when someone came to you for help or make up an example of a problem, identify the attachment style, and, finally, explain how you would direct that person to help.

HOW TO BE A GOOD LISTENER

"Understand this, my dear brothers and sisters: You must all be quick to listen, slow to speak, and slow to get angry."
—James 1:19

Listening to understand another's experience is a complex task requiring concentration, selflessness, and skill. Listening to understand someone who is emotionally distressed or perhaps experiencing some form of mental illness requires an even greater degree of patience and skill. The Bible teaches us that listening is important (e.g., Prov. 18:13, Prov. 19:27). All too often, however, we find ourselves talking and lecturing when we should be listening and paying attention to nonverbal cues. The following concepts are fundamental components of being a good listener, and although basic in nature, they will assist you in better understanding the internal experiences of you parishioners and to triage more complex mental health issues.

Active Listening

Although the phrase **active listening** has taken on various interpretations, Topornycky and Golparian (2016) describe five key techniques of active listening that are generally agreed upon by most disciplines: 1) paying attention, 2) showing that you are listening, 3) providing feedback, 4) deferring judgment, and 5) responding appropriately.

- *Paying attention*—accomplished through good eye contact, attention to body language, and active dismissal of distracting thoughts
- *Showing that you are listening*—accomplished through facial expression, including smiling and nodding and nondistracting verbal expressions (e.g., uh-huh, I see, yes)
- *Providing feedback*—accomplished through summarizing, asking clarifying questions, and reflection
- *Deferring judgment*—accomplished by delaying competing perspectives, noninterruption, and grace

- *Responding appropriately*—accomplished by remembering your role in the congregant's life and speaking the truth in love but with requisite humility that reflects our limited perspectives and biases

Active listening can be a powerful antidote to feelings of isolation and pain—feelings that many counselees may present with. These are skills that must be practiced, however, and can feel very unnatural when first being implemented. Fortunately, these skills can be practiced in nearly any conversation and do not have to be limited to pastoral counseling or other formal listening contexts. Ongoing practice of active listening skills will typically result in a more natural and meaningful flow to a conversation with a greater potential to access deeper and more vulnerable cognitions and emotions.

Sitting With Difficult Emotions

Those who experience mental health struggles nearly always wrestle with difficult and complex emotions (American Psychiatric Association, 2013). Sitting with another's difficult emotions can oftentimes activate complicated feelings within the listener. These emotionally loaded situations can easily become "combustible" and require a high degree of emotional self-awareness within the listener so as to avoid a painful and disheartening conversation with an emotionally vulnerable parishioner. Although this is a complex topic and a thorough treatment is beyond the scope of this text, three listening principles may help you when interacting with someone who is experiencing intense emotions or is evoking intense emotions within you.

First, know thyself. Each of us has a variety of situations that are often linked to our past that evoke intense or little understood emotional reactions. Knowing which situations may dysregulate us, what our typical reaction may be, and what it is linked to in our past may help us re-regulate when these scenarios arise. Assistance from a therapist, spiritual director, or trusted mentor may be an important component in better understanding how and why these situations affect us.

Second, know your limitations. It is very easy to become frustrated with counselees' who seem resistant to your input. Resistance has many facets and often reflects a person's inner anxieties, many of which are subconscious in nature. When confronted with resistance in its various forms, as well as your own counseling limitations, it may be important to simply retreat to the active listening skills listed earlier in the chapter. Moreover, one should attempt to respond empathically and with prayer when appropriate and consider a referral to a professional therapist if needed.

Third, know when to let go of your agenda. Parishioners who are struggling with mental health issues may meet with you for many reasons, some of which you are aware and some which you are not. Oftentimes, the presenting problems are long-standing in nature and not fully understood even by the parishioners themselves. Letting go of your agenda simply means to make space for whatever the parishioner may bring to the appointment and responding nonjudgmentally while inviting God's Spirit into the conversation. The counselor's role at this point is to trust that His Spirit will both convict and guide.

The Role of Empathy

"Be happy with those who are happy, and weep with those who weep."
—Romans 12:15

The definition of **empathy** in the counseling context has evolved significantly over the past several decades. Basic empathy is simply the ability to feel and understand the approximate emotional experience of another (Neukrug, Bayne, Dean-Nganga, & Pusateri, 2013). Moreover, we now know that empathy is both a cognitive and emotional experience, as well as a neurological process whereby neurons appear to become activated in the listener when one empathizes (Lohmar, 2006). This activation of a parallel neural process is referred to as mirroring and appears to be a highly developed capacity in virtually all non-brain-injured humans (Thomson, 2018). Empathy of any type is considered a foundational component of counseling, and in both its most basic and more advanced forms, it appears to affect counseling outcomes significantly and positively (Neukrug et al., 2013).

Basic empathy is very similar to the application of the active listening skills addressed earlier in the chapter, but it is also combined with our internal affective experience that parallels the counselee. Although basic empathy can come quite easily to some, a more advanced form of empathy that is helpful, if not necessary, in a counseling context typically results from seasons of training and practice (Neukrug et al., 2013). The gift of expressed empathy cannot be overstated and is perhaps the foundational healing component of many counseling experiences. No one can take away the emotional pain of another; however, an attuned pastor or counselor can join with those who struggle and "share in their burden" (Gal. 6:2). Having the knowledge that we are not alone in our suffering can be a powerful salve to a broken spirit.

KEY TERMS

Empathy: the ability to feel and understand the approximate emotional experience of another person

Active listening: an active strategy of communication that attempts to engage the speaker fully

Discussion Questions

1. Describe the five components of active listening.

2. List three listening principles that will help you sit with a counselee who is experiencing difficult emotions.

BRIEF, HISTORICAL OVERVIEW OF PSYCHOLOGY'S COMPLICATED RELATIONSHIP WITH CHRISTIANITY

Having explored two of the rich areas of theory and practice developed in the field of psychology (attachment and active listening), this final introductory topic of psychology's complicated relationship with Christianity is important, as it highlights areas of tension and addresses how pastors and therapists might work together toward the common goal of helping to alleviate suffering. It is assumed that any member of the clergy or a Christian professional wants to strive in his or her calling to serve God to the best of his or her ability. This section attempts to offer a historical overview of working toward this mutually shared goal.

It was 1993, and I (Robyn) had just completed several years of school earning a doctorate in psychology from Biola University. One Sunday, I was sitting in my home church, and I was stunned at what I was hearing from my own pastor. He told the congregation that if they were experiencing depression or anxiety or felt God was distant, they only had themselves to blame. He went on to say, in so many words, if they were to seek help from a counselor, instead of God, that meant they had weak faith. I do agree that God *is* the answer to all of mankind's problems; however, my pastor's message made me very sad for the people he was unintentionally shaming in his own congregation. Ironically, the way he was addressing hurt people was not itself biblical. It did not meet them in their time of need, and it did not acknowledge or address their infirmities (depression, for example, is not an attitude—it is an illness).

In his work with the disenfranchised of society, Jesus Himself established **rapport**, a psychological (and biblical) principle of building trust through care, with the woman at the well before He lovingly spoke the truth to her (John 4).

There are two essential questions that must be answered regarding the relationship between psychology and Christianity:

1. Can anything psychological be compatible with the Bible?
2. What is the debate Christian counselors have over the role of scripture within the work of therapy?

The first issue addresses the question of whether there can be such a thing as a Christian therapist. The second addresses the concern of whether the Bible is completely sufficient to inform counseling practices.

Are Christianity and Psychology Compatible?

A few issues give concern to some Christians as to whether psychological principles can be congruent with the biblical perspective. One problem is the idea that Christian therapists who subscribe to secular psychology are promoting **humanism**, a belief that people are basically good and have the capacity to help themselves with the right encouragement. Most of the significant contributors to the field of psychology would be considered humanistic. The second concern is that Christian therapists might subscribe to the psychological emphasis of building an individual's self-image as the primary goal for treatment. Some Christians may wonder if this emphasis on self-esteem is in direct opposition to the scripture that teaches us "all have sinned and fall short of the glory of God" (Rom. 3:23).

It is impossible to speak for the whole Christian therapist community, so I offer my personal response to these concerns. In regard to humanism, God's Word clearly tells us that man is sinful and our only redemption is through Jesus Christ. While keeping this in mind, I further take into consideration the Bible passages that tell us we have a responsibility for what we have been given (Matt. 25:14–30). This means that although our righteousness is like filthy rags (Is. 64:6), we do have a responsibility to find value in and attempt to redeem the life we have been given. We are to discover the direction God has for us and to use our gifts and callings (Eph. 4:11–13). Therefore, it is possible to hold simultaneously that man is seriously depraved and in need of God's redemptive work and that we have a purpose for being here, which is to glorify God by identifying and fulfilling our calling. We are to apply ourselves by recognizing that Jesus gifted each of us with something that we are to share with mankind (Eph. 4:11–13). In addition, Genesis 1:27 tells us that we are made in the image of God. All of these things are what give every person great value! It may be that if you have an opportunity to counsel someone, God is using you to help that person sort through the debris of his or her life to identify that person's value and calling.

This brings us to the second concern that building self-esteem, as opposed to glorifying God, is the primary goal of therapy. Sadly, oftentimes, people do struggle to see their worth in Christ because of the hardships in their lives. The Christian counselor's role should not be to make a person love him or herself above all else, but rather to see him or herself the way God does (Ps. 139:13, Luke 12:7). Pursuing good self-esteem in and of itself is a dead end. We will always be able to find something disappointing in ourselves. Christians know that, among many things, our significance comes from being made in God's image, being loved by Him, being redeemed by Him, and understanding each of us is here for a reason.

Integrationists Versus Biblical Counselors

Generally speaking, there are two main camps of Christian therapists. **Integrationists** are counselors who subscribe to the use of biblical principles as well as secular psychological information. They believe both sources are required to best inform their work. On the other hand, **biblical or nouthetic counselors** argue that scripture alone is sufficient for any type of therapy. While some consider the notion that secular information could be informative, they do not believe it is necessary (Lambert, 2013).

One of my first integration courses, the study of how the disciplines of psychology and theology fit together, was taught by Drs. Bruce Narramore and John Carter. They were among the first Christian psychologists to write and provide thoughtful direction for Christian therapists. A fundamental principle of Christian integrationists is the concept that "all truth is God's truth" (Carter & Narramore, 1979). In other words, while we look to the Bible first. Carter and Narramore argue that there are also valuable extra biblical sources of information that should be considered as long as they are not contradictory to scripture. For example, we learn in scripture that worry is fruitless (Matt. 6:25). However, secular researchers in psychology have provided research-based tools to help people better manage their anxiety, allowing them, perhaps, to experience the love of God in a more profound way. Therefore, although most prominent psychologists who contribute to this field do not hold a biblical worldview, integrationists believe we can learn valuable principles from their research. God's truth stands whether it is recognized by a person or not.

In their book *Integrative Psychotherapy* (2007), integrationists McMinn and Campbell further discuss what it means to believe all truth is God's truth. They agree that general and special revelation both have merits, but they also point out that sometimes one source may be more authoritative, simply because more information is available. For example, there are plenty of scientific findings that contribute to the field of medicine and most would agree that those findings would be more authoritative in treating a disease than the Bible. This would be true simply because the Bible does not offer specific medical advice. While they hold the Bible offers plenty of guidance for relationships, they also hold that many psychotherapists provide invaluable insights used to help treat people (McMinn & Campbell, 2007).

On the other side of the isle, Heath Lambert and David Powlison, both current biblical counselors and authors, suggest that perhaps integrationists have incorrect theological foundations (Heath, 2017). Their work expands on the ideas initially expressed by Jay E. Adams in his book *Competent to Counsel* (1970). He was among the first to question whether any extra biblical sources are necessary to competently help those in need. To be fair, Adams did seem to give some concession to scientific findings.

Lambert has written and taught on this subject, and offers some insight into this position. He would say that integrationists and biblical counselors actually agree on many things such as

- both are conservative;
- both have a genuine heart to help those in pain;
- both do recognize some value in secular psychology and that it is not all correct; and
- both consider spiritual issues as a possible source of problems.

While recognizing these potential areas of agreement, Heath also agrees with Adams's concerns with regard to the integrationists. Heath asks any Christian counselor to consider whether secular psychology's contributions are essential in helping others. Biblical counselors believe that while extra biblical information may be helpful, it is not required. Heath is further concerned that Christian therapists may have an unstable theological foundation when not standing on God's Word alone. Biblical counselors contend that the Bible is completely sufficient for any counselor to use in helping others (Heath, 2017).

A discussion on the integration of psychology and theology is not complete without mentioning a couple of other sources that have had a significant influence on my practice as a Christian psychologist. I was blessed to have a chance to be trained in **spiritual direction/soul care,** which is the practice of a mature Christian helping other believers focus on their relationship with God, while sometimes using various spiritual disciplines (Calhoun, 2005). This helped me become more aware of the fact that God is already at work in people's lives, and we as therapists or pastors are just tuning into where He is inviting them. This understanding can significantly affect how we pray for and approach those we help. Lastly, I have taken classes from people who do **prayer counseling.** This is a method of helping others through prayer. The prayer counselor relies on God the Father, to Jesus and the Holy Spirit to reveal what needs attention in the person's life (Jerome, 1990). Some may also refer to this as a form of spiritual warfare. It appears that prayer counselors understand many of the same concepts that therapists may implement. I believe educating myself in both of these ministries has given me more tools to address the problems people face.

Counseling Techniques as a Complement to Biblical Wisdom

As you prepare to read through the rest of this book and the collective wisdom these Christian therapists offer, I suggest you consider the following thoughts. We are all here for the same purpose—that is, to direct people toward God and what He is doing in their lives. Some of the people we help have open hearts to God and are able and willing to hear from Him directly. They may need help from a caring believer whom the Holy Spirit uses to put the pieces of their lives together with the right scriptures to make sense of what God is saying to them. We also know that other people, like some unbelievers and less mature Christians or someone who has experienced significant trauma, may not be able or willing to talk about God. God deeply cares about them too. The information you will learn in the pages that follow all serves the purpose of trying to meet people where they are, as Jesus did, and responding to them in a way that they can hear. For some, that may mean starting with milk before we introduce them to solid food (1 Cor. 3:2). Our prayer is that you consistently develop your biblical wisdom and prayerfully consider what the Holy Spirit may be teaching you in these pages to develop your calling and to glorify Him.

KEY TERMS

Integration: the study of how the disciplines of psychology and theology complement each other to help people in pain and to glorify God

Humanism: belief that man is basically good and can improve himself in his own strength

Rapport: psychological principle of building trust through care

Integrationists: therapists who purport that the use of biblical principles as well as secular information are both required to best inform their work

Biblical counselors: believe that scripture alone is sufficient for any type of therapy and secular information could be informative but not necessary

Spiritual direction/soul care: the practice of a mature Christian helping other believers focus on their relationship with God and how that relationship relates to the other issues in individuals' lives

Prayer counseling: being guided through healing by someone who relies on Jesus and the Holy Spirit through prayer to reveal what needs attention and how God wants to intervene to help an individual

Discussion Questions

1. What has been your belief about the role of psychology in Christian culture?

2. Have you ever tried to share a Bible verse or scriptural principle with someone who needed help, and they rejected your assistance? Provide a real or imagined example of this and how you would or did respond.

3. Think of someone you know who needs help and then review the attachment styles. Apply your understanding of early bonding and how it would affect your offer of help to this person.

4. Explain the main difference between integrationists and biblical counseling when it comes to biblical revelation. Provide an example of how each would approach the same problem.

REVIEWING THE CONCEPTS

Learning Objectives

- Describe the foundational aspects of being a good listener
  - Capacity to experience empathy with the speaker
  - Use of active listening techniques to maximize listener engagement
  - How to be with a parishioner who is experiencing difficult emotions

- Articulate a biblically constructed view of attachment
  - The four styles of attachment
  - The neurobiology of attachment

- Conceptualize ministry to those suffering with mental health issues as a fundamental care ministry within the church
  - Rates of mental illness, suicide, and addiction in the U.S. population
  - Care ministries that are oriented toward those struggling with emotionally complex issues or who may be mentally ill
  - Know the differences between various types of mental health professionals and when and why to refer
  - Conceptualizing a pastoral role for those who suffer from mental health issues

- Define a spiritually integrated approach to care
  - Differences and similarities in the psychological and Christian views
  - Biblical versus integrationist approaches
  - How psychology complements biblical wisdom

Chapter Review Questions

Level 1: Knowledge (True/False)

1. One in 5 adults live with some form of mental illness.
2. Suicide is the 15th leading cause of death in the United States.
3. Psychiatrists and psychologists have essentially the same training.
4. Celebrate Recovery is a church-based, 12-step-type program for those dealing with addiction and other emotional struggles.
5. Basic empathy is very similar to the application of active listening skills.
6. Intimacy is an attachment style.
7. Disorganized attachment encompasses two of the other attachment types.
8. One's attachment experience is determined for life.
9. Brain development in infancy significantly affects attachment.
10. Integrationists and biblical counselors both consider problems to be possibly primarily spiritual.

Level 2: Comprehension

1. The necessity for a professional referral should be discussed when
   a. significant clinical symptoms become evident
   b. thoughts of self-harm are shared
   c. you clearly know that you are beyond your level of competency
   d. all of the above

2. Which of the following is not a key technique of active listening as described in the text?
   a. Paying attention
   b. Expressing empathy
   c. Providing feedback
   d. Deferring judgment

3. Suicide is the _____ leading cause of death among 35- to 54-year-olds.
   a. 2th
   b. 4th
   c. 6th
   d. 10th

4. To avoid becoming an *unintentional therapist* you should

    a. have a small window installed on your office door

    b. only counsel parishioners of the same gender

    c. limit your counseling sessions to a maximum of five

    d. all of the above

5. Which of the following is not a mental health care ministry described in this text?

    a. Celebrate Recovery

    b. GriefShare

    c. Alcoholics Anonymous

    d. Stephen Ministries

6. Anxious attachment may result when all of the following occur except

    a. there is some good attachment experience

    b. the parent avoids emotional connection

    c. the parent-child interactions are too inconsistent

    d. the parent is often nervous

7. Disorganized attachment is not

    a. anxious

    b. avoidant

    c. abusive

    d. argumentative

8. Dissociation is best defined as

    a. short-term memory loss

    b. long-term memory loss

    c. emotional memory loss

    d. medical memory loss

9. Of the following, who is not known for aligning with an integrationist viewpoint?

    a. Bowlby

    b. Carter

    c. McMinn

    d. Narramore

10. Biblical counselors and integrationists agree on which of the following:

    a. Psychology offers what the Bible cannot answer.

    b. Therapists are more equipped to help those in pain.

    c. There is some value in secular psychology.

    d. Biblical counselors are more equipped to deal with spiritual issues.

Level 3: Application

1. Propose the development of a mental health care ministry at your church. Include a description of the need, potential costs, and necessary training for leaders.

2. Create a PowerPoint presentation that you might use to teach active listening techniques to church staff.

3. Prepare a brief lesson defining the four attachment styles and explain why understanding these might help your staff interact with someone in need.

4. Pick one attachment style and write a vignette of how that person may interact with others and how a pastor can respond to help that individual.

5. If a congregant with a mental health issue approached you regarding your thoughts on pursuing psychological help, write out how you would respond to this person.

ANSWERS

LEVEL 1: KNOWLEDGE

1. T
2. F
3. F
4. T
5. T
6. F
7. T
8. F
9. T
10. T

LEVEL 2: COMPREHENSION

1. d
2. b
3. b
4. c
5. c
6. b
7. d
8. c
9. a
10. c

RESOURCES

Online Resources

- GriefShare—https://www.griefshare.org
- Celebrate Recovery—https://www.celebraterecovery.com
- DivorceCare—https://www.divorcecare.org
- DivorceCare for Kids—https://www.dc4k.org
- Center for Marriage and Relationships—http://cmr.biola.edu/resources/mentors/
- Marriage Mentoring—https://www.marriagementoring.com
- The Dementia Friendly Church—https://www.umcdiscipleship.org/resources/the-dementia-friendly-church
- Hope for Mental Health—http://hope4mentalhealth.com
- Stephen Ministries—http://www.stephenministries.org
- National Alliance on Mental Illness (NAMI)—https://www.nami.org
- National Institute of Mental Health (NIMH)—https://www.nimh.nih.gov/index.shtml
- Attachment style screening test—https://dianepooleheller.com/attachment-test/

Readings

- *Strategic Pastoral Counseling*—David Benner
- *The Lost Art of Listening*—Peter Nichols
- *Skills for Effective Counseling*—Sbanotto, Gingrich, and Gingrich
- *Theories of Attachment: An Introduction to Bowlby, Ainsworth, Gerber, Brazelton, Kennell, and Klaus*—Carol Mooney
- *Integrative Psychotherapy: Toward a Comprehensive Christian Approach*—Mark McMinn and Clark Campbell

Video Resources

- *Neurobiology of the Brain*—https://www.youtube.com/watch?v=vHrmiy4W9C0

CLASSROOM ACTIVITIES

1. Break students into listening triads (listener, speaker, observer) and have them role-play the application of active listening techniques.

2. Have students discuss what it is like for them to sit with a counselee verbalizing difficult emotions.

3. Ask students to sit in small groups to discuss the four attachment styles and share which ones they identify with.

REFERENCES

Adams, J. E. (1970). *Competent to counsel.* Grand Rapids, Michigan: Zondervan.

Ainsworth, M. (1989). Attachments beyond infancy. *American Psychologist, 44*(4), 709–716.

Ainsworth, M., & Bowlby, J. (1991). An ethological approach to personality development. *American Psychologist, 46*(4), 333–341.

American Psychiatric Association (2013). *Diagnostic and statistical manual of mental disorders* (5th ed.). Washington, DC: Author.

Arden, J., & Linford, L. (2009). *Brain based therapy with adults.* Hoboken, NJ: John Wiley & Sons

Benoit, D. (2004). Infant-parent attachment: Definition, types, antecedents, measurement and outcome. *Pediatrics Child Health, 9,* 541–545. NCBI (Accessed July 2, 2018).

Benner, D. G. (2003). *Strategic pastoral counseling: A short-term structured model.* Grand Rapids, MI: Baker Academic.

Bohlin, G., Eninger, L., Brocki, K. C., & Thorell, L. B. (2012). Disorganized attachment and inhibitory capacity: Predicting externalizing problem behaviors. *Journal of Abnormal Child Psychology, 40*(3), 449–458.

Calhoun, A. A. (2005). *Spiritual disciplines handbook: Practices that transform us.* Downers Grove, IL: Intervarsity Press.

Carter, J., & Narramore, B. (1979). The integration of psychology and theology. Grand Rapids, MI: Zondervan.

Crittendon, P. M. (2017). Gifts from Mary Ainsworth and John Bowlby. *Clinical Child Psychology and Psychiatry, 22*(3), 436–442. doi.org/10.1177/1359104517716214

De Lauretis, T. (2008). *Freud's drive: Psychoanalysis, literature and film.* New York, NY: Palgrave MacMillan.

Ghashghaei, H. T., Hilgeag, C. C., & Barbas, H. (2007). Sequence of information processing for emotions based on the anatomic dialogue between prefrontal cortex and amygdala. *Neuroimage, 1:34*(3), 905–923. doi: 10.1016/j.neuroimage.2006.09.046

Gmel, G., Mohler-Kuo, M., Dermota, P., Gaume, J., Bertholet, N., Daeppen, J., & Studer, J. (2013). Religion is good, belief is better: Religion, religiosity, and substance use among young Swiss men. *Substance Use & Misuse, 48*(12), 1085–1098.

Hall, B. B., Webb, J. R., & Hirsch, J. K. (2018). Spirituality and suicidal behavior: The mediating role of self-forgiveness and psychache. *Psychology of Religion and Spirituality.* doi:10.1037/rel0000182

Jerome, S. (1990). *Seek me find me: Clearing the heart debris that separates us from God.* Nashville, TN: Thomas Nelson Publishers.

Lambert, H. (2011). *The biblical counseling movement after Adams.* Wheaton, IL: Crossway.

Lambert, H. (2017, September 30). Biblical counseling versus Christian counseling: What is the difference? Zondervan Academic. Retrieved from https://zondervanacademic.com/blog/biblical-counseling-vs-christian-counseling-whats-the-difference/

Lester, D., Leitner, L. A., & Posner, I. (1983). Recent life events and stress scores: an examination of the Holmes and Rahe scale. *Psychological Reports, 53,* 70. Retrieved from http://search.ebscohost.com/login.aspx?direct=true&db=eue&AN=507507359&site=eds-live

Lifeway Research (2014). Study of acute mental illness and Christian faith: Research report. Lifeway Research. Retrieved from http://lifewayresearch.com/wp-content/uploads/2014/09/Acute-Mental-Illness-and-Christian-Faith-Research-Report-1.pdf

Lohmar, D. (2006). Mirror neurons and the phenomenology of intersubjectivity. *Phenomenology and the cognitive sciences, 5*(1), 5–16.

McMinn, M., & Campbell, C. (2007). *Integrative psychotherapy: Toward a comprehensive Christian approach.* Downers Grove, IL: Intervarsity Press.

Mooney, C. (2010). Theories of attachment: An introduction to Bowlby, Ainsworth, Gerber, Brazelton, Kennell & Klaus. St. Paul, MN: Redleaf Press.

National Center on Addiction and Substance Abuse at Columbia University (2001, November). *So help me God: Substance abuse, religion and spirituality.* Center on Addiction. Retrieved from https://www.centeronaddiction.org/addiction-research/reports/so-help-me-god-substance-abuse-religion-and-spirituality

Neukrug, E. E., Bayne, H., Dean-Nganga, L., & Pusateri, C. (2013). Creative and novel approaches to empathy: A neo-Rogerian perspective. *Journal of Mental Health Counseling, 35*(1), 29–42.

Proeschold-Bell, R. J., Eisenberg, A., Adams, C., Smith, B., Legrand, S., & Wilk, A. (2015). The glory of God is a human being fully alive: Predictors of positive versus negative mental health among clergy. *Journal for the scientific study of religion, 54*(4), 702–721. doi:10.1111/jssr.12234

Reisz, S., Duschinsky, R., & Siegel, D. (2017). Disorganized attachment and defense: Exploring John Bowlby's unpublished reflections. *Attachment and Human Development, 20*(2), 107–134. Retrieved from https://www.ncbi.nlm.nih.gov/pmc/articles/PMC5782852/

Schore, J. R., & Schore, A. N. (2008). Modern attachment theory: The central role of affect regulation in development and treatment. *Clinical Social Work Journal, 36*(1), 9–20. doi: 10.1007/s10615-007-0111-7

Siegel, D. (2008). *The mindful brain.* New York, NY: W.W. Norton & Co. Inc.

Slavich, G. M., & Auerbach, R. P. (2018). Stress and its sequelae: Depression, suicide, inflammation, and physical illness. In American Psychological Association (Ed.). *APA handbook of psychopathology: Psychopathology: Understanding, assessing, and treating adult mental disorders, Vol. 1* (pp. 375–402). Washington, DC: American Psychological Association. doi:10.1037/0000064-016

Steele, H., & Steele, M. (2008). *Clinical applications of the adult attachment interview.* New York, NY: Guilford Press.

Taylor, C. A., Bouldin, E. D., & McGuire, L. C. (2018). Subjective cognitive decline among adults aged ≥45 years—United States, 2015–2016. *MMWR: Morbidity & Mortality Weekly Report, 67*(27), 753–757. doi:10.15585/mmwr.mm6727a1

Topornycky, J., & Golparian, S. (2016). Balancing openness and interpretation in active listening. *Collected Essays on Learning & Teaching, 9,* 175–184.

Thomson, H. (2018). Social monkeys sync their brains. *New Scientist, 238*(3172), 15.

U.S. Department of Health and Human Services, National Institutes of Health, National Institute of Mental Health. (2014). National Institute of Mental Health. Substance use and mental health. Retrieved from https://www.nimh.nih.gov/health/topics/substance-use-and-mental-health/index.shtml#part_152565

U.S. Department of Health and Human Services, National Institutes of Health, National Institute of Mental Health. (2017). National Institute of Mental Health. Mental illness. Retrieved from https://www.nimh.nih.gov/health/statistics/mental-illness.shtml

U.S. Department of Health and Human Services, National Institutes of Health, National Institute of Mental Health. (2018). National Institute of Mental Health. Suicide. Retrieved from https://www.nimh.nih.gov/health/statistics/suicide.shtml

Vacek, H. H. (2015). *Madness: American protestant responses to mental illness.* Waco, TX: Baylor University Press. Retrieved from http://ebookcentral.proquest.com/lib/biola-ebooks/detail.action?docID=2100951

Wang, M., Wong, Y. J., Nyutu, P. N., Spears, A., & Nichols, W. I. (2016). Suicide protective factors in outpatient substance abuse patients: Religious faith and family support. *The International Journal for the Psychology of Religion, 26*(4), 370–381. doi:10.1080/10508619.2016.1174568

Winston, R., & Chicot, R. (2016). The importance of early bonding and the long-term mental health and resilience in children. *London Journal of Primary Care, 8*(1), 12–14. doi: 10.1080/17571472.2015.1133012

IMAGE CREDITS

Depression

Jaclyn Yorkey, LMFT

LEARNING OBJECTIVES

Upon completion of this chapter, readers will be able to

1. explain the different types of depression;

2. have specific insight into crisis assessment and intervention;

3. identify treatment strategies for depression; and

4. understand the need for self-care when caring for depressed people.

*"It's difficult to describe depression to someone who's never been there,
because it's not sadness. I know sadness. Sadness is to cry and to feel.
But it's that cold absence of feeling—that really hollowed out feeling."*
—J.K. Rowling, author of the Harry Potter series

AN INTRODUCTION TO THE NATURE OF DEPRESSION IN ITS MANY FORMS

*"If I can't feel, if I can't move, if I can't think, and I can't care,
then what conceivable point is there in living?"*
—Kay Redfield Jamison

DEPRESSION, IN ITS many forms, is one of the most paralyzing mental disorders affecting the population, with more than 18 million people affected in the United States alone in 2016 (National Institute of Mental Health, 2017a). It has been found that 10% of visits to primary care physicians include prescriptions for **antidepressants** and that in the United States alone, depression is one of the most frequently listed causes of **disability** (Bromley, Kennedy, Miranda, Sherbourne, & Wells, 2016). Depression carries with it many names: major depressive episodes, persistent depressive disorder, bipolar I and II, cyclothymia, seasonal affective disorder (SAD), and postpartum depression.

FIGURE 2.1   **Loneliness in depression**

In its more severe states, the feelings of hopelessness one experiences can lead to **ruminating thoughts of suicide**, extreme isolation, loneliness, and actual attempts to end one's life. Symptoms of depression can fluctuate between **manic states** and low, hopeless states. They can come on strong and then leave after a few weeks' time. Conversely, they can be persistent all throughout someone's life. Depression can be seen in any race, economic standing, gender, or age. Even young children experience symptoms of depression as often as adults; the presentation, however, is different and includes irritable mood. The very nature of depression, in all of its forms, can cause impairment in one's ability to function in the workplace, school setting, and relationships.

Seeking help can be difficult for depressed individuals for many reasons that will be explored later in this chapter. Something of concern is the care and management they may receive when they make an attempt to reach out for help. Research has suggested that physicians tend to overlook the symptoms of depression in half of their patients, properly treating only 9% of depressed patients and only seeing remission occur in 6% of these patients. Furthermore, it was found that 40% of patients stopped antidepressant use within 30 days of starting it, and 30% more patients discontinued taking it by 90 days of starting the medication (Bromley et al., 2016). This research is showing us that the care and management being received for depression isn't effective in the majority of cases.

Depression is a complicated condition to diagnose and treat effectively. It can be difficult to identify because some of the symptoms include problems concentrating and articulating oneself. It is common for symptoms to be underreported or misunderstood. Depressed individuals may seek medical attention to address their symptoms and leave with a prescription that ignores what is really going on internally in response to external stressors. They already feel hopeless but may be willing to give medicine a try if it is the only option that is presented to them. When specific external stressors aren't relieved by antidepressants, they are at risk of abruptly discontinuing them without consulting their prescribing doctor, making medication compliance a common problem.

Depression can look different from one person to the next, contributing to the difficulty of properly identifying it. A man who recently lost his job of 25 years as a prestigious engineer may now struggle to get out of bed. A new mom who has a healthy and seemingly perfect little baby may be overcome with sadness, crying all the time and unable to care for her family. A child may seem moody, irritable, sad, tired, and begin falling behind in school. A pastor who may feel completely overwhelmed may not be able to understand why he feels so down despite lovingly serving in the church. And another person may say he or she feels incredibly lonely, sad without reason, and completely worthless. All of these scenarios illustrate depression.

Considering the percentages of "reported" depression mentioned earlier being at 10%, which is likely an underrepresentation, for every 100 people in a church, 10 will suffer from depression. A larger church of 4,000 would have 400 depressed individuals in it. Depression is so pervasive that pastors can expect to minister to people suffering from it regularly. Pastors may experience symptoms of depression as well. It is no secret that many pastors at times feel overwhelmed by the demands of ministry. Studies that will be presented later in the chapter reveal to us a direct correlation between burnout and subsequent depression.

Several screening tests have been created to help assess depression and corresponding severity, and to bring clarity to different symptoms. Two well-known screenings are the Beck Depression Inventory (BDI) and the Major Depression Inventory (MDI). Both inventories are user friendly, easily accessible online, and simple to score. Looking at the questions from the MDI, it's easy to see how common depressive symptoms can be:

1. Have you felt low in spirits or sad?
2. Have you lost interest in your daily activities?
3. Have you felt lacking in energy and strength?
4. Have you felt less self-confident?
5. Have you had a bad conscience or feelings of guilt?
6. Have you felt that life wasn't worth living?
7. Have you had difficulty concentrating?
8. Have you felt very restless?
9. Have you felt subdued or slowed down?
10. Have you had trouble sleeping at night?
11. Have you suffered from reduced appetite?
12. Have you suffered from increased appetite?

The MDI has a person score on frequency for each of the earlier questions within the last 2 weeks, with options of "all the time," "most of the time," "slightly more than half time," "slightly less than half time," "some of the time" and "at no time" (Psychology Tools, n.d.). These questions not only demonstrate how common symptoms of depression are but also how easily overlooked they can be. Sadness is a universal human emotion that is sometimes dismissed instead of investigated to see how often it is experienced. Fatigue is common in a fast-paced society, another easily overlooked symptom of depression. Trouble sleeping at night might be blamed on having coffee late in the day. Changes in appetite are seldom thought of as being significant. Depression can be hard to see when some of the symptoms seem so common.

It can be challenging to identify symptoms of depression, understand its causes, and meet with someone who is lost in hopelessness. Understanding and recognizing the symptoms of depression will require patience and compassion on the part of the counselor. The goal of this chapter, therefore, is to educate those who minister to depressed individuals on the presentation of different types of depression and provide a set of tools to use in helping them.

KEY TERMS

Depression: a mood disorder characterized by feelings of sadness that impairs daily life

Ruminating thoughts: upsetting or negative thoughts that are thought about repetitively

Antidepressants: pharmaceutical drugs used to relieve symptoms of depression

Suicide: the act of intentionally causing one's own death

Disability: an impairment that affects a person's activities and quality of life

Manic state: a mood state marked by mania/manic episodes

Discussion Questions

1   What are the BDI and MDI used for?

2   List at least five assessment questions from the MDI that you could use in a meeting with someone who you suspect is depressed.

3   In what areas of life would you expect to see impairment in functioning because of depression?

4   How many questions from the MDI can you say you have experienced in life?

MAJOR DEPRESSIVE DISORDER

Symptoms

Major depressive disorder is one of the more well-known types of depression. The *Diagnostic and Statistical Manual of Mental Disorders, 5th edition* (*DSM-5*) defines it as follows:

- Occurring over a 2-week period (or longer) with the tendency for reoccurrence
- Includes feelings of sadness and a general loss of interest or pleasure in activities that were once meaningful in a person's daily life
- The feelings of depression and sadness occur all day, every day during the 2-week period, with a marked decline of interest in several activities
- Additional symptoms can include weight gain or loss because of an increase or decrease in appetite, difficulty sleeping or waking at normal hours, appearing slower than normal to others, fatigue, lethargy, feelings of worthlessness and guilt, clouded thoughts, difficulty concentrating, indecisiveness, and **suicidal ideation** (American Psychiatric Association, 2013)

Case Example

Martha has come to pastoral counseling initially requesting help because she just "hasn't been herself lately." She reports to her pastor that for several weeks she has been feeling sad and hopeless but has no idea why. She can't make sense of it, but reports that life doesn't feel the same. She used to wake up with a sense of joy and great anticipation for the day ahead. She looked forward to her work, walks with a friend at lunchtime, and her bible study meetings.

   Now she struggles to get out of bed, even though she is sleeping more than ever before and states that she just doesn't care about work, seeing friends, or getting outside. She reports that everything seems to take longer to do and wears her out faster. She tells her pastor that she feels "empty" and "hollow" on the inside. She reports eating "maybe" one meal a day. The pastor notices her hair is unusually unkempt and that she looks exhausted. She expresses feeling like something is wrong with her, and she is embarrassed by her behavior.

Case Assessment

One of the key ways to recognize depression is a drastic change in lifestyle. In this vignette, Martha went from being actively engaged in relationships and activities to barely getting out of bed and looking exhausted. It would be tempting to think she just needs rest and had maybe worn herself out recently; however, it is clear that she has lost joy and interest in activities, which is a clear sign of depression being present. At this point, the pastor would want to gather information from Martha and understand what was going on when this shift occurred to rule out trauma, other types of depression, or something that could have caused an adjustment disorder with depressed features.

Suicidality and Self-Harm

This vignette would have taken a drastic and alarming turn if Martha had said to her pastor that she was engaging in **self-harm/cutting behaviors** and had lost all desire to continue living. Common phrases of potential suicidal ideation include "there's no point in living anymore," "death would be a relief," "I just don't want to be here anymore," and "I can't see a way out of my sadness." Any statement made that discusses the idea of dying needs to be approached with sensitivity and should be taken seriously. Oftentimes, people are afraid to ask directly if someone is thinking about hurting him or herself; they worry that this could lead to the idea of committing suicide. However, this is not the case, and it is imperative that the following questions are asked to assess risk of self-harm:

- Are you thinking about hurting yourself or committing suicide?
- Have you tried to commit suicide in the past?
- Do you have a plan for hurting yourself?
- If there is a plan, ask questions about accessibility to the method of choice. For example, if a person says he or she plans to shoot him or herself, you would ask whether he or she has access to a gun and where that gun is currently located.
- Has anyone in your family ever committed suicide?
- Do you regularly drink or do drugs?
- Do you want to go to the hospital?

After asking these assessment questions, consider the **SAD PERSONS** assessment tool and determine the person's risk score. If it turns out that the person is feeling hopeless and helpless but has a low risk score and no plans to harm him or herself, your next step will be to determine appropriate self-care practices and to help develop a plan to alleviate the depressive symptoms (see the interventions section). If the risk is high and there is a plan and set time to execute the plan for suicide, ask the person if he or she is willing and able to go to the hospital for an evaluation (and likely a **5150 hold** for treatment and observation). Another option would be to call a **mobile crisis unit** or 911 if the threat is imminent.

SAD PERSONS Suicide Assessment

S—Sex. Men have a higher likelihood of suicide.

A—Age. Individuals over 65 years of age have an elevated risk.

D—Depression. Clinical depression increases the chance of suicide by 20%.

P—Prior History. Prior attempt may be the best indicator that another attempt will be made.

E—Ethanol Use. Alcohol and drug use increase the risk of suicide.

R—Rational Thinking Loss. Psychosis (hearing voices) increases risk of suicide.

S—Support System Loss. Loss of an important attachment figure by separation or death.

O—Organized Plan. Having a plan to commit suicide increases the risk of suicide.

N—No Significant Other. Lack of support because of loss, isolation, or negligence.

S—Sickness. Terminal illness increases the risk of suicide by 20%.

Scoring system—1 point for each positive answer.
Score/Risk

0–2 Refer to counseling services, person allowed to go home

3–4 Encourage counseling services, follow up closely, evaluate need for hospitalization

5–6 Consider hospitalization voluntarily/involuntarily depending on level of trust that client will return for another meeting

7–8 Hospitalize

(G.A., 1996; G. E. Juhnke, 1994)

KEY TERMS

Major depressive episode: depression that lasts a minimum of 2 weeks characterized by a loss of interest or pleasure in activities and feelings of sadness

Suicidal ideation: ruminating thoughts of death and dying

Self-harm: a nonsuicidal act of purposely harming one's body, most commonly through cutting behaviors

Cutting behaviors: deliberately creating small cuts on the skin of the body

SAD PERSONS: a suicide risk assessment acronym: sex, age, depression, prior attempts, ethanol use, rational thinking loss, support system loss, organized plan, no significant other, sickness

Mobile crisis unit: a mental health service that provides immediate evaluations at the location of a crisis

5150 hold: an involuntary psychiatric hold lasting 72 hours when a person is believed to be a grave danger to him or herself or others

Discussion Questions

1   What would be the hardest symptom of a major depressive episode for you to notice?

2   What fears do you have about meeting with someone who is expressly suicidal?

3   What are the main symptoms of major depressive disorder?

4   What kinds of physiological symptoms would be present with major depressive disorder?

5   Where will you be challenged to remain compassionate in meeting with a depressed individual?

PERSISTENT DEPRESSIVE DISORDER

When a person's symptoms of depression extend for a longer period of time, at least 2 years, he or she is diagnosed with **persistent depressive disorder**. The *DSM-5* tells us that persistent depressive disorder is

- the presence of ongoing depressed mood for more days than not;
- includes changes in appetite, **sleep disturbances**, **lethargy**, a low view of self, difficulty concentrating, **indecisiveness**, and **hopeless** feelings; and
- may include relief from symptoms lasting up to 2 months at a time (American Psychiatric Association, 2013).

Case Example

Mark's mom brought him to meet with his youth pastor. He is 15 years old. His mom shares with the pastor that her son has been "on edge," "sensitive," and irritated by most things recently. She has noticed that he hasn't seemed happy for over a year now and doesn't know why. She brought him to see the pastor now because the last few weeks have been "more intense."

When pressed for more information, she reports that Mark hasn't been eating; he has been lazy and only wanting to sleep, and his grades have dropped from straight As to Cs and Ds, and that he looks exhausted all the time. When asked about his own experience, Mark reports that its true he's been irritable—everything just bugs him these days. He tells the pastor that he is more tired recently, and so he can't concentrate on his studies. He feels down in the dumps but doesn't think it's a big deal because it's "always been this way."

Case Assessment

This vignette highlights for us the key differences between adult and adolescent symptoms of depression. Although they have similarities, two main differences are present here. First, irritability is a common experienced mood in adolescents instead of expressed sadness. Second, length of time required to make a diagnosis is shorter—1 year instead of 2 to qualify. It is normal for parents to initiate the discussion of their experience with the child's fluctuating mood states and struggle to understand them. Oftentimes, as is the case here, children and adolescents are referred to as moody and lazy when in all actuality they are experiencing depression. Two key phrases mentioned by Mark help us to see that he is depressed: he can't concentrate on his studies, and he has felt down in the dumps for a while now. This makes it clear that his depression is ongoing and is likely persistent depressive disorder.

KEY TERMS

Persistent depressive disorder: persistent depression lasting a minimum of 2 years or longer

Hopeless: feeling despair, resigned, or inadequate

Lethargy: low energy and enthusiasm

Sleep disturbances: changes in the sleep-wake cycle characterized by insomnia, excessive sleeping, or difficulty waking during usual time frames

Indecisiveness: an inability to make decisions or settle an issue effectively

Discussion Questions

1   What is the key difference between persistent depressive disorder and major depressive disorder?

2   In what ways will it be difficult for you to hear about child/adolescent depression?

3   What are two main differences in adult and child/adolescent depression?

BIPOLAR I, BIPOLAR II, AND CYCLOTHYMIC DISORDERS

This category represents a unique form of depression known for its fluctuations between classic depressive symptoms and mania. Bipolar disorder is fairly pervasive in society, accounting for approximately 3% prevalence worldwide (Aldinger & Schulze, 2017). The depressive symptoms are the same as those previously mentioned under major depressive disorder. In order to understand the difference between these three types of depression, one must understand mania (**manic episodes** and **hypomanic episodes**).

Manic episodes last at least 1 week and have the following symptomology as outlined in the *DSM-5*:

- Obvious and abnormal fluctuations in mood that present as excessively happy, expansive, or irritable
- High levels of activity or energy fixated on a certain goal
- **Narcissism**
- Decreased sleep or insomnia
- Pressured speech, excessive talking, racing thoughts and multiple new ideas
- Distractibility
- Increased focus on goal-directed activities and greater involvement in reckless, dangerous, or other activities that typically include painful consequences
- Mood disturbance present is typically severe enough to warrant hospitalization in order to protect the person or those around him or her (American Psychiatric Association, 2013)

Hypomanic episodes are similar to manic episodes in symptomology. The *DSM-5* outlines the following differences:

- Hypomanic episodes have a shorter duration (4 days)
- Symptoms tend to be less severe
- Hypomanic episodes are associated with changes in behavior, mood, and ability to function that are observable by others. They are not, however, severe enough to warrant hospitalization or cause an inability to function socially or occupationally (American Psychiatric Association, 2013)

Bipolar I

Bipolar I is the more commonly referred to type of bipolar disorder. It is known for being more extreme in the way it fluctuates between depression and mania. For someone to receive this diagnosis, he or she must meet the criteria for a manic episode. Before or after manic episodes, there may be major depressive episodes or hypomanic episodes. It is not necessary for there to be a major depressive episode to have a diagnosis of bipolar I, it is, however, very common for it to occur (American Psychiatric Association, 2013).

Case Example

Charles is a 25-year-old who has met with his pastor before when he was feeling severely depressed and even suicidal. His pastor is surprised when he sees that Charles appears to be extremely happy. Charles quickly says that he came to see the pastor because he has so much to share. He begins by saying that he feels more alive than ever before—like he's on top of the world, and the world is his oyster. He is so excited and energized that he doesn't even need sleep because all of his best ideas have been coming to him in the middle of the night for days now. The pastor is having a hard time keeping up with Charles because he is talking fast and can't be interrupted. Charles tells him that God himself has told him that he is directly related to Jesus—they share the same DNA, and so now Charles knows how great and powerful he is. One night, for example, he knew he was supposed to sleep on the streets with prostitutes to bring them healing. The next day he realized he was supposed to go to Hollywood because God wanted him to find and marry a celebrity. He tells his pastor he couldn't find any celebrities so instead he performed a social experiment in a local grocery store where he offered his extraordinary organizing services to organize people's shopping carts. He reports that people gave him weird looks, so he left and decided to go to a bar to find a wife. He says he met a girl who liked how enthusiastic, smart, and strong he is, so he brought her home to meet his parents that very night and to share the good news of finding a wife. He doesn't understand why they weren't happy for him because this is better for him than sleeping with prostitutes, and besides, he is going to be rich by next week because he has five inventions in the works. He says he came in to see the pastor because he needs help getting his parents to understand how great he is doing.

Case Assessment

So much of this vignette is alarming and disturbing. Charles's behavior is incredibly reckless, senseless, and dangerous to his well-being. Key manic qualifiers are met in this presentation—insomnia, pressured speech, racing ideas, high goal-focused energy, expansive mood, narcissism, and reckless behavior. Sitting with Charles would feel chaotic, overwhelming, and concerning. Charles presented to the counselor while manic at his parents' request. It would be of upmost importance to remember his previous suicidal presentation when considering next steps for him.

Bipolar II

Bipolar II is distinct in that it is necessary for there to be hypomanic episodes and major depressive episodes currently or historically. In order to have this diagnosis, there cannot be a current or historical manic episode. With this disorder, it is typical for someone to seek help during a depressive episode and not during a hypomanic episode. This is due to the fact that hypomanic episodes in and of themselves do not cause significant impairment in functioning. Depression and unpredictable mood changes are more likely to cause distress (American Psychiatric Association, 2013).

Case Example: Martha Returns

It has been 3 months since the pastor has seen Martha. He had heard from her family members that not long after their last visit, she seemed to take a turn toward feeling happier. In fact, they had told him she had more energy than normal, was very talkative with them, sleeping much less, had been very driven to achieve new work and fitness goals, had invested money into a few companies that were promising, had been shopping a lot for "a new look," and updating the house. The pastor assumed this meant she was doing well and was back to normal, so he was therefore perplexed to see Martha depressed again. She reports that she has had some highs and lows in the last 3 months and can't understand why she keeps feeling great and then becomes depressed again.

Case Assessment

Overall, it appears Martha had taken a turn away from depression and toward positive, goal-oriented behavior. None of which was alarming to subjective viewers. Although her hypomanic state was seemingly productive for her, it is important to understand that she was indeed hypomanic and not functioning at a "normal" pace. The key piece to understand in this vignette was her cycling through hypomania and major depressive episodes over the 3-month period. Acknowledging the pattern will help her make sense of what is happening to her while also helping inform the counselor of the best course of action to care for her.

Cyclothymic Disorder

Cyclothymic disorder is the least severe form of depression in this category. For this diagnosis to occur, a person must have experienced numerous instances when symptoms of major depressive episodes and hypomanic episodes that don't fully meet the criteria take place for at least a 2-year period. The hypomanic and depressive symptoms will have been present at least 50% of the time with no more than a 2-month break in symptoms (American Psychiatric Association, 2013).

Case Example

Cindy, 22 years old, has asked to meet with her church's college pastor. She is feeling frustrated by her "personality" lately. She tells you that for the last 3 years, she has had periods of being lazy, lethargic, struggling to get out of bed, and even feeling sad for no reason. Then out of nowhere, she has energy, is very talkative, and becomes very focused on socializing. She reports struggling with friendships because her friends tell her it is hard to know which version of her they will experience. People have prayed for her, but she still keeps fluctuating between times of fatigue and sadness and times of having the energy she needs to be engaged socially.

Case Assessment

Initially, it could be perplexing to understand why Cindy is fluctuating between feeling okay and feeling down. Overall, she seems to be functioning well but can't understand her mood fluctuations. Her depression is not severe, and her hypomania is observable but focused on energy levels for social engagement, which doesn't meet full hypomanic criteria.

KEY TERMS

Manic episodes (mania): extreme fluctuations in mood that include excessive happiness or irritability, insomnia, fixation on a goal, racing thoughts, and reckless behavior for 1 week or longer

Hypomanic episode (hypomania): fluctuation in mood similar to mania but less severe with a 4-day duration

Bipolar I: a form of depression that includes manic episodes

Bipolar II: a form of depression that includes hypomanic episodes and major depressive episodes

Cyclothymic disorder: a form of depression that cycles between symptoms of major depressive episodes and hypomanic episodes, neither of which meet the full criteria of symptoms

Narcissism: having an inflated ego or grandiose sense of self

Discussion Questions

1 What is the major difference between bipolar I and bipolar II?

2 What types of behavior would be considered reckless or dangerous during a manic episode?

3 When you suspect someone has had a manic or hypomanic episode, what types of information will you want to begin gathering?

4 What worries you about potentially meeting with someone who is currently manic?

OTHER FORMS OF DEPRESSION/POTENTIAL CAUSES

So far, we have covered the most common forms of depression. Two additional types of depression with potential to be observed by a pastor are **seasonal affective disorder** and **postpartum depression**. The criteria for each are listed next, followed by a brief overview.

Seasonal Affective Disorder

Seasonal affective disorder (commonly referred to as SAD) can be found in the *DSM-5* (American Psychiatric Association, 2013) listed as recurrent major depressive disorder with seasonal pattern. The *DSM-5* defines the seasonal pattern specifier as

- having regular onset times of major depressive episodes at particular times of the year;

- having full remission also occur at specific times of the year;
- within the last 2 years, two major depressive episodes have demonstrated a seasonal pattern as described earlier; and
- the majority of lifetime major depressive episodes have occurred seasonally as opposed to out of season.

In short, SAD, is a form of depression that changes with the seasons. Typically, fall or winter is when the onset of depression occurs and spring or summer is when it goes into remission. The American Psychiatric Association (2017) links SAD to a biochemical imbalance in the brain that occurs because of a change in the amount of sunlight in a day that changes a person's circadian rhythm and consequently leaves him or her feeling out of step with his or her normal patterns and schedules.

Postpartum Depression

Postpartum depression is a form of depression affecting women shortly after childbirth. The National Institute of Mental Health (NIMH; n.d.) lists the following as symptoms of postpartum depression:

- Feeling sad, distressed, and/or overwhelmed
- Crying often without a known reason as to why
- Anxiety
- Feeling moody and/or irritable
- Sleep disturbances
- Indecisiveness, foggy memory, or difficulty concentrating
- Experiencing anger and/or rage
- Loss of interest in activities that previously brought joy
- Somatic symptoms
- Changes in eating patterns
- Social isolation
- Difficulty attaching and forming a bond with the new baby
- Doubting ability to care for the new baby
- Thoughts of self-harm or harm to the baby

Symptoms of postpartum depression are generally severe and need professional intervention because of the nature of the disorder interfering with a woman's ability to care for her family and keep her and baby safe. Typically, onset of postpartum depression is within a month of childbirth. NIMH reports that 80% of mothers experience something known as "baby blues," which is characterized by fatigue, worry, and unhappiness in mild ways that tend to dissipate within a week or two without intervention. Although baby blues are common, they are different than postpartum depression, which is more severe, is ongoing without intervention, and affects a woman's ability to function (NIMH, n.d.).

Possible Causes of Depression

Causes of depression are often wondered about and include a range of possibilities engendered externally, internally, or a combination of both. External causes of depression include work-related stress, worrying about family members who have severe problems (drug addiction, severe illness, etc.), financial strain, relational problems, and guilt about certain life situations. (Bromley et al., 2016). This type of depression is referred to as **exogenous** (or reactive) **depression**. Research has demonstrated a strong correlation between burnout and depression. One hundred percent of teachers who had reported high frequencies of burnout were found to have diagnosable depression, with 36% of them having suicidal ideations. Conversely, when someone reported experiencing low levels of burnout, they reported low or no symptoms of depression (Bianchi, Mayor, Schonfeld, & Laurent, 2016). Etiologically speaking, general unresolvable stress experiences, including those in the workplace, have been causally linked to symptoms of depression. Unresolvable stress includes chronic stressors, feeling a lack of control in an environment, feeling trapped in a difficult situation, and some sense of losing one's status or role (Bianchi et al., 2016).

In bipolar disorder, childhood **trauma** has occurred in 50% of patients. The trauma is said to affect the onset of bipolar disorder at an earlier age and increases the chances of **psychotic features**, rapid cycling, suicidal ideations and attempts, and the overall lifetime number of episodes experienced. Studies have demonstrated that childhood trauma can cause many biological and molecular changes that can interplay on genetic factors. Positive and negative life events can trigger depression or mania, as well as **bereavement**, illness, interpersonal relationship struggles, financial problems, and environmental factors (Aldinger & Schulze, 2017). Furthermore, research into causes of bipolar disorder have revealed immune factors related to specific viruses, elevated inflammation markers, and gastrointestinal inflammation, as all playing a role in bipolar disorder (Dickerson et al., 2015). Significant life events that cause social rhythm changes can lead to changes in biological rhythms (sleep-wake cycle), making them unstable, which can contribute to somatic changes and subsequent mood disturbances in people with other risk factors for bipolar disorder (Pinho et al., 2016). What we see in bipolar disorder causes includes exogenous depression and **endogenous** (biochemical) **depression,** wherein serotonin levels are lower, affecting mood.

With regard to postpartum depression, there may be a combination of physical, emotional, and hormonal causes. When hormones change rapidly, this can lead to chemical changes in the brain (endogenous depression). The result of this can lead to mood dysregulation. (NIMH, 2017, & NIMH, n.d.). The NIMH (n.d.) specifies that the quick and dramatic fluctuation in progesterone and estrogen levels after childbirth can cause chemical changes in the brain that are responsible for mood changes, especially when paired with sleep deprivation and physical discomfort.

Sometimes, people wonder if depression is the result of a lack of trust in God. They may even wonder if the root of depression is sin and selfishness. It is common to hear people who are encountering a depressed person to use a phrase similar to "depression is selfish." Understandably, the symptoms of depression can appear to be focused solely on the depressed individual and can leave those around them feeling neglected and unimportant. In caring for and experiencing depressed individuals, it will be important to remember that depression can be a reaction to a disheartening and distressing situation (exogenous),and/or it can be the result of chemical changes in the brain (endogenous).

Any believer helping someone with depression wants to have an opportunity to help that person see God in the process and have a better understanding of him or herself as well. They may even desire to help the depressed person see that God can be trusted during such a challenging time. Unfortunately, sometimes well-meaning people may say the wrong thing. One of the most disheartening stories of someone seeking pastoral help for severe depression included the pastor telling the person that by taking antidepressant medication, the person wasn't trusting God. At this, the individual discontinued medication use and became so severely depressed that the person ended up committing suicide shortly thereafter.

In this case, it is highly likely that the person's depression was endogenous and required medication to manage it and keep it in remission. This case is an excellent reminder to all of us working with depressed people to proceed with compassion, a listening ear, and patience. Biblically, we can see the wisdom in taking the time to listen and understand before intervening. Proverbs 18:2 and 13 (NIV) remind us that "fools find no pleasure in understanding; but delight in airing their own opinions. ... To answer before listening— that is folly and shame." James 1:19 reminds us, "My dear brothers and sisters, take note of this: everyone should be quick to listen, slow to speak, and slow to become angry."

KEY TERMS

Seasonal affective disorder: a type of depression with regular onset and relief patterns based on changes in seasons

Postpartum depression: a severe mood disorder that affects some women with onset after childbirth characterized by sadness, exhaustion, and difficulty caring for and attaching to her newborn baby

Exogenous depression: a form of depression that is reactive to life circumstances

Endogenous depression: a form of depression that is biochemical in nature

Trauma: a deeply distressing and/or disturbing event

Psychotic features: losing touch with reality, which includes hallucinations and delusions

Bereavement: a period of mourning that includes intense grief, typically occurring after the loss of a loved one

Burnout: feelings of hopelessness and displeasure as a result of being in a constant state of stress

1 What are different causes of depression?

2 Do you have any reactions to the different causes of depression?

3 What are the differences between SAD and postpartum depression?

COMMON BARRIERS TO RECOVERY AND INTERVENTIONS

Barriers

Given the severity of depressive symptoms, it can be difficult to understand why some people choose against seeking help. Here we break down the barriers to treatment into three categories: **stigmas**, **family**, and **internal struggles**, all of which can be interrelated.

Stigmas are significant barriers to treatment. For our purposes here, a stigma is anything that represents a mark on a person that causes him or her to have a diminished value and discounts the person as being abnormal with a tainted and weak identity. The stigma of depression can cause delays in approaching treatment, include low disclosure rates of symptoms, and contribute to noncompliance with treatment (not taking medications as prescribed and missing appointments). The fear of losing "normal" social value, along with status and power, make it difficult to reach out for help (Bromley et al., 2016).

Family and other close relationships represent another significant barrier to treatment and highlight the intense threat of relational loss. For some, the family unit is strong, and an individual's needs are less important than overall family needs. If one member of the family struggles with depression but also feels like he or she would let down the family if he or she can't perform as a "normal" family member should, then that person is likely to conceal the depressive symptoms. The person may perceive a threat of being exiled from family relationships and having a diminished value in the eyes of others (Bromley et al., 2016).

Depression is perceived to have the power to break relationships, and therefore seeking professional help will only confirm an individual's weakness and increase the risk of relational ruptures if the weakness is exposed (Bromley et al., 2016). Even when the threat of losing a relationship isn't experienced, symptoms may be minimized (if shared) so as to not burden family members with the severity of depression.

The threat of losing relationships can lead to the concealment of help-seeking behaviors from family and friends, a common occurrence. Concealment includes hiding medications and professional treatment in an effort to preserve relationships. The recurrent hiding theme is oftentimes based in fears of being labeled, devalued, and even being avoided. A person may feel that taking medication is the "easy way out" and brings a sense of shame. Concealment feels easier than sharing the shame he or she feels for seeking help.

Some studies have revealed that depressed individuals experience ambivalence from family members when their help-seeking behavior isn't concealed. Family members may express a dislike of medication and professional help while also acknowledging their effectiveness in reducing the symptoms of depression in the depressed individual. When family members express disliking medication and professional help, it can lead to the depressed person being less compliant with medications (choosing to reduce the amount/dosage or discontinuing use without consulting a doctor), avoiding therapeutic help, and further concealment from family and the prescribing doctor to avoid a feeling of judgment from them. All of this is done in an effort to prevent relational loss—a heavy burden that would feel incredibly lonely to carry. Thus this is a significant barrier to the successful treatment of depression (Bromley et al., 2016).

Being that relationships are highly valued and can be central to the cause of depression, some depressed individuals feel as though medication alone is not helpful to them. They feel the root cause of their depression is overlooked since medication doesn't address their relational distress. They may believe medication can help reduce symptoms but can't fix their concerns, fears, or attachment injuries (Bromley et al., 2016).

Internal struggles also represent several barriers to treatment. When an individual seeks help, the person can feel as though he or she is weak and damaged. In an effort to avoid additional negative feelings about themselves beyond what they are already experiencing with depression, these individuals may avoid treatment. They may have difficulty accepting a diagnosis of depression—a diagnosis that makes them believe they are weak, tainted, deficient, undesirable, and lacking personal strength and self-control—all of which can significantly interfere with seeking help (Bromley et al., 2016).

They may feel judged for their feelings about their diagnosis and disliking the recommended plan for treatment. Their internal struggle with whether to accept help includes weighing the potential benefit of help with the previously mentioned fears of what that might do to their relationships. They may feel too overwhelmed to even know how to share what is happening to them and how they are feeling. It is possible that they will set out to seek help, arrive at the appropriate office, and then leave because of how overwhelming it feels to try and articulate their symptoms of depression (which they may not yet know is depression) (Bromley et al., 2016).

Finally, they may believe that they should be able to handle their problems without help. This doesn't mean that they don't want help, but they may feel pressured to be strong. Sometimes previous negative experiences seeking help have led to the view that the problem is within them, and they just need to learn to view things as manageable, try cognitive-behavioral therapies to fix themselves, and practice relaxation exercises (Bromley et al., 2016).

Interventions

Because depression can be potentially life threatening and debilitating, the first course of action when recognizing someone is depressed is to assess the pervasiveness of his or her depression (what areas of life are being affected), gather information about the depth of despair and sadness the person is experiencing, and assess their level of safety through direct questions about self-harm and reviewing the SAD PERSONS assessment to determine a risk score.

If it is determined that suicidal thoughts are present, and a plan is in place for the person to take his or her life, proceed with seeking outside help: call 911 or a mobile crisis unit, encourage hospitalization, and use social support systems available to the person (family, friends, church, group therapy). Trusted outside relationships can be used to establish a 24/7 watch over the person when suicidal thoughts are present but there is no plan to harm him or herself nor a desire to do so. To determine who would feel safe and containing, ask the individual who he or she trusts to support him or her in this way.

The next step would be to ask if the person would allow you to reach out to that safe individual on his or her behalf. If the person agrees to this, be thorough in explaining what you will be sharing about his or her situation. The phone call can be made with the depressed individual present and should include the basic facts that he or she is experiencing depression that is currently severe with some suicidal thoughts and needs support and check-ins.

Once safety issues have been assessed, the next step would be to provide a sense of containment in the room through the use of gentle questions and responses, empathy, and validation for how hard this struggle must be for the depressed person. As the afore-mentioned research has demonstrated, it is hard for someone to open up about his or her sad and hopeless feelings. The person is taking a risk by being open and vulnerable—a risk that threatens the individual's sense of dignity and self-worth. The most kind and helpful thing you can do is provide a safe, supportive, listening ear. Allow the person to take their time sharing with you; this will help him or her to trust that you care to hear about their sadness instead of rushing through so you can get to something else.

Take the person seriously and believe his or her lonely struggle. Acknowledge the loneliness the individual must feel carrying this by themselves. Reflect the feelings you hear the person saying and allow him or her the space to be the expert on those feelings, experiences, and struggles. Phrases that will help the depressed individual feel validated and understood would sound like this: "It has been so hard for you lately." "I see you and hear that this has been such a difficult time for you." "It must be lonely to carry the weight of your depression by yourself." "Can you help me understand what this sadness has been like for you to experience?" And, "It makes sense to me that you would be feeling sad and down after going through so many stressful situations."

As you listen carefully to the person's depression and how the symptoms are manifesting, determine to the extent possible whether the depression is endogenous or exogenous. Educate the individual on the different causes of depression and ask what seems to fit for him or her. It is possible that a combination of external stressors and chemical imbalances could be the cause of his or her depression. The purpose in evaluating the potential cause of the person's depression is so that you can provide some understanding as to what is happening to them and give the individual an idea of what might be most helpful in the form of next steps.

For example, if together you determine that the person's depression is the result of **burnout** and stress, referring the individual for antidepressants may not be the solution. Instead, he or she would need more social support and self-care in place to balance the burnout/stress. If, on the other hand, you determine that the person's relationships are fulfilling, his or her job is satisfactory and low stress, and life is as he or she would want it to be, and yet the person has unexplainable sadness, low production of serotonin in the brain or other chemical imbalances may be responsible for the sadness and a referral to a psychiatrist would be an appropriate next step.

It is possible when working with depressed individuals to begin feeling frustrated, stuck without any traction, helpless, and even hopeless. These feelings may evoke a need to fix the person sitting in front of you. **Countertransference** is a common experience when meeting with depressed individuals. It occurs when the individual is redirecting his or her experience of emotions and feelings onto you (**transference**), and then you experience a reaction to them (the frustration, stuck feeling, hopeless feeling, need to fix). When this takes place, it is important to ask yourself questions about what you are feeling, why you might be feeling it, and determine whether the feelings belong to you or the person you are meeting with. It could be possible that something the person is sharing is triggering a wound or experience from your own life.

If this is true, it is important for you to find a safe place to process your own experiences and bring healing to them. Taking time for your own internal work is important and will allow you to work more effectively with those you minister to. If you determine that what you are feeling belongs to the person you are meeting with, you can find a way to use that to the person's benefit. For example, if the feeling you are experiencing is hopelessness, you can say, "I wonder if what you are going through right now feels hopeless to you." From there you can hear more about them feeling the way they do and discuss what might be needed to feel differently.

When someone has depression, the person is not functioning how he or she typically has in the past. The individual can dramatically change from being an active, lively person, to an isolated, slow-paced, withdrawn person. This can be frustrating to witness and sit with. When frustration is growing, it can be tempting to try to fix the person through the use of spirituality—giving him or her bible verses in an effort to bring the person comfort or to solve his or her problems, telling the individual to pray more, talk to God more, or to trust God more.

The desire to see a person move from feeling depressed to remission is valid. Praying with the depressed individual and pointing him or her to God's truth is important. The way to make this most effective is to start by attuning to the person's sadness, struggles, and shame. Help the individual to feel known and understood first by you. Starting with prayer and bible verses may bring more shame to the depressed person and make him or her continue to feel weak and deficient. Ending with this, however, may feel comforting. You will know how to attend specifically to the person's heart in prayer and offer verses that can give him or her hope in between meetings with you.

Depression, being complex and debilitating as it is, typically needs outside help. With research showing how families tend to be against treatment for depression, an important step to take when ministering to a depressed individual will be to guide him or her to individual therapy, group therapy, and/or a psychiatric consultation. In addition to these forms of professional help, any church group experiences that cover the topic of depression in a safe supportive environment can also be encouraged.

Finally, evaluate the level of **self-care** the depressed individual engages in. Self-care is any deliberate activity that is meant to take care of one's mental, emotional, physical, or spiritual well-being. Practically speaking, self-care can be journaling, exercising, spending time with friends, resting, etc. With exogenous depression, it is possible that there is an imbalance in focusing on upsetting and stressful problems that lead to burnout and not enough focus on self-care activities.

In one research study, it was discovered that positive life events (nutritious eating, exercise, agreement with others) had an inverse relationship with depression. Furthermore, this study identified that savoring those positive life events was also associated with a decrease in depression and increase in well-being. Savoring was defined as having the following components: anticipating a positive life event, savoring the event in the moment, and reminiscing about what took place in the positive life event. Two weeks of practicing savoring resulted in a significant decrease in depressive symptoms (Chen & Zhou, 2017). When self-care is low in the person a minister is meeting with, he or she can begin educating and encouraging the person to discover what self-care looks like for that individual. A minister can also educate and encourage the act of savoring positive life events.

In review, interventions will include assessing the level of depression and any self-harm; providing containment, understanding, empathy and validation; identifying potential causes of depression and providing education on how depression affects someone's life, checking in on one's own countertransference, managing personal frustration, avoiding quick attempts to fix the problem with spirituality, making necessary referrals, and assessing for and educating about self-care.

Self-Care

Caring for those suffering from any form of depression has the potential to be deeply rewarding and satisfying work. However, it is also true that it can lead to burnout and **compassion fatigue**. It is important to understand what burnout and compassion fatigue are, why they happen, and how to practice self-care in an effort to minimize the potential risk of them occurring.

Exposure to stress, suffering, depression, and suicidality all increase the risk of both burnout and compassion fatigue (Jacobson, Rothschild, Mirza, & Shapiro, 2013). Burnout refers to living in an enduring and constant state of stress, and has been shown to gradually create feelings of hopelessness and displeasure in the workplace. Compassion fatigue has been defined as "a natural, predictable, treatable, and preventable consequence of working with suffering people" (Jacobson et al., 2013). Compassion fatigue stems from exposure to traumatic stories and crisis, and can be felt suddenly or slowly over time and can take on an appearance of post-traumatic stress disorder (PTSD).

Ultimately, burnout and compassion fatigue can lead to the very same depression occurring in ministers and counselors as the people they are attempting to help. In fact, a few studies demonstrate this. Of those ministering to depressed individuals in the Evangelical Lutheran Church in America and the Roman Catholic Church, they found that they were more likely to report having depressive symptoms in their clergy than in their general congregation (Jacobson et al., 2013).

Currently, there is no simple way to predict who may become burned out by ministering to those who suffer with depression. However, there are a number of risk factors that have been identified. They include a lack of proper training to handle mental illness and crisis, feeling incompetent to provide care for depression and suicidality, being of a younger age, having fewer years of experience, being in a smaller congregation, having a lower salary, and having a recent decline in church attendance and church-based support (Jacobson et al., 2013).

Experiencing burnout and/or compassion fatigue are often a sign that self-care is being overlooked. It is important that self-care be an ongoing practice and not limited to only taking place once burnout or compassion fatigue has occurred. There are many ways to implement self-care: spending time in self-reflection, journaling, pursuing training and education that builds a sense of competence within oneself, maintaining proper nutrition, getting regular exercise, resting, meditating, nurturing relationships apart from the work environment, pursuing interests and hobbies that bring pleasure and a sense of fulfillment (that aren't related to working with depression), and reflecting on joys that are experienced on the job (such as accomplishments achieved) (Jacobson et al., 2013; Streets, 2015).

In addition to practicing self-care, there are other ways to reduce the stress that working with mental illness includes. First, it is important to reexamine current expectations and goals for helping others to see if they are reasonable and achievable (Streets, 2015). There is also research that suggests that there is a lack of collaboration between ministers and social workers, psychologists, and marriage and family therapists (Jacobson et al., 2013). Regular collaboration with trusted outside assistance will help prevent burnout and compassion fatigue by providing resources that can further help the depressed individual and at the same time take pressure off the ministers as the only source of support for them.

KEY TERMS

Burnout: feelings of hopelessness and displeasure as a result of being in a constant state of stress

Compassion fatigue: fatigue experienced as the result of exposure to traumatic stories over time that can take on the appearance of PTSD

Self-care: deliberate actions taken to care for one's physical, mental, and emotional well-being

Stigma: anything that represents a mark on oneself causing personal diminished value

Countertransference: the emotional reaction toward someone as a result of transference

Transference: the transfer of ones' own emotions and feelings onto someone else

1   What are three significant barriers to successful treatment of depressed individuals?

2   What do you imagine will be the most challenging approach to treatment for you to provide?

3   What is self-care and who should practice it?

REVIEWING THE CONCEPTS

Learning Objectives

- Explain the different types of depression.
  - Major depressive disorder: depression that lasts a minimum of 2 weeks that is characterized by feelings of sadness and a loss of interest or pleasure in activities
  - Persistent depressive disorder: depression that lasts longer than 2 years (1 year for children/adolescents) that includes having depressed mood more days than not, with periods of relief lasting no longer than 2 months
  - Bipolar 1 disorder: a mood disorder marked by manic episodes. Manic episodes last one week minimum with abnormal fluctuations in mood that include excessive happiness, irritability, and expansive mood. It includes the following behavior changes: insomnia, narcissism, pressured speech, racing thoughts, distractibility, goal-directed activity, and involvement in reckless and/or dangerous behavior
  - Bipolar II disorder: a mood disorder that cycles between major depressive episodes and hypomania. Hypomanic episodes last 4 days and are similar to, but less severe than, manic episodes
  - Cyclothymic disorder: a mood disorder lasting a minimum of 2 years that has symptoms of major depressive episodes and hypomania, neither of which fully meet the criteria
  - Seasonal affective disorder: a mood disorder wherein major depressive episodes occur during seasonal shifts (fall/winter) at the same time each year and go into remission during other seasonal shifts (spring/summer)
  - Postpartum depression: depression affecting some women after giving birth to a child that causes difficulty attaching to a newborn child and interferes with the woman's ability to care for her newborn and family

- Have specific insight into crisis assessment and intervention.
  - Ask specific questions to understand what suicidal/self-harm thoughts may be taking place.
  - Evaluate the severity of risk of suicide using the SAD PERSONS assessment.
  - Evaluate outside support systems.

- o If risk assessment is low, determine appropriate self-care practices that the depressed individual can begin doing. Encourage regular contact with the outside support system.
- o If risk assessment is high, ask the person if he or she can take him or herself to the hospital or call 911 or a mobile crisis unit for assistance.

- Identify treatment strategies for depression.
  - o Assess level of safety.
  - o Provide containment, support, empathy, and validation.
  - o Ask questions to understand the type of depression and causes.
  - o Provide education on depression and self-care.
  - o Refer to professional therapy and psychiatric consultation.

- Understand the need for self-care when caring for depressed individuals.
  - o Working with depressed individuals can lead to burnout, compassion fatigue, and symptoms of depression.
  - o Self-care is a deliberate act to attend to one's well-being mentally, emotionally, and physically.
  - o Examples of self-care include journaling, exercising, evaluating goals to make sure that they are realistic, consuming proper nutrition, resting, obtaining further education, and building relationships apart from the work environment.

Chapter Review Questions

Level 1: Knowledge (True/False)

1. Depression is the number-one listed cause of disability.
2. Depressed individuals typically adhere to prescribed medication use.
3. Asking someone if he or she feels like committing suicide will likely trigger them to do so.
4. For children to receive a diagnosis of depression, they typically need to be depressed for longer periods of time than adults.
5. Loss of pleasure in usual activities is a key indicator of depression.
6. A manic episode is usually severe enough to warrant hospitalization.
7. Postpartum depression is the same as having "baby blues."
8. A common barrier to successful treatment for depression is the threat of relational loss.
9. Burnout does not play a role in causing depression.
10. Self-care is an important practice for pastors to manage compassion fatigue.

Level 2: Comprehension

1. Which of the following is not a type of depression?
   a. Bipolar I
   b. Cyclothymia

    c.   Manic depressive disorder

    d.   Persistent depressive disorder

2.   When a pastor suspects that a person he is meeting with is suicidal, what should he do?

    a.   Nothing yet, asking about it will only give someone the idea to harm him or herself.

    b.   Call 911 or a mobile response unit.

    c.   Ask a series of assessment questions to see if they are feeling suicidal.

    d.   Give them a few referrals to therapists in the area.

3.   Which type of depression is known for lasting for 2 years or longer, with depressed mood occurring more days than not?

    a.   Major depressive disorder

    b.   Bipolar ll

    c.   Persistent depressive disorder

    d.   SAD

4.   Which of the following represent exogenous causes of depression?

    a.   Financial strain

    b.   Hormonal changes

    c.   Relational problems

    d.   Chemical changes in the brain

    e.   a and c

    f.   b and d

5.   Which of the following is not a symptom of mania?

    a.   Fluctuations of mood

    b.   Racing thoughts

    c.   Reckless behavior

    d.   An increased need for sleep

6.   Which type of depression fluctuates between hypomania and depression?

    a.   Bipolar ll

    b.   Bipolar l

    c.   Cyclothymia

    d.   Persistent depressive disorder

7.   Which of the following could be a cause of depression?

    a.   Childhood trauma

    b.   Change in seasons

c. Hormonal changes

d. All of the above

8. Which type of depression can cause disability?

a. Major depression disorder

b. Bipolar l

c. Postpartum disorder

d. All of the above

9. What can happen to pastors who work with depressed people?

a. Compassion fatigue

b. Burnout

c. Vicarious trauma

d. Depression

e. a and b

10. Major depressive disorder is characterized by

a. feelings of sadness

b. loss of interest or pleasure in activities

c. fatigue

d. difficulty concentrating

e. all of the above

ANSWERS

LEVEL 1: KNOWLEDGE

1. T
2. F
3. F
4. F
5. T
6. T
7. F
8. T
9. F
10. T

LEVEL 2: COMPREHENSION

1. c
2. c
3. c
4. e
5. d
6. a
7. d
8. d
9. e
10. e

Level 3: Application

1. A member of your congregation arrives to an appointment with you and mentions that he or she has been depressed all of his or her life and currently don't see the point in living anymore. Describe the course of action you would take to assess the person's level of depression and potential suicidal thoughts, as well as what steps you would take to ensure his or her safety.

2. Describe the different causes of depression and how you might explain them to someone who is meeting with you and struggling to understand why he or she is feeling so down.

3. Describe a thorough intervention plan for someone who has persistent depressive disorder.

4. Describe the hallmarks of bipolar II disorder. How might you use these while meeting with someone to determine how to help them? How would you know when to refer them to a professional?

5. While meeting with someone from your church, it becomes clear that the person suffers from cyclothymia. The individual shares that he or she feels a lack of faith and trust in God, which is why the person is unable to stay happy. Describe how you would educate the individual about depression and how you would integrate faith into the conversation.

RESOURCES

Online Resources

- National Alliance on Mental Illness—https://www.nami.org
- NIMH—https://www.nimh.nih.gov
- International Association for Suicide Prevention—iasp.info

Readings

- *Darkness Visible: A Memoir of Madness*—William Styron
- *An Unquiet Mind: A Memoir of Moods and Madness*—Kay Redfield Jamison
- *Reasons to Stay Alive*—Matt Haig
- *Manic*—Terri Cheney
- *Speaking of Sadness*—David Karp

Phone Resources

- National Suicide Prevention Hotline—800-273-8255
- National Youth Crisis Hotline—800-448-4663
- National Hopeline Network—800-784-2433

Video Resources

- *Silver Linings Playbook* (2012): The Weinstein Company, Rated R—A film that highlights the everyday realities of bipolar disorder following the release of the main character from a psychiatric mental institution.
- *Men and Depression*: NIMH—https://www.nimh.nih.gov/news/media/2017/men-and-depression-bill-maruyama-lawyer.shtml
- *Men and Depression*: NIMH—https://www.nimh.nih.gov/news/media/2017/men-and-depression-rodolfo-palma-lulion-college-student.shtml
- *Postpartum Depression*: NIMH—https//www.youtube.com/watch?v=6kaCdrvNGZw

CLASSROOM ACTIVITIES

1. Interview a fellow student regarding a depression experience. Encourage the student to discuss what they found helpful as well as unhelpful in moving through the depression process.

2. Role-play depression counseling sessions.

3. Brainstorm ways in which Christians "overly spiritualize" responses to depression as well as compassionate pastoral responses.

REFERENCES

Aldinger, F., & Schulze, T. G. (2017). Environmental factors, life events, and trauma in the course of bipolar disorder. *Psychiatry & Clinical Neurosciences, 71*(1), 6–17.

American Psychiatric Association. (2013). *Diagnostic and statistical manual of mental disorders* (5th ed.). Washington, DC: Author.

American Psychiatric Association. (2017). *Seasonal Affective Disorder (SAD)*. Retrieved from https://www.psychiatry.org/patients-families/depression/seasonal-affective-disorder

Bianchi, R., Mayor, E., Schonfeld, I. S., & Laurent, E. (2016). Burnout-depression overlap: A study of New Zealand schoolteachers. *New Zealand Journal of Psychology, 45*(3), 4–11.

Bromley, E., Kennedy, D. P., Miranda, J., Sherbourne, C. D., & Wells, K. B. (2016). The Fracture of Relational Space in Depression. *Current Anthropology, 57*(5), 610–631. doi:10.1086/688506

Chen, J., & Zhou, L. (2017). Savoring as a moderator between positive life events and hopelessness depression. *Social Behavior & Personality: An International Journal, 45*(8), 1337–1344. doi: 10.2224/sbp.6235

Dickerson, F., Katsafanas, E., Schweinfurth, L. B., Savage, C. G., Stallings, C., Origoni, A., & ... Yolken, R. (2015). Immune alterations in acute bipolar depression. *Acta Psychiatrica Scandinavica, 132*(3), 204–210. doi: 10.1111/acps.12451

Jacobson, J. M., Rothschild, A., Mirza, F., & Shapiro, M. (2013). Risk for burnout and compassion fatigue and potential for compassion satisfaction among clergy: Implications for social work and religious organizations. *Journal of Social Service Research, 39*, 455–468. doi: 10.1080/01488376.2012.744627

Juhnke, G. A. (1996). The adapted-SAD PERSONS: a suicide assessment scale designed for use with children. *Elementary School Guidance & Counseling, 30*(4), 252.

Juhnke, G. E. (1994) SAD PERSONS scale review. *Measurement & Evaluation in Counseling & Development, 27*,(1) 325.

National Institute of Mental Health. (n.d.). *Postpartum depression facts*. NIMH. Retrieved from https://www.nimh.nih.gov/health/publications/postpartum-depression-facts/index.shtml

National Institute of Mental Health. (2017). *Major depression.* NIMH. Retrieved from https://www.nimh.nih.gov/health/statistics/major-depression.shtml

National Institute of Mental Health. (2016). *Seasonal affective disorder*. NIMH. Retrieved from https://www.nimh.nih.gov/health/topics/seasonal-affective-disorder/index.shtml

Pinho, M., Sehmbi., M., Cudney, L. E., Kauer-Sant'anna, M., Magalhaes, P.V., Reinares, M., & ... Rosa, A. R. (2016). The association between biological rhythms, depression, and functioning in bipolar disorder: a large multi-center study. *Acta Psychiatrica Scandinavica, 133*(2), 102–108. doi: 10.1111/acps.12442

Psychology Tools. (n.d.). *Major depressive inventory*. Retrieved from https://psychology-tools.com/major-depression-inventory/

Streets, F. (2015). Social work and a trauma-informed ministry and pastoral care: A collaborative agenda. *Social Work & Christianity, 42*(4), 470–487.

IMAGE CREDITS

Anxiety and Panic

Steve Gioielli, PsyD

LEARNING OBJECTIVES

Upon completion of this chapter, readers will be able to

1. differentiate generalized anxiety disorder and panic attacks from other expressions of anxiety and fear;

2. describe the phenomenological experiences of generalized anxiety and panic;

3. facilitate a pastoral response to anxiety and panic among parishioners;

4. identify common etiological and predisposing factors; and

5. identify risk factors for those who may be vulnerable to experiencing generalized anxiety and panic.

"And no Grand Inquisitor has in readiness such terrible tortures as has anxiety, and no spy knows how to attack more artfully the man he suspects, choosing the instant when he is weakest, nor knows how to lay traps where he will be caught and ensnared, as anxiety knows how, and no sharp-witted judge knows how to interrogate, to examine the accused as anxiety does, which never lets him escape, neither by diversion nor by noise, neither at work nor at play, neither by day nor at night."

(Kierkegaard, 1980, p. 139)

"The truth is that anxiety is at once a function of biology and philosophy, body and mind, instinct and reason, personality and culture. Even as anxiety is experienced at a spiritual and psychological level, it is scientifically measurable at the molecular level and the physiological level. It is produced by nature and it is produced by nurture. It's a psychological phenomenon and a sociological phenomenon. In computer terms, it's both a hardware problem (I'm wired badly) and a software problem (I run faulty logic programs that make me think anxious thoughts). The origins of a temperament are many faceted; emotional

dispositions that may seem to have a simple, single source—
a bad gene, say, or a childhood trauma—may not."

(Stossel, 2014, pp. 14–15)

FIGURE 3.1 **The desperation of fear**

THE STORY OF MARK

Mark has been a member of his church congregation since he was a teenager. Now married with three young children, Mark works as a general manager at a local grocery store, where he landed his first job as a stock clerk. Mark is a soft-spoken, friendly guy who is well liked by others. However, he has few close friends and is often inconsistent in his participation at church services and ministry events. People who have known Mark over the years may notice the ways in which he often seems distracted and tense despite his insistence that he is "fine."

Mark is the middle child in his large family of seven. His parents are immigrants from Eastern Europe, who left their countries of origin because of economic depression and lack of employment opportunities. While growing up, his mother and father worked hard to provide for their family, each often working two jobs to make ends meet and put food on the table. Once the eldest siblings were old enough, they were in charge of babysitting the youngest ones while their parents picked up extra shifts at night or on the weekends. Despite his parents' reassurance, Mark often worried about his family. He has always been a rather perceptive person, and he used this innate skill to monitor his parents' moods to try to assess at times the severity of his family's financial situation, or if his parents' marriage would withstand the pressures of family life. Even as a young child, Mark would pray regularly for God to help his family and to make his parents happy by taking away the burdens weighing them down. He would express his longing to God for his father to find a higher paying job so that he would not have to work so much and could spend more time with him and his siblings.

"Great potential," was often the phrase used by Mark's teachers to put a positive spin on his average academic performance. They witnessed glimmers of his brilliance, but were often left disappointed and confused by his seeming lack of effort or motivation to succeed. The truth of the matter was that Mark loved school and dreamed of becoming an architect. His preoccupation with his family's well-being kept him from devoting himself to his studies or pursuing extracurricular activities or friendships. He just wanted to be home where he could keep an eye on things and help out when his parents needed him. Following high school graduation, he opted to stay local and attend community college while continuing to work at the grocery store to support his family.

As Mark entered into adulthood, his anxiety only seemed to worsen. Despite his family's growing financial stability, he continued to worry about them. As he entered marriage and became a father, he found more and more things to be worried about: his children's safety, his health, natural disasters, political issues, conversations at work, the list seemed endless. Mark started having difficulty sleeping because he just could not stop thinking about his fears. He sought out medical professionals for unusual muscle aches and migraines, and began to doubt God's goodness and faithfulness.

AN INTRODUCTION TO ANXIETY

Anxiety is part of the universal human experience. For nearly all, the experience of anxiety is uncomfortable at best and utterly paralyzing at its worst. Symptoms usually include disturbances in one's thought life, including worry, catastrophic or "worst-case-scenario" thinking, ruminative thought patterns, and difficulty concentrating. Other symptoms include disturbances experienced in the body, including physical agitation, restlessness, muscle tension, increased heart rate, and tiredness. Some degree of anxiety is normal in human experience and is to be expected. In fact, research indicates that for some people, anxiety is an important factor in promoting learning and motivation (Strack, Lopes, Esteves, & Fernandez-Berrocal, 2017). However, for others who experience elevated levels of anxiety or chronic anxiety warranting a clinical diagnosis, it leads to negative effects on health and well-being.

The most current statistics indicate that in the past year, an estimated 19.1% of adults in the United States suffered from an anxiety disorder (Harvard Medical School, 2007). It is also estimated that nearly 1 in 3 (31.1%) U.S. adults will experience an anxiety disorder in their lifetime (Harvard Medical School, 2007). Despite it being such a widely shared experience, anxiety is commonly misunderstood. In some instances, the experience of anxiety can be elusive or disguised. For example, it is quite common for someone who is experiencing a panic attack to mistake anxiety for a heart attack. In other cases, it may be expressed in idiosyncratic ways or overshadowed by other, perhaps more obvious, symptoms or feelings (e.g., frustration, anger). Cultural factors often influence the presentation or experience of anxiety as well.

Many philosophers, spiritual leaders, and mental health professionals throughout history have attempted to address the problem of anxiety, offering hypotheses as to its causes as well as possible cures. Perspectives on understanding anxiety have included moral or spiritual issues, environmental factors, biological imbalances, and genetic heredity. Despite these historical collective efforts, today's most prominent researchers and professionals continue to offer varying explanations and treatments to address anxiety. Most treatments work for some; none work for all. So how has such a common human experience evaded understanding by some of the brightest people throughout time?

Perhaps one reason is that the human experience of anxiety is complex and intimately intertwined with many dimensions of one's personhood. Certainly, progress has been made in differentiating types of anxiety, classifying them into distinct anxiety disorders. In the fifth and current edition of the *Diagnostic and Statistical Manual of Mental Disorders, 5th edition* (*DSM-5*) published by the American Psychiatric Association (2013), there are seven different disorders of anxiety, each with its own criteria of symptoms. This chapter aims to help pastoral counselors cultivate a deeper understanding of the experience of those who suffer from anxiety so that they may know best how to care for them. This chapter will articulate the complexity of anxiety and provide more detailed understanding of two of the most common anxiety disorders, generalized anxiety disorder and panic disorder.

Anxiety and Fear

There is no universally agreed upon definition for anxiety. However, there is an important distinction that most make between anxiety and fear. **Fear** is an immediate response to a current threat of danger. One experiences fear when approached by a bear while hiking in the mountains or during a natural disaster, such as a hurricane or earthquake. In these instances, the **fear stimulus**, or perceived threat of danger (e.g., wild animal or natural disaster), is real and occurring in the present moment. The human body's natural response to fear is to mobilize its strategy for survival by activating hormones in the sympathetic nervous system, which increases heart rate and respiration to prepare for a response to the threat.

Anxiety is a response to a stimulus that is either not occurring in the present or is not immediately a threat of danger (Hyman, 2013, p. x). One may experience anxiety about a final exam next week or a court trial starting at the end of the month. In these scenarios, the future-based event is perceived as threatening or dangerous, but has yet to occur. Nonetheless, the person experiences anxiety in the present moment and may continue to until the stimulus is somehow neutralized as a threat. When these threats are real (e.g., a high grade is needed to pass the class, or the court decision may lead to the loss of child custody), the anxiety experienced may be helpful to motivate one to prepare appropriately for the upcoming situation (e.g., study hard or rehearse for testimony), or it may have deleterious effects, such as sleep disturbance, worry, or muscle tension. When the future-based stimulus does not pose a realistic threat, then the anxiety experienced is unhelpful and contributes to unnecessary pain and suffering. People who struggle with chronic anxiety tend to hold a posture of vigilance for potential threats of danger, which leads them to adopt behavioral patterns to try to protect themselves (e.g., avoidance, hypervigilance). However, anxiety is often not the problem. Experiencing anxiety is a normal and appropriate response to danger. The problem lies in the relationship one has with one's experience of anxiety. People with anxiety disorders tend to have ineffective strategies for dealing with their anxious response and strong emotions of fear.

Anxiety disorders tend to differ in their duration, complexity, and constellation of symptoms. Some anxiety disorders, such as a specific phobia, which is fear or anxiety related to a specific object or situation (American Psychiatric Association, 2013), can be of shorter duration, less complex, and more easily treatable. Other disorders, such as generalized anxiety disorder or panic disorder, are often more complex, harder to treat, and more chronic in nature. Panic disorder involves intense fear along with mostly bodily symptoms, while generalized anxiety disorder is characterized by excessive worry that is difficult to control and avoidance. Social anxiety disorder is fear or anxiety restricted to social situations in which one may be scrutinized by others (American Psychiatric Association, 2013), whereas generalized anxiety disorder is fear or anxiety about several situations or events, spanning across different domains of one's life (e.g., work, school, social relationships, finances, health). Like other mental illness, anxiety disorders have powerful and debilitating effects that significantly affect people's lives. It can feel like a full-time job trying to manage anxiety or avoid situations that evoke it.

Anxiety and the Christian Life

It is not difficult to locate examples or explicit teachings on anxiety and fear in scripture. A popular New Testament example is found in the teaching of Jesus from the Sermon on the Mount:

> Therefore I tell you, do not be anxious about your life, what you will eat or what you will drink, nor about your body, what you will put on. Is not life more than food, and the body more than clothing? Look at the birds of the air: they neither sow nor reap nor gather into barns, and yet your heavenly Father feeds them. Are you not of more value than they? And which of you by being anxious can add a single hour to his span of life? And why are you anxious about clothing? Consider the lilies of the field, how they grow: they neither toil nor spin, yet I tell you, even Solomon in all his glory was not arrayed like one of these. But if God so clothes the grass of the field, which today is alive and tomorrow is thrown into the oven, will he not much more clothe you, O you of little faith? Therefore do not be anxious, saying, 'What shall we eat?' or 'What shall we drink?' or 'What shall we wear?' For the Gentiles seek after all these things, and your heavenly Father knows that you need them all. But seek first the kingdom of God and his righteousness, and all these things will be added to you. Therefore do not be anxious about tomorrow, for tomorrow will be anxious for itself. Sufficient for the day is its own trouble (*Matt 6:25–34, ESV, 2002*).

Jesus appears to be communicating quite clearly that anxiety and worry are not only unhelpful but also not what God desires for creation. The most tragic consequences of clinical anxiety are the limits it imposes on experiencing the fullness of life God intends for human beings. Jesus draws the connection that fear is extinguished in the reality of God's love for creation. But for those with clinical anxiety or anxiety disorders, fear and anxiety significantly affect their lives, including their capacities to experience the love of God and others.

But how does one differentiate between sin and psychological suffering from anxiety disorders? Counselors need to take care to make thoughtful distinctions between sin and pathology, or suffering, although there is often overlap between them (Cooper-White, 2007). It may be easy to say that all pathology is a result of sin, or vice versa, but neither of those statements is fully accurate or helpful to those who suffer. Counselors who suggest that anxiety is solely a result of sin or lack of faith hold grave misunderstandings of the human condition and are a risk to others. Of course, there is something to say for also taking sin as "moral failure" seriously (Cooper-White, 2007, p. 118).

Attachment Style, Trauma, and Interpersonal Relationships

Past experiences and parent-child relationships have influence over how people experience anxiety. Early childhood relational bonds and caregiver experiences create a template, or attachment style, for how one will relate generally with oneself and others throughout life. Attachment styles are classified into two main categories, secure and insecure. Secure attachment develops in relationships in which caregivers are consistently attuned and responsive to the needs of their infants (Wallin, 2007). Individuals who have experienced secure attachment with caregivers tend to show greater resilience when confronted with stress and problems than those with insecure attachment (Wallin, 2007). Insecure attachment styles develop when the caregivers are either inconsistent in attuning and responding to the needs of their children or rejecting or unavailable when their children express a need for comfort or nurture (Wallin, 2007; see Chapter 1 in this volume for more information on attachment theory).

Individuals with secure attachment styles generally report experiencing lower levels of anxiety and depression than individuals with insecure attachment styles (Marganska, Gallagher, & Miranda, 2013). People who experience anxiety related to issues of attachment tend to display greater levels of avoidance behaviors and lower levels of self-directedness, cooperativeness, energy, and emotional stability (Picardi, Caroppo, Toni, Bitetti, & Di Maria, 2005). Therefore, the quality of attachment relationships between children and caregivers can have substantial effects on the levels of anxiety one may experience throughout life. When counselors sit and listen to the problems of others, it is crucial to have an ear for how attachment issues may be playing a role in suffering.

In the case of Mark, it is rather obvious that his childhood experiences of anxiety are related to the environmental stressor of his family's financial instability. Perhaps not as obvious are the attachment issues involved. Mark was much too young to be concerned about family finances. He was unable to manage the fear he was experiencing. Despite his parents' best efforts, they were unable to meet his needs for comfort; he needed more from them. They also failed to help him see that he was not responsible for his family's financial situation, and, in fact, his "job" was to explore and play, to be a kid. Mark longed for quality time with his father, which would have helped to foster a sense of self-esteem and positive experiences of relational intimacy. Instead, he was left with the distorted belief that his needs and interests were not important, and, as an adult, he continued to struggle to find a sense of purpose aside from worrying about potential threats of danger.

Symptoms of anxiety are often tied to experiences of trauma and almost always coincide with trauma- and stress-related disorders (American Psychiatric Association, 2013). Traumatic experiences are often tied to events relating to death, serious injury, or sexual violence. It is important for counselors to be curious about what lies beneath one's experience of anxiety. If there is evidence or suspicion of trauma related to one's anxiety, it may have to be addressed in appropriate ways, including specific psychotherapy treatments, to aid in the alleviation of anxiety (see Chapter 4 in this volume for more information on trauma).

Whether stemming from attachment issues or trauma-related factors, anxiety disorders often affect how people interact socially. Almost all anxiety disorders listed in the *DSM-5* have symptoms related to social functioning. At some point in their lives, most people experience mild anxiety before a public speech or performance, or at a social gathering or party. For others, their experiences of anxiety in social situations are so debilitating that they have difficulty managing their distress or may even avoid social situations altogether. Severe cases may include people who have difficulty holding interpersonal conversations, going out in public, or keeping a job.

People with attachment-related anxiety also tend to misperceive social interactions or hold distorted or unrealistic beliefs about how others may treat them or what people may think about them (Şirin, 2017). These distorted beliefs or misperceptions can lead to avoidance of feared social interactions or cause relational distress and dissatisfaction. Studies have shown that individuals who score high on levels of attachment-related anxiety may be particularly sensitive to the threat of rejection in romantic relationships (Besser & Priel, 2009).

Neurobiological Disturbances

People who suffer from anxiety disorders can experience a multitude of disturbances of their personhood. The brains of people with clinical anxiety tend to display abnormalities in areas that process and regulate memories, emotions (especially fear), and hormones in the body (Shin & Liberzon, 2010). These abnormalities include the size of these areas (abnormally large or small) as well as metabolic rates (how often or fast these areas are working). Other brain abnormalities include differences in the processing and amounts of neurotransmitters, or chemicals, in the brain that affect mood, sleep, and arousal, as well as other processes governed by the central nervous system, such as the body's fight-or-flight response.

These brain abnormalities suggest that treatment for people with anxiety usually involves more than just changing thoughts and beliefs. It involves literally changing the brain or nervous system through carefully constructed interventions. For counselors, awareness of brain differences is crucial to holding a healthy and realistic perspective on how the process of healing or change may happen. Often, healing takes much longer than people hope or expect it to.

Emotion Regulation

Emotions are vital to daily life experience. Emotions are filled with meaning, value, and energy that serve to organize and direct human life. When a person's capacities to experience, regulate, and express his or her emotions are impaired, it can lead to substantial human suffering. **Emotion regulation** involves the processes responsible for monitoring, evaluating, and modifying emotional reactions, especially in respect to their duration and intensity, to meet one's goals (Thompson, 1994).

People who suffer from anxiety disorders tend to have deficits in emotion regulation. Pastors and counselors often encounter people in emotionally dysregulated states seeking help. This includes people who appear emotionally out of control, numb, or unstable. Therefore, it is important to have some understanding of the normal and abnormal processes by which people relate to their emotional experience, as it may inform how best to provide care (see Siegel, 2015). People who suffer with anxiety often find benefits from making intentional efforts to build capacities in emotion regulation through practices such as mindfulness meditation, for example.

KEY TERMS

Fear: an immediate response to a current threat of danger

Fear stimulus: a perceived threat of danger

Anxiety: a response to a stimulus that is either not occurring in the present or is not immediately a threat of danger

Emotion regulation: the processes responsible for monitoring, evaluating, and modifying emotional reactions, especially in respect to their duration and intensity, to meet one's goals

Discussion Questions

1   What are areas of anxiety in your own life? How would you describe your experience of anxiety (e.g., thoughts, bodily sensations)?

2   How do you understand the causes of your own anxiety? What may be the underlying factors (e.g., trauma, attachment)?

3   Given what you know about Mark thus far, how would you describe his emotion regulation capacities?

4   How do you understand anxiety and anxiety disorders in light of scripture and your spiritual tradition?

UNDERSTANDING GENERALIZED ANXIETY DISORDER

Taking a deeper look into Mark's internal world will detail the suffering related to **generalized anxiety disorder (GAD),** an anxiety disorder characterized by excessive worry about a variety of activities or events that is difficult to control. Mark's fears about potential danger and catastrophe keep him on high alert. He rarely feels free to relax or "stop and smell the flowers," despite his desire to be a person who is present for the gifts that God has given to him. He knows on some level that his worries are irrational and unlikely to lead to catastrophe, but that awareness does not stop his worrisome thoughts from racing. If his mind is not consumed by developing strategies to ward off danger, he is involved in activities that serve to distract him or alleviate his anxiety, such as completing yard work or researching the best retirement plans. He often feels the pressures of life are closing in on him, like a blood pressure cuff that keeps getting inflated but never entirely releases to feel comfortable. Despite his best efforts, he cannot quite reach a place of balance and calm, like everyone around him seems to. Every few months, he has a string of darker days when he feels like throwing in the towel. He begs God for relief but despairs that life will ever change. (Indeed, many people with anxiety disorders have an active faith and prayer life, but this does not reduce their symptoms).

Intolerance of Uncertainty

Life is full of uncertainty. It is an existential aspect of being human that can be disliked and difficult to accept. Much time and energy are devoted to trying to predict the future, from the weather to the stock market. It is perfectly normal to be concerned at times about what may happen in the future. However, people with GAD have significant difficulty coping with uncertainty. The **intolerance of uncertainty** is defined as the inability to cope with the fearful response triggered by uncertain situations (Carleton, 2016). This includes problematic ways in which an individual thinks, feels, and behaves in response to ambiguous or uncertain situations (Dugas, Gagnon, Ladouceu, & Freeston, 1998). Intolerance of uncertainty includes three key components: positive beliefs about worry, negative problem orientation, and cognitive avoidance (Dugas et al., 1998, Bottesi et al., 2016).

Positive beliefs about worry include beliefs such as "worrying helps me to get things sorted out in my mind," "worrying helps me to solve my problems," and "worrying helps me to avoid problems in the future" (Wells & Cartwright-Hatton, 2004). People who hold positive beliefs about worry generally attempt to use worry as a form of problem solving. However, it turns out that it's not very effective and only reinforces worrying thought patterns, making them difficult to stop or change and often increasing anxiety. Mark's pattern of worrying is centered on uncertain situations, which began in childhood with the uncertainty of his family's financial security. On some level, he believes that worrying about the uncertainty of his life situations makes him more prepared for those dangers, should they become reality.

Negative problem orientation is a general posture of negativity toward problems, including thoughts and emotions that are evoked by problematic situations (Bottesi et al., 2016). People with GAD do not like to be faced with problems. Whereas some people see problems as opportunities for learning or challenge, individuals with GAD feel that they are unable to use problem-solving strategies effectively, leaving them lacking in confidence that they are equipped to manage problems when they arise. They may quickly feel overwhelmed and helpless, and tend to be pessimistic that the problems they encounter can be solved.

The third component of the intolerance of uncertainty is **cognitive avoidance**, thought processes used to avoid or alter uncomfortable thoughts and imagery that may also be associated with unwanted feelings (Bottesi et al., 2016). Since worrying is a hallmark symptom of GAD, it is believed that worry also functions as a maladaptive strategy to avoid more distressing emotions or experiences (Lee, Orsillo, Roemer, & Allen, 2010). In the case of Mark, his worry likely prevented him from experiencing his sadness over his family's situation or his anger at his father for never being around to play with him. Since avoidance is such a problematic aspect of GAD, it will be expanded upon in the next section.

Unbearable Affective Experience, Experiential Avoidance, and Worry

An aspect of the anxious response in GAD is an intense fear that arises in anticipation of feelings and emotions that are perceived as unbearable. **Unbearable affective experiences** are emotional experiences that are fundamentally painful (e.g., grief, loneliness), of great potential to threaten the self (e.g., rage leading to loss of control), or elicit negative emotional responses from one's relational environment (e.g., expression of sexual feelings met with shaming responses) (Fosha, 2000). Unbearable affective experiences arise from traumatic events, relational losses (e.g., loss of a parent/caregiver), and insecure child-parent attachment relationships. The human mind has amazing capacities to defend itself against unbearable affective experiences. These defensive strategies are usually highly effective in the short-term to reestablish a sense of safety in the face of overwhelming emotions, but when they are used regularly as strategies to respond to daily life experience, they become highly problematic and lead to suffering. Examples of defensive strategies include denial, avoidance, and substance use.

A common defensive strategy in GAD is **experiential avoidance**, a defensive strategy involving a person's unwillingness to connect with particular private experiences (e.g., bodily sensations, emotions, thoughts, memories, behavioral predispositions) and intentional efforts to circumvent events and contexts that trigger them (Hayes, Wilson, Gifford, Follette, & Strosahl, 1996). As outlined previously, people with GAD are highly sensitive to stimuli perceived to be dangerous and capable of leading to unbearable affective experiences, when, in fact, the stimuli pose no realistic threat or danger. With GAD, these stimuli trigger an anxious response that is highly uncomfortable. Experiential avoidance is used to defend against this anxious response, which provides temporary relief from the discomfort. However, experiential avoidance perpetuates suffering, as it keeps individuals from understanding what drives their anxious response, such as past traumatic experiences, painful memories, or family of origin influences. They are unwilling to explore or be curious about their thoughts, emotions, memories, and bodily sensations evoked by the stimuli, which prevents change. It is often only by a process of exploration and increasing awareness of one's anxious response that opportunities are created for healing and change (Tompkins, 2013).

Chronic, excessive worry is the hallmark symptom of GAD (American Psychiatric Association, 2013). **Worry** is a flurry of negative verbal thoughts (as opposed to imagery) about negative events feared to happen in the future (Borkovec, Ray, & Stöber, 1998). Worry is a form of experiential avoidance because it involves mainly thoughts, which block a person from being in touch with his or her bodily and emotional experiences, and prevents healthy emotional regulation of fear (Foa & Kozak, 1986). Because worry causes people to disengage with their bodily sensations and emotions, it has positive short-term effects of relief from discomfort. This temporary relief from discomfort reinforces the need to worry, making it difficult to control. Because of the avoidant nature of worry, people with GAD often have little understanding about the nature of their worry (e.g., why they worry), which only exacerbates their fear and anxiety (Starcevic, 2005).

Etiological, Predisposing, and Related Factors

As mentioned earlier, GAD can arise from insecure early attachment relationships, trauma, and unbearable affective experiences. Studies have indicated that people with severe GAD report significant deficits in early attachment relationships (e.g., Cassidy, Lichtenstein-Phelps, Sibrava, Thomas, & Borkovec, 2009). These include childhood experiences of role reversal, low maternal love, and high maternal rejection (Cassidy et al., 2009). Childhood experiences of role reversal involve not only the failure of the parent to meet the needs of the child but also the demand that the child care for the parent. Such responsibility is developmentally inappropriate for a child and likely emotionally overwhelming. Low maternal love and high maternal rejection are emotionally painful and often terrifying to young children. Other types of child maltreatment have also been associated with GAD, including harsh discipline, changes in primary caregiver, and exposure to physical abuse or unwanted sexual contact (Moffitt et al., 2007). These types of unbearable affective experiences early in life likely set a course of avoidant behaviors that persist into adulthood (Cassidy et al., 2009).

In the United States, sociodemographic factors, including gender, race, age, marital status, and socioeconomic status, are associated with differentiated risks for GAD (Grant et al., 2005). Women are twice as likely to be diagnosed with GAD as men. People in middle age (30–64) also have much higher rates of GAD than young adults and those in later life stages. Asian Americans have the lowest rate of GAD in the United States, while whites and Native Americans have the highest rates. Individuals who are widowed, divorced, or separated are twice as likely to have GAD than people who are married or cohabiting. Income also plays a major role, with low-income earners at much greater risk. Some minority populations have significantly elevated risk for anxiety disorders, including transgender individuals (Budge, Adelson, & Howard, 2013).

It is also likely that GAD has a genetic component, although it is hard to disentangle genetic factors from environmental ones, since family influences co-occur in these ways. Some studies show evidence of genetic factors in individuals who have GAD with co-occurring major depression (e.g., Hettema, Neale, & Kendler, 2001). GAD also seems to have a developmental pattern, which means there are often signs of anxiety in childhood and adolescence that seem to grow in severity over time, until they peak in adulthood. Some of these early signs, aside from the attachment-related ones previously mentioned, may include conduct problems, such as fighting, bullying, stealing, and lying (Moffitt et al., 2007).

Diagnostic and Statistical Manual of Mental Disorders Diagnostic Criteria

GAD is a diagnostic term created by the American Psychiatric Association (1980) in attempt to capture a constellation of anxiety symptoms that differentiate GAD from other anxiety disorders, as well as normal expressions of anxiety. The hallmark of GAD is the presence of excessive worry nearly every day for 6 months or more. The worry spreads over several domains of life, usually including work or school, relationships, and home life. Whereas other types of worry come and go, those with GAD experience much difficulty stopping the worry. They struggle to relax, rarely experiencing calm and peace. Typically, these individuals have difficulty with sleep, leaving them fatigued and often tense and irritable (American Psychiatric Association, 2013).

Awareness of GAD symptoms can help you effectively differentiate GAD from other anxiety disorders, as well as normal expressions of anxiety. Such familiarity with the symptoms and complexity of GAD will also aid in determining the appropriate course of action for care, including possible referrals to mental health professionals.

Comorbidity

Comorbidity, or co-occurring medical disorders, is a common feature of GAD. This means that most people who have GAD also have at least one other psychological or medical disorder. This adds a great deal of complexity to the appearance of a person's symptoms and suffering, and often makes it difficult to see clearly what is going on in a person. Common comorbid psychological diagnoses include depressive disorders, substance abuse and dependence, personality disorders, and other anxiety disorders, including panic disorder (Grant et al., 2005). GAD and major depressive disorder have the highest rates of comorbidity, with estimates between 40% and 98% (Zbozinek et al., 2012). Comorbid medical diagnoses include cancer, asthma, irritable bowel syndrome, chronic pain, and cardiovascular disease (Roy-Byrne, et al., 2008).

As a counselor, being curious and patient in understanding the complexity of someone's suffering will not only help you avoid harming someone by overlooking or simplifying aspects of their suffering but also empower you to make informed and discerning decisions about how best to care for them. In the case of Mark, not only does he display symptoms of GAD, but he also shows signs of depression (i.e., hopelessness/despair). It is good practice to refer those under one's care for a comprehensive medical evaluation by a physician to rule out other issues.

KEY TERMS

Generalized anxiety disorder: an anxiety disorder characterized by excessive worry about a variety of activities or events that is difficult to control

Intolerance of uncertainty: the inability to cope with the fearful response triggered by uncertain situations

Positive beliefs about worry: beliefs that worrying has benefits

Negative problem orientation: a general posture of negativity toward problems, including thoughts and emotions that are evoked by problematic situations

Cognitive avoidance: thought processes used to avoid or alter uncomfortable thoughts and imagery that may also be associated with unwanted feelings

Unbearable affective experiences: emotional experiences that are fundamentally painful (e.g., grief, loneliness), of great potential to threaten the self (e.g., rage leading to loss of control), or elicit negative emotional responses from one's relational environment (e.g., expression of sexual feelings met with shaming responses)

Experiential avoidance: a defensive strategy involving a person's unwillingness to connect with particular private experiences (e.g., bodily sensations, emotions, thoughts, memories, behavioral predispositions) and intentional efforts to circumvent events and contexts that trigger them

Worry: a flurry of negative verbal thoughts (as opposed to imagery) about negative events feared to happen in the future

Discussion Questions

1   How do positive beliefs about worry, negative problem orientation, and cognitive avoidance contribute to the experience of anxiety in GAD?

2   How is worrying a form of avoidance?

3   In the case of Mark, how did his early childhood experiences possibly play a role in the development of GAD?

4   What is the most common comorbid diagnosis with GAD?

TREATMENT APPROACHES FOR GENERALIZED ANXIETY DISORDER

As with many psychological disorders, the two main approaches to the treatment of GAD are psychological treatment and psychopharmacological treatment. Psychological treatment generally takes the form of "talk therapy," although for some disorders, such as phobias, treatment may be in vivo, or outside the therapist's office. The three main types of psychological treatment for GAD include cognitive-behavioral therapies (CBTs), acceptance-based therapies, and emotion-focused/psychodynamic therapies. As a pastoral counselor, knowledge of these differing types of psychological treatment will aid you in finding the best approach for the person you are trying to help.

CBTs are the most recognized type of psychological treatment for GAD (Timulak & McElvaney, 2016). CBT treatment for GAD usually focuses on some or all of the following: education about anxiety, early detection of anxious cues, monitoring of anxious responding, relaxation exercises, imaginary exposure to feared stimuli, desensitization, and construction of better coping skills (Roemer & Orsillo, 2002). The focus of CBT treatment is on working with thoughts and behaviors relevant to a person's experience of anxiety, but may also include space for emotional processing. However, CBT treatment may not be the most helpful choice when a person's experience of anxiety is rooted in attachment-related issues because it does not promote the use of the therapy as a new relational experience (between the therapist and client) that may serve as a source of healing of one's pain.

One major critique of CBT treatment for GAD is that it does not usually include components focused on the acceptance of a person's anxious experience. Acceptance is being "experientially open" to the reality of the present moment rather than focusing on evaluation or judgment of what one is experiencing (Roemer & Orsillo, 2002). Within the last few decades, CBT treatment has shifted to recognize and include the importance of acceptance as a means of working with anxiety (Rosales & Tan, 2016; Tan, 2011). Acceptance can be such an important aspect of GAD treatment because it targets the person's avoidance, which, as mentioned earlier, is what fuels anxiety and underlies worry in GAD. One example of an acceptance-based treatment is acceptance and commitment therapy (ACT). ACT involves three main components: decreasing the use of avoidant strategies through increasing acceptance of one's experience, reducing the responses to one's thoughts through a posture of mindfulness, and increasing one's commitment to behavioral change based on one's values and beliefs (Hayes, 2005). This last component provides space for the person's spiritual values and beliefs to be incorporated specifically into their psychological treatment.

Although CBT treatments are often used and have been shown in studies to be effective in treating GAD, there is a growing body of research to support the effectiveness of emotion-focused and short-term psychodynamic therapies (e.g., Crits-Christoph, Gibbons, Narducci, Schamberger, & Gallop, 2005; Leichsenring et al., 2009; Lilliengren, Johansson, Town, Kisely, & Abbass, 2017; Timulak & McElvaney, 2016). These treatment models may be particularly effective in treating GAD because they focus on emotional processing, especially with respect to interpersonal relationships (e.g., negative attachment-related experiences, interpersonal trauma, loss). This focus on emotional processing may be key in reducing experiential avoidance in GAD, because it is often the fear of triggering events or experiencing certain emotional states that causes people to avoid situations and relationships.

Understanding Panic

Almost immediately after his first child was born, Mark entered into a season of height-ened anxiety. He would often awaken in the middle of the night in a state of alarm to check to see if his infant daughter was still breathing. He had read a newspaper article about sudden infant death syndrome that ignited new fears about his daughter's seeming fragility. To make matters worse, the local grocery store he was managing was strug-gling financially, which pressured him to find ways to cut costs, or he would be forced to lay off some of his employees. One afternoon while he was in his work office, one of his employees brought him the daily mail. As Mark sifted through the various letters, he came across an unexpected bill from one of his vendors. Instantly, his heart began to race. Something felt lodged in his throat. Gasping for air, he felt as if his office walls were caving in on him. A cashier returning from her break noticed his face was flushed and his eyes were wide as she walked past his office window. She poked her head in to see if he was okay, but Mark was unable to piece together a sentence. His mind was racing and blank all at once. She called 911 and paramedics rushed him to the local emergency room.

Panic Attacks and Panic Disorder

The word "panic" is used often in common language to describe the experience of intense fear that is accompanied by irrational or frantic behavior. In clinical terminology, a **panic attack** is an experience of sudden and intense anxiety with associated physiological, or bodily, symptoms, including, sweating, dizziness, increased heart rate, difficulty breath-ing, and thoughts that often include a fear of imminent death or loss of mental control (Pilecki, Arentoft, & McKay, 2011). People who experience panic attacks, like Mark, usually misinterpret their bodily sensations as signs of serious medical issues, such as a heart attack, when in reality they are experiencing anxiety. They often incur large medical bills because of ambulance trips to hospital emergency rooms or primary care appointments when, in fact, there are no medical explanations for their experiences. Rather, the root of the issue is psychological in nature.

Some people may experience a sole panic attack in their lifetime. Others experience recurrent panic attacks that may warrant a clinical diagnosis of panic disorder. **Panic disorder** is the experience of unexpected recurrent panic attacks, one of which is followed by at least 1 month of worry about having more panic attacks or their consequences (e.g., "it may kill me"), or significant behavioral change because of the panic attacks (e.g., avoidant behaviors; American Psychiatric Association, 2013). Every year, approximately 2%–3% of adults living in the United States are diagnosed with panic disorder, while approximately 11.2% experience panic attacks (American Psychiatric Association, 2013). Therefore, it is much more likely for people to experience panic attacks without meeting criteria for panic disorder. Women are more likely to experience panic attacks than men, and they are twice as likely to develop panic disorder (American Psychiatric Association, 2013). Panic attacks can occur in adolescence, but are very rarely seen in children.

Expected and Unexpected Panic Attacks

An important distinction to be made is the difference between expected and unexpected panic attacks. An **expected panic attack** is a panic attack that is evoked by an obvious cue or trigger (e.g., flying on an airplane; driving over a bridge; American Psychiatric Association, 2013). This means that the panic attack is bound to a specific situation, and subsequent panic attacks may occur in the same or very similar situations. On the other hand, an **unexpected panic attack** is a panic attack that occurs "out of the blue" with no obvious cue or trigger (American Psychiatric Association, 2013). Unexpected panic attacks are not bound by a situation or event and may even occur during sleep (i.e., nocturnal panic attack). Recurrent unexpected panic attacks are required to be diagnosed with panic disorder. Sometimes, it can be difficult to determine if a panic attack is expected or unexpected. Mental health professionals are trained to make these careful judgments through diagnostic interviews. Mark's panic attack described earlier would be considered unexpected. He had opened plenty of bills in the past. In fact, it was a regular aspect of his daily routine.

Agoraphobia

As a pastoral counselor, being acquainted with associated disorders and symptoms that accompany GAD and panic disorder is a vital aspect of understanding and approaching these experiences of human suffering. Much like depressive disorders are commonly associated with GAD, agoraphobia is one associated anxiety disorder that occurs commonly with panic attacks and panic disorder. **Agoraphobia** is characterized by an intense fear and anxiety of situations in which escape may be difficult, and intentional efforts made to avoid such situations. These situations include the use of public transportation (e.g., buses, trains, planes), open spaces (e.g., parking lots, bridges), enclosed spaces (e.g., grocery stores, malls, movie theaters), standing in line or in a crowd, and being outside of one's home (American Psychiatric Association, 2013). The intense fear and anxiety involved in agoraphobia usually includes catastrophic thoughts about horrible things happening, as well as the fear of experiencing embarrassing or debilitating symptoms with no one to help. Estimates indicate that 30%–50% of people experience panic attacks or meet criteria for panic disorder prior to developing agoraphobia (American Psychiatric Association, 2013).

Diagnostic and Statistical Manual of Mental Disorders Diagnostic Criteria

The *DSM-5* (American Psychiatric Association, 2013) provides diagnostic criteria for both panic attacks and panic disorder. Panic attacks involve a sudden onset of significant fear accompanied by substantial changes in the body. These may include rapid heart rate, shortness of breath, chest pain, numbness, and dizziness, as well as other symptoms. It is also common to experience catastrophic thinking, including the thought that one is about to die. These symptoms tend to reach the height of greatest intensity within minutes. Panic disorder is diagnosed when there is a history of multiple panic attacks and a person experiences ongoing worry about having more attacks in the future. Often, this includes significant changes in a person's behavior to avoid future panic attacks from occurring.

Comorbidity

Panic attacks can occur alongside any other psychological disorder. Like GAD, individuals with panic disorder tend to have high rates of comorbidity with other psychological disorders, including other anxiety disorders (e.g., agoraphobia, GAD, specific phobia, social anxiety disorder), mood disorders, somatic disorders, and alcohol use disorders (Starcevic, 2005). People with panic disorder also tend to have higher rates of suicide and suicidal ideation than people with many other psychological disorders (American Psychiatric Association, 2013).

It is important for counselors to be aware that some people who experience panic attacks also may have serious medical conditions underlying their bodily symptoms that exacerbate their anxiety. Some of these conditions include cardiac arrhythmias, hyperthyroidism, vestibular dysfunction, mitral valve prolapse, epilepsy, and hypoglycemia (Barlow, 2014; Starcevic, 2005). Therefore, it is crucial that counselors, who attempt to care for individuals who appear to be experiencing panic attacks refer to medical professionals for comprehensive medical evaluations to rule out medical issues.

KEY TERMS

Panic attack: an experience of sudden and intense anxiety with associated physiological, or bodily, symptoms, including, sweating, dizziness, increased heart rate, difficulty breathing, and thoughts that often include a fear of imminent death or loss of mental control

Panic disorder: the experience of unexpected recurrent panic attacks, one of which is followed by at least 1 month of worry about having more panic attacks or their consequences (e.g., "it may kill me"), or significant behavioral change because of the panic attacks (e.g., avoidant behaviors; American Psychiatric Association, 2013)

Expected panic attack: a panic attack that is evoked by an obvious cue or trigger (e.g., flying on an airplane; driving over a bridge)

Unexpected panic attack: a panic attack that occurs "out of the blue" with no obvious cue or trigger

Agoraphobia: an anxiety disorder characterized by an intense fear and anxiety of situations in which escape may be difficult, and intentional efforts made to avoid such situations

Discussion Questions

1   What is the difference between a panic attack and panic disorder?

2   How does one differentiate between unexpected and expected panic attacks?

3   What is agoraphobia and how does it relate to panic disorder?

4   In the case of Mark, which symptoms of a panic attack was he likely experiencing?

TREATMENT APPROACHES FOR PANIC DISORDER

The two most used approaches for treatment of panic disorder are CBT and pharmacotherapy treatment. CBT is considered the treatment of choice for panic disorder (Reichenberg & Seligman, 2016). Many research studies support the effectiveness of CBT for panic disorder, with 70%–80% of people reporting no symptoms of panic at the end of treatment (Barlow, 2014). Although there are different forms of CBT for panic disorder, most CBT treatments include the following elements: education about anxiety, self-monitoring exercises, respiratory/breathing training, applied relaxation exercises, cognitive restructuring to address anxiety sensitivity and catastrophic misinterpretations, and exposure to feared bodily sensations (Barlow, 2014; Starcevic, 2005). Pharmacotherapy treatment is also highly used mostly because of people with panic seeking help in medical care settings (e.g., emergency room, primary care). Selective serotonin reuptake inhibitors and tricyclics are the two types of antidepressants most commonly prescribed for panic disorder (Starcevic, 2005). Short-acting benzodiazepines (e.g., Alprazolam, Clonazepam) are also commonly used, but should be considered with strong caution because of their addictive nature.

Panic-focused psychodynamic psychotherapy (PFPP) also has been shown to be effective in treating panic disorder, although the research support is not as robust as for CBT (Beutel, Stark, Pan, Silbersweig, & Dietrich, 2010; Busch, Milrod, & Singer, 1999; Milrod et al., 2001; Milrod et al., 2007). PFPP has three phases. Phase one works to address acute panic symptoms through exploration and processing of unconscious emotions and personal meanings to achieve relief. Phase two focuses on panic vulnerability by working through underlying conflicts, which are theorized to involve separation/autonomy and the experience and expression of anger. Phase three involves termination of the therapy, using the relational aspects of the therapy to further address underlying conflicts relevant to panic.

FACILITATING A PASTORAL RESPONSE TO ANXIETY

The following guiding principles are offered as considerations for pastoral counselors to use and integrate with their specific spiritual traditions, theological perspectives, and cultural community contexts. It is not the opinion of this author that there is a "right" way to integrate psychological approaches with pastoral ministry, but rather that each pastoral counselor must take responsibility for the careful task of thoughtful integration in his or her specific contexts. Although these guiding principles are in light of the topic of anxiety and panic, they may be applied to other presentations of suffering as well.

- *Containment.* People with high levels of anxiety often seek help in moments of emotional dysregulation. This means they may enter the counseling relationship in a frantic state, which can be overwhelming to the counselor. Therefore, it can be helpful to the counselee (and counselor) to offer responses that provide **containment** of the person's anxiety. Often this simply involves an empathic and kind presence that takes seriously the person's suffering. Other helpful responses include statements that are reflective, educational, or offer steps to address their concerns. Such a statement may sound like, "You've been experiencing a lot of anxiety and worry about a variety of issues. That sounds really challenging. Perhaps it would be helpful for us to think about getting you connected with a good psychotherapist."

- *Openness and curiosity.* It is far more helpful to take a posture of openness and curiosity to a person's anxiety than to simply jump into problem solving. Sometimes asking thoughtful and discerning questions about a person's experience can begin the healing process. It will also help to prevent missing vital aspects of someone's experience, including comorbid disorders and histories of abuse or attachment-related wounds. Being interested in the experience of someone's suffering rather than jumping to diagnostic labels or reducing the person to a disorder is honoring to their personhood and uniqueness.

- *Content versus relationship.* A common mistake when attempting to alleviate someone's fears is to engage in a rational argument to dispel the person's concerns. More often than not, and especially for those with GAD, simply addressing the surface content, or object, that is feared (e.g., fear of social rejection, fear of uncertain future events) through reasoning or reassurance will not lead to long-term relief. Rather, it is the relationship to their anxiety and fear (e.g., worrying, avoidance, intolerance of uncertainty, attachment-related issues) that is problematic and is in need of being addressed. For example, a pastor may encourage someone struggling with anxiety to increase his or her distress tolerance through building skills in the areas of self-soothing, acceptance, and mindfulness practices.

- *Spirituality and spiritualization.* Research clearly indicates an important connection between a person's spirituality and mental health issues (e.g., DiPierro, Fite, & Johnson-Motoyama, 2018; Koszycki, Bilodeau, Raab-Mayo, & Bradwejn, 2010; Wilt, Grubbs, Lindberg, Exline, & Pargament, 2017). Perhaps this is obvious to the pastoral counselor. However, much care and wisdom are needed in how such issues are handled. Although theological teaching, spiritual disciplines, and communal fellowship are vital aspects to the spiritual lives of most people, simple recommendations along these lines to people struggling with anxiety disorders rarely addresses the roots of their anxiety. Yarhouse, Butman and McRay, drawing on the insight of Brennan Manning, write, "It becomes readily apparent to most pastors or Christian workers that meditation on key Scriptures rarely 'fixes' serious anxiety struggles, any more than the regular singing of 'Amazing Grace' helps a struggling person feel like he or she is God's beloved" (p. 112, 2005). Similarly, there are often important spiritual meanings related to people's experiences of anxiety, but counselors should take care not to overly **spiritualize** the anxiety a person experiences or reduce a person's suffering to a matter of inaccurate theological beliefs or "lack of faith."

- *Embodiment and dualism.* There are some Christian traditions that uphold theological doctrine pertaining to body/soul dualism, or some other bifurcation of the material and immaterial aspects of personhood. Such dualism has been used historically to dismiss the importance of the role of the body in a person's psychological experience, or **embodiment.** However, recent advances in neuroscience have made claims for the importance of the body (e.g., genes, neuroplasticity, mirror neurons) in human lived experience and its relationship to suffering, flourishing, and mature spirituality (see Hogue, 2014). To provide adequate care, it is imperative that counselors be educated about and take seriously the role of the body in suffering so that they may integrate such knowledge into a thoughtful pastoral response that will be honoring to the experiences of those under their care.

- *Know thyself.* Perhaps the greatest capacity in working with people who struggle with anxiety is the counselor's own self-awareness. Knowing and practicing mindfulness of one's own anxiety and emotional regulation experiences, past and present, affords the counselor an empathic presence that will likely allow others to feel cared for and understood.

KEY TERMS

Containment: the capacity to manage or limit distressing thoughts, feelings, and imagery

Embodiment: the emphasis on the role of the body in an individual's psychological experience

Discussion Questions

1 Which principles listed earlier do you imagine will be most challenging for you in your role as counselor?

2 Think of an example in which you reached out for someone for help in processing a stressful or anxiety-provoking situation. What aspects of the person's response were helpful to you? Which were not?

REVIEWING THE CONCEPTS

Learning Objectives

- Differentiate GAD, panic attacks, and panic disorder from other expressions of anxiety and fear
  - GAD is an anxiety disorder characterized by excessive worry about a variety of activities or events that is difficult to control.
  - Panic attacks are experiences of sudden and intense anxiety with associated physiological, or bodily, symptoms, including, sweating, dizziness, increased heart rate, difficulty breathing, and thoughts that often include a fear of imminent death or loss of mental control.
  - Panic disorder is the experience of unexpected recurrent panic attacks, one of which is followed by at least 1 month of worry about having more panic attacks or their consequences (e.g., "it may kill me"), or significant behavioral change because of the panic attacks (e.g., avoidant behaviors).

- Describe the symptoms of generalized anxiety and panic
  - GAD is characterized by excessive anxiety and worry, which is a flurry of negative verbal thoughts (as opposed to imagery) about negative events feared to happen in the future. It is difficult to control and is usually accompanied by symptoms of restlessness, fatigue, difficulty concentrating, irritability, muscle tension, and sleep disturbance.
  - Panic is an abrupt surge of intense fear or intense discomfort that reaches a peak within minutes and is usually accompanied by accelerated heart rate, sweating, trembling, shortness of breath, feelings of choking, chest discomfort, nausea, dizziness, numbness/tingling, and hot/cold sensations. It can also include feelings of unreality, being detached from oneself, and fears of losing control or dying.

- Facilitate a pastoral response to anxiety and panic among parishioners
  - We reviewed six guiding principles for facilitating a pastor response to parishioners with presentations of anxiety and panic.
  - Educational and support resources are provided at the end of the chapter.

- Identify common etiological, predisposing, and risk factors
  - For GAD, factors include deficits and relational injuries in early attachment relational experiences and other environmental factors, as well as genetic heredity. Risk factors for GAD are also related to race, gender, age, marital status, and socioeconomic status.
  - For panic, genetic heredity may be a substantial factor. Other factors include family history of mental illness, various negative environmental factors, and cognitive factors—namely, catastrophic misinterpretations of bodily sensations, anxiety sensitivity, and panic self-efficacy.

Chapter Review Questions

Level 1: Knowledge (True/False)

1. All anxiety has the same root causes and is easily treated.

2. Nearly everyone agrees that anxiety and fear are the same.

3. Cultural factors have little to no influence on the experience and manifestation of anxiety.

4. Symptoms of anxiety are almost always experienced by individuals who meet criteria for trauma- or stress-related disorders.

5. Emotional regulation involves nonconscious processes that may have profound effects on an individual's experience of anxiety as well as emotions.

6. In individuals with GAD, worry is considered a form of experiential avoidance.

7. GAD has very low rates of comorbidity when compared with other disorders.

8. Panic attacks always lead to the development of panic disorder.

9. Panic attacks can occur alongside any psychological disorder.

10. There is only one effective treatment for panic disorder.

Level 2: Comprehension

1. Without much access to consciousness,

   a. people are generally happier

   b. people risk living their lives on "automatic pilot," leaving them little room to choose or influence how nonconscious processes affect them

   c. people will never lead fulfilling lives

   d. people experience much greater levels of freedom and rarely ever experience distressing anxiety

2. Which of the following is the disorder that most commonly occurs with panic attacks and panic disorder?

   a. Attention-deficit/hyperactivity disorder

   b. Agoraphobia

   c. Schizophrenia

   d. Anorexia nervosa

3. Which of the following is a defensive strategy involving a person's unwillingness to connect with aspects of one's experience?

   a. Intolerance of uncertainty

   b. Experiential avoidance

   c. Psychopharmacology

   d. Cognitive distortions

4. Neurobiological differences in individuals with chronic anxiety include all of the following except
   a. complete absence of specific brain regions
   b. abnormalities in the size of specific brain regions
   c. abnormalities in the metabolic rates in specific brain regions
   d. neurotransmitter abnormalities

5. Agoraphobia
   a. always occurs prior to the onset of panic disorder
   b. is preceded by panic attacks or panic disorder in 30%–50% of cases
   c. always occurs subsequent to the onset of panic disorder
   d. never occurs in the case of panic disorder

6. Evidence-based psychological treatments for GAD include
   a. CBT, acceptance-based therapies, and emotion-focused/psychodynamic therapies
   b. CBT only
   c. acceptance-based therapies only
   d. none of the above

7. Which is not a guiding principle to consider when facilitating a pastoral response?
   a. Providing simple spiritual answers to people's problems
   b. Openness and curiosity
   c. Taking seriously human embodiment
   d. Developing and maintaining mindful self-awareness

8. Which treatments for panic disorder are most used?
   a. Biofeedback and pharmacotherapy
   b. Electroconvulsive therapy and pharmacotherapy
   c. Psychoanalysis and CBT
   d. CBT and pharmacotherapy

9. Which of the following is not a symptom of a panic attack?
   a. Chest pain
   b. Sweating
   c. Fear of dying
   d. Memory loss

10. Factors that contribute to an individual's experience of anxiety include all of the following except
    a. insecure attachment issues
    b. traumatic experiences
    c. genetic factors
    d. blood type

Level 3: Application

1. A parishioner approaches you wanting to get your thoughts on how to make sense of anxiety in light of the Christian faith. In 500 words or less, craft a response to this person's request in light of the chapter material and your own spiritual/ theological tradition.

2. Find an example of someone who may be suffering from GAD or panic disorder in television or film. How might you respond to this person if he or she approached you for counseling? What guiding principles may be most helpful?

3. Compare and contrast generalized anxiety and panic.

4. A parishioner approaches you after a sermon you just preached. He is extremely anxious about some aspects of your teaching that may have future implications on his life. How would you respond? What questions might be helpful to ask to ascertain what might be going on in this person?

5. Given that anxiety is a common human experience, how would you determine when you might need to refer a parishioner to see a mental health professional for treatment? What information would inform this decision?

ANSWERS

LEVEL 1: KNOWLEDGE

1. F
2. F
3. F
4. T
5. T
6. T
7. F
8. F
9. T
10. F

LEVEL 2: COMPREHENSION

1. b
2. b
3. b
4. a
5. b

6. a

7. a

8. d

9. d

10. d

RESOURCES

Online Resources

- National Alliance on Mental Illness—https://www.nami.org
- National Institute of Mental Health—https://www.nimh.nih.gov/index.shtml
- Anxiety and Depression Association of America—https://adaa.org
- American Psychological Association—http://www.apa.org/topics/anxiety/

Readings

- *My Age of Anxiety: Fear, Hope, Dread, and the Search for Peace of Mind*—Scott Stossel
- *The Meaning of Anxiety*—Rollo May
- *Be Not Anxious: Pastoral Care of Disquieted Souls*—Allan Hugh Cole Jr.
- *Modern Psychopathologies: A Comprehensive Christian Appraisal*—Mark Yarhouse and Richard Butman

Video Resources

- *Anxiety: 11 Things We Want You To Understand*—Psych2Go: https://www.youtube.com/watch?v=E35O0nxOUy4
- *The Do's of Assisting With Panic Attacks*—Psych2Go: https://www.youtube.com/watch?v=t7VjFfsZKE4
- *Living With High-Functioning Anxiety*—Jordan Raskopoulos—TEDxSydney: https://www.youtube.com/watch?v=JUedQ0_EGCQ
- *Surviving Anxiety: Solome Tibebu at TEDxTC*—https://www.youtube.com/watch?v=8PcdRyB8YJY

CLASSROOM ACTIVITIES

1. Role-play counseling sessions involving anxiety and panic presentations.

2. Consider a circumstance in your life in which you experienced anxiety. As you recall the memory, articulate the ways in which you experienced anxiety in both your body and thought life. Share your experience with a classmate.

3. In small groups, consider ways in which Christians tend to spiritualize experiences of anxiety or reduce the complexity of anxiety to simplistic explanations. What sorts of language have you heard in this regard? How might this affect the person who suffers with anxiety?

REFERENCES

American Psychiatric Association. (1980). *Diagnostic and statistical manual of mental disorders* (3rd ed.). Washington, DC: Author.

American Psychiatric Association. (2013). *Diagnostic and statistical manual of mental disorders* (5th ed.). Washington, DC: Author.

Barlow, D. H. (Ed.). (2014). *Clinical handbook of psychological disorders: A step-by-step treatment manual.* New York, NY: Guilford Publications.

Beutel, M. E., Stark, R., Pan, H., Silbersweig, D., & Dietrich, S. (2010). Changes of brain activation pre-post short-term psychodynamic inpatient psychotherapy: An fMRI study of panic disorder patients. *Psychiatry Research: Neuroimaging, 184*(2), 96–104.

Besser, A., & Priel, B. (2009). Emotional responses to a romantic partner's imaginary rejection: The roles of attachment anxiety, covert narcissism, and self-evaluation. *Journal of Personality, 77*(1), 287–325.

Borkovec, T. D., Ray, W. J., & Stöber, J. (1998). Worry: A cognitive phenomenon intimately linked to affective, physiological, and interpersonal behavioral processes. *Cognitive Therapy and Research, 22*(6), 561–576.

Bottesi, G., Ghisi, M., Carraro, E., Barclay, N., Payne, R., & Freeston, M. H. (2016). Revising the intolerance of uncertainty model of generalized anxiety disorder: Evidence from UK and Italian undergraduate samples. *Frontiers in Psychology, 7*(1723).

Budge, S. L., Adelson, J. L., & Howard, K. A. S. (2013). Anxiety and depression in transgender individuals: The roles of transition status, loss, social support, and coping. *Journal of Consulting and Clinical Psychology, 81*(3), 545–557.

Busch, F. N., Milrod, B. L., & Singer, M. B. (1999). Theory and technique in psychodynamic treatment of panic disorder. *Journal of Psychotherapy Practice and Research, 8*(3), 234.

Carleton, R. N. (2016). Into the unknown: A review and synthesis of contemporary models involving uncertainty. *Journal of Anxiety Disorders, 39*, 30–43.

Cassidy, J., Lichtenstein-Phelps, J., Sibrava, N. J., Thomas Jr, C. L., & Borkovec, T. D. (2009). Generalized anxiety disorder: Connections with self-reported attachment. *Behavior Therapy, 40*(1), 23–38.

Cooper-White, P. (2007). *Many voices: Pastoral psychotherapy in relational and theological perspective*. Minneapolis, MN: Fortress Press.

Crits-Christoph, P., Gibbons, M. B. C., Narducci, J., Schamberger, M., & Gallop, R. (2005). Interpersonal problems and the outcome of interpersonally oriented psychodynamic treatment of GAD. *Psychotherapy: Theory, Research, Practice, Training, 42*(2), 211.

DiPierro, M., Fite, P. J., & Johnson-Motoyama, M. (2018). The role of religion and spirituality in the association between hope and anxiety in a sample of Latino youth. *Child & Youth Care Forum, 47*(1), 101–114. doi: 10.1007/s10566-017-9421-2

Dugas, M. J., Gagnon, F., Ladouceur, R., & Freeston, M. H. (1998). Generalized anxiety disorder: A preliminary test of a conceptual model. *Behaviour Research and Therapy, 36*(2), 215–226.

ESV. (2002). *The bible*. Wheaton, IL: Crossway.

Foa, E. B., & Kozak, M. J. (1986). Emotional processing of fear: Exposure to corrective information. *Psychological Bulletin, 99*(1), 20.

Fosha, D. (2000). *The transforming power of affect: A model for accelerated change*. New York, NY: Basic Books.

Grant, B. F., Hasin, D. S., Stinson, F. S., Dawson, D. A., Ruan, W. J., Goldstein, R. B., ... & Huang, B. (2005). Prevalence, correlates, co-morbidity, and comparative disability of *DSM-IV* generalized anxiety disorder in the USA: Results from the national epidemiologic survey on alcohol and related conditions. *Psychological Medicine, 35*(12), 1747–1759.

Harvard Medical School. (2007). National comorbidity survey (NCS). Retrieved from https://www.hcp.med.harvard.edu/ncs/index.php

Hayes, S. C. (2005). *Get out of your mind and into your life: The new acceptance and commitment therapy*. Oakland, CA: New Harbinger Publications.

Hayes, S. C., Wilson, K. G., Gifford, E. V., Follette, V. M., & Strosahl, K. (1996). Experiential avoidance and behavioral disorders: A functional dimensional approach to diagnosis and treatment. *Journal of Consulting and Clinical Psychology, 64*(6), 1152.

Hettema, J. M., Neale, M. C., & Kendler, K. S. (2001). A review and meta-analysis of the genetic epidemiology of anxiety disorders. *American Journal of Psychiatry, 158*(10), 1568–1578.

Hogue, D. A. (2014). Sometimes it causes me to tremble: Fear, faith, and the human brain. *Pastoral Psychology, 63*(5–6), 659–671. doi: 10.1007/s11089-013-0593-x

Hyman, S. (Ed.). (2013). *Fear and anxiety: The science of mental health*. New York, NY: Routledge.

Kierkegaard, S. (1980). *The concept of anxiety*. (R. Thomte, Trans.). Princeton, NJ: Princeton University Press. (Original work published 1844).

Koszycki, D., Bilodeau, C., Raab-Mayo, K., & Bradwejn, J. (2014). A multifaith spiritually based intervention versus supportive therapy for generalized anxiety disorder: A pilot randomized controlled trial. *Journal Of Clinical Psychology, 70*(6), 489–509. doi: 10.1002/jclp.22052

Lee, J. K., Orsillo, S. M., Roemer, L., & Allen, L. B. (2010). Distress and avoidance in generalized anxiety disorder: Exploring the relationships with intolerance of uncertainty and worry. *Cognitive Behaviour Therapy, 39*(2), 126–136.

Leichsenring, F., Salzer, S., Jaeger, U., Kächele, H., Kreische, R., Leweke, F., ... & Leibing, E. (2009). Short-term psychodynamic psychotherapy and cognitive-behavioral therapy in generalized anxiety disorder: A randomized, controlled trial. *American Journal of Psychiatry, 166*(8), 875–881.

Lilliengren, P., Johansson, R., Town, J. M., Kisely, S., & Abbass, A. (2017). Intensive short-term dynamic psychotherapy for generalized anxiety disorder: A pilot effectiveness and process-outcome study. *Clinical Psychology & Psychotherapy, 24*(6), 1313–1321.

Marganska, A., Gallagher, M., & Miranda, R. (2013). Adult attachment, emotion dysregulation, and symptoms of depression and generalized anxiety disorder. *American Journal of Orthopsychiatry, 83*(1), 131–141.

Milrod, B., Busch, F., Leon, A. C., Aronson, A., Roiphe, J., Rudden, M., ... & Shear, M. K. (2001). A pilot open trial of brief psychodynamic psychotherapy for panic disorder. *Journal of Psychotherapy Practice and Research, 10*(4), 239.

Milrod, B., Leon, A. C., Busch, F., Rudden, M., Schwalberg, M., Clarkin, J., ... & Graf, E. (2007). A randomized controlled clinical trial of psychoanalytic psychotherapy for panic disorder. *American Journal of Psychiatry, 164*(2), 265–272.

Moffitt, T. E., Caspi, A., Harrington, H., Milne, B. J., Melchior, M., Goldberg, D., & Poulton, R. (2007). Generalized anxiety disorder and depression: Childhood risk factors in a birth cohort followed to age 32. *Psychological Medicine, 37*(3), 441–452.

Picardi, A., Caroppo, E., Toni, A., Bitetti, D., & Maria, G. (2005). Stability of attachment-related anxiety and avoidance and their relationships with the five-factor model and the psychobiological model of personality. *Psychology and Psychotherapy: Theory, Research and Practice, 78*(3), 327–345.

Pilecki, B., Arentoft, A., & McKay, D. (2011). An evidence-based causal model of panic disorder. *Journal of Anxiety Disorders, 25*(3), 381–388.

Reichenberg, L. W., & Seligman, L. (2016). *Selecting effective treatments: A comprehensive, systematic guide to treating mental disorders.* San Francisco, CA: John Wiley & Sons.

Roemer, L., & Orsillo, S. M. (2002). Expanding our conceptualization of and treatment for generalized anxiety disorder: Integrating mindfulness/acceptance-based approaches with existing cognitive-behavioral models. *Clinical Psychology: Science and Practice, 9*(1), 54–68.

Rosales, A., & Tan, S. Y. (2016). Acceptance and commitment therapy (ACT): Empirical evidence and clinical applications from a Christian perspective. *Journal of Psychology and Christianity, 35*(3), 269.

Roy-Byrne, P. P., Davidson, K. W., Kessler, R. C., Asmundson, G. J., Goodwin, R. D., Kubzansky, L., ... & Stein, M. B. (2008). Anxiety disorders and comorbid medical illness. *General Hospital Psychiatry, 30*(3), 208–225.

Shin, L. M., & Liberzon, I. (2010). The neurocircuitry of fear, stress, and anxiety disorders. *Neuropsychopharmacology, 35*(1), 169.

Siegel, D. J. (2015). *The developing mind.* New York, NY: Guilford Press.

Şirin, H. D. (2017). The predictive power of adult attachment patterns on interpersonal cognitive distortions of university students. *Educational Research and Reviews, 12*(18), 906–914.

Starcevic, V. (2005). *Anxiety disorders in adults: A clinical guide.* New York, NY: Oxford University Press.

Stossel, S. (2014). *My age of anxiety: fear, hope, dread, and the search for peace of mind.* New York, NY: Random House Press.

Strack, J., Lopes, P., Esteves, F., & Fernandez-Berrocal, P. (2017). Must we suffer to succeed? When anxiety boosts motivation and performance. *Journal of Individual Differences, 38*(2), 113.

Tan, S. Y. (2011). Mindfulness and acceptance-based cognitive behavioral therapies: Empirical evidence and clinical applications from a Christian perspective. *Journal of Psychology and Christianity, 30*(3), 243.

Thompson, R. A. (1994). Emotion regulation: A theme in search of definition. *Monographs of the Society for Research in Child Development, 59*(2–3), 25–52.

Timulak, L., & McElvaney, J. (2016). Emotion-focused therapy for generalized anxiety disorder: An overview of the model. *Journal of Contemporary Psychotherapy, 46*(1), 41–52.

Tompkins, M. A. (2013). *Anxiety and avoidance: A universal treatment for anxiety, panic, and fear.* Oakland, CA: New Harbinger Publications.

Wallin, D. J. (2007). *Attachment in psychotherapy.* New York, NY: Guilford Press.

Wells, A., & Cartwright-Hatton, S. (2004). A short form of the metacognitions questionnaire: Properties of the MCQ-30. *Behaviour Research and Therapy, 42*(4), 385–396.

Wilt, J. A., Grubbs, J. B., Lindberg, M. J., Exline, J. J., & Pargament, K. I. (2017). Anxiety predicts increases in struggles with religious/spiritual doubt over two weeks, one month, and one year. *International Journal for the Psychology of Religion, 27*(1), 26–34. doi: 10.1080/10508619.2015.1098820

Yarhouse, M. A., Butman, R. E., & McRay, B. W. (2005). *Modern psychopathologies: A comprehensive Christian appraisal.* Downers Grove, IL: Inter-Varsity Press.

Zbozinek, T. D., Rose, R. D., Wolitzky-Taylor, K. B., Sherbourne, C., Sullivan, G., Stein, M. B., ... & Craske, M. G. (2012). Diagnostic overlap of generalized anxiety disorder and major depressive disorder in a primary care sample. *Depression and Anxiety, 29*(12), 1065–1071.

IMAGE CREDITS

CHAPTER 4

Trauma and Post-Traumatic Stress Disorder

Holly Morris, LMFT

LEARNING OBJECTIVES

Upon completion of this chapter, readers will be able to

1. identify risk and vulnerability factors to contribute toward adaptive or intensified traumatic reactions;

2. understand the functions of the limbic system when activated in the survival-oriented stress response to perceived threat; and

3. differentiate between acute stress disorder, post-traumatic stress disorder and complex post-traumatic stress disorder.

"Trauma, by definition, is unbearable and intolerable."
(van der Kolk, 2014, p. 1)

THE STORY OF BILLY AND JORDAN

Late one night, Billy was driving through a neighborhood when a dog darted out into the road. He swerved to avoid the dog, lost control of the vehicle, and hit a tree. After the deployed airbags deflated and the debris in the air started to clear, Billy noticed that his passenger, Jordan, was moaning in pain. Billy felt a surge of panic as his heart was racing, and he felt his palms and forehead beginning to perspire. He was also speechless. After what felt like several minutes, he noticed Jordan's leg was pinned under the dashboard, and he was unable to dislodge it. Billy was struggling to decide what to do when he heard sirens in the distance and someone trying to open his door from the outside. When he opened the door, a man stood outside who stated he had called 911.

Firemen removed Jordan from the vehicle, and he was taken by ambulance to the hospital. Billy, with a few burns from the airbag and cuts from a shattered windshield, rode in the ambulance with Jordan. Jordan, while still in pain, seemed relieved to be in the care of medical professionals. Billy, doing his best to support his friend on the outside, felt overwhelmed, afraid, and guilty inside. At the hospital, Billy was treated for minor injuries and released. Jordan was admitted and taken into emergency surgery for a compound break to his femur.

Waiting at the hospital for Jordan to get out of surgery, Billy called Nathan, the pastor for the college group that both Billy and Jordan attended regularly. Both young men were students at a local university and states away from their families. Nathan drove to the hospital to meet Billy and wait for Jordan to get out of surgery.

FIGURE 4.1 **The pervasiveness of trauma**

INTRODUCTION TO TRAUMA

Trauma may be experienced as a single incident, several incidents intermittently, or a chronic experience. It may involve a single person, a group or massive number of people. The actual crisis event(s) may last a short time, such as a motor vehicle accident, or over the course of months, as in combat, a kidnapping, or domestic violence. It could also continue over the course of many years, as in childhood abuse. The experience of post-traumatic stress may be present for a number of days, months, years, and sometimes decades. Research reflects that when traumatic event details include chronic frequency, long-lasting duration of incident(s), physical injury, and/or the perpetrator is known to the victim, the severity of post-traumatic stress increases (American Psychiatric Association, 2013). However, the nature of traumatic response is individualistic, informed by objective details of the event and subjective individualistic historical experiences and current life circumstances. These include relational, cognitive, emotional, physiological, and faith beliefs/practices. To understand the effect of trauma on an individual, it is imperative to consider each of these indicators as a lens to be used in concert with the details of the incident to get the fullest understanding of the person. Such is the nuance of understanding trauma.

The diagnosis of post-traumatic stress disorder (PTSD) was first introduced in 1980 and published in the *Diagnostic and Statistical Manual of Mental Disorders*, 3rd edition (*DSM-III*). It was the first *DSM* diagnosis to reflect compounded and lasting psychological symptomology caused by "a distressing event that is outside the range of usual human experience" (American Psychiatric Association, 1980). The criteria made a demarcation between experiences deemed with a level of traumatic intensity expected to generate lasting symptomology and those expected to resolve naturally. The *DSM* continued to define "the precipitating stressor must not be one which is usually well tolerated by most other members of the cultural group" (American Psychiatric Association, 1980). This definition limited the people who may be included in this diagnostic category. However, there was an important shift in the mental health community and culture by addressing the severity of impact from traumatic events. Combat veterans and rape victims were able to label the post-traumatic manifestations they were experiencing. This reduced some of the stigmatization (Collins, 2017) and disbelief of their conditions. It also continued to provoke further research and study of the etiology and effect of stress response on individuals.

This chapter will explore trauma and the human experience of post-traumatic stress. It will discuss the nature of crisis experiences that may cause traumatic stress and traumatic symptomology, two stress- and trauma-related disorders as defined by the *Diagnostic and Statistical Manual of Mental Disorders, 5th Edition* (*DSM-5*; American Psychiatric Association, 2013). In addition, the concept of complex post-traumatic stress disorder (C-PSTD) will be discussed as a condition widely accepted and used among trauma specialists, but it is not included in the *DSM-5*. This chapter will explore risk factors to the further development of trauma symptoms and resiliency factors to influence adaptive resolution of negative traumatic impacts. It will also address the risks and vulnerabilities involved for persons working alongside traumatized people. Ultimately, this chapter will address the realities of living in a fallen world involving tragedies of small and great magnitude. The scientific and clinical data suggest that 50%–89% (Owens, 2016) of the population will experience traumatic stress at some point throughout their lives. In consideration of the number of natural and human-made disasters, veterans returning from war, families effected by divorce and rate of child abuse, it appears the realities of the general human experience fall closer to the later end of the statistical range.

The Fallen World

The book of Genesis (Chapter 3) includes the story of the fall of Adam and Eve. They lived in the harmonious Garden of Eden until evil and temptation entered in. They ingested forbidden fruit and consequently their eyes were opened, and their world was thrown into disequilibrium. In a moment, their cognitive, emotional, relational, and physiological lives were forever altered. In a sequence of events, and in one moment, there was a radical loss of innocence. Evil and shame were introduced into their hearts and into the story of humanity. Their shame was reflected in the affixing of fig leaves, covering of their bodies, and hiding from God. They experienced a loss of freedom, a need to hide, and the birth of secrecy. Consequently, they had a desperate need to manage their newly developed scarcity of resources. One pivotal moment ignited a surge of internal changes to influence the course of their lives and, in their case, the course of humanity.

In a foundational sense, trauma is an unexpected, life-altering, inescapable, and shattering loss of innocence. It creates an "opening of eyes" to the experiential knowledge of good and evil. The affect often places a person in an unexpected position: he or she may feel ill equipped to handle or process emotionally, physically, mentally, or spiritually. The degree of traumatic stress is influenced by details of the event(s), historical experiences of the individual, and current life circumstances. However, response to a traumatic crisis is idiosyncratic and unfolds in person-specific ways.

Categories of Trauma

Most traumatic experiences can be classified into at least one of four circumstantial categories: individual, interpersonal, natural, or human-made and developmental. While this list is not exhaustive, it will provide a context for conceptualizing categories of trauma (Center for Substance Abuse Treatment, 2014).

Individual traumatic events are single-incident events, as in a rape or attack, or prolonged events, as in multiple assaults or chronic illness involving one victim. If victims experience the trauma without a witness known to them, victims may not disclose the event or personal impact from the event. This dynamic of secrecy minimizes access to support and may result in shame. It also decreases accessibility to process traumatic reactions, thus prolonging negative effects and feelings of isolation.

Interpersonal traumatic events may include those listed earlier when they are experienced, instigated, or perpetrated by people within a trusted, relational context. The post-traumatic stress experienced after this type of trauma is complicated with betrayal. These events occur within romantic relationships, marriages, families, communities, organizations, and church bodies. All forms of abuse, domestic violence, infidelity, sexual or physical violence within a relationship, or the death of a loved one would be considered interpersonal traumas. Because of the complexity, events within interpersonal and developmental categories tend to have the most severe effect in the relational belief system of the individual (Pressley & Spinazzola, 2015).

Natural or human-caused events may be unintentional or intentional. Natural events include catastrophic disasters, such as hurricanes, wildfires, and floods. Human-caused events involve one or a few people, as in a robbery or assault, to massive amounts of people, as in war, shootings/bombings, or terrorist attacks. When these traumas occur, the degree of devastation, level of losses, and required effort for recovery influence personal traumatic impact. Victims often need to process through anger and blame as part of their reaction. The quality of response to immediate and extensive needs by relief agencies contributes to or reduces personal recovery from the event.

Developmental trauma occurs within the childhood years of an individual. Child abuse in any form—physical, verbal, emotional, sexual, or neglect—would be defined in this category. Developmental trauma can also occur from the consistent lack of emotional engagement and nurture from primary caretakers.

Uniqueness of Each Person

The uniqueness of an individual will be described in five categories organized by this author: attachment style, developmental stage, current life stressors, support system, and meaning-making (see Figure 4.2). The five categories collectively create a representation of a person's current condition of functioning. In the wake of trauma, it also creates insight to factors of predisposition to support or hinder healthy mitigation during and after a traumatic event. Understanding these categories can inform meaningful ways to provide and solicit support for parishioners during post-traumatic phases.

FIGURE 4.2   **Uniqueness of Man**

Attachment theory is the primary consideration, as it provides relational context for how an individual may navigate his or her experience during and after a traumatic event. Included in the innate response to a traumatic event is a need for others, activating the attachment system of an individual. For a securely attached person, the qualities of self-awareness, positive self-concept, and belief in the availability of support by others will instigate proximity-seeking behaviors (Laible, 2004). This engagement promotes ongoing adaptation through comfort, externalization of the event, and reception support. Consequently, "the emotional regulating effect of secure attachment explains why some individuals are able to confront affectively charged life events in all their complexity and work toward a full and coherent explanation of distressing situations" (Miner, 2008, p. 228).

In contrast, for insecurely attached individuals, the nature of need can be conflict inducing (Hollidge & Hollidge, 2016). Anxious-avoidant attached individuals may become angry or self-loathing because of their need of others. They may be more inclined to retreat, isolate, and be independent. Anxious-ambivalent attached persons may pursue others to meet their needs and become preoccupied in the fear that their needs will be unmet (Hollidge & Hollidge, 2016), producing hypervigilance, rumination, or anger. Lastly, a person disorganized in his or her attachment style commonly has a history of caretakers who were emotionally frightening, unpredictable, and/or abusive in presentation. "They are unable to identify any point of security in a relational world that they constantly perceive as dangerous" (Hollidge & Hollidge, 2016, p. 132) and consequently may appear fearful and fragile, and be difficult to engage. Any current trauma is coupled with a history of developmental trauma, thus increasing susceptibility to intensified traumatic reactions.

The second consideration is the broad category of the person's **developmental stage**. This will include demographic information, such as age, gender, ethnicity, level of education, and level of maturity. These factors will greatly inform how a person will conceptualize the experience based on his or her cognitive ability to metabolize varying aspects of the event(s). Children, elderly, and dependent adults generally have a level of dependency exposing them to greater risk of abuse (Levine, 1997). Populations with lower socioeconomic status and lower levels of education commonly have decreased accessibility to resources, creating risk for increased and elongated traumatic stress (Caramanica, Brackbill, Liao, & Stellman, 2014). "Women have twice the risk of developing PTSD following a trauma than men do" (van der Kolk, 2003).

The third consideration includes **current life stressors**. Current and ongoing life stressors create a barometer for the internal capacity to successfully navigate the physical, emotional, mental, relational, and spiritual demands that trauma initiates. Additional stressors, occurring during and after the event, influence a person's ability to process the trauma adaptively (Brewin, Andrews, & Valentine, 2000). Examples of common life stressors are financial strain, lack or loss of employment, life-stage transitions, divorce, psychiatric diagnoses, or preexisting medical conditions. Research highlights prior traumatic events as a primary vulnerability factor to compounded traumatic impact to individuals (Weinberg & Gil, 2016).

The fourth consideration is the condition of the current **support system**. A research study conducted in three waves post-9/11 reflected at 10–11 years after the terrorist attack that persons without or with one "source of social integration reported the highest prevalence" (Caramanica et al., 2014, p. 684) of experiencing PTSD and depression. The utilization of a support system(s) is one of the biggest predictors of adaptive navigation through traumatic stress. The capacity of the support system(s) to join in the healing of post-traumatic stress is imperative to positive outcomes. Some considerations to evaluate the quality of the support system(s) are as follows (Matsakis, 1996): Is the system open to soliciting help from outside sources or closed to the inclusion of others? What are the cultural expectations for how to navigate healing? Is there emotional and physical capacity within the system for the traumatized person to externalize his or her experience? Is the system supportive or blaming? Compatibility of the needs of the individual and qualities of the support system(s) are essential.

Finally, the fifth consideration is the concept of **meaning-making**. The value assigned by the individual to any losses associated with the trauma will inform a level of distress. The "subjective experience of the trauma as a threat" (Weinberg & Gil, 2016, p. 137) will inform the level of emotional reaction the individual will face post-trauma. Exploration of meaning for individuals is often layered in beliefs, sentiment, and worldview. Relational losses or abuses contain a layer of betrayal; physical losses may have sentimental value; first responders and military have layers of loyalty evoked by a loss of one of their own. If details of the event challenge a person's worldview or values, it may cause more distress (Pressley & Spinazzola, 2015) to the individual.

KEY TERMS

Individual: trauma involving one victim

Interpersonal: trauma experienced, instigated, or perpetrated by people within a trusted relational context

Natural or human-made: events including natural disasters and events instigated against small or large numbers of people

Developmental: trauma occurring in childhood

Attachment style: style of navigating connection within relationships

Developmental stage: inclusion of a person's demographic information and level of maturity

Current life stressors: ongoing and transient conditions or circumstances evoking stress

Support system: people and resources providing support to a person's well-being

Meaning-making: value assigned to an event by belief system, sentiment, or worldview

Discussion Questions

1   Discuss the concept of the discovery of knowledge between good and evil that a person may experience after a life-altering event.

2   Describe the four categories of trauma.

3   Applying one example from each uniqueness of man category, create a scenario of a person vulnerable to becoming severely affected by a traumatic event.

EXPERIENCE OF TRAUMA

Assault to Functioning: Life-Threatening Event(s)

Crisis events are considered traumatic when they include four key elements: an experience of serious threat, perceived inescapability, preexisting vulnerable biopsychosocial traits, and significant loss from the event (Ruden, n.d.). During a traumatic experience, victims feel that the collective damages from the trauma exceed the perceived resources available, creating feelings of helplessness, powerlessness, and fear.

The Survival-Oriented Stress Response System

The neurophysiological process involved in the survival-oriented stress response to threat is commonly known as **fight-flight-freeze** (FFF). A basic understanding of this system by both the counselor and counselee is critical in fostering empowerment. This empowerment is gained through a recognition and appreciation of the body's automatic survival response.

The Emotional Brain: The Limbic System

The **limbic system**, which is just above the brain stem, is imperative for survival. It is the part of the brain responsible for regulating emotions and the formation of memories (Painter & Scannapieco, 2013). It is very important for the development of relational attachment and for monitoring danger. This system functions as the gatekeeper for assessing whether there is safety or danger present in the environment and/or social interactions.

When an experience of perceived threat occurs, the limbic system is activated, igniting four brain regions (amygdala, thalamus, hippocampus, and hypothalamus) by working in collaboration to engage the body in the FFF response. The FFF response is a biological engagement of the sympathetic nervous system (SNS) preparing the body to fight or flee. When activated, the body experiences contracting of muscles in the limbs, increased heart rate, perspiration in palms, metabolism and digestion slow, and breathing quickens. In circumstances when fighting or escape are perceived as impossible, the parasympathetic nervous system (PNS) is employed, creating a freeze response in the system (Tyler, 2012). This response is typically evoked in situations perceived as most dangerous, wherein the last hope for survival is immobility (Levine, 1997). There is often a numbing sensation or dissociation that occurs, wherein mind and body experience a type of separation.

Encoding of Traumatic Memory

In natural memory processing, memories are stored in the limbic system for the short-term until processed adaptively and transported to the neocortex (Painter & Scannapieco, 2013). Traumatic memories are encoded in the limbic system itself in fragmented form with sensory details of sight, sound, smell, taste, and touch (Tyler, 2012). These memories become problematic to healthy integration post-trauma. Sensory input in the environment, related or seemingly unrelated, trigger the traumatic experience. The limbic system is void of a time regulator. Consequently, when sensory memories are triggered, the person may re-experience the trauma as if it were happening in the here and now. This creates a constant state of hypervigilance, contributing to a stressful and confusing environment for the traumatized to feel and be well.

When traumatic memories are encoded in the limbic system, it becomes overactive and lacks regular modulation, releasing frequent doses of stress hormones. Over time, this may increase social inhibition and impair healthy psychological functioning. In addition it can cause damage to other biological systems, producing medical issues such as the following (D'Andrea, Sharma, Zelechoski, & Spinazzola, 2011):

- Cardiovascular illness
- Immune functioning
- Gastrointestinal conditions

- Reproductive disorders
- Pain disorders

Symptoms of Post-Traumatic Stress

"PTSD is an entirely normal reaction to an abnormal amount of stress."
(Matsakis, 1996, p. 2)

TRAUMATIC SYMPTOMS
in Phases of Development

PHASE 1	PHASE 2	PHASE 3
Hyperarousal	Panic attacks, anxiety and phobias	Excessive shyness
Constriction	Mental "blankness" or "spaciness"	Muted or diminished emotional responses
Dissociation	Avoidance behavior	Inability to make commitments
Denial	Attraction to dangerous situations	Chronic fatigue or very low physical energy
Feelings of helplessness	Frequent crying	Immune system problems and certain endocrine problems such as thyroid dysfunction
Hypervigilance	Exaggerated or diminished sexual activity	Psychosomatic illnesses, particularly headaches, neck and back problems, asthma, digestive spastic colon, severe premenstral syndrome
Intrusive imagery or flashbacks	Amnesia and forgetfulness	Depression, feelings of impending doom
Extreme sensitivity to light and sound	Inability to love, nurture or bond with other individuals	Feelings of detachment, alienation and isolation
Hyperactivity	Fear of dying, going crazy or having a shortened life	Diminished interest in life
Exaggerated emotional and startle responses		Rage, temper tantrums, shame
Nightmares and night terrors		Feelings and behaviors of helplessness
Abrupt mood swings		Reduced ability to formulate plans
Reduced ability to deal with stress		
Difficulty sleeping		

FIGURE 4.3 **Symptoms of Post-traumatic Stress**

Figure 4.3 reflects a list of typical post-traumatic symptoms experienced in three phases and was created using symptom lists from a book by a leading trauma expert, Peter Levine (1997) *Waking the Tiger: Healing Trauma* (pp. 147–149). Figure 4.3 is intended as a reference guide to provide support for counselors who may be conceptualizing the symptoms of a counselee. Noting the phase of symptoms the counselee is experiencing will assist the counselor to determine the level of intervention and support necessitated. It can also be used as a tool to normalize the experience of a person who has experienced a trauma. The provision of symptom language can solicit a sense of empowerment for a person feeling powerless.

For diagnostic purposes of acute stress disorder (ASD) and PTSD, symptoms of post-traumatic stress are designated into five clusters (American Psychiatric Association, 2013): intrusion, negative mood, dissociative, avoidance, and arousal. Symptoms of **intrusion** involve spontaneous thoughts, dreams, or memories of the traumatic event. Reminders in the environment or internal thoughts or feelings may trigger these symptoms. **Flashbacks** are included in this cluster wherein a traumatic memory activates the system as if the event is happening in real time. Flashbacks can include still-frame memories or internal "movies" remembered as a sequence of events. They can also be experienced somatically, wherein the body re-experiences the trauma through physical sensation, smell, or taste (van der Kolk, 2014). Flashbacks may also be emotionally cued by a current experience, activating the combination of emotional states experienced at the time of traumatic incident. **Negative mood** is a lack of feeling positive emotional states. **Dissociative** symptoms produce disconnection from the present moment, feeling "checked out" and often being checked in to another time or space internally. **Avoidance** symptoms are attempts to circumvent internal and external reminders of the event. Finally, **arousal** symptoms are restlessness in the form of agitation, startle response, lack of focus, aggression, and disruption of sleep patterns.

The experience of loss of control, helplessness, and powerlessness are hallmark features of trauma. In desperate attempts to avoid, people may display erratic or risky behavior, such as driving recklessly, excessive substance use, or gambling. They may isolate in an attempt to eliminate sensory input and emotionally shut down or become enraged. These are the efforts of a traumatized person to regain some control (Levine, 1997).

Stages of Post-Traumatic Response

Shock

The stage of shock is typically the time from the incident through the first several days. Intervention during this stage involves safety, support, and assessment of need (Myer, Lewis, & James, 2013). The presence of trusted others as mediators will promote feelings of emotional and physical safety. Inquiry about the provision of basic needs is typically helpful, as a parishioner may be disconnected from his or her hunger or need for sleep. Keeping communication uncomplicated is supportive, as the person may have difficulty with focus and retention. If information is important, provide a written reminder. Letting the parishioner know when you will be in contact with him or her again and following through will build trust. If any immediate action is needed, talk it through step-by-step. Gaining permission before disclosing the situation to others will empower the parishioner with choice. Well-meaning communal responses, such as adding a situation to a prayer chain or setting up meal delivery, will only be helpful if there is agreement.

The First Month

With the decrease of shock, an increase of traumatic distress typically develops. During this month, the prevalence of ASD is varied depending on the nature and severity of the event. For example, 13%–21% of people involved in accidents and 20%–50% of interpersonal trauma victims meet the criteria for ASD (American Psychiatric Association, 2013). Assisting a parishioner to understand the importance of honoring his or her experience while incorporating aspects of his or her life prior to the event is invaluable to the resolution of negative impact (Levine, 1997). A plethora of negative effects may include psychological, physiological, relational, emotional, spiritual, or vocational factors. A counselor may contribute to the movement toward health by being a safe, open, nonjudgmental presence. By doing so, space for the person's experience to be expressed becomes cultivated.

People with a religious affiliation and/or spiritual conviction may express a feeling of shame about their reaction. They may doubt God's omnipresence and presence in their world (Walker, Courtois, & Aten, 2015). They may doubt His love for them or their value to Him. People need to know in view of their current life experiences that their questions, doubts, fears, and anger are valid. Recovery from a traumatic event(s) is a process that often includes revisiting previously held beliefs about themselves, others, the world, and God (Pressley & Spinazzola, 2015). It is during these times that pastoral counselors and ministry leaders have an opportunity to interrupt the traumatic reactions that may build internally, often leading to guilt and isolation. Connecting them with others in a support group setting and or counseling can help them continue processing the traumatic experience and promote momentum toward increased health.

Evaluation of Ongoing Adaptive Process

When post-traumatic symptoms persist and intensify, they effect the overall functioning of the individual. The person's world becomes smaller in attempts to avoid any stimuli of the event. The role of guilt and shame may dominate thoughts, thus effecting relationships and the person's faith. Issues of safety may become pertinent as engagement in risky behaviors, such as substance abuse, eating disorders, or suicidal ideation, may develop in the person's attempt to distance him or herself from the pain. In this phase, the degree of impact to a person's life functioning is to be evaluated to determine if the intervention of professional therapy or a support group is necessary.

KEY TERMS

Fight-flight-freeze: a survival-oriented biological response to threat

Limbic system: "the emotional brain" functions to evaluate the environment for threat or safety and activates physiological response accordingly

Intrusion: spontaneous memories of traumatic events

Flashbacks: re-experiencing of trauma in real time

Negative mood: lack of positive feelings

Dissociative: mental and emotional disconnection from the present moment

Avoidance: attempts to circumvent reminders of the trauma

Arousal: symptoms of restlessness

1 Describe the biological process that occurs when the FFF response becomes activated.

2 Referring to the story of Billy and Jordan, identify two post-traumatic stress symptoms reflected in Billy's experience.

3 It is a common occurrence for a person who has experienced trauma to question his or her faith in the goodness, protection, or love of God. How would you respond to a counselee struggling with these doubts?

TRAUMA AND STRESSOR-RELATED DISORDERS

The *DSM-5* (American Psychiatric Association, 2013) contains six diagnoses that are classified into the category of trauma and stressor-related disorders. These are defined as "disorders in which exposure to a traumatic or stressful event is listed explicitly as a diagnostic criterion" (American Psychiatric Association, 2013). This section will include discussion of two of the six diagnoses, ASD and PTSD. Post-traumatic symptoms may fit the diagnosis of ASD or PTSD and/or may resonate in categories of depressive disorders, anxiety disorders, eating disorders, and/or addictions. The co-occurrence of PTSD and other diagnoses is 80% (American Psychiatric Association, 2013), respectively.

The first criterion to be met for a diagnosis of ASD or PTSD is a traumatic or stressful event. As defined by the *DSM-5* (American Psychiatric Association, 2013), it is an "exposure to actual or threatened death, serious injury or sexual violation" by experiencing the event directly, being a witness to the event occurring to others, learning the event occurred to a person related through familial or friendship ties, or being persistently exposed to the details of the event(s).

Acute Stress Disorder

When using the *DSM-5*, a diagnosis of ASD is given when a person who has experienced a traumatic event as described earlier is also experiencing any nine of 14 symptoms designated in the five defined clusters: intrusion, avoidance, dissociation, negative mood, and arousal.

Case of Billy

Pastor Nathan became concerned when 3 weeks had passed since he had seen Billy at any church events. Nathan called Billy, and he agreed to meet. When Billy arrived, Nathan immediately noticed his downcast mood. Typically an engaging young man, Billy walked slowly and made minimal eye contact. When they sat down, Nathan expressed that he had been concerned about him. Billy apologized for not being in attendance at church events or visiting Jordan at the hospital. He became quiet, his eyes appeared to focus on the corner of the office; his face became expressionless, and he stopped speaking. Nathan leaned in toward Billy and gently called his name. When Billy looked back at Nathan and caught his eyes, he began shaking. His eyes appeared afraid; his movements were erratic, and he kept repeating, "It was all my fault."

Discussion

In that moment, dissociated, Billy was in a flashback of the auto accident. He was recalling feeling paralyzed, with his mind blank and staring at Jordan's pinned leg. He was remembering the man at the car door, hearing the sirens and the shame that washed over him. He had not called 911. When Nathan called his name, Billy came back into the present moment, and his stress response system was still activated. Billy was shaking, heartbeat racing, breaths shallow, and arms and legs cramping. He verbalized his belief in the moment of the accident, and in the weeks to follow the event, "it was all my fault." Nathan, based on his awareness of Billy's absence and in initiating the meeting, communicated concern and care for Billy. Nathan's warm presence created space for Billy to speak his heart. Nathan shared with Billy the changes he had noticed in him, demonstrating concern for his well-being. Because of feelings of guilt and unworthiness, Billy had isolated himself. This had perpetuated the weight of negative self-messages of self-deprecation, helplessness, and fear. While the symptoms he had experienced after the accident were not outside the norm, they had become compounded in his isolation.

Intervention and Support

Social engagement is imperative to decrease dissociation in someone experiencing post-traumatic stress. Although adaptive during traumatic exposures, dissociation becomes a liability to processing the trauma and reengagement into life (van der Kolk, 2014). Dissociation is a coping strategy all people employ to one degree or another. Imagine yourself driving home from work and realizing as you pull into the driveway that you do not recall the details of the drive home. You have been on "auto pilot" and used procedural memory to get you there. This has been an experience of dissociation. In response to trauma, dissociation is a state internally developed as a way of escape when it was perceived to be physically impossible (Tyler, 2012; van der Kolk, 2014). It is a defensive strategy used primarily by children, who have limited strength and resources, as well as victims of sexual crimes. Scaer, (2006) discusses a concept of dissociative encapsulated internal states. These are defined as partial traumatic memories containing factual and emotional information. When a person becomes triggered by traumatic internal or external stimulus, the system becomes overridden and dissociates into one of the encapsulated states. The emotional response may range from flat to heightened; these moments can be a surprising and frightening experience for both the counselee and the counselor.

When counseling someone who becomes dissociative, inviting them to participate in **grounding techniques** will help bring them out of him or her internal state into the present moment. Facilitating grounding exercises with your parishioner will help him or her to feel more comfortable and help to ground the counselor if distressed. Francine Shapiro, the founder of Eye Movement Desensitization Reprocessing (EMDR), describes a four-step protocol for grounding the biological system into the present moment from the bottom (ground) to the top (mind) in her book *Getting Past Your Past* (Shapiro, 2012, pp.

261–262). Figure 4.4 consists of a combination of protocols from the book and additions from this author. The four stages are categorized by the names of the four elements: earth, air, water, and fire, and they are designed to be practiced in the aforementioned order.

EARTH:
GROUNDING, SAFETY IN THE PRESENT/REALITY

• Place both feet on the ground and feel the ground beneath you.

• Shift weight between sides of your body and notice the ground supporting you.

• Look around and notice 3 new things.

• Listen and identify 3 sounds.

AIR:
BREATHING FOR CENTERING

• Use deep belly breath technique:
  INHALE FOR A COUNT OF 4,
  HOLD FOR 4, EXHALE FOR 4
  AND WAIT 4, DO THIS 4 TIMES.

• Take the breaths deep into your lower lungs and diaphragm.

• Notice the way the air feels as it fills your lungs and exhales from them.

• Feel your belly rise and fall with each breath.

WATER:
CALM AND CONTROLLED, TO SWITCH ON RELAXATION RESPONSE

When 'fight or flight' stress response is activated, the digestive system begins to shut down creating dry mouth.

• Reactivate your digestive system:
  GET A DRINK OF WATER
  CHEW A PIECE OF GUM
  SUCK ON A MINT OR HARD CANDY

FIRE:
LIGHT UP THE PATHWAY TO YOUR IMAGINATION TO FEEL SAFE

• Go to a place in your mind you feel calm.
• Imagine being with someone you love.
• Remember doing something you enjoy.

How do you feel and where do you feel it in your body?

FIGURE 4.4   Earth, Air, Water, and Fire

Other risk factors to impede ongoing adaptation post-trauma may include collateral damage, as in losses of money or property; legal decisions to press charges in burglary, assault, or rape; or job loss or medical bills. The process of rebuilding what was lost through trauma has a stealthy nature of keeping people reliving their experience. Once physical damages are rectified, a host of triggers may become minimized or resolved, which assists the traumatized in continuing toward wholeness (Matsakis, 1996).

Post-Traumatic Stress Disorder

A diagnosis of PTSD is evaluated when symptoms have persisted for 1 month or longer. The criteria to be met for a diagnosis includes one symptom of intrusion, one symptom of avoidance, two symptoms of negative thoughts and mood, and two symptoms of arousal.

The symptoms must cause significant decrease in quality of life and must not be caused by any substance or other medical condition (American Psychiatric Association, 2013).

PTSD is a condition of the limbic system that is locked on high alert. The development of symptoms can quickly become severe and debilitating or slow and insidious. The symptoms of PTSD can surface within the first month after a traumatic event or lay dormant for months, years, or sometimes decades before surfacing. In the case of a **delayed expression**, symptoms surface 6 months or longer after traumatic event (American Psychiatric Association, 2013). The anniversary of a traumatic event, children becoming the age a parent was when he or she experienced trauma, or the exiting of the perpetrator of abuse out of the victim's life may be triggers. For professions that involve chronic traumatic exposure, as in combat veterans, PTSD symptoms may intensify in retirement (Schnurr, Lunney, Sengupta, & Spiro, 2005).

Case of Billy

Two months after the accident, Billy stopped by the church office to meet with Pastor Nathan. He described a steady decline in life functioning after the accident. Nightmares disrupted his sleep and loud noises had become distressing. He was feeling apathetic and spent most of his time in his room. Too afraid to drive, he quit his job and classes. Being unable to pay his rent and dropping out of school left him without reason to stay, and he would be moving back home.

Discussion

Billy's symptoms steadily increased and broadened in complexity, impacting his ability to function in multiple areas of his life. In addition, there were several vulnerability factors with the potential to negatively affect Billy's recovery process. He was away from home and support; he had current stressors of managing school and a job. He "felt overwhelmed, afraid, and guilty inside" while being transported to the hospital, suggesting a possible insecure attachment style. He also stopped attending church and stopped visiting Jordan shortly after the accident, suggesting avoidance and possible isolation. An evaluation of Billy's safety would be imperative in this case, as suicidal thoughts, self-harming behaviors, and substance abuse may be used to numb or distance from post-traumatic stress.

Intervention and Support

The nature of PTSD often tends to devitalize a person. People with PTSD live in a state of fear of being activated in their memories. The symptoms impacting their ability to regulate their emotional states, maintain focus, get proper rest, and regularly remain cognitively and emotionally engaged in present circumstances is compromised. These struggles greatly affect their ability to maintain interpersonal relationships, create and retain employment, manage health care, and navigate ongoing life skills. This makes the PTSD population vulnerable to suicidality, self-injury, acts of aggression, addiction, depression, and anxiety (van der Kolk, 2014).

When counseling someone who is experiencing PTSD, it is important to assess for abuse of any substances or engagement in self-harm behaviors, as early intervention may decrease the progression toward further harm. In some cases of suicidality, assessment may preserve a life. Direct questions about suicidal thoughts can be difficult to broach, but most often if a person is contemplating suicide, the questions will open a door to more candid discussion and the potential for support. (Please see the chapter on depression for a suicide assessment protocol).

KEY TERMS

Grounding techniques: methods for engaging the mind and body into the present moment

Delayed expression: PTSD symptoms that have met the criteria for diagnosis 6 months or longer after traumatic event

Discussion Questions

1   Increased dissociation contributes toward increased symptoms and may disrupt ongoing healing of post-traumatic symptoms. Social engagement appears to be a positive mediator to disrupt dissociation. If Billy were your parishioner, how would you address the benefit of social engagement with him?

2   Grounding techniques are one way to invite someone who is dissociative to engage in the present moment. Review the chart of grounding techniques, discuss them, and practice each step.

3   PTSD, delayed expression, can be triggered by current events in a person's life that surface symptoms from an event that occurred in the past. How would you describe and normalize this experience for a parishioner who was confused by it?

4   Consider yourself in the position of Pastor Nathan. How would you approach the safety concerns about Billy? Using the suicide protocol in the chapter on depression, role-play asking Billy the safety assessment questions.

5   The experience of Billy developing PTSD and returning home would be difficult for any pastor. If this occurred in your church body, what would be your approach to attending to the loss for yourself? For the church body?

COMPLEX POST-TRAUMATIC STRESS DISORDER

The term Complex Post-Traumatic Stress Disorder (**C-PTSD**) is a widely accepted and used term among health professionals who work with people who have been traumatized. The term is credited to Judith Herman, MD, and dates back to the early 1990s (Herman, 1992). Seventy-nine percent of people diagnosed with PTSD have one co-occurring diagnosis and 44% have three or more additional diagnoses (Nemcic-Moro, Franciskovic, Britvic,

Klaric, & Zecevic, 2011). C-PTSD is used as one diagnosis to include PTSD diagnostic symptoms and other prominent symptoms of chronic trauma survivors: depression, aggression, dissociation, and interpersonal and intrapersonal complications.

Nature of Development

C-PTSD is developed in individuals exposed to repetitive, prolonged, chronic trauma imposed by someone in close proximity with an unequal distribution of power between perpetrator and victim. The typical two scenarios for this type of abuse are within the family system or an organizational system (Herman, 1992). A 19th-century playwright originally used the term "**soul murder**" to describe the pervasive effect on the sense of self of a person who experiences complex trauma. He defined it as "the destruction of another human being's love for life" (as cited in Van Deusen & Courtois, 2015, p. 35).

Childhood is a time in life when humans first learn about themselves, their connection to others, and the world around them. Children with attuned, nurturing caretakers experience a feeling of safety, which fosters the development of a sense of self with internalized value. In the case of a child raised in an environment with abuse of a physical, sexual, verbal, or emotional nature or neglect, the safety is replaced by insecurity, instability, and distress. The neurological and relational development expected to occur is stunted by a constant state of threat. Energy is displaced from learning and growing to survival, which often converts into core developmental deficits (Walker, 2014, p. 11). This dynamic often imprints a disorganized attachment style in the child to believe people are unsafe, unpredictable, and untrustworthy. This typically informs the way they navigate relational attachments with themselves, others, and God.

The second form of chronic abuse is in the form of an organizational structure as experienced in combat, prisons of war, ritual abuse, or domestic violence (Herman, 1992). These atrocities often shake the worldview of the victim and may deconstruct their existing identity. Their recovery often includes an exploration of existential questions, rebuilding a sense of safety and life purpose.

Symptoms of Complex Post-Traumatic Stress Disorder

The profound effect on the identity formation from developmental trauma and the degeneration of identity from organizational trauma, C-PTSD may best be understood as a disorder of attachment. The pervasive quality of symptoms incorporates features of personality, mood, and somatization disorders (Herman, 1992; van der Kolk, 2003):

- Alterations in emotional regulation: episodes of rage or inhibited anger, lack of joy, being self-destructive
- Alterations in attention and consciousness: dissociation, unable to remember or rumination on past traumatic events
- Alterations in self-perception: fixation in comparison with others, chronic guilt, shame, or self-blame
- Alterations in relationships with others: difficulty trusting others, may become easily wounded in relationships, difficulty feeling intimate with others.

- Alterations in systems of meaning: loss of sustaining faith, hopelessness, and despair
- Somatization: feeling emotional and/or traumatic memories in the body

Case of Billy

When Billy returned home, he met with his high school pastor who had known him for years. While processing his experience after the auto accident, they also talked about Billy's upbringing. Billy had a younger brother who was struck by a car as a toddler and suffered irreparable brain damage. Billy, also a child at the time of that occurrence, had always felt responsible, as he did not stop his brother from going into the street. His parents frequently abused alcohol, and he was intermittently physically abused throughout his childhood. Billy grew up trying to "make up for his mistake" and "wondered if he would ever be worthy of love by anyone, including God."

Discussion

In this case, Billy is describing an experience of **toxic shame**, a distinctive feature of C-PTSD. Toxic shame is experienced as an emotional flashback wherein a person becomes captured by a belief that they are unworthy, despicable, unlovable (Walker, 2014) and sometimes overwhelmed by a feeling of being evil or chronically guilty (Pressley & Spinazzola, 2015).

The circumstances surrounding the accident triggered Billy into memories of the past. As the church group surrounded Jordan with support and visitation, Billy felt conflicted. Although he also needed support, he felt guilty because he was not physically injured. The church group dynamic reminded Billy of his family in childhood when his brother was given the most attention, and Billy felt overlooked and isolated. Billy suffered with guilt for not doing enough and being unharmed in childhood when his brother experienced life-altering damage. That guilt became triggered by the circumstances of the auto accident when Jordan was injured, and Billy only suffered minor injuries. In an attempt to avoid the internal conflict and guilt, he stopped going to the hospital and participating in church activities.

Intervention and Support

People who suffer with C-PTSD often struggle to feel intimate in their relationship with God. God, as another attachment figure, is often assigned similar character traits as their relationships with early caretakers (Pressley & Spinazzola, 2015). God may be seen as rageful, judgmental, and accusatory or distant and unreachable (Walker et al., 2015). At the core of attachment disorders is an inability to securely attach to another; this also may include God. This internal experience may evoke feelings of guilt and shame in parishioners desiring to have emotional closeness to God. They may assume others have a relationship with God that feels out of reach for them, compounding their shame.

By being a generous listener who empathizes with a parishioner, an individual involved in ministry can create an opening for the parishioner to continue to explore his or her relational struggle. When a parishioner who has not had a safe relationship with an authority or parental figure during his or her life is wrestling to have one for the first time, acknowledging the risk toward growth can be empowering. The admission of troubling thoughts and feelings, as in the case of Billy, can be an important step in breaking the shame and creating connection.

In his book, *Shame and Grace* (1993), Lewis Smedes writes, "The simplest of all remedies for shame is the discovery that we are in spite of everything accepted by the grace of someone we most need to accept us" (p. 60). Pastors and ministry leaders often have the tender opportunity to extend grace and acceptance to a parishioner along his or her transformative journey. The church can be a place of conversion and transformation for individuals and communities. It can also be a system similar to a family with persons in positions of authority, cultural norms, expectations, and relational connections. People who suffer with C-PTSD are often both drawn to and triggered by experiences within church communities. A desire to experience the security they lacked in early relationships, God and "church family" may provide an opportunity for redemption of lost nurture, acceptance, and love. Conversely, they may become triggered within the relational dynamic of trust and intimacy, and may have sensitivity to perceived or actual indiscretions by persons in church leadership. When noticing a parishioner has deep and repetitive questions about his or her place within the church community, in the absence of any actual conflict, or has difficulty navigating relationships, a referral to a trusted professional therapist may be the support needed. Processing the pain often fosters growth in a parishioner's unique gifts to invest more fully in his or her life and church community.

Wounds created within relationship require healing within relationship (Walker, 2014). For some people with C-PTSD, the level of trauma has created such relational injury and distrust that allowing someone to get close enough to assist on their journey of healing may initially be too triggering (Walker, 2014). Book recommendations, online support groups, or a professional **trauma therapist** available by Skype or other Internet-based services may be a tolerable beginning. For some joining a support group with others who experienced similar trauma and referral to a therapist who specializes in working with C-PTSD would be most helpful.

KEY TERMS

C-PTSD: complex post-traumatic stress disorder—a single diagnosis including symptoms of PTSD with relational, mood, and somatic symptoms

Soul murder: destruction of ability to freely express emotion and enjoy life

Toxic shame: feeling of being unlovable, guilty, unworthy

Trauma therapist: a professional therapist who specializes in assisting in the healing and recovery of persons who have post-traumatic symptoms and/or disorders

1 Discuss the relational dynamic between a caretaker and a child to develop a disorganized attachment style in the child.

2 Toxic shame is a common experience among persons who struggle with C-PTSD. How might you respond to a parishioner who was describing this experience?

3 If you were Billy's pastor who had a long-term relationship with him, how would you approach referring him to see a professional therapist?

TOOLS AND CONSIDERATIONS TO ASSIST IN THE PROVISION OF CARE

Impacts From Counseling the Traumatized: A Case for Self-Care

A vital consideration for helpers of all types working with traumatized individuals and groups is the possible development of personal secondary impacts. Pastors and others in ministry may be among the group of first responders in times of crisis. This may include being called directly to the scene of an incident or being the receiver of a first disclosure of trauma from a parishioner. The personal emotional and cognitive reactions to these circumstances can have a cumulative negative effect on the well-being of the person in the role of helper. This can manifest in the form of **compassion fatigue**, **secondary traumatic stress,** or **vicarious trauma**.

The experiences of compassion fatigue, secondary traumatic stress, and vicarious trauma are experienced uniquely and vary in definition (Knight, 2013). The following definitions are informed by an article on indirect trauma by Carolyn Knight (2013) written in the *Clinical Supervisor.* First, compassion fatigue is the experience of decline in ability to empathize with parishioners. Often a sense of restlessness in the helper, becoming "short fused," and dissatisfaction in work can ensue. Second, secondary traumatic stress is an experience similar to PTSD in the helper. It can include intrusive thoughts, nightmares, and hypervigilance. It may include overwhelming concern for the parishioner outside of usual meeting times, a sense of over-responsibility, and difficulty disengaging from the thoughts causing concern. Finally, vicarious trauma is defined as a helper's internal experience of altered personal, spiritual, and worldview perceptions in response to empathic engagement with traumatic stories (Courtois, 2015). Engagement in self-awareness to notice internal shifts and strains is crucial in the ongoing balance of serving others and being emotionally, spiritually, and relationally replenished.

Self-Care Practices

Self-care is an integral exercise that engages the helper in cognitive, emotional, physical, relational, and spiritual practices to cultivate a fulfilling personal life (Knight, 2013). For a person of faith, a practice in self-care that was modeled by Jesus was to be alone and pray. Luke 5:16: "But Jesus often withdrew to lonely places and prayed" (Holy Bible, New

International Version). He engaged in this practice frequently and unapologetically to connect with His most secure and perfect attachment, Father God. Another self-care practice can be times of silence and/or meditative prayer, being ministered to by the Holy Spirit, and prayerfully surrendering the care of parishioners into His loving hands (Nouwen, 1981). There may also be times that a parishioner is processing a traumatic experience that evokes personal feelings from a history of the helper's own trauma. Self-care may include seeking the counsel of a trusted person or a therapist.

Some other common self-care strategies are exercise, relational connectedness, pleasure, and enjoyment (Miller, 2015). For self-care practices that will be meaningful for a helper, engaging in a self-inventory of relationships, activities, and hobbies can be a good place to start. The life of a pastor or ministry leader can be demanding and relationally and emotionally taxing. Consider your spiritual, relational, emotional, and physical health as important for you as you would encourage a parishioner. Create margins in your schedule to replenish your soul.

Collaboration of Care

The collaborative approach to the support of persons who have experienced trauma is the most preferred method. Consistent with information in the chapter, most people who experience a single-incident trauma may have post-traumatic distress resolve within several weeks. With the support of a church community extending warmth and emotional support, assisting with tasks, and being received lovingly for some will be enough. In cases of increased severity, the need for care and support may extend through a longer duration of time and require collaborative services to support the individual toward healing. At the end of the chapter, there are resources for individuals who have experienced specific traumas. Generally, support groups for either the specific trauma or co-occurring symptoms as anger management, addictions, or eating disorders can be helpful.

Treatment by Mental Health Professionals

Clinical Approach

The overarching clinical goals are (1) to feel safe and increase stability from post-traumatic symptoms, (2) to create and discover meaning from experiences, and (3) to reintegrate into the world with new hope and possibilities. This is a complex and unique journey for each person who has been traumatized (Herman, 1992; Shapiro, 2001).

The first phase of safety is paramount to beginning any journey toward healing. Often, people affected by PTSD and C-PTSD feel terrified or shut down. An integral part of healing for the traumatized is to feel safe in their bodies, in relationships with others, and in their surroundings (van der Kolk, 2014). It is only after therapeutic rapport and safety have been established that people will begin to risk facing their trauma in order to heal. Safety and stabilization are the foundational clinical focus throughout treatment.

With the high correlation of co-occurring disorders and probability of self-harming behaviors, this first phase includes crisis management and persists throughout the process of healing. This phase also includes psychoeducation about the effects of trauma and development on coping strategies to manage negative symptoms. Sometimes this is the entire treatment, for some progression through the next two stages is necessary.

Processing the trauma and grieving the losses connected to it facilitates a sense of increased freedom and creation of meaning from the experience(s). Sometimes the positive changes "surpass the individual's state before the trauma" (Dekel, Hankin, Pratt, Hackler, & Lanman, 2016, p. 315) referred to as **post-traumatic growth**. This is the hope for each person in his or her healing. The third phase of reintegration is when the trauma has been integrated into the person's life story and does not define him or her. It is in this phase when the trauma may be transformed and repurposed. Many advocates for social causes, developers of nonprofit foundations, and helpers are survivors who have experienced their own healing and crusade for the healing of others.

Methodology

Discoveries in the field of neuroscience addressed in this chapter support the methodologies of treatment of trauma to include psychotherapy and **psychosensory** approaches to treatment. Essentially, this involves a combination of approach to include the mind and the body. Trauma-focused cognitive-behavioral therapy is reflected in research as an efficacious psychotherapy treatment involving exposure and cognitive structuring techniques (Ponniah & Hollon, 2009). Psychosensory approaches are "the application of sensory input to alter behavior, mood and thought" (Ruden, 2005, p. 155). The goal of somatic interventions is to release tension in parts of the body that became frozen at the time of the traumatic event, resulting in a decrease of negative symptoms (van der Kolk, 2014).

EMDR is the gold standard for empirical research supporting the success in the treatment of PTSD. The psychosensory approach includes doses of exposure to the traumatic experience in the form of recall coupled with bilateral stimulation through eye movements, taps, or sounds. This causes the brain to reprocess the cognitive, somatic, and emotional post-traumatic stressors (Shapiro, 2001) to adaptive resolution.

Psychopharmacological Approaches

Psychopharmacological approaches to the treatment of trauma target the complex symptoms of depression, anxiety, and sleep disturbance. They are often prescribed in conjunction with psychotherapy and help the client tolerate facing the traumatic memories throughout his or her healing journey. For specific medications prescribed for varied PTSD symptoms, please see the chapter on psychopharmacology.

Conclusion

Experiencing trauma firsthand or supporting someone else through their trauma puts a person face-to-face with sin and evil. It creates moments of intimate connection to when sin entered the world and the current life circumstance of living in a fallen world. In the process of this facing, existential questions often surface about the meaning of life; the existence, kindness, or goodness of God; and the worth of an individual. Conversely, in the facing is an opportunity to experience, witness, or be a part of miracles. When traumatized people come through their pain to engage in the richness of life again, it is a sacred, restorative journey unlike anything else. And the story of redemption is one of inspiration and hope.

KEY TERMS

Compassion fatigue: a decline in ability to share the feelings of parishioners

Self-care: practices engaged in by a helper to cultivate a fulfilling personal life

Secondary traumatic stress: PTSD-like symptoms experienced in the helper

Post-traumatic growth: positive changes that surpass the individual's state before the traumatic experience

Vicarious trauma: the helper's altered personal and/or spiritual worldview perception in response to empathic engagement with traumatic stories

Psychosensory: application of sensory input targeting the healing of trauma in the limbic system and body

Discussion Questions

1   What are the differences between compassion fatigue, secondary traumatic stress, and vicarious trauma?

2   How do you currently practice self-care? What are two additional practices you could incorporate?

3   Describe the three phases of treatment for persons seeking healing for trauma.

REVIEWING THE CONCEPTS

Learning Objectives

- Identify risk and vulnerability factors to contribute to adaptive or intensified traumatic reactions
  - Attachment style: secure versus insecure traits
  - Developmental stage: consideration of demographic information, maturity level, and history of diagnoses
  - Current life stressors: ongoing and transient stressors
  - Support system: compatibility of the need of the traumatized person and his or her support system(s)
  - Meaning-making: subjective beliefs about the event and self, sentimental losses, physical losses

- Understand the functions of the limbic system when activated in the survival-oriented stress response
    - The limbic system is activated in times of perceived threat.
    - The limbic system engages the SNS to fight or flee or the PNS to freeze.
    - The system is activated for the survival of the person.

- Differentiate between ASD, PTSD, and C-PTSD
    - ASD is a diagnosis of post-traumatic stress meeting nine diagnostic criteria within the first month of a post-traumatic event.
    - PTSD is a diagnosis when symptoms last 1 month or longer defined by symptoms of intrusion, negative mood, dissociation, avoidance, and arousal.
    - C-PTSD is a diagnosis including PTSD symptoms and symptoms of mood, somatization, and relational difficulties.

Chapter Review Questions

Level 1: Knowledge (True/False)

1. PTSD was included in a *DMS* for the first time in 1990.

2. A person with an ambivalent-avoidant attachment style will typically respond to trauma with proximity-seeking behaviors with members of their support system.

3. The FFF response is initiated in the limbic system.

4. An example of an intrusive symptom would be a nightmare.

5. The co-occurrence of PTSD and other psychological disorders is 60%, respectively.

6. A risk factor that may impede a person's adaptive process through acute stress is unfinished resolution to collateral damages.

7. C-PTSD is a diagnosis in the *DSM*.

8. People often assign characteristics of their childhood primary caretakers to God.

9. Secondary traumatic stress can include intrusive thoughts, nightmares, and hypervigilance.

10. The goal of somatic interventions is to release tension in parts of the body that became frozen at the time of a traumatic event.

Level 2: Comprehension

1. Which of the following is not a category of traumatic experience?
    a. Interpersonal
    b. Developmental
    c. Complex
    d. Individual

2. Which of the following categories within the uniqueness of man section includes the subjective experience of the trauma as a threat?

    a. Attachment

    b. Meaning-making

    c. Support system

    d. Life stressors

3. The post-traumatic stress symptom category to include attempts to circumvent reminders of the event is

    a. dissociative

    b. arousal

    c. intrusive

    d. avoidance

4. In the shock stage, any of these would be helpful in the care of a person who has just experienced trauma except

    a. inquire about provision of basic needs

    b. write down any important information

    c. speak in noncomplicated language

    d. include the situation on the prayer chain (without the person's permission)

5. Dissociation, while adaptive at the time of trauma, creates struggle in the process of healing. What activity helps decrease dissociation?

    a. Social engagement

    b. Avoidance

    c. Grounding techniques

    d. Both a and c

6. A diagnosis of PTSD, delayed expression is used when symptoms of PTSD do not surface or become intensified to meet diagnostic criteria until _____ months or longer:

    a. 2

    b. 4

    c. 6

    d. 8

7. The attachment style often developed by a child when his or her primary caretaker is a source of fear is

    a. Disorganized

    b. Anxious-ambivalent

    c. Avoidant

    d. Secure

8. Which category of symptoms was not included in the C-PTSD symptom list:

    a. Dissociative

    b. Socioeconomic

    c. Relational

    d. Physiological

9. The experience of feeling unable to empathize with a parishioner is

    a. Secondary traumatic stress

    b. Survivor guilt

    c. Compassion fatigue

    d. Vicarious trauma

10. Self-care may be

    a. meditative prayer

    b. counsel of a trusted friend

    c. exercise

    d. all of the above

Level 3: Application

1. There are several references to traumatic events throughout scripture. Select one person from the Bible who experienced trauma and write about it through one of the four trauma categories. Include observations of how his or her trauma impacted others.

2. A parishioner is reporting symptoms of traumatic stress and asks to meet with you. How would you incorporate an understanding of post-traumatic stress symptoms and FFF response to comfort, empower, and assess the parishioner?

3. Compare the symptoms of PTSD and C-PTSD diagnoses. What makes them different?

4. The transformative faith journey of each person is personal and unique. Consider a situation when symptoms of C-PTSD may be recognized within a parishioner's process of desiring to become more intimate in his or her relationship with God. Discuss how you would counsel someone disheartened by his or her experience.

5. Why is self-care essential to support the meaningful, ongoing care of a church body? What are signs that you may be experiencing secondary stress? List practical self-care strategies that are meaningful to you.

ANSWERS

LEVEL 1: KNOWLEDGE

1. F
2. F
3. T
4. T
5. F
6. T
7. F
8. T
9. T
10. T

LEVEL 2: COMPREHENSION

1. c
2. b
3. d
4. d
5. d
6. c
7. a
8. b
9. c
10. d

RESOURCES

Online Resources

- Gift From Within—https://giftfromwithin.org (nonprofit organization for trauma survivors)
- Nation Center for PTSD—https://www.ncptsd.org
- My PTSD—https://myptsd.com (a forum for online support and information on PTSD)

- Wounded Warrior Project—https://woundedwarriorproject.org (an organization that supports the military)

Readings

- *I Can't Get Over It: A Handbook for Trauma Survivors*, 2nd ed.—Dr. Aphrodite Matsakis
- *Waking the Tiger: Healing Trauma*—Dr. Peter Levine
- *Complex PTSD: From Surviving to Thriving*—Pete Walker
- *The Wounded Heart: Hope for Adult Victims of Childhood Sexual Abuse*—Dr. Dan Allender
- *Shame and Grace: Healing the Shame We Don't Deserve*—Lewis Smedes
- *The Relaxation & Stress Reduction Workbook*, 6th Ed.—Dr. Martha Davis; Elizabeth Eshelman, MSW; and Dr. Matthew McKay (2008)

Video Resources

- *EMDR*—https://youtu.be/hDivEv1U3Pg (a documentary film)
- *Understanding PTSD's Effects on Brain, Body, and Emotions, Janet Seahorn, TEDxCSU*—https://www.youtube.com/watch?v=BEHDQeIRTgs&t=5s
- CALM-electronic application that guides in relaxation and breathing techniques—http://www.calm.com

CLASSROOM ACTIVITIES

1. Role-play with a fellow student a scenario where a parishioner is reporting post-traumatic stress symptoms. Discuss what was helpful and challenging in each role.

2. Have a student volunteer to facilitate the students in grounding exercises. Discuss what the experience was like and when they may use them.

3. Have students create a self-care list of meaningful practices. Have them get into groups to share their lists and discuss self-care value.

REFERENCES

American Psychiatric Association. (1980). *Diagnostic and statistical manual of mental disorders* (3th ed.). Washington, DC: Author.

American Psychiatric Association. (2013). *Diagnostic and statistical manual of mental disorders* (5th ed.). Washington, DC: Author.

Brewin, C., Andrews, B., & Valentine, J.D. (2000). Meta-analysis of risk factors for posttraumatic stress disorder in trauma-exposed adults. *Journal of Consulting and Clinical Psychology, 68*(5), 748–766.

Carmanica, K., Brackbill, R., Liao, T., & Stellman, S. (2014). Comorbidity of 9/11-related PTSD and depression in the world trade center health registry 10–11 years postdisaster. *Journal of Traumatic Stress, 27,* 680–688.

Center for Substance Abuse Treatment. (2014). *Trauma-informed care in behavioral health services* (Chapter 2, "Trauma awareness"). NCBI. Retrieved from http://www.ncbi.nlm.nih.gov/books/NBK207203/

Collins, T. (2017). Historical trajectory of military PTSD and the psychosocial impacts on families: A literature review. *Canadian Social Work, 19*(1), 9–27.

Courtois, C. (2015). First, do no more harm: Ethics of attending to spiritual issues in trauma treatment. In D. Walker, C. Courtois, & J. Aten (Eds.), *Spiritually oriented psychotherapy for trauma* (pp. 55–75). Washington, DC: American Psychological Association.

D'Andrea, W., Sharma, R., Zelechoski, A., & Spinazzola, J. (2011). Physical health problems after single trauma exposure: When stress takes root in the body. *Journal of the American Psychiatric Nurses Association, 17*(6), 378–392.

Davis, M., Eschelman, E., & McKay, M. (2008). *The stress & relaxation reduction workbook* (6th ed.). Oakland, CA: New Harbinger Publications, Inc.

Dekel, S., Hankin, I., Pratt, J., Hackler, D., & Lanman, O. (2016). Posttraumatic growth in trauma recollections of 9/11 survivors: A narrative approach. *Journal of Loss and Trauma, 21*(4), 315–324.

Herman, J. (1992). *Trauma and recovery: The aftermath of violence—From domestic abuse to political terror.* New York, NY: Basic Books.

Hollidge, C. & Hollidge, E. (2016). Seeking security in the face of fear: The disorganized dilemma. *Psychoanalytic Social Work, 23*(2), 130–144.

Knight, C. (2013). Indirect trauma: Implications for self-care, supervision, the organization, and the academic institution. *Clinical Supervisor, 32*(2), 224–243. doi: 10.1080/07325223.2013.850139

Laible, D. (2004). Mother-child discourse in two contexts: Links with child temperament, attachment security, and socioemotional competence. *Developmental Psychology, 40*(6), 979–992.

Levine, P. (1997). *Waking the tiger: Healing trauma: The innate capacity to transform overwhelming experiences.* Berkeley, CA: North Atlantic Books.

Matsakis, A. (1996). *I can't get over it: A handbook for trauma survivors* (2nd ed.). Oakland, CA: New Harbinger Publications, Inc.

Miller, J. (2015). Seven self-care strategies. *Reflections: Narratives of Professional Helping, 21*(1), 52–58.

Miner, M.H. (2008). Healthy Questing and Mature Religious Reflection: Critique, Antecedents, and Relevance of Attachment Theory? *Journal of Psychology and Theology, 36*(3), 222–233.

Myer, R., Lewis, J. S., & James, R. (2013). The introduction of a task model for crisis intervention. *Journal of Mental Health Counseling, 35*(2), (95–107).

Nemcic-Moro, I., Franciskovic, T., Britvic, D., Klaric, M. & Zecevic, I. (2011). Disorder of extreme stress not otherwise specified (DESNOS) in Croatian war veterans with posttraumatic stress disorder: Case-control study. *Croatian Medical Journal, 52*(4), 505–512. doi: 10.3325/cmj.2011.52.505

Nouwen, H. (1981). *The way of the heart.* New York, NY: Ballantine Books.

Owens, G. (2016). Predictors of posttraumatic growth and posttraumatic stress symptom severity in undergraduates reporting potentially traumatic events. *Journal of Clinical Psychology, 72*(10), 1064–1076.

Painter, K. & Scannapieco, M. (2013). Child maltreatment: The neurobiological aspects of posttraumatic stress disorder. *Journal of Evidence-Based Social Work, 10,* 276–284. doi: 10.1080/15433714.2011.566468

Ponniah, K. & Hollon, S. (2009). Empirically supported psychological treatments for acute stress disorder and posttraumatic stress disorder: A review. *Depression and Anxiety (1091-4269), 26*(12), 1086–1109.

Pressley, J. & Spinazzola, J. (2015). Beyond survival: Application of a complex trauma treatment model in the Christian context. *Journal of Psychology & Theology, 43*(1), 8–22.

Ruden, R. (n.d.). Harnessing synaptic plasticity to treat the consequences of emotional traumatization by amygdala depotentiation techniques: An electrochemical model. Retrieved from https://www.havening.org

Ruden, R. (2005). A neurological basis for the observed peripheral sensory modulation of emotional responses. *Traumatology, 11*(3), 145–158.

Scaer, R. (2006). The dissociative capsule. Retrieved from https://www.traumasoma.com.

Schnurr, P., Lunney, C., Sengupta, A., & Spiro III, A. (2005). A longitudinal study of retirement in older male veterans. *Journal of Consulting and Clinical Psychology, 73*(3), 561–566.

Shapiro, F. (2001). *Eye movement desensitization and reprocessing (EMDR): Basic principles, protocols, and procedures* (2nd ed.). New York, NY: The Guilford Press.

Shapiro, F. (2012). *Getting past your past: Take control of your life with self-help techniques from EMDR therapy.* New York, NY: Rodale Books.

Smedes, L. (1993). *Shame and grace: Healing the shame we don't deserve.* New York, NY: HarperCollins Publishers.

Tyler, T. (2012). The limbic model of systemic trauma. *Journal of Social Work Practice, 26*(1), 125–138.

van der Kolk, B. (2003). Posttraumatic stress disorder and the nature of trauma. In M. Solomon & D. Siegel (Eds.), *Healing trauma: Attachment, mind, body and brain* (pp. 168–195). New York, NY: W.W. Norton & Company.

van der Kolk, B. (2014). *The body keeps the score.* New York, NY: Penguin Group.

Van Deusen, S. & Courtois, C. (2015). Spirituality, religion, and complex developmental trauma. In D. Walker, C. Courtois, & J. Aten (Eds.), *Spiritually oriented psychotherapy for trauma* (pp. 29–54). Washington, DC: American Psychological Association.

Walker, D., Courtois, C., & Aten, J. (2015). Basics of working on spiritual matters with traumatized individuals. In D. Walker, C. Courtois, & Aten, J. (Eds.), *Spiritually oriented psychotherapy for trauma.* Washington, DC: American Psychological Association.

Walker, P. (2014). *Complex PTSD: From surviving to thriving.* Berkeley, CA: Pete Walker.

Weinberg, M. & Gil, S. (2016). Trauma as an objective or subjective experience: The association between types of traumatic events, personality traits, subjective experience of the event, and posttraumatic symptoms. *Journal of Loss and Trauma, 21*(2), 137–146.

IMAGE CREDITS

CHAPTER 5

Grief, Mourning, and Loss

Kevin Van Lant, PhD

LEARNING OBJECTIVES

Upon completion of this chapter, readers will be able to

1. differentiate between common grief, complicated grief, and depression;

2. define the typical process of grief;

3. facilitate a pastoral response to grief and loss among parishioners; and

4. identify risk factors for those who may be vulnerable to more complicated bereavement outcomes and know how to respond accordingly.

*And who's to say which is more incredible—a man who raises
the dead ... or a God who weeps?*
(Gire, 1998, p. 252)

*We find a place for what we lose. Although we know that after such a loss
the acute stage of mourning will subside, we also know that we shall remain
inconsolable and will never find a substitute. No matter what may fill the gap,
even if it be filled completely, it nevertheless remains something else.*
(Freud, 1961, p. 386)

THE STORY OF PASTOR JAKE

At the conclusion of a long journey through seminary, Jake was recently recruited to pastor a small church in rural California. This was Jake's first pastorate and marked a transition from his previous job as an insurance adjuster. In many ways, this transition to pastoral ministry represented the fulfillment of a long-term sense of calling that both Jake and his wife, Katie, had felt since they served together in a college ministry many years prior. Jake and Katie have three school-aged children who were deeply rooted in their church and school communities, and very connected to their grandparents who lived nearby. Despite the sadness related to leaving their long-term home, Jake and his family appeared to be adjusting reasonably well to their new community and felt quite confident that the move had been a success.

FIGURE 5.1   **Jesus Weeps Upon Hearing the News of Lazarus's Death**

During his first year as a pastor, Jake's church community was severely affected by two significant losses. Josiah, a 15-year-old boy from their youth ministry drowned at an annual church-sponsored 4th of July event. In addition, Frank, an 80-year-old beloved elder of the church, who had befriended Jake early in his ministry, suddenly passed away from a severe cardiac event. This had been particularly hard on Jake, as he had become quite attached to Frank who had functioned much like a father figure during his transition to the pastorate.

Throughout this season of loss and pain for his new church family, Jake could not shake the feeling that he should be able to do more to shepherd his congregation through the individual and communal process of grief and mourning. In addition, Jake also began to re-experience feelings of loss related to the death of his father a number of years earlier and wondered if his decision to pursue pastoral ministry was perhaps misguided. At the encouragement of his elder board, Jake reached out to a local pastor who also functioned as a chaplain for a hospice organization in the area. Through his time with the local pastor and several sessions with a grief counselor, Jake was able to begin to understand the nature of grief and loss, both within his own heart and among those he shepherds.

AN INTRODUCTION TO THE NATURE OF GRIEF, MOURNING, AND LOSS

Loss is an inevitable part of life. No one, regardless of age, position, or privilege will avoid confronting a lifetime of loss experiences. Loss takes many forms: loss through divorce or death, loss of health or independence, loss of a job or relationship, loss of confidence or a sense of security, loss of faith in others or even in God. Although loss is inevitable, its impact is frequently misunderstood and sometimes, not even recognized. However, when losses are grieved and mourned "well," they can ultimately result in a transformative experience. Understanding and recognizing the loss experience in all its permutations requires patience, empathy, and wise discernment on the part of the counselor. The goal of this chapter, therefore, is to equip those who minister to others during times of loss and mourning to help bring about comfort, healing, and growth.

What Is the Purpose of Grief and Mourning, and Why Are They Necessary?

As Pastor Jake attended to the grieving individuals and families in his congregation, he was confronted with the reality that people grieve, or avoid grieving, in many different ways. For some, grieving and mourning were an instinctual and natural response to the loss of their loved ones. Some, however, were overtly resistant to grieving their losses. One member told Pastor Jake that his elderly friend Frank was better off now that he was in heaven with God and saw no reason to be sad or mournful. Jake felt conflicted because although on one level he agreed with the parishioner, he also knew that something about the parishioner's response felt incomplete or unhealthy. Why, he wondered, is it important to grieve lost loved ones, and should he just accept the notion that the "dead in Christ" are better off?

Grief is defined as the primarily emotional response to the loss of a loved one through death (Stroebe, 2008). Grief is a broadly felt emotion, however, and can be a normal reaction to nearly any type of loss or serious life change. In fact, grief resulting from forms of loss other than death may be quite confusing and perhaps difficult for the parishioner to label as such. Grieving individuals typically experience a complex and even contradictory set of feelings that are oftentimes difficult to articulate. Those around them may see the physiological expression of these emotions (i.e., tearfulness, lethargy, and other vegetative symptoms), but may have very limited access to their actual emotional process. Conversely, **mourning** is defined primarily as an external expression of grief (Stroebe, 2008). Because mourning often takes place in a relatively public context, it's manifestation in the individual is highly influenced by personality, social and religious culture, and family history. Although the words grief and mourning are often used interchangeably, as there are areas of overlap, it is important that the counselor remains aware of the differences and attempts to honor the cultural expectations relevant to the person's context and personality variables.

Grief, then, is an emotional process involving the realization of what has been lost as well as what the loss actually represents within the context of one's life. One's initial experience of grief is vital in that it represents the beginning of an important awareness and the start of a long process of letting go. We often describe the lack of grief as denial. **Denial**, in this context, results from the emotionally overwhelming nature of loss and an unconscious attempt to psychologically avoid the disorienting and painful reality of the situation. Denial may be a natural initial response to loss; however, it is not a healthy, long-term coping mechanism. Although some may experience periods of numbness following the loss, denial of one's emotional experience is different and can interfere with resolving the grief process.

Grief's purpose, therefore, is to help the individual emotionally confront the reality of who and what has been lost in a manner that ultimately allows him or her to move forward with what life still has to offer. Those who do not grieve typically become psychologically and relationally "trapped" between a past reality that no longer exists and an unrealized future with the potential for new relationships and growth experiences. The avoidance of grief can become its own form of death, often resulting in depression and despair.

Attachment as a Mediator for Loss

As in the discussion of anxiety earlier in this text, it is difficult to comprehend the nature of loss experiences without first understanding the nature of human attachment. Human attachment, or bonding, begins within the womb (Laxton-Kane & Slade, 2002). Mothers and their babies develop prenatal emotional bonds through the sound of the mother's voice as well as the sensation of physical rhythms, which serve to soothe and comfort the developing child in utero (Lefkovics, Baji, & Rigó, 2014). Once born, a child's early experiences with primary caregivers continue to shape his or her attachment style. Although early relational experiences tend to be the most impacting, the nature of these attachments develop over the entire course of one's life, becoming the foundation for how one experiences intimacy and safety, or the lack thereof, in day-to-day relationships.

As presented in Chapter 1, human attachment can be summarized in three common patterns: (1) **Secure attachment** is characterized by a general sense of security and relational trust. (2) **Anxious-ambivalent attachment** often manifests as an insecure, anxious relational style combined with feelings of unworthiness of love or trust. (3) **Anxious-avoidant or dismissive attachment** often results in a typically distant or detached style of interaction (Blalock, Franzese, Machell, & Strauman (2015). These patterns have significant implications for how an individual grieves the loss of a loved one.

Although there is much variability in how an individual will react to a loss experience, securely attached mourners are less likely to report feelings of abandonment and helplessness (Jerga, Shaver, & Wilkinson, 2011). Their grieving process will often reflect the nature of their attachments more broadly. Individuals demonstrating an anxious-ambivalent attachment style commonly experience more distress and fear over typical relationship tensions, which can result in a clingy or overly dependent relational style, particularly in intimate or romantic relationships. As a result, anxiously attached individuals tend to experience prolonged grief symptoms when compared to those who report a more secure attachment style. Those with anxious-avoidant or dismissive attachment styles tend to minimize the nature of their losses and may demonstrate minimal evidence of mourning or grief.

When attempting to assess the nature of a parishioner's grief reaction, it may be beneficial to understand the person's attachment to the deceased as well as his or her general attachment style, particularly when the grieving individual is presenting with what appears to be a more unusual or incongruent reaction to the loss. Such an assessment need not be comprehensive or time-consuming. Oftentimes a few open-ended and situationally appropriate questions regarding the nature of the relationship with the deceased will bring some level of clarity to the person's attachment experiences. Use this as an opportunity to understand and "be with," rather than to comment or evaluate verbally, with the grieving individual. If needed, an ongoing counseling relationship will provide time and space to help the grieving individual better understand the nature of his or her attachment, who or what is actually lost, and the opportunity to grieve in a healthy and productive manner.

The Universality of Loss

Although this chapter will primarily focus on the nature of grief and mourning through loss experiences related to death and dying, it is important to at least briefly address the universality of loss in nearly every aspect of daily life as well as the likelihood that the typical pastoral counselor will frequently attend to these more common losses in his or her day-to-day work with parishioners. Examples of common loss may include

- divorce;
- children leaving home for college or the military;
- loss of a job;
- illness and aging;
- moving;
- financial, economic, or material losses; or
- loss of dreams or expectations.

These common, and uncommon, experiences of loss punctuate the lives of all people and are often later described as life altering or even life defining. The pain of loss can leave us feeling quite vulnerable and exposed, which highlights the need for pastors and pastoral counselors to be sensitive to the effect of loss experiences and remain mindful of the potential grieving process that may ensue. Perhaps through the awareness of his or her own micro- and macro-losses, the pastoral or ministerial counselor can better empathize with the breadth and universality of loss experiences within his or her congregation. In the case of Pastor Jake, the losses associated with leaving his former job and church communities were significant personal losses that were quickly overshadowed by the loss of Josiah and Frank. It was through conversation with his grief counselor that the broader extent of Jake's loss experiences became evident, making it possible for him to grieve these significant losses and to share them with his wife, who was also experiencing a very similar grief.

KEY TERMS

Grief: the primarily emotional response to the loss of a loved one through death

Mourning: a primarily external expression of grief and loss

Denial: an unconscious attempt to psychologically avoid the unpleasant and painful reality of a difficult experience

Secure attachment: relational style characterized by a general sense of security and trust

Anxious-ambivalent attachment: an insecure, anxious relational style leaving one feeling unworthy of love or trust

Anxious-avoidant (dismissive) attachment: a typically distant or detached style of relational interaction

Discussion Questions

1   Jake felt conflicted about his parishioner's dismissal of the need to grieve their loved one. How might you respond to someone who meets with you and says he or she really doesn't need to grieve because his or her loved one is in a "better place"?

2   What is the purpose of grief?

3   What are some biblical examples of grief and mourning?

4   Attachment styles appear to affect grief outcomes. How might someone with an anxious-avoidant attachment style differ from someone who has a generally secure attachment style as it relates to his or her grief response?

TYPES OF GRIEF REACTIONS

Grief can take many forms. At times, grief can take the form of sadness and despair, while at other times, it may look more like anger and bitterness toward the deceased, toward life, or toward God. Grief tends to diminish over time; however, for many, grief manifests as a variety of conflicting emotions and thoughts that are exceedingly difficult to reconcile with one's faith, relationships with others, and one's confidence in the nature of life. The following sections will describe the different common grief reactions and more complicated forms of grief and bereavement with the goal of equipping ministers to come alongside the bereaved and skillfully minister during a time of tragedy and loss.

Normal or Common Grief

Normal grief, which may also be referred to as common or uncomplicated grief, can manifest as a broad range of behaviors and emotional experiences that are somewhat typical after a loss. The nature of these behaviors and emotional experiences are highly affected by culture and societal norms and expectations; therefore, understanding and acknowledging the cultural norms of the mourner will be crucial to understanding the nature of a congregant's loss experience. Common reactions to loss across most cultures can be placed into four broad categories: emotions, physical sensations, cognitions, and behaviors (Worden, 2009). It is vital that pastors and grief counselors understand these categories and recognize how experiences within each category may present. Common emotional responses to loss include sadness, anxiety, guilt, loneliness, helplessness, and anger. Tearfulness is a typical response to sadness; however, many variables may affect the freedom or willingness of an individual to shed tears over a loss.

When counseling someone who appears sad, but not tearful, it may be important to help the counselee put words to his or her sadness and to make emotional space for tears to be expressed. My experience suggests that many people fear the depth of their sadness, however, and may actively attempt to avoid expressing it, lest they become overwhelmed by pain. In these moments, the counselor's judgment is crucial. It is important to honor the counselee's situation while giving him or her the opportunity to express the depth of his or her grief and sorrow. A simple comment such as, "I notice that you feel deep sadness and wonder if there are times when you find yourself tearing up or even weeping?" This type of comment acknowledges the emotional experience while respecting the counselee's containment of his or her tears. Conversely, the ongoing and inconsolable emotional expression of pain may be attached to an unresolved trauma or a preexisting and/or developing mental health issue, such as major depression, and may suggest the need for a referral to a mental health professional.

For many, a common and frequently confusing emotional experience after a significant loss is the feeling of anger. Anger can feel complicated, as it may be experienced as a situationally inappropriate emotion. For several months after Josiah's death, his mother, Sarah, experienced waves of anger directed at Josiah himself for not listening to her warning about the depth of the lake, toward her husband for not being attentive to his whereabouts, toward herself for failing to go with him, and toward God for taking her son. Sarah's anger was so intense that Pastor Jake had a difficult time counseling her through it. He would often vacillate between subtly avoiding her expressions of anger to defending God and his interpretation of his sovereignty. This approach only seemed to intensify Sarah's anger. Only upon taking the counsel of his chaplain friend did Jake change approaches and give space and empathic responses to Sarah's anger. He didn't understand why it worked, but over time, he noticed that her anger was slowly becoming less intense, being replaced with more tears and sorrow. (While outside the scope of this chapter, many resources are available for improving counseling skills for working with anger.)

Despite the complicated nature of angry feelings after a loss, it is important for the grief counselor to make space for feelings of anger since unresolved or unexpressed anger may contribute to a more complicated grief experience later on. Anger appears to primarily emanate from two sources: powerlessness over one's inability to prevent a loved one from dying and a primitive, regressive experience that is perhaps more related to a type of fear or panic (Worden, 2009). Either way, it is important to allow those who grieve to put language to their anger without fear of shame or guilt. Anger that is suppressed can frequently turn inward, resulting in a depressive experience that may include thoughts of suicide or self-harm. It is imperative that the counselor remain attentive to depressive or suicidal language and respond in a manner that is congruent or "fits" with the person's presentation. Although this will be developed later in the chapter, such responses may include a referral to a medical doctor or therapist, as well as other community resources that may meet the needs of the person's specific situation. Pastors should not attempt to counsel such an individual without consultation and professional support.

Common thought processes, or cognitions, that follow the loss of a loved one may include confusion, disbelief, idealizing, and even types of auditory or visual hallucinations. Because of the disorienting nature of severe grief, it is important that the pastoral counselor understand the complexity and normalcy of these thought processes so that he or she remains a stabilizing and accepting presence in the grieving person's life. In many ways, the belief systems that bring coherency and stability to one's life are often highly disrupted by the nature of loss and death. This disruption may result in a questioning of reality, including the nature of God and the meaning of life, that can be quite frightening and confusing in-and-of itself. Isolation during these cognitively confusing times will often exacerbate the disrupted connection to reality. Connection to you as a counselor as well as a broader church community is irreplaceable and can act to ground the grieving individual during such seasons of time. In addition, the appropriate use of prayer and scripture, particularly the Psalms, appear to give solace and hope when the counselee's sense of reality feels a bit shaky (e.g., Psalm 23, Psalm 46, and Psalm 139).

Lastly, it is common for people to "see" or "hear" their deceased loved ones in the weeks and early months following their loss (Worden, 2009). Although pastors and lay counselors will likely have many uncertainties about the theological validity of such experiences, I find that many counselees experience these moments as quite comforting, particularly when they feel "visited" in a dream. In addition, dream visitation experiences may be culturally normative, particularly for some Latin, Native American, and Asian cultures. These experiences rarely last beyond the first several weeks following the death and do not appear to suggest a more complicated or pathological grief outcome. A referral to a mental health professional should be considered if the hallucinatory experiences persist, create problematic outcomes, or existed prior to the loss.

Normal grief also elicits common behavioral responses. These behaviors may include sleeplessness, loss of appetite, withdrawal, avoidance or obsession with objects or reminders of the deceased, extreme restlessness, and, of course, crying. Although these behaviors are common after a loss, the severity and extent of such behaviors should be monitored quite closely as a part of the counseling process. A quick review of their overall well-being and some questioning about how they spend their time throughout the week will frequently give the counselor a good sense of their behavioral life. In addition, family members can be an important resource for behavioral information, as the counselee may not have reliable recollection or insight into the grieving person's behavior. When appropriate, a family member's participation in aspects of the counseling process may provide a level of insight that would otherwise be difficult to obtain.

Grief affects the entirety of one's being, and physical complaints are common after a significant loss. Common physical sensations after a loss may include

- gastrointestinal discomfort;
- tightness in the chest or throat;
- high sensitivity to sensory input; or
- fatigue and sluggishness.

Although these symptoms are common and should generally be normalized, it is important that you advise someone describing such symptoms to consult with a medical doctor, as they may be indicators of a more serious illness. In addition, a medical evaluation may result in possible interventions to relieve some the more unpleasant physical symptoms, such as gastrointestinal discomfort or fatigue. It is relatively common for grieving individuals to become quite ill in the weeks and months following a loss. This may be related to the compromising effect of stress on the immune system or personal health neglect. Regardless, it is helpful for the counselor to be prepared for this likelihood and encourage the parishioner to pursue good health care.

With time, most people who experience "normal grief" will begin to see a reduction in the intensity and frequency of their grief symptoms (Jacobs, 1993). Mourners will begin to notice that times of tearfulness and sadness will be experienced with briefer duration and less regularity. Although feelings of pain will likely always be present in one form or another, grief recovery is typically accompanied by a general reduction in symptoms, a renewed interest in life, and a general sense of moving forward while letting go of the person or thing that was lost. This recovery process can present its own challenges, however, as the recovering individual may also experience conflicting feelings of guilt or betrayal about moving forward with life without his or her loved one. Talking about these conflicting feelings can often help normalize and bring clarity to what feels complicated and even troubling.

Although there is no definitive agreement among researchers as to a specific time period for grief recovery, most individuals appear to experience a reduction in symptoms between 6 months and 2 years following a significant loss. A normal grief response occurs in 50% to 85% of individuals following a loss and typically resolves in 1 to 2 years (Grief, Bereavement, and Coping With Loss, 2017).

Prolonged or Complicated Grief

The notion of common or normal grief suggests that the process of loss and grief can be experienced in an uncommon or abnormal manner. Indeed, between 15% and 31% of those who confront a significant loss will develop some form of complicated grief reaction (Crunk, Burke, & Robinson, 2017). Although a clear and agreed upon definition of **prolonged or complicated grief** appears to be somewhat elusive, **minimal grief reaction** and **chronic grief** are two types of complicated grief supported by empirical studies

(Bonanno, 2004). Minimal grief reaction, which is experienced by approximately 15% of persons during the first 2 years post-loss, is evidenced by the absence of emotional distress or impairment. Many contextual factors may contribute to a minimal grief reaction and, for some, may be a reasonable response to loss. Chronic grief is a pattern in which the person exhibits the symptoms of normal grief, but does so over a much longer period of time. Chronic grief occurs in about 15% of the bereaved population. Those experiencing chronic grief may also appear to be suffering with symptoms of major depression and anxiety. A chronic grief reaction will almost certainly require a referral to a mental health professional to determine the extent of the co-occurring symptoms and to assess the cause of the extended grief reaction.

The *Diagnostic and Statistical Manual of Mental Disorders* (5th ed.; *DSM-5*; American Psychiatric Association, 2013) includes a diagnostic code for **persistent complex bereavement disorder** (PCBD) and codifies a number of symptoms related to prolonged and complicated grief problems. The diagnosis of PCBD includes a variety of maladaptive and prolonged bereavement symptoms that impair healing and suggest signs of significant distress, isolation, and preoccupation with the deceased. As a counselor, familiarity with PCBD symptoms can help you effectively distinguish between normal and complex or complicated bereavement. These distinctions will allow you to facilitate the counseling process better as well as to determine the potential need for professional intervention.

Common Risk Factors for Those Who May Suffer With Complicated Grief

Although it is impossible to predict who will suffer from PCBD or more complicated grief outcomes, research does appear to indicate that some individuals may be at a higher risk than others (Tomarken et al., 2008). Common factors associated with poorer grief outcomes include

- difficult circumstances of the death;
- social support;
- unsupportive religious practices;
- younger or older age groups;
- severity of stressful life events;
- low income; or
- history of depression or current depression.

Historically, those who experience the sudden and unexpected death of a loved one were assumed to be more vulnerable to complicated grief outcomes. However, Stroebe and Schut (2001) suggest that one's response to a sudden or unexpected death might be moderated by a strong sense of self-worth as well as a sense that life overall is not out of control. Those with a poor sense of self-worth and a feeling that life is out of control appear to experience higher rates of depression and physiological (somatic) complaints than those with higher levels of self-worth and situational confidence. For many, perceived levels of social support are strongly correlated to grief outcomes (Cherry et al.,

2015). Those with higher levels of social support report lower rates of depression and fewer symptoms of mental illness more broadly.

Unsurprisingly, those who attend church on a frequent and consistent basis also report better grief outcomes. The strength of one's personal religious beliefs, however, appear to be less of a factor than the nature of one's connections within a church community. Clearly, the "Body of Christ," as represented within the church community, can be a source of strength and support for those who are suffering with loss and grief, affecting not only their current state of mourning but also their longer term mental health.

Age and gender also appear to be factors affecting grief outcomes. Men, particularly those under 60 years of age, report higher rates of depression and increased frequency of complicated bereavement than women (Grief, Bereavement, and Coping With Loss, 2017). Although various theories have been proposed for this gender discrepancy, it appears that lower levels of social support experienced by bereaved men may be a primary factor. Pastoral counselors, therefore, would be well advised to be aware of perceived levels of social support among all counselees, but with particular attention given to males who appear somewhat isolated or less connected within a church community.

In addition, both males and females who are younger in age appear to report higher rates of complicated grief during the initial stages of loss, particularly when the death was sudden or unexpected. Complicated grief in younger adults seems to be shorter lived, however, and may reflect a greater level of access to social supports that older adults may not have.

Pre-loss levels of mental health and attachment style affect grief outcomes for nearly all people (Schenck, Eberle, & Rings, 2016). As a result, those who experience higher rates of depression, stress, and anxiety prior to losing a loved one will be at a significantly higher risk of developing complicated grief and commonly see an exacerbation of clinical symptoms.

Grieving individuals may display many symptoms found in people who are depressed, and the two experiences can be difficult to differentiate. One approach to differentiating between depression and grief is to evaluate the person's sense of self-worth. People struggling with depression often have a poor sense of self-worth, while grieving individuals seldom mention feeling badly about who they are. They tend to feel badly about the situation, but don't feel like they themselves are bad. Pastoral counselors should pay particular attention to mourners with complicated mental health or attachment backgrounds and be prepared to refer to mental health professionals should these symptoms increase in severity or disruption.

Stage Models of Grief

Grief is often organized around process. When we think of a process, we normally imagine a somewhat linear and predictable series of stages and steps. Experts often attempt to describe the process of grief while simultaneously acknowledging the inherent limitations of any theory that attempts to predict an experience as complex as grief, loss, or mourning. For example, some persons experiencing grief and loss do not report each and every stage of a particular theory or perhaps experience various stages in a different order than presented in the literature (Neimeyer, 2014). That being said, there is evidence that the process of grieving does contain a number of common experiences reported by most individuals when confronted with the reality of significant loss. Stage theories, therefore, are not to be held to with great rigidity or allegiance. They are, simply, a helpful tool to inform a counselor (and others) of potential movement within a process that can at times feel abstract, disorienting, and difficult to understand.

The **five stages of grief**, otherwise referred to as the Kübler-Ross model, presents a set of emotions typically experienced by those who are terminally ill as well individuals who have lost loved ones (Kübler-Ross, 1969). Kübler-Ross' five stages of grief include the following:

- Denial—A subconscious attempt to deny the reality, extent, or meaning of the diagnosis or loss.
- Anger—When denial is no longer a viable defense, persons often become quite angry at the reality of their loss and the feelings of helplessness it evokes.
- Bargaining—An attempt or promise to make compensatory life changes to undo the prospect of or reality of a loss or disease process.
- Depression—The full reality of loss has taken hold, resulting in feelings of great sadness and despair.
- Acceptance—This involves acknowledging the reality of the loss in a manner that brings about healing and a stability of emotions.

The five-stage theory of grief has been applied to nearly all experiences of loss, including divorce, substance abuse recovery, job loss, and infertility, to name but a few. It is perhaps the best-known model by the general population and may create common language from which to counsel those who come to you seeking help with their grief experiences. In my clinical work, I have found that many of the bereaved experience some or all of the five stages in repetitive cycles with varying degrees of intensity, typically decreasing in frequency and intensity as time progresses, although rarely extinguishing completely.

While processing the nature of his own grief after the loss of his wife, C. S. Lewis described the repetitiveness and confusion of the grieving process as follows:

> For in grief nothing "stays put." One keeps on emerging from a phase, but it always recurs. Round and round. Everything repeats. Am I going in circles, or dare I hope I am on a spiral? But if a spiral, am I going up or down? How often—will it be for always?—how often will the vast emptiness astonish me like a complete novelty and make me say, "I never realized my loss till this moment"? The same leg is cut off time after time. The first plunge of the knife into the flesh is felt again and again. (Lewis, 1961, p. 67)

This is a compelling description of the repetitive and disorienting nature of grief, which both highlights the nature of a grieving process and the lack of uniformity to such a process.

The concept of tasks that must be completed during the process of mourning is presented as an alternative to the stages of grief model (Worden, 2009). In the task approach, counselors and mourners are given a model that is active and hopeful rather than passive and immutable. The **four tasks of mourning** (Worden, 2009) are as follows:

- Task 1: To Accept the Reality of the Loss
- Task 2: To Process the Pain of Grief
- Task 3: To Adjust to the World Without the Deceased
- Task 4: To Find an Enduring Connection With the Deceased in the Midst of Embarking on a New Life

Notice that each of the four tasks asks the mourner to participate actively in a process with definable boundaries. In Task 1 of this approach, the person experiencing the loss is encouraged to participate in activities that bring the reality of the loss to consciousness rather than to simply wait for the denial stage to end. Although the process of accepting reality may be slow and must honor the nature of the loss and the mental and emotional health of the mourner, gentle and scalable encouragement on the part of the counselor can empower the individual to move toward this reality rather than to avoid the actual nature of the loss.

Much of grief counseling, however, is oriented toward accomplishing Task 2, Processing the Pain of Grief. This work involves moving toward pain rather than away from it. It is important that in your work as a counselor that you do not unintentionally participate in the avoidance of such pain. As studies of compassion fatigue indicate, you are not immune from the hurt, particularly when you counsel an individual with whom you have a pastoral relationship or when his or her loss correlates to a past loss in your own life. Pastor Jake found himself doing just that when counseling Josiah's father, Peter. The devastating nature of Josiah's death, as well as the reminder of his own son's near drowning experience, initially resulted in Jake's subconscious avoidance of Peter's pain. At one point during a counseling session, Peter asked Jake to give him more time to discuss what he was feeling rather than he and his wife's marital struggles post-loss. Jake realized in that moment that he was avoiding discussing the rather overwhelming nature of Peter's obvious pain and moving toward their marital difficulties, which were much easier for him to process.

J. William Worden (2009) describes Task 3 as Adjusting to the World Without the Deceased. This task consists of three components: external adjustments, internal adjustments, and spiritual adjustments. It may take considerable time to adjust to all of the external realities one might experience after a loss. Many of these external adjustments appear to become increasingly evident after the initial experiences of loss diminish.

Pastor Jake noticed that a few months after Frank's funeral, his widow, Marjorie, became increasingly confronted with the external realities of his death. She described confusion and despair as she attempted to adjust to sleeping in a bed alone, paying bills online, and hiring a plumber, as well as a myriad of other tasks she had never needed to do when Frank was alive. These adjustments can be quite demanding and are rarely understood immediately after a death.

In his book on bereavement in adult life, C. M. Parkes (1972, p. 7) states, "In any bereavement, it is seldom clear exactly what is lost. A loss of a husband, for instance, may or may not mean the loss of a sexual partner, companion, accountant, gardener, baby minder, audience, bed warmer, and so on, depending on the particular roles normally performed by the husband." As a counselor, you may often find yourself empathizing with the bereaved over the external reality of his or her loss as well as providing practical assistance when needed. For example, Jake was able to connect Marjorie with a fellow parishioner who assisted her with online bill paying and locating a plumbing contractor. These practical ways of coming alongside Marjorie were an important part of ministering to her very real needs.

Although adjusting to the internal realities of loss is certainly less concrete than the external, these internal adjustments can be far more complex. Much of this adjustment may relate to self-worth and self-definition. After the loss of a child or spouse, the bereaved may have a difficult time defining who they are relative to their shifting role. They may no longer be a wife or a husband, a role that has at least partially defined them for many years. Their role as a parent may suddenly cease to exist upon the death of a child. Worden suggests that the internal adjustments after a loss often revolve around the questions, "Who am I now" and "How has this loss redefined me?" The counselor's role in helping the mourner put words to these questions as well as to assist in exploring different types of answers may be extremely beneficial as they move through this disorienting process of rediscovering a new sense of self.

Spiritual adjustments to a world without the deceased may be particularly relevant in your role as a pastoral counselor. After the loss of a loved one, parishioners may find themselves questioning every aspect of their view of God as well as a belief in his essential goodness. Shortly after Josiah's death, Jake met with his older brother Paul. For many years, Paul had been an active participant in their high school youth group and was now part of the worship team for their college ministry. Although Paul had been a Christian for many years, the death of Josiah had created great angst in his foundational belief in God and left Jake feeling ill equipped to respond to his questions about how a "good God" can allow someone like his brother to die at such a young age.

Counseling parishioners who are struggling with doubt may be a fairly common experience for pastors and pastoral counselors; however, doubts about God after a significant loss may differ in key ways that create new challenges for a pastoral counselor. Doubts about God after the loss of a loved one may be intricately tied to a mourner's sense of self as well as his or her personal sense of self-worth in the eyes of God. In addition, feelings of anger and powerlessness toward God may surface, which are crucial to accommodate and empathize with. Each of these aspects may be highly influenced by such things as the mourner's age, maturity, capacity of self-reflection, and life stage. This is not a time for simple answers, a poorly timed bible verse, or a defense of God. The counselor's capacity to "sit with" the mourner's pain, anger, and fear with compassion, wisdom, and empathy while making space for the Spirit of God to do His work on the mourner's heart is oftentimes the most meaningful and productive stance a counselor might take in such a situation. Attending to spiritual adjustments after a loss will take time and patience on the part of the counselor, and it may be during these times that seeking your own spiritual counsel and direction may be of particularly value.

The fourth, and final task in Worden's (2009) model is to "find an enduring connection with the deceased in the midst of embarking on a new life." For some, this task can seem a bit counterintuitive. After all, aren't we typically told that the completion of the grief process results in a "letting go and moving on?" Although this may be the case for some, it is often quite reassuring that the completion of task four makes space for an enduring connection while finding avenues to embark upon a new life. A year after Josiah's death, his parents and siblings planted a tree near the walking path that they had frequented as a family throughout his childhood. In fact, Josiah's mother has fond memories of pushing him in a stroller along this path as well as watching him toddle a bit erratically as he was learning to walk and run nearby.

Josiah's parents will always feel a sense of sorrow and pain when remembering him; however, "his tree," as they call it, and the area nearby are a location where they are reminded of their loss while simultaneously experiencing a sense of enduring connection. The capacity to embark upon a new life is often intertwined with a right remembering that includes a sense of connection to those that we lose.

KEY TERMS

Normal grief: also referred to as common or uncomplicated grief describing the typical range of emotions and behaviors after a loss

Prolonged or complicated grief: an atypical grief reaction accompanied by intensified and prolonged or absent grief reactions

Minimal grief reaction: the absence of emotional distress or impairment after a loss

Chronic grief: person exhibits symptoms of normal grief, but does so over a much longer period of time

Persistent complex bereavement disorder: *DSM-5* disorder that codifies a number of symptoms related to prolonged and complicated grief issues

Five stages of grief: also known as the Kübler-Ross model, identifies a five-stage model of grief consisting of denial, anger, bargaining, depression, and acceptance

Four tasks of mourning: model proposed by J. William Worden consisting of four active grief tasks important to grief resolution

Discussion Questions

1   Cultural expectation plays a significant role in the grief response. How might your subcultural expectations related to a grief response differ from other subcultures you have knowledge of?

2   What are the four broad categories of the grief response?

3   Describe the common emotional processes one would expect to see in a person who is grieving?

4   Describe the two primary sources of anger experienced by many who are grieving?

5   What are the four physiological complaints often described by grieving people?

6   Describe the various personal and contextual factors associated with poorer grief outcomes.

7   Describe various spiritual adjustments that are often confronted after a significant loss. How might you respond to a counselee who is experiencing such spiritual tensions?

COMMON APPROACHES TO CARE, TREATMENT, AND SUPPORT

Although many pastors are trained to perform funerals, too few are adequately trained to emotionally shepherd those who are suffering from the loss of a loved one or to create ministries that respond to their specific needs. Ministering to this population can at times be painful, confusing, and even traumatizing. In spite of this, pastors and pastoral counselors must be prepared to respond to losses within their ministries and congregations. Pastor Jake was completely ill prepared for the losses that took place within his congregation. As a result, he initially minimized the severity of the emotions his congregants were experiencing as a way to protect himself from his own feelings of being overwhelmed. Through the hours spent with a more experienced local pastor and grief counselor, Jake was able to develop several ministry strategies that attended to the needs of grieving congregants and to contain his own insecurities. The following approaches to care, treatment, and support are meant to address the breadth of the grief experience, including community professionals who can assist with more complex scenarios.

Church-Based Grief Ministries

As noted earlier in the chapter, a sense of social support can be a key indicator of how one experiences the process of grief. Strong levels of social support are positive indicators for healthy grief outcomes, while a lack of social support may leave one vulnerable to complicated grief. **Church-based grief ministries** can be a significant help to those who are grieving. Broad categories of church-based grief ministries include the following:

- Individual pastoral counseling
- General lay ministries with grief-trained counselors
- Christian-oriented grief groups based on purchased curriculum
- Secular grief curriculum adapted for church use

Many churches develop lay counseling ministries in which a parishioner struggling with a particular personal or emotional issue is paired with a trained lay counselor. The tradition of members of the church body caring for one another is as old as Christianity. In John 13: 34 and 35 (English Standard Version), Jesus instructs his disciples to "love one another: just as I have loved you, you also are to love one another. By this all people will know that you are my disciples, if you have love for one another." Training individuals within the church body to care for and counsel those who are grieving will not only be a blessing for those who are ministered to but also a living out of the gospel message. Lay counseling ministries require thoughtful preparation, careful screening, and ongoing training.

Because comprehensive lay counseling programs can require a significant investment of time and energy, many churches purchase or develop a packaged grief-oriented counseling program. These programs can be quite effective and are typically video based with associated discussion questions that are provided with the materials (Goodman & Stone, 2009). Training for this type of program is relatively minimal and designed to be led by congregants, lay counselors, or church staff. Much of the effectiveness of such programs may be associated with the communal aspects of shared grief, mutual support, spiritual encouragement, and grief education. Secular grief support training materials are also available and can be effectively modified for use in a church or overtly Christian setting.

Extended Grief Care

For many, the immediate aftermath of losing a loved one consists of funeral arrangements; hosting family members; financial confusion; responding to expressions of support, including phone calls, text messages and e-mail; and entering the very beginning stage of confronting the reality of their loss. Most people describe feeling well supported during the early stage of loss. Community members deliver meals, family members are attentive, the pastor calls, and in one respect or another, the "space" left empty by the deceased feels somewhat filled.

In my experience, many church communities unintentionally begin to withdraw connection from the grieving member once the daily demands of ministry again take precedence. Much of this is normal, as it would be difficult or impossible to maintain the intensity of contact typically offered during the first few weeks or months after a loss. The bereaved, however, can feel deeply lonely and disoriented after the initial activity following a loss begins to quiet down. It is incumbent upon the pastor or lay counselor to develop an **extended grief care** plan for those who are in need. This plan can range from promoting ongoing grief groups to simple monthly calendar reminders to check in with members of the congregation who have lost loved ones, particularly on important dates, such as the anniversary of the death or various birthdays and holidays. These follow-ups often become a significant time to disciple and minister to the grieving congregant who, by virtue of his or her loss, is often open to spiritual guidance, direction, and insight that is unique to the person's circumstance. It is important that these points of contact are preceded by prayer and are experienced by the congregant as genuine and unrushed. In addition, each congregant may need something unique from the pastor or church body. It is during these moments of contact that the pastor can assess these needs as well as encourage the bereaved to define his or her specific desire for ongoing support and community connection.

Facilitating Initial Grief and Mourning

Pastors and pastoral counselors are often among the first to be contacted when a loved one passes away. Because of this, the pastor's approach to facilitating these initial grief experiences can be crucial to the trajectory of the congregant's grief process. Although not exhaustive, the following guidelines for both the initial contact with the congregant and the ongoing follow-up will set the tone for a potentially healthy grief process. First, be **knowledgeable** about the process of grief and loss, including the many forms of expression it may take. Grief and loss are frequently disorienting experiences, and your congregant is typically looking to you for reassurance and stability. Knowing what to expect can help you provide this need in a calm and compassionate manner. Second, **normalize** the range, intensity, and sometimes conflicted nature of the mourner's affect during the grieving process. Emotions will vary widely from moment-to-moment, and it is quite helpful to simply acknowledge the normalcy of this experience. Third, encouraging the mourner to **talk** with you about the experience of losing his or her loved one, including the nature of how the person died, may help to moderate the potential for a complicated grief outcome. Of course, this process requires sensitivity to the nature of your relationship with the grieving individual as well as an awareness of appropriate timing. Fourth, you don't need to have all the **answers**. Your presence, compassion, spiritual attentiveness, and willingness to listen are often more than adequate. Fifth, be emotionally and spiritually **accessible**. Although you cannot choose the moment when you will be called upon, you can be ready for any moment through preparation and an awareness of the absolutely crucial need to be emotionally and spiritually accessible when present with the mourner. If accessibility is something you personally wrestle with, it may be helpful to consider having an elder or lay leader accompany you during these important first visits. Lastly, **resist** the urge to share too much. This is an important time to listen and ask questions. These situations can be awkward, and we often feel compelled to talk when we feel anxious or when there is a difficult silence. It is during these times that silent or verbal prayer may be the most appropriate, and healing, response.

Therapy for Complicated Bereavement

Pastoral and lay counselors should remain vigilant to indications that the grieving individual's symptoms or life circumstances may necessitate the need for a referral to a professional **grief therapist**. Not all people who grieve need therapy; however, those who display symptoms of depression beyond normal grief, including severe anxiety or trauma reactions, suicidal ideation, or experiences consistent with prolonged and complicated grief described earlier in the chapter, should be referred out for more in-depth care. Although most professional therapists have experience with grief and loss issues, only a relatively small number will consider themselves "grief therapists." Connecting congregants with the right therapist can be a vital part of your role during this complex and vulnerable time. Therefore, developing relationships with therapists in your locale should include locating an individual who has expertise as a grief counselor or therapist. Ideally, this will be someone who shares, or at least respects, the nature of the congregant's Christian worldview.

Pharmacological Treatment

Pharmacological treatment of those experiencing complicated grief reactions is not unusual and should be supported when necessary. When a psychiatrist or medical doctor feels that the nature or severity of the mourner's symptoms have reached a critical level, medications such as antidepressants or anxiolytics (antianxiety medication) are commonly prescribed. A general knowledge about how these medications work, including common side effects and terminology, can make you a more effective counselor. Some parishioners may feel ashamed about needing such medications, and your understanding and valuing of their potential benefit will help facilitate a safe and open dialog about their grief experiences, psychological symptoms, and spiritual process. A thorough reading of Chapter 12 will provide you with adequate information regarding the basics of psychopharmacology so that you can recognize or anticipate the effect of medication on your own work with the bereaved individual.

KEY TERMS

Church-based grief ministries: individual- or group-oriented ministries designed to assist parishioners with the process of grief

Extended grief care: ministries designed to meet the longer term needs of grieving parishioners

Grief therapy: clinical intervention provided by professional therapists

Pharmacological treatment: use of psychopharmacological interventions to relieve symptoms of complicated grief

Discussion Questions

1 Church-based grief ministries can play a significant role in supporting grieving parishioners. Describe two types of church-based grief support ministries.

2 Describe the key ingredients of an extended grief care ministry.

3 What are the six guidelines a pastor should keep in mind when considering the healthy facilitation of a parishioner's grief process?

4 What are some indications that a referral to a professional counselor should be considered?

SELF-CARE FOR THE GRIEF COUNSELOR

Being emotionally and spiritually present for those who are going through the grief process can at times become mentally and physically exhausting. Because of this, self-care must be a priority for those who minister to others during these difficult and demanding times. Attention to one's own emotional process, grief, and spiritual experience are fundamental necessities to a long-term and successful ministry to those who are grieving.

Attending to Your Own Grief and Seeking Support

Grieving is a personal *and* communal experience that affects all members of a community in some manner. Pastoral counselors are often intimately involved in processing the grief and loss experience of those in their ministries. Because of the frequency and proximity to death via the experiences of their parishioners, pastoral counselors must confront the cumulative effect of loss and vicarious trauma on their personal and emotional lives in a unique and thoughtful manner (Hendron, Irving, & Taylor, 2014; Spidell et al., 2011). Emotions that are dismissed or disowned tend to increase in intensity and impact. Therefore, pastoral counselors who find themselves regularly ministering to congregants within the context of death and dying must take particular care of their own emotional well-being in a manner that reflects the long-term effect of such work.

Self-care for the pastoral counselor who is exposed to frequent and significant loss begins with **self-awareness**. Oftentimes, self-awareness begins with being open to the influence and insights of others as well as to the Holy Spirit. Feedback from others is crucial to self-awareness and should be invited rather than avoided. When seasons of loss and death enter your role as a pastoral counselor, it can be a beneficial time to seek out the guidance and counsel of others. Perhaps a season of time with a therapist or pastoral counselor may help you give words to the cumulative aspects of loss and pain that you have participated in and witnessed. Also, participation in a grief group, rather than leading a grief group, may be a time of grace and restoration for you as a pastoral leader. Finally, a season of prayer focused on inviting God's Spirit to illuminate and attend to your hidden heart and to guide you in your process of self-awareness and seeking support for you as a caregiver, counselor, and shepherd may result in a renewed sense of spiritual and professional vitality rather than fatigue and burnout. Although one might endeavor upon a season of prayer alone with God, it may be beneficial to consider teaming with a professional spiritual director who can guide you through this complex and disorienting season. The demands of ministry can be intense. When seasons of grief and loss affect you and your congregation, it can be easy to neglect yourself and your family. Despite the consuming nature of these experiences, it is crucial that you remain conscious of you own needs, emotional health, and spiritual vitality, and prioritize them as an essential part of your own longevity as a shepherd and counselor.

KEY TERMS

Self-awareness: insight into one's personal level of functioning

Self-care: personal attention to one's emotional, physical, and spiritual well-being

Discussion Questions

1 What are the unique exposures that many pastors and pastoral counselors have to the personal and vicarious experiences of grief and loss?

2 How might a pastor or pastoral counselor seek support for the longer term implications of cumulative grief and vicarious trauma?

3 Based on personal experience, how might you build your prayer life during such times?

REVIEWING THE CONCEPTS

Learning Objectives

- Differentiate between common grief, complicated grief, and depression
  - Common grief is an emotionally healthy process of grieving and mourning a death or significant loss.
  - Complicated grief outcomes are atypical and may include various prolonged symptoms described as PCBD.
  - The significant decrease of the subjective experiences of self-worth and self-image often differentiate clinical depression from the sadness of common grief.

- Define the typical process of grief
  - Kübler-Ross stage model (Kübler-Ross, 1969)—denial, anger, bargaining, depression, and acceptance
  - Worden "task" model (Worden, 2009)
  - Task 1: To Accept the Reality of the Loss
  - Task 2: To Process the Pain of Grief
  - Task 3: To Adjust to the World Without the Deceased
  - Task 4: To Find an Enduring Connection With the Deceased in the Midst of Embarking on a New Life
  - Typical process of grief resolves in 6 months to 1 year

- Facilitate a pastoral response to grief and loss among parishioners
  - Six points of facilitating initial grief and mourning
  - Developing grief support ministries (e.g., GriefShare)
- Identify risk factors for those who may be vulnerable to more complicated bereavement outcomes
  - Common risk factors include the circumstances of death, religious faith, lack of social support, age, and gender
  - Pre-loss mental health, including depression and severe stress

Chapter Review Questions

Level 1: Knowledge (True/False)

1. Grief is primarily an external manifestation of loss.
2. The terms grief and mourning are generally interchangeable.
3. Those with anxious-ambivalent attachment styles are at risk of developing prolonged grief symptoms.
4. Grief symptoms are often experienced through losses other than death.
5. Emotions, physical sensations, and cognitions make up the broad categories of response to grief.
6. A grieving person who feels he or she was visited by the deceased in a dream should be referred to a mental health professional immediately. PCBD is a *DSM-5* diagnosis.
7. Females report higher rates of depression after a loss than males.
8. High levels of social support are a strong predictor of positive grief outcomes.
9. It's important that you have all the correct answers when visiting the bereaved.

Level 2: Comprehension

1. Which of the following is not a quality that pastors should have to help facilitate the initial grief process?
   a. Knowledgeable
   b. Accessible
   c. Talkative
   d. Normalizing

2. When a mourner's symptoms become severe, it is not unusual for a medical doctor or psychiatrist to prescribe

   a. antipsychotics

   b. antihypertensives

   c. analgesics

   d. anxiolytics

3. Self-care for a pastor who is exposed to frequent or significant loss begins with

   a. self-awareness

   b. therapy

   c. a thorough medical evaluation

   d. emotional health

4. Mourning is defined primarily as

   a. a deep state of sorrow

   b. an external expression of grief

   c. an emotional response to the loss of a loved one

   d. a symptom of grief

5. Secure attachment is characterized by

   a. feelings of love

   b. appropriate detachment

   c. relational trust

   d. gratitude

6. Examples of common loss may include

   a. moving

   b. illness

   c. divorce

   d. job loss

   e. all of the above

7. Kübler-Ross's five stages of grief include

   a. denial, anger, bargaining, depression, acceptance

   b. denial, anger, fear, depression, acceptance

   c. fear, denial, anger, bargaining, acceptance

   d. denial, mourning, anger, bargaining, acceptance

8. Which of the following is not one of J. William Worden's "Tasks of Grief?"

   a. To Process the Pain of Grief

   b. To Accept the Reality of the Loss

   c. To Adjust to the World Without the Deceased

   d. To Embark on a New Life Without the Deceased

9. Categories of church-based grief ministries include

   a. grief groups

   b. Celebrate Recovery

   c. lay counseling with grief-trained volunteers

   d. both 1 and 3

10. Which of the following is the key predictor of healthy grief outcomes?

   a. Pre-loss levels of functioning

   b. History of depression

   c. High levels of social support

   d. Deep spiritual faith

Level 3: Application

1. Write a 5-minute minisermon integrating what you have learned about healthy grieving with what the biblical text says about loss and restoration.

2. A recently divorced parishioner asks to meet with you for pastoral counseling. She's confused about the differences between grief and depression, and wonders if she'd depressed. How might you help her distinguish between the two?

3. Describe the four "Tasks of Grief." How might you conceptualize these tasks when counseling a grieving parishioner?

4. Describe a church-based grief ministry. How might this assist someone who is dealing with a significant loss?

5. You arrive at the hospital shortly after a parishioner's death and are asked to meet with the grieving family members. Describe the six components of facilitating the initial grief and mourning process.

ANSWERS

LEVEL 1: KNOWLEDGE

1. F
2. F
3. T
4. T
5. F
6. F
7. T
8. F
9. T
10. F

LEVEL 2: COMPREHENSION

1. c
2. d
3. a
4. b
5. c
6. d
7. a
8. d
9. d
10. c

RESOURCES

Online Resources

- GriefShare—https://www.griefshare.org
- Hope for Mental Health—http://hope4mentalhealth.com
- New Hope Grief Support—http://www.newhopegrief.org
- The Grief Recovery Method—https://www.griefrecoverymethod.com
- Stephen Ministries—http://www.stephenministries.org

- National Alliance on Mental Illness—https://www.nami.org
- National Institute of Mental Health—https://www.nimh.nih.gov/index.shtml

Readings

- *Grief Counseling and Grief Therapy: A Handbook for the Mental Health Practitioner*, 4th Ed.—J. William Worden
- *The Slavery of Death*—Richard Beck
- *Necessary Losses*—Judith Viorst
- *Experiencing Grief*—H. Norman Wright
- *When Breath Becomes Air*—Paul Kalanithi

Video Resources

- *Understanding Grief: Hospice Foundation of America*— https://www.youtube.com/watch?v=NlwQn4nmzYY
- *What Comes After Grief? TED Talks*—Ted.com https://www.ted.com/playlists/526/what_comes_after_grief
- *Lars and the Real Girl* (2007): MGM Studios, PG-13—An unusual film that highlights loss, trauma, grief, and the role of community in the healing process

CLASSROOM ACTIVITIES

1. Interviews—In groups of three, have students discuss the nature of their own loss experiences and the way in which their process followed the stage-loss sequence. Encourage students to only discuss loss experiences that have been well grieved.

2. Role-plays—Break into triads and role-play a counseling session with a counselee who has recently experienced the death of a close friend. Each person in the triad will play the role of the counselor, counselee, and observer.

3. Small groups—Break into small groups and brainstorm common ways in which Christians might "overly spiritualize" their grief process.

4. Personal loss paper/list—Take time to write a list of life-long loss experiences (both actual and symbolic) and the ways in which you have resolved them. How has your experience of God effected how you have addressed these losses?

REFERENCES

American Psychiatric Association. (2013). *Diagnostic and statistical manual of mental disorders* (5th ed.). Washington, DC: Author.

Blalock, D. V., Franzese, A. T., Machell, K. A., & Strauman, T. J. (2015). Attachment style and self-regulation: How our patterns in relationships reflect broader motivational styles. *Personality and Individual Differences, 87*, 90–98. doi: 10.1016/j.paid.2015.07.024

Bonanno, G. A. (2004). Loss, trauma, and human resilience: Have we underestimated the human capacity to thrive after extremely aversive events? *American Psychologist, 59*(1), 20–28.

Cherry, K. E., Sampson, L., Nezat, P. F., Cacamo, A., Marks, L. D., & Galea, S. (2015). Long-term psychological outcomes in older adults after disaster: Relationships to religiosity and social support. *Aging & Mental Health, 19*(5), 430–443. doi: 10.1080/13607863.2014.941325

Crunk, A. E., Burke, L. A., & Robinson, E. M. (2017). Complicated grief: An evolving theoretical landscape. *Journal Of Counseling & Development, 95*(2), 226–233. doi: 10.1002/jcad.12134

Freud, S. (1961). *Letters of Sigmund Freud* (E. L. Freud, Ed.). New York, NY: Basic Books.

Gire, K. (1998). *Incredible moments with the savior.* Grand Rapids, Mich.: Zondervan Publishing Co.

Goodman, H., Jr., & Stone, M. H. (2009). The efficacy of adult Christian support groups in coping with the death of a significant loved one. *Journal of Religion & Health, 48*(3), 305–316. doi: 10.1007/s10943-008-9201-2

Grief, bereavement, and coping with loss (PDQ), PubMed Health. (2017, April 20). A service of the National Library of Medicine and National Institutes of Health.

Hendron, J. A., Irving, P., & Taylor, B. J. (2014). Clergy stress through working with trauma: A qualitative study of secondary impact. *Journal of Pastoral Care & Counseling, 68*(4), 1–14.

Jacobs, S. (1993). *Pathologic grief: maladaptation to loss.* Washington, DC: American Psychiatric Press.

Jerga, A. M., Shaver, P. R., & Wilkinson, R. B. (2011). Attachment insecurities and identification of at-risk individuals following the death of a loved one. *Journal of Social And Personal Relationships, 28*(7), 891–914. doi: 10.1177/0265407510397987

Kübler-Ross, E. (1969). *On death and dying.* New York, NY: Macmillan Publishing Company Inc.

Lefkovics, E., Baji, I., & Rigó, J. (2014). Impact of maternal depression on pregnancies and on early attachment. *Infant Mental Health Journal, 35*(4), 354–365.

Laxton-Kane, M., & Slade, P. (2002). The role of maternal prenatal attachment in a woman's experience of pregnancy and implications for the process of care. *Journal of Reproductive & Infant Psychology, 20*(4), 253–266. doi: 10.1080/0264683021000033174

Lewis, C. S. (1961). *A grief observed.* New York, NY: Bantam Books.

Neimeyer, R. A. (2014). The changing face of grief: Contemporary directions in theory, research, and practice. *Progress in Palliative Care, 22*(3), 125–130. doi:10.1179/1743291X13Y.0000000075

Parkes, C. M. (1972). *Bereavement: Studies of grief in adult life.* International New York, NY: Universities Press.

Schenck, L. K., Eberle, K. M., & Rings, J. J. (2016). Insecure attachment styles and complicated grief severity. *Omega: Journal of Death & Dying, 73*(3), 231–249. doi: 10.1177/0030222815576124

Spidell, S., Wallace, A., Carmack, C. L., Nogueras-Gonzalez, G. M., Parker, C. L., & Cantor, S. B. (2011). Grief in healthcare chaplains: An investigation of the presence of disenfranchised grief. *Journal of Health Care Chaplaincy, 17*(1/2), 75–86. doi: 10.1080/08854726.2011.559859

Stroebe, W., & Schut, H. (2001). Risk factors in bereavement outcome: A methodological and empirical review. In M. S. Stroebe, R. O. Hansson, W. Stroebe, H. Schut, M. S. Stroebe, R. O. Hansson, H. Schut (Eds.), *Handbook of bereavement research: Consequences, coping, and care* (pp. 349–371). Washington, DC, US: American Psychological Association. doi: 10.1037/10436-015

Stroebe, M. S. (2008). *Handbook of bereavement research and practice: Advances in theory and intervention.* Washington, DC: American Psychological Association.

Tomarken, A., Holland, J., Schachter, S., Vanderwerker, L., Zuckerman, E., Nelson, C., & Prigerson, H. (2008). Factors of complicated grief pre-death in caregivers of cancer patients. *Psycho-Oncology, 17*(2), 105–111. doi: 10.1002/pon.1188

Worden, J. W. (2009). *Grief counseling and grief therapy. [Electronic resource]: A handbook for the mental health practitioner.* New York, NY: Springer Pub. Co.

IMAGE CREDITS

Fig. 5.1: Source: https://commons.wikimedia.org/wiki/File:Brooklyn_Museum_-_Jesus_Wept_(Jésus_pleura)_-_James_Tissot.jpg.

CHAPTER 6

Addiction

Lauren Richardson, PhD

LEARNING OBJECTIVES

Upon completion of this chapter, readers will be able to

1. broadly define substance use addiction and understand the key areas of functioning that are affected by substance addiction;

2. understand the differences between intoxication, addiction, and withdrawal;

3. be familiar with typical treatment for addiction;

4. gain insight into ways individuals with addiction can be supported and maintain their sobriety; and

5. identify ways that churches can provide specific support for individuals maintaining sobriety.

"The worst part about anything that's self-destructive is that it's so intimate. You become so close with your addictions and illnesses that leaving them behind is like killing the part of yourself that taught you how to survive."
—Anonymous

LUKE'S STORY

Just after you wrap up your Sunday service, a new member of the church approaches you and introduces himself as Luke. He shares that he recently detoxed from opiates and would like to meet with you to get some direction on how to move forward with his sobriety. He shares that he is married in his early 30s, has one child, and lost his job with an online advertising agency just last month. In the few brief minutes that you chat with him, you learn that his struggle with opiates has been ongoing. You decide to set up a time to meet with Luke so that you can hear his story and learn how best to support him on his journey of recovery.

FIGURE 6.1   **The Isolation of Addiction**

Over coffee with Luke during the week, he shares his struggle with opiate addiction. His addiction started in college when he enjoyed partying, which included weekend binge drinking and occasional meth use. At one point in college, he had surgery on his knee because of a sports injury, and his doctor prescribed him Vicodin to manage the pain. Luke shares that he remembered what those first Vicodin pills did to his body, and he wanted to do everything he could to replicate the feeling. The opiate use progressed to stronger pain pills and eventually heroin. He confesses that he is embarrassed to share with you that he was using his parents' money to buy drugs—money that was supposed to be for "college expenses." But with pressure from his family as to why he was unable to get a job after graduating, Luke disclosed his addiction issues to them. They stopped supporting him financially, so Luke made a decision to enter a facility to detox, and he immediately started attending 12-step meetings.

Luke proceeds to share that this point in the journey was not the end of his struggles. He explains that he has relapsed several times on Oxycontin and other prescription pills, but with the help of his sponsor, he was able to recover quickly. He notes that this most recent relapse has been the hardest. He explains that it all started when he and his wife had just welcomed their newborn daughter home; he felt pressure to be a caring husband, and his work stress was increasing. He tried everything he knew to manage the stress, but it did not feel like enough. He ended up connecting with an old friend who later offered him some Oxycontin. He told himself it was no big deal, and he just needed to relieve the work stress for one night, and then he would be back to normal. Luke shares that, at that time, he was unable to stop with just one night of relief. He believed the drug made him feel more like himself, and he reports that he was able to complete his work more effectively. He also thought the drug use made him a better dad and husband. It was easy for him to contact his concierge doctor, a fee for care doctor, and fill his prescription.

As you sit with Luke and hear his story, he feels compelled to share more about how his drug use progressed. He explains that his days became very focused on managing how often he needed to pop some pills, and his weekends were spent finding the pharmacy that would fill his prescription and not become suspicious. His wife began to persistently ask him to spend more time with her and their daughter. Being with his family became difficult because he believed he needed to be high to best support her. He shares that he wishes he would have stopped then, but felt like there was no way out. His wife began to question how he spent his time and money. Even his job performance rapidly decreased, which caught the attention of his supervisors. They decided to "let him go," which eventually forced him to come clean to his wife regarding his drug use. In a state of dismay, he shares that he never wants to get to that place again and needs your direction on how to stay sober.

Because of the extent of his use, you decide to refer him for individual therapy. He sets up an appointment right away and stays committed to treatment. In therapy, Luke learns more about himself regarding his desire to be known, his need for acceptance and validation of his emotional experience, and his tendency to hide behind his ability to perform his job well, along with his desire to be the perfect parent. This level of insight helps Luke stay sober for 3 years, and he is hopeful that it will continue.

Much like the experiences of Luke, opioid addiction is on the rise and has now been labeled as an epidemic. In 2015, 2 million Americans over the age of 12 had an addiction to prescription pain relievers (Opioid Addiction 2016 Facts and Figures, n.d.). In addition, 590,000 Americans over the age of 12 had an addiction to heroin. Overall, the prevalence of addiction has been on the rise for the past several years. In 2014, 21.5 million Americans over the age of 12 had an addiction, substance use disorder, to either alcohol or drugs (Mental Health and Substance Use Disorders, 2017). Given these statistics, we can assume that addiction affects many people from many different backgrounds.

With the earlier stated prevalence, we are aware that church communities will often experience members and possibly staff who are struggling with addiction. A common misunderstanding of substance use and addiction is that it is an issue that does not affect "average" or "good" people. My hope is to destigmatize addiction and offer some thoughts that help you feel equipped to work through this mental health issue within your community.

This chapter will give an overview of some of the key concepts and core ideas relevant to understanding addiction. The information discussed applies to a general understanding of addiction to alcohol and drugs as a whole rather than to the unique components within specific drug classes. Therefore, the term **substance** is used to describe the general umbrella of alcohol and classes of drugs, including opioids, simulants, sedatives, inhalants, hallucinogens, and marijuana (American Psychiatric Association, 2013). It is important to note that there are unique features and considerations for each class of drug (see the "Resources" section). For the purpose of this chapter, the discussion will focus on addiction to substances in general.

THE IMPACT OF ADDICTION

Mental health professionals, theorists, and researchers have paid particular attention to how the term addiction is defined. Because of the complex nature of addiction, no single definition exists. In part, this is due to the fact that there are several models describing the origins of addiction and the multifaceted impact of addiction on the individual. We will take a closer look at two popular definitions of addiction and the primary components of personhood that are impaired as a result of addiction.

Defining Addiction

A common model of addiction is the **disease model**. This model is a medical model that seeks to encompass several key areas that are impaired as a result of addiction. The American Society of Addiction Medicine provides the following brief definition of addiction:

> Addiction is a primary, chronic disease of brain reward, motivation, memory and related circuitry. Dysfunction in these circuits leads to characteristic biological, psychological, social and spiritual manifestations. This is reflected in an individual pathologically pursuing reward and/or relief by substance use and other behaviors. (Definition of addiction, 2011)

This model focuses on the chronic impairments of certain neurobiology in the brain, which have a global effect on the individual. A direct correlation is made between the pursuit of a "reward" (e.g., positive experience) or relief and substance use behaviors, thus resulting in a disease, or as some theorists propose, a "chronic condition" (DiClemente, 2018).

Another model that is often referenced to explain addiction is the **biopsychosocial model**. This model focuses on several key factors—biological, psychological, and social—that are correlated with the presence of substance use behaviors. These areas include "genetic predisposition; psychological vulnerabilities; personality traits and temperaments; cognitive expectations about the anticipated benefits derived from drinking, drug use or engaging in other addictive behaviors; and lack of adequate coping skills and an attendant low level of self-efficacy" (Donovan & Marlatt, 2005, p. 32). Some examples of personality traits and temperament factors are impulsivity or propensity to risky behaviors. The presence of anxiety or depression would be an example of a psychological vulnerability. The role of genetics tends to vary between substances, but the highest genetic correlation is observed for alcohol addiction (McGue & Irons, 2013). Some theorists have proposed a biopsychosocial model that includes the idea that psychological and social factors interact with and effect the expression of genetic/biological factors (e.g., Buchman, Skinner, & Iles, 2010). The benefit of the biopsychosocial model is that it captures several areas that contribute to the presence of substance use addiction. For example, one might explain that the development of addiction is related to genetic factors, early attachment injuries, and limited social support. It is a broad and all-encompassing definition; however, some argue that this model needs to be improved to account for the integrative layers of the factors (DiClemente, 2018).

Global Impact of Addiction on Personhood

Because of the many factors contributing to the presence of substance addiction, the resulting effect of these behaviors is global. This means that many, if not all, areas of an individual's personhood become impaired. This may include negative biological, psychological, social, and spiritual effects.

Biological impairments include physiological and neurological issues that can result from chronic substance use. Brain regions and the neurochemistry of the brain can be significantly altered (DiClemente, 2018). The physiology of an individual changes not only during the experience of a "high" but also over longer-term use. Physical health is significantly affected as well. The specific symptoms are dependent on the specific class of substance that is being used. For example, Luke's opioid use will likely cause him to experience nausea, vomiting, and liver damage. In addition, individuals with addiction issues will experience physical dependence, tolerance, and withdrawal, which will be discussed in a subsequent section. Cognitive abilities are also affected, such as memory and processing speed (American Psychiatric Association, 2013).

A common physical symptom of addiction is the presence of **cravings**. This is a symptom that is experienced during periods of use as well as sobriety. It is similar to craving sweets, but much stronger. Addicted individuals will have a physiological sensation of desiring to use the substance. This physiological symptom, as well as other psychological symptoms, fosters the continued cycle of use. Once someone is sober, there are various coping skills as well as medications (e.g., Naltrexone) that can be used to manage cravings.

Addiction has a significant effect on the psychological and social functioning of the individual. The addict's life starts to center on use, which was the case for Luke, and other regular activities or responsibilities adopt less priority. Psychological symptoms, such as anxiety and depression, might exacerbate, resulting from the ineffective "coping skill" of substance use. Social support becomes limited to those who are using with the addicted person and/or those supporting the addict's use, which can often include the addict's family and friends (DiClemente, 2018). In addition, relationships with family and the addict's support community (e.g., church community support) can become strained due to the negative effect of the substance use behaviors, such as the strain Luke experienced in his marriage with his wife. In some cases, the addict's only "support" system is the people with whom he uses. Occupational and legal issues can also develop, such as inability to secure or maintain employment or receiving a ticket for driving under the influence of a substance, such as having a blood alcohol content above .08 while driving in the state of California (American Psychiatric Association, 2013).

A common psychological and relational issue experienced by addicted individuals is **denial**. The addicted person is actively engaging in denial when he or she is unable to recognize the unpleasant experiences of the addiction or cannot take in evidence that highlights his or her distorted reality (Roget & Fisher, 2009). Ultimately, the addicted person does not think he or she has a problem, which allows for a continued pattern of substance use. At times, denial functions as a protective mechanism because the pain of knowing the reality of the addiction or the affect it has had on others is too great to bear. Overall, denial reflects an "ambivalence and resistance to change" (Roget & Fisher, 2009, p. 272) despite evidence and experiences indicating a necessity for change. As ministry workers, you will want to remember that you cannot reason someone out of a place of denial. The recommended way to approach an addicted person in a place of denial is to come alongside the individual and explore the purpose of the addiction to foster motivation to change. I will discuss this further next.

The addict's **spiritual health** is also impaired as a result of substance addiction. The addicted person might experience a disconnection from his or her faith community as well as a disconnection from God. The idol of the addicted person then becomes the substance, as all time and energy focus around it. The alcohol or drug is "worshiped." In addition, the addicted person is no longer honoring God's creation, his or her body, as he or she engages in addictive behaviors. For example, before he was aware of it, Luke developed a pattern of turning to drugs for comfort in place of God.

Addiction Issues Often Co-occur With Other Mental Health Issues
Oftentimes, a complex entanglement of addiction and mental health issues are present in the addicted person. Mental health professionals describe the presence of a mental health disorder along with an addiction as a **co-occurring disorder**. Some common examples of co-occurring disorders are generalized anxiety disorder (GAD), major depressive disorder, post-traumatic stress disorder, and bipolar disorder. In fact, a greater risk of developing addiction issues is present for individuals who have a mental health disorder (e.g., Zimmerman, et al., 2003). In these cases, the substance can be used as a coping strategy to cover up, numb, or detach from the mental health symptoms. For example, an individual might use alcohol to numb or avoid feelings of hopelessness. The presence of a co-occurring disorder adds a layer of complexity to substance use and recovery, as the addicted person will need to learn to cope with emotions in new ways. Typically, this requires more extensive treatment, such as residential treatment and ongoing outpatient psychotherapy.

KEY TERMS

Substance: alcohol and all classes of drugs, including opioids, simulants, sedatives, inhalants, hallucinogens, and marijuana

Disease model: a medical model of addiction that emphasizes chronic impairments of certain neurobiology as well as a correlation between the pursuit of relief/rewards and substance use behaviors

Biopsychosocial model: a model of addiction that focuses on impairments in biological, psychological, and social functioning in correlation to substance use behaviors

Cravings: a physiological sensation of desiring the use of the substance that is experienced during periods of use and sobriety

Denial: the inability to recognize the unpleasant experiences of addiction or resistance to taking in evidence that highlights one's distorted reality of substance use

Co-occurring disorder: the presence of a mental health disorder in addition to a substance use disorder

1   How are the disease model and biopsychosocial model of addiction similar and different? Are there other ways of defining addiction that might be helpful to consider?

2   Discuss and provide specific examples of the various areas of impairment experienced by Luke.

DIFFERENTIATING INTOXICATION, ADDICTION, AND WITHDRAWAL

The term addiction is often used loosely to reference anything done in excess. An individual might say he is addicted to television, and it is assumed that he means that he views television too much; however, it is important to assess whether his viewing of television is to the point of interfering with all areas of his life. In the substance addiction community, mental health professionals make clear distinctions between three levels of substance use that negatively affect human functioning.

Intoxication

Intoxication is a term that is used to differentiate a level of substance use that does not result in persistent global functioning issues. According to the *Diagnostic and Statistical Manual of Mental Disorders, 5th Edition* (*DSM-5*), intoxication is defined as the development of physiological and psychological symptoms and problematic behaviors shortly after the ingestion of the substance (American Psychiatric Association, 2013). Examples of psychological symptoms and problematic behaviors include impaired judgment, belligerence, aggressive behavior, and shifts in mood. Physiological symptoms are specific for each type of substance. With alcohol intoxication, physiological symptoms can include slurred speech, lack of coordination, unsteady gait, and impairment in memory. Symptoms most often alleviate after the substance is no longer in the body.

It is important to differentiate addiction from intoxication in that frequent intoxication does not automatically indicate an addiction. While it might be a barrier to the person's overall well-being, frequent intoxication (e.g., weekly) is not considered an addiction; however, it is possible that someone with a diagnosis of substance addiction does experience frequent intoxication. Within the church community, it might be helpful to think critically through how the word addiction is used and its implications. Especially for churches that have recovery ministries, it would be important for staff and volunteers to have an understanding of the implications of the term. If the term addiction is used incorrectly, then individuals might make incorrect assumptions about themselves and others regarding the necessity of treatment and recovery.

Substance Addiction

As discussed earlier, addiction typically involves a global effect on a person's life functioning. Three other key features differentiate substance addiction from intoxication:

dependence, tolerance and withdrawal. These features indicate the experience of a physiological and psychological need for substances on a regular basis.

An individual experiences **dependence** when he or she "needs" the substance to function or exist. Dependence can be experienced on both a physiological and psychological level (DiClemente, 2018). An addicted person might continue to use because of a physiological need for the substance. In other words, the addicted person uses because the body "needs" the substance. One might say that the body does not know how to function without it, meaning severe physiological symptoms are experienced in absence of the substance. For example, with severe alcohol addiction, the individual is at risk of experiencing seizures if he or she immediately ceases drinking. Thus, the addicted person is using to avoid the symptoms of withdrawal (American Psychiatric Association, 2013).

Dependence might also be experienced on a psychological level, which includes the experience of thinking that one cannot exist without the substance. Some addicted individuals describe feeling more like themselves when they are using the substance. For example, some heroin addicted individuals will describe a sense of being more complete when using this drug. They will describe feeling calmer, more confident, and better able to function at work. This type of thought process indicates psychological dependence on a substance, even to the point of substance use becoming a core part of the person's identity.

Tolerance is also a key feature of addiction that is defined by the need to use larger amounts of a substance to feel the effects of the substance (American Psychiatric Association, 2013). For example, an individual, over time, might need to drink more alcoholic beverages in a day in comparison to months prior. Increased tolerance is interwoven with increased dependence. It is likely that as tolerance to a substance is increasing so too is physiological dependence. The body needs more of the substance and requires that substance to function.

Withdrawal

Withdrawal is a term that is used to indicate the symptoms experienced when someone is reducing or ceasing prolonged and heavy substance use (American Psychiatric Association, 2013). Withdrawal includes cognitive and physiological symptoms that affect behavior. Symptoms are typically specific to the type of substance. For example, typical alcohol withdrawal symptoms include high blood pressure, sweating, insomnia, hand tremors, nausea, hallucinations, anxiety, and seizures. In addition to physical symptoms, the individual experiences impairment in functioning such as difficulties with social or occupational well-being. For example, individuals going through withdrawal are likely to experience limited ability to complete tasks related to their occupations. It is important to note that withdrawal symptoms are differentiated from symptoms present after intoxication. The defining difference is the effect on functioning and the severity of symptoms (American Psychiatric Association, 2013).

KEY TERMS

Intoxication: the development of physiological and psychological symptoms and problematic behaviors shortly after the ingestion of a substance

Dependence: physiological and psychological need for continued use of a substance

Tolerance: the need to use larger amounts of a substance to feel the same effects of the substance

Withdrawal: the presence of physiological and psychological symptoms when reducing or ceasing prolonged and heavy substance use

Discussion Questions

1 What is the purpose of correctly using the term addiction?

2 How might you explain the difference between frequent intoxication and substance addiction to someone in your church community?

MORAL FAILURE VERSUS DISRUPTION IN ATTACHMENT STYLE

Misconception That Addiction Is the Result of a Moral Failure

Before the holistic and integrative models were introduced, addiction was understood to be an issue of morality, both within the Christian community and among Western society at large. In recent decades, mental health and medical professionals have made advances to the field that have dispelled the idea that addiction is only a **moral failure**: the act of engaging in negative behaviors that go against God's desire for humanity. Rather than simply addressing the issue of a moral failure, addiction is now treated from a holistic perspective, addressing all areas in an individual's life that require healing and health (Mignon, 2015). This may include addressing the relevant physiological, psychological, social, and spiritual issues.

This idea that addiction should only be addressed as a moral failure is an attitude sometimes found in the church. For example, when helping an addict, a pastor or church volunteer may only expect the person to engage in regular confession of his or her sins and Scripture reading. While these are helpful tools, it is important to address all areas of impairment, including biological, psychological, and social, in the process of recovery. It is necessary to also address the global impact and the brokenness experienced by an addicted person. In Genesis 3, Adam and Eve's sin affected all human experiences, resulting in an enduring brokenness apart from the grace of God. Thus, it might be helpful to consider addiction as an issue of brokenness. For example, the first step in Alcoholic Anonymous is to admit that one is powerless over the substance and addiction. This expression of brokenness has been found to be beneficial for individuals in recovery, as they regularly identify various ways in which they need support. For successful recovery, the addicted person needs his or her spiritual, physical, and psychological needs addressed.

Addiction as the Result of Insecure Attachment

In connection to the idea of permeating brokenness, addiction can be understood through the lens of attachment theory. Insecure (broken) attachments often precede the development of substance use disorder (Fairbairn, et al., 2018). **Insecure attachment** involves the quality of early connection experiences that have been discussed in the previous chapters. Individuals with insecure attachment styles can also have difficulties with regulating emotions (Fairbairn et al., 2018; Mikulincer & Florian, 1998), thus potentially relying on coping mechanisms to avoid the emotional experience (e.g., drug use). For example, an individual with an anxious-ambivalent attachment style might think his or her needs for love and trust are a burden or not valuable to others. This belief might lead to seeking substances to numb the needs. An individual with an anxious-avoidant attachment style might be detached from the need for love and trust, and use substances to connect with this need. Heroin is sometimes described as the "love" drug, producing a warm effect of completeness. The injuries resulting from early childhood experiences are managed through substance use. Although **secure attachment** styles, ones that are characterized by a sense of trust and secure dependence, tend to be a protective factor for the development of substance addiction, individuals with this attachment style also develop addiction issues. This is due to the complex nature of the etiology of addiction.

The correlation between insecure attachment styles and substance use addiction demonstrates an example of the nature of human brokenness, as early childhood relational experiences continue to have profound effects on adulthood. This level of relational brokenness permeates all areas of personhood and predisposes the potential development of an addiction issue. Therefore, addiction is often the result of family system dynamics in combination with genetic predisposition. Addictive behaviors become a way to cope with great suffering that is connected to the attachment injuries. This can feel like desperate emotional survival to the person, while the idea of moral choice is not likely in one's awareness.

KEY TERMS

Moral failure: the act of engaging in negative behaviors that go against God's desire for humanity

Secure attachment: a way of relating that is characterized by a sense of trust and secure dependence on others

Insecure attachment: a way of relating that is characterized by a sense of distrust in or disconnection from others.

Discussion Questions

1   What is the benefit and the challenge of understanding addiction as a moral failure? As an issue of brokenness related to attachment injuries?

2   How might your approach to an individual with addiction issues change based on your beliefs about addiction?

THE PATH OF HEALING: TREATMENT, RECOVERY, AND LOVE

Seeking some form of treatment or recovery program is an imperative component of an individual's journey toward health and healing from addiction issues. Treatment can take on many forms based on the needs of the individual; there is no "one-size-fits-all" method of treatment. It is generally understood by medical and mental health professionals that individuals with addiction must identify the treatment and recovery components that best fit their unique issues, personalities, and health needs; thus, treatment can be understood as eclecticism that is formed based on scientific evidence (Miller & Hester, 1995). Although identifying a unique path of healing is crucial, several key components of treatment and recovery are generally necessary. These core elements will be discussed next.

Motivation to Seek Treatment

Taking a step toward treatment and recovery can be very challenging for those struggling with addiction. At times, those abusing alcohol or drugs might not think treatment is necessary, and instead they continue to remain in a place of denial. The individuals supporting the addicted person who are watching the path of destruction are often far readier for the addicted person to get treatment than the individual. Family members might pressure or plea with the addicted person to seek help, but if not ready, the addicted person will continue to use substances. This is often the case when there is no risk or imminent motivation, such as change in values (e.g., religious beliefs), developmental life stage (e.g., becoming a parent), or health issues (e.g., serious health issues resulting from use) that push the addicted person toward change (DiClemente, 2018).

As ministry workers, you do not need to feel pressure to convince someone that sobriety is the path to take. Instead, your role will take one of many possible forms. You will likely step into one of the following relational postures:

- Engage the individual in exploratory conversations about his or her addiction (e.g., costs and benefits).
- Assist the individual in identifying his or her ability to overcome the addiction and his or her choice to access regular support and resources.
- Provide a space within the church for individuals with addiction to develop community.
- Seek to understand and listen to the individual's story and experience.
- Embody and express the love of Christ.

These suggestions allow a ministry worker to step into the role of "coming alongside" rather than directing or giving advice to the individual with addiction. Maintaining a posture of embodying Christ's love and grace may be the central and most important component for ministry workers to maintain.

As mentioned, taking the first step toward treatment can be one of the hardest and intensely challenging times for the individual actively using substances. To understand the process, we will review the **Stages of Change Model** (also known as the Transtheoretical Model; DiClemente, 2018; Prochaska & DiClemente, 1984), which is the primary theory that treatment specialists use to assess and understand an addict's posture toward treatment. This theory is made up of five stages that describe an individual's motivation and state of mind regarding the necessary change. The following are the five stages with a brief description of the mind-set and goal required for each (DiClemente, 2018).

- Precontemplation—no intention toward action, does not see problematic nature of behaviors
  - Goal: consider changing behavior through increased awareness and concern for change of problematic behavior

- Contemplation—intention to take action, examination of the risks and benefits of behavior
  - Goal: decision to take action through examining behavior and potential change

- Preparation—ready to take action, might take small steps or develop plan toward action
  - Goal: action plan is set along with increased commitment

- Action—changes have been made with behavior and intention to make forward progress with behavior change (e.g., treatment program)
  - Goal: successfully changing behavior for a prolonged period of time

- Maintenance—changes in behavior are continued, intention to keep this change moving forward (e.g., regular attendance of 12-step meetings)
  - Goal: long-term change in behavior that extends into the individual's lifestyle

Holding this model in mind helps those supporting addicted individuals to manage their expectations of those seeking change and treatment. For example, when interacting with an individual regularly using drugs, in the precontemplation stage, it would be important not to expect the individual to identify or engage in a plan for sobriety as if in the action stage. Also, a ministry worker is likely to be able to set boundaries around his or her provisions and support for the addicted person if she or he is able to remember this model of motivation. Empathy is also fostered as ministry workers remember how much effort, thinking, praying, and preparation it takes just to move toward that first little step of recovery.

A technique commonly used by counselors and therapists to assist addicted individuals in setting an intention toward and engaging in change is **motivational interviewing** (DiClemente, Corno, Graydon, Wiprovnick, & Knoblach, 2017; Lundahl & Burke, 2009;

Miller and Rollnick, 1991;). Motivational interviewing is the process of asking the addicted person questions that will help him or her overcome ambivalence and resistance to change, determine the necessity of change, and make a commitment to change. One of the key features of this technique is developing a supportive and trusting relationship with the addicted person so that the addicted person can arrive at the intention to change her or himself rather than have the change imposed. The relational posture held within this framework allows the ministry worker to come alongside the addicted person to help him or her identify his or her own motivating factors for seeking change. Ministry workers regularly engaging with individuals actively using might consider seeking out further information and resources about this technique (see the "Resources" section at end of chapter).

A phrase often used in the addiction community is **"hitting rock bottom."** This phrase is often used to describe the experience of reaching an ultimate low emotionally, legally, financially, physically, and/or spiritually. This idea assumes the necessity of an ultimate low for changes to occur with addictive behaviors. The problem with is assumption is that it is an overgeneralization. A "rock bottom" is not a *necessary* part of the recovery journey to overcoming addiction (Patterson, n.d.). But what is helpful about this idea is that oftentimes, addicted individuals do experience some type of significant loss or negative consequence of their behavior that then leads to increased motivation. To use the previous example, Luke lost his job, which further pushed him in the direction of seeking help. He did not necessarily call this "rock bottom" because he still had a roof over his head and a relationship with his family, although strained. Essentially, a consequence or negative event often presupposes motivation to seek treatment, but this event does not need to be an ultimate low.

Treatment

Treatment is typically a long-term process and takes significant commitment from the addicted person. Generally, seeking treatment is the first major step on the road of recovery and sobriety. A typical course of treatment includes several components: detoxification, residential or intensive outpatient program, sober living facility, and sobriety maintenance through outpatient therapy and/or participation in a recovery support group.

The first step in treatment is **medical detoxification (detox),** which involves removing the substance from the body. Detox is typically done with pharmaceutical assistance, thus requiring formal medical treatment (Mignon, 2015). The goal is to evaluate and obtain medical stability of the individual. The type of pharmaceutical assistance depends on the substance used by the addicted person. For example, detox from alcohol, opiates, and heroin require medical assistance to manage withdrawal symptoms that can pose serious threats (e.g., seizures) to the health and safety of the addicted person. In other cases, pharmaceutical assistance is used to ease the withdrawal symptoms, but it is not necessary for the physical safety of the addicted person (e.g., methamphetamine). Detox typically lasts 3 to 5 days.

After detoxification, the next step is to enact some type of plan that allows for continued change in addictive behavior. Some individuals might seek support groups, while others might attend a program at a treatment facility. Individuals need to engage in the treatment that best fits their needs; however, formal treatment is generally recommended.

If taking this route, the next step is to attend a **residential treatment** program or an **intensive outpatient program (IOP).** These are typically known as rehabilitation programs (rehab). A residential program requires the individual to stay at a treatment facility typically for 30 days or more. This involves immersion in 24/7 care that includes group therapy, individual therapy, family therapy, psychiatry, case management, and staying at the residential housing provided by the facility. The benefit of a program like this is that the addicted person puts all of her or his attention and energy into her or his recovery. Most often, individuals will seek treatment in another state or distant city so that this focus can be maintained without the distractions of a familiar area or family nearby. In addition, residential treatment facilities tend to offer programs that simultaneously address co-occurring issues. The challenge of taking this route is that is requires significant financial means, either private or insurance funding. (Mignon, 2015)

An IOP is a type of treatment that requires the attendance of group and individual therapy for 2–5 hours per day for 3–5 days per week. Services such as medication management and family therapy are also provided. IOPs are typically 4–6 weeks in length. The frequency and length of treatment depends on the need of the individual. The positive of this program is that the individual can still maintain a job or other daily activities while also working on her or his recovery. Most often, individuals who are enrolled in an IOP will also stay at a sober living facility (Crane, 2016).

Some addicted individuals will choose to stay in a **sober living facility,** which is a residence occupied by several sober individuals and managed by some type of addiction treatment service provider. Individuals are required to commit to maintaining sobriety as well as participating in other activities, such as maintaining a job, attending IOP treatment, and/or attending 12-step meetings. This type of living situation can be great for individuals who would like to have access to a recovery community. The challenge with sober living facilities is that it can be difficult for individuals to witness their peers relapse. In general, sober living facilities are a great option for individuals who would like to maintain access to a supportive community after detox or rehab (Mignon, 2015).

A variety of medications are typically used throughout the treatment process. Some medications are used to treat continued withdrawal or physiological symptoms (e.g., Suboxone). Other medications might be prescribed to treat subsequent psychological symptoms during the initial stages of sobriety. For example, an individual might be prescribed a selective serotonin reuptake inhibitor for symptoms of anxiety and depression. Medications are sometimes used during periods of sobriety maintenance to help with curbing cravings (e.g., Naltrexone) (Mignon, 2015).

Another path of treatment is self-detoxification immediately followed by regular attendance at a recovery support group (e.g., Alcoholics Anonymous, Celebrate Recovery). A medical professional must be consulted before engaging in self-detoxification to ensure the safety of the individual. After detox, some individuals elect to begin a 12-step program such as Alcoholics Anonymous rather than attend a formal treatment program (Mignon, 2015). Individuals taking this route will typically attend meetings anywhere from 4 to 7 days a week or more. I have known some individuals to attend two times per day in the early stages of their recovery and regularly meet with their sponsors. Although this method is not the standard of practice among mental health professionals, I have seen many individuals have great success with this process. The only down side to this approach is that if there are co-occurring issues, such as anxiety and depression, then they are not likely to get formally addressed through the 12-steps as they would in individual therapy or other forms of treatment. The positive of this approach is that the addicted person is able to make a choice on the best type of treatment program she or he wants and quickly establishes a long-term community through meeting attendance.

Sobriety Maintenance

Remaining sober from substances is an ongoing process and often a life-long journey. The long-term goal for the addicted person is to develop a healthy lifestyle that includes wellness in biological, psychological, social, and spiritual areas of life. From my Christian worldview, I consider this a journey toward shalom, where all aspects of the person are in order as God intends given our brokenness in this fallen world. Thus, the journey of sobriety must continue to focus on all areas of personhood, including spiritual, psychological, relational, and biological. The task includes restoration of the body, mind, and relationship with God as the addicted person actively participates in elements of sobriety maintenance.

Typically, sobriety maintenance includes two key elements: regular attendance at **support groups** such as Alcoholics Anonymous or Celebrate Recovery and engagement in some form of **psychotherapy**. Support groups are made up of a community of individuals who are committed to their recovery and supporting others in the process (Mignon, 2015). Some examples are Alcoholics Anonymous/Narcotics Anonymous, Celebrate Recovery, and SMART Recovery (Table 6.1). Each of these programs focus on a particular "step program" that highlights keys elements and exercises for the individual to engage on the path of sobriety/recovery. The variety of recovery programs offers the opportunity to the addicted person to pick what fits best for him or her. Several meetings are typically available in one's surrounding community, both in person and online; an individual might need to try a few to find the right fit. Overall, support groups offer a great source of community and a place to continue to make lifestyle changes.

TABLE 6.1   **Types of Support Groups**

Alcoholics/Narcotics Anonymous	• Twelve-steps and principles found in the Big Book • Concept that each person is powerless over his or her addiction • Placing hope in higher power (e.g., God)
Celebrate Recovery	• Christian 12-step program • Christ at the center of steps and principles
SMART Recovery	• Mental health support group • Emphasizes change of behaviors, emotions, and thoughts for the purpose of reaching an abstinent lifestyle • Does not require participant to agree to a particular religious or spiritual belief

Psychotherapy, in the form of individual, group, or family, is another avenue in which the addicted person can have support in the recovery journey (Mignon, 2015). Psychotherapy, especially individual therapy, can allow the addicted person to have an intentional space to gain insight and make changes about how he or she approaches him or herself and his or her relationships on a holistic level. Co-occurring issues can also be addressed that underlie the addictive behaviors. Engaging in psychotherapy allows the individual to have a space to focus in on the specific and unique issues that need to be addressed for recovery. While some might choose therapy as an intentional space to work on maintaining sobriety, others might choose to have a good sponsor relationship. This is dependent on the needs of the individual and the best fit for the person's recovery journey.

Cultural factors also have a significant influence on an individual's approach to and process in treatment. Cultural components, such as socioeconomic status, ethnicity and race, and family upbringing and values, affect substance use and understanding of health (Mignon, 2015). Of these factors, one's access to services and treatment is primarily dependent on socioeconomic status (Wells, Klap, Koike, & Sherbourne, 2001). In addition, treatment approaches need to address the sociocultural layers, such as age, gender, race, and ethnicity (Abbott & Chase, 2008; Mignon, 2015). Ministry workers need to hold this in mind as they come alongside individuals in their healing process. Seek to understand the unique components of recovery and health for the individual.

It is key to remember that **relapse**, returning to regular engagement in substance use behaviors, can often be a component of sobriety maintenance. For the addict, walking this new path of sobriety can be a very challenging process that has its fair share of suffering and struggles. As ministry workers, we need to keep this struggle in mind and understand that relapse does not indicate a failure of sobriety; it is a part of the terrain to be navigated on the sobriety path.

Love and Acceptance

If we pause here for a moment and reflect on the journey of sobriety and recovery, we can acknowledge that the process is one that requires much work and effort. As I was reflecting on the many individuals with whom I have worked and the many components to recovery and health, I was reminded of how overwhelming and exhausting treatment and recovery can be for the addicted person as well as the supporting community. There are so many pieces to remember, layers to dissect, and components to constantly juggle in the air. The focus can become about managing all the pieces and keeping that goal of sobriety. As ministry workers, we might have a tendency to check in with addicted individuals and ask them several detailed questions regarding what they are *doing* to stay sober and "work the program." For example, you might find yourself asking, "How many days have you been sober?" and want to do everything possible to keep the addicted person sober. While this question might be helpful for some, it has the potential to put undue pressure on the addicted person. Our vision of support can become clouded by tasks, leading us to forget one essential component. We must *listen* and *be* with the addicted person. We understand that the most helpful component for individuals in treatment and recovery from addiction is experiencing acceptance and love from Christ Jesus. We must remember to embody God's love for the individual first.

One of the core experiences of many addicted individuals in recovery is the feeling of shame. This results from the consequences of their actions during periods of substance use, particularly how they hurt people along the way (Luoma, Kohlenberg, Hayes, & Fletcher, 2012). As a result of their past behaviors, addicted individuals might struggle to think and believe that they are worthy of love and acceptance. Thus, the addicted person might have a persistent sense of shame and struggle to acknowledge his or her value, especially in the eyes of Christ.

In addition to shame for past behaviors, addicted individuals often experience shame for their needs. These needs might include the need to be understood, loved, accepted, known, or seen, just to name a few. This shame is not only connected to past behaviors but also connected to attachment injuries. For example, addicted individuals might think that they are not worthy of love and acceptance, not just because they stole money from their families to buy drugs but also because they were verbally abused as children. It can be very difficult for addicted individuals to accept their own emotional and relational needs and readily step into getting those needs met by others. Engaging in healthy relational dependency is often felt as counter to the addict's prior experience. Needs can then become veiled or hidden by the addicted person. In addition, the addicted person might resort to past coping strategies, substance use, to manage the insurmountable shame (Hayes, Luoma, Bond, Masuda, & Lillis, 2006). It is helpful to remember that experiencing and receiving love and acceptance from God and others is how shame is overcome and healed.

Thus, it is imperative that the church community embody Christ's love and acceptance. This is also balanced with an embodiment of God's truth, depending on the needs of the individual. I believe this embodiment of love is the core form of healing that all addicted individuals need. In 1 John 4, we read that it is through the embodiment of love in relationships that we experience Christ's love for us.

> This is how God showed his love among us: He sent his one and only Son into the world that we might live through him. This is the love: not that we loved God, but that he loved us and sent his Son as an atoning sacrifice for our sins. Dear friends, since God loved us, we also ought to love one another. No one has ever seen God; but if we love one another, God lives in us and his love is made complete in us. (1 John 4:9–12 NIV)

The image that God's love is perfected in us as we are in loving relationship with one another is very powerful. The opportunity for healing within Christ's unconditional love is made manifest in relationship. Therefore, we must hold at the core of how we support those struggling with addiction the love of Christ. Before we focus on the tasks of sobriety, we must approach the recovering individual from a posture of love and grace. This occurs through listening, empathy, understanding, and acceptance, as well as asking questions of the addict's experiences rather than giving advice. Even in the role of accountability partner, Christ's love must remain central. Ultimately, this expression of Christ's love is foundational to the stability of the addict's sobriety.

KEY TERMS

Stages of Change Model: a set of stages used to assess and understand motivation and the state of mind toward change

Motivational interviewing: process of asking the addicted person questions to overcome ambivalence and resistance to change, determine the necessity of change, and make a commitment to change

"Hitting rock bottom": the experience of reaching an ultimate low emotionally, legally, financially, physically, and/or spiritually, but it is not necessary for change in addiction behaviors

Medical detoxification (detox): removing the substance from the body typically by medical and pharmaceutical assistance

Residential treatment: immersion in 24/7 care that involves group therapy, individual therapy, family therapy, psychiatry, case management, and staying at the residential housing provided by the facility

Intensive outpatient program: treatment that requires attendance of group and individual therapy typically for 2–5 hours per day for 3–5 days per week

Sober living facility: a residence occupied by several individuals committed to sobriety and managed by an addiction treatment service provider

Support groups: a community of individuals who are committed to their recovery and supporting others in the process

Psychotherapy: an intentional space to gain insight and make changes to addictive behaviors at a holistic level

Relapse: returning to regular engagement in substance use behaviors

Discussion Questions

1 Given the Stages of Change Model, how might you respond to someone who does not think his or her substance use is an issue, yet family and friends think otherwise?

2 What are key components to keep in mind when referring an individual with addiction issues to treatment and/or therapy?

3 Why might it be important to understand the connection between shame, addiction, and Christ's love?

NAVIGATING ADDICTION ISSUES IN THE CHURCH

Navigating addiction issues within the church community can be difficult for pastors and ministry workers. This challenge can occur for a wide variety of reasons, ranging from having the resources available to working through personal addiction issues as a ministry worker. Ministry workers will need to make important decisions about how to address the addiction issues present within their church community and staff.

One common challenge is creating a support network within the church community. On one level, it might be difficult for the addicted person to feel safe to be vulnerable about his or her struggles within the church community. This might be out of fear of judgment, not feeling accepted, or ultimately feeling a sense of shame. Some addicted individuals might struggle to find their place and feel supported. They might even feel like they are outcasts or that no one can relate to what they have experienced in life. Thus, it might be very hard for the addicted person to experience a safe community within the church. In addition, it is just as challenging for the church to create a community of safety and acceptance for those struggling with addiction issues. Creating this type of community within the church requires resources and commitment to investing relationally. This community can be created informally by building relationships with those in the church or by launching a recovery group such as Celebrate Recovery. Both options require time, relational investment, setting healthy boundaries, and training.

Another consideration is that ministry workers might also need support for addiction issues. It requires a significant amount of strength and vulnerability for a ministry worker to acknowledge his or her need for support and healing from his or her personal addiction issues. In addition, as a leader, one can sometimes feel the pressure to appear to "have it all together." Thus, ministry workers who also struggle with addiction issues are likely to experience a level of shame given the felt pressures of their leadership roles. Other church staff might also find it difficult to navigate these issues with other leaders. An experience of trauma might be present for all parties involved (see the chapter on trauma). Many complex dynamics are present such as re-evaluating leader responsibilities, processing the effect of the addiction on the staff and church community, and reconciling and establishing boundaries and expectations for the future. All these layers need to be intentionally addressed, especially from a place of love and grace as discussed earlier.

As you walk with those working through addiction and recovery, it is important to remember to seek your own support. It is helpful to receive care and support from others as you step into places of darkness with the person struggling with addiction and offer the presence of Christ. It can be challenging to keep your focus on Christ's love and grace all on your own. Remember that God's love is perfected in relationship, and you need supportive relationships as you are supporting individuals with addiction issues.

1   Describe two different types of support ministries for addicted individuals that might be offered within a church community.

2   What types of support might one seek while navigating addiction issues with a fellow church leader/staff member?

REVIEWING THE CONCEPTS

Learning Objectives

- Broadly define substance use addiction and understand the key areas of functioning that are impacted by substance addiction.
  - Substance addiction can be defined as a disease using the medical model of addiction.
  - A biopsychosocial model of addiction that encompasses many factors leading to addictive behaviors can also be used to define substance addiction.
  - Addiction affects several key areas of functioning, including biological, psychological, social/relational, and spiritual health.

- Understand the differences between intoxication, addiction, and withdrawal.
  - Intoxication includes physiological and psychological symptoms shortly after substance use.
  - Addiction includes the experience of physiological and psychological dependence, increased tolerance, and avoidance of withdrawal symptoms.
  - Withdrawal is the experience of physiological and psychological symptoms when reducing or ceasing prolonged substance use.

- Be familiar with typical treatment for addiction.
  - The first step in treatment typically includes medical detoxification.
  - Following detox, an individual is likely to seek residential treatment or an IOP.
  - Another route includes frequent and regular attendance at support groups following detox.
  - An individual might also elect to stay in a sober living facility.

- Gain insight into ways individuals with addiction can be supported and maintain their sobriety.
  - Given the Stages of Change Model, addicted individuals need to be support based on their readiness for change.
  - Support groups are often a key source of guidance and community during the recovery journey.
  - Psychotherapy might be a component of sobriety maintenance based on the unique needs of the individual.

- Identify ways that the churches can provide specific support for individuals maintaining sobriety.
    - ○ Given the common experience of shame for addicted individuals, embody Christ's love within a supportive relationship with the addicted person.
    - ○ Create an intentional community and support network for addicted individuals within the church either informally or formally (e.g., Celebrate Recovery).

Chapter Review Questions

Level 1: Knowledge (True/False)

1. Addiction is best defined using only the medical model.
2. Often, individuals with substance addiction experience impairments in biological, psychological, social, and/or spiritual functioning.
3. A co-occurring disorder is a mental health disorder that is present alongside the substance addiction and can add a layer of complexity to recovery.
4. Intoxication can always be classified as substance addiction.
5. Physiological and psychological dependence can be characterized by avoidance of withdrawal and the belief that one needs the substance to function.
6. The only cause of addiction issues is moral failure.
7. Given the Stages of Change Model, it can be understood that most addicted individuals are ready to change their addiction behaviors.
8. Treatment can include a variety of different components depending on the needs of the individual.
9. Engaging in support groups such as Alcoholics Anonymous or Narcotics Anonymous is the only way addicted individuals can maintain their sobriety.
10. Shame is a common experience for individuals in recovery.

Level 2: Comprehension

1. Which of the following can be impaired/impacted by substance addiction?
    - a. Physical health
    - b. Spiritual well-being
    - c. Family relationships
    - d. All of the above
2. A common barrier to seeking treatment is
    - a. denial
    - b. support from family
    - c. desire to make a change
    - d. ability to get time off from work

3. An individual who is actively working on changing his or her addiction behaviors is in which stage of change?

   a. Precontemplation

   b. Contemplation

   c. Preparation

   d. Action

4. Which of the following is typically the first step in treatment?

   a. Psychotherapy

   b. Support groups

   c. Detoxification

   d. Intensive outpatient program

5. Which of the following can be a key component of *treatment* for substance addiction?

   a. Engaging in a supportive community

   b. Residential treatment

   c. Intensive outpatient program

   d. All of the above

6. Substance addiction includes the following, except

   a. using to avoid withdrawal symptoms

   b. occasional intoxication

   c. dependence

   d. increased tolerance

7. Which of the following is correlated with higher rates of substance addiction?

   a. Secure attachment

   b. Insecure attachment

   c. Absence of other mental health issues

   d. Race and ethnicity

8. An example of a Christian-based recovery support group is

   a. Alcoholics Anonymous

   b. Al-Anon

   c. Celebrate Recovery

   d. SMART Recovery

9. Challenges that churches might encounter regarding substance addiction include

   a. creating a community to support addicted individuals

   b. navigating addiction issues among leaders and staff

   c. accessing support for self as one supports others in recovery

   d. all of the above

10. The following are examples of co-occurring disorders, *except*

    a. GAD

    b. major depressive disorder

    c. frequent stress disorder

    d. bipolar disorder

Level 3: Application

1. Compare and contrast the idea that addiction is the result of moral failure and/ or the result of early childhood attachment injuries.

2. Describe a potential ministry program for substance addiction that you could implement at your church. Identify three important components of the ministry based on what you learned from this chapter.

3. You encounter a member of your church who does not think his addiction to pain pills is an issue; however, his family wants him to seek treatment. How do you approach and support this individual? What is your role and expectations?

4. Discuss three key components of substance addiction that differentiate it from other forms of recreational substance use (e.g., intoxication). Reflect on the purpose of clearly defining addiction.

5. From your personal Christian worldview, discuss the potential importance of the embodiment of Christ's love as a core component of supporting those in recovery from addiction.

ANSWERS

LEVEL 1: KNOWLEDGE

1. F

2. T

3. T

4. F

5. T

6. F

7. F

8. T

9. F

10. T

LEVEL 2: COMPREHENSION

1. d
2. a
3. d
4. c
5. d
6. b
7. b
8. c
9. d
10. c

RESOURCES

Online Resources

- Alcoholic Anonymous—https://www.aa.org/
- Narcotics Anonymous—https://www.na.org/
- Al-Anon (support for family of addicted individuals)—http://al-anon.org/
- Celebrate Recovery—http://www.celebraterecovery.com/
- SMART Recovery—https://www.smartrecovery.org/
- Types of substance use disorders—https://www.samhsa.gov/disorders/substance-use

Readings

- *Motivational Interviewing: Helping People Change*, 3rd Edition—W. R. Miller and S. Rollnick
- *Twelve Steps and Twelve Traditions*—Alcoholics Anonymous
- *Just for Today: Daily Meditation for Recovering Addicts*—Narcotics Anonymous World Services
- *Courage to Change: One Day at a time in Al-Anon*—Al-Anon Family Group Headquarters
- *Hope for Today*—Al-Anon Family Group Headquarters
- Any personal account, memoir, or biography written by an addicted person in recovery. For example, *Drinking: A Love Story* by Caroline Knapp

CLASSROOM ACTIVITIES

1. Within a counseling session, what types of questions and responses might be helpful for a person in each stage of change? Using these questions, role-play a counseling session where you seek to identify the stage of change from which the congregant is operating.

2. Reflect on your experience of how your church or denomination views and responds to addiction issues. Share your reflections with a classmate.

3. In small groups, design/create a recovery ministry program. Identify several core components of the ministry program.

REFERENCES

Abbott, P., & Chase, D. M. (2008). Culture and substance abuse: Impact of culture affects approach to treatment. *Psychiatric Times*. Retrieved from https://pro.psychcentral.com/culture-and-substance-abuse-impact-of-culture-affects-approach-to-treatment/

American Psychiatric Association. (2013). *Diagnostic and statistical manual of mental disorders* (5th ed.). Arlington, VA: American Psychiatric Publishing.

Buchman, D. Z., Skinner, W., & Illes, J. (2010). *Negotiating the relationship between addiction, ethics, and brain science. AJOB Neuroscience, 1*(1), 36–45. doi: 10.1080/21507740903508609

Crane, M. (2016, July 29). Intensive outpatient treatment for substance abuse. Retrieved from https://www.recovery.org/topics/intensive-outpatient-treatment/

Definition of addiction. (2011, April 19). *American Society of Addiction Medicine*. Retrieved from https://www.asam.org/resources/definition-of-addiction

DiClemente, C. C. (2018). *Addiction and change: How addictions develop and addicted people recover* (2nd ed.) New York, NY: Guilford Press.

DiClemente, C. C., Corno, C. M., Graydon, M. M., Wiprovnick, A. E., & Knoblach, D. J. (2017). Motivational interviewing, enhancement, and brief interventions over the last decade: A review of reviews of efficacy and effectiveness. *Psychology of Addictive Behaviors, 31*(8), 862–887. doi: 10.1037/adb0000318

Donovan, D. M., & Marlatt, G. A. (Eds.). (2005). *Assessment of addictive behaviors* (2nd ed.). New York, NY: Guilford Press.

Fairbairn, C. E., Briley, D. A., Kang, D., Fraley, R. C., Hankin, B. L., & Ariss, T. (2018). A meta-analysis of longitudinal associations between substance use and interpersonal attachment security. *Psychological Bulletin, 144*(5), 532–555, doi: 10.1037/bul0000141

Hayes, S. C., Luoma, J., Bond, F., Masuda, A., & Lillis, J. (2006). Acceptance and commitment therapy: Model, processes, and outcomes. *Behaviour Research and Therapy, 44*(1), 1–25. doi: 10.1016/j.brat.2005.06.006

Lundahl, B., & Burke, B. L. (2009). The effectiveness and applicability of motivational interviewing: A practice-friendly review of four meta-analyses. *Journal of Clinical Psychology, 65*(11), 1232–1245. doi: 10.1002/jclp.20638

Luoma, J. B., Kohlenberg, B. S., Hayes, S. C., & Fletcher, L. (2012). Slow and steady wins the race: A randomized clinical trial of acceptance and commitment therapy targeting shame in substance use disorders. *Journal of Consulting and Clinical Psychology, 80*(1), 43–53. doi: 10.1037/a0026070

McGue, M., & Irons, D. E. (2013). Etiology. In B. S. McCrady & E. E. Epstein (Eds.), *Addictions: A comprehensive guidebook* (pp. 36–72). New York, NY: Oxford University Press.

Mental health and substance use disorders (2017). *Substance Abuse and Mental Health Services Administration.* Retrieved from https://www.samhsa.gov/disorders

Mignon, S. I. (2015). *Substance abuse treatment: Options, challenges, and effectiveness.* New York, NY: Springer Publishing Company.

Mikulincer, M., & Florian, V. (1998). The relationship between adult attachment styles and emotional and cognitive reactions to stressful events. In J. A. Simpson & W. S. Rholes (Eds.), *Attachment theory and close relationships* (pp. 143–165). New York, NY: Guilford.

Miller, W. R., & Hester, R. K. (1995). Treatment for alcohol problems: Toward an informed eclecticism. In R. K. Hester & W. R. Miller (Eds.), *Handbook of alcoholism treatment approaches: Effective alternatives* (pp. 1–11). Needham Heights, MA: Allyn & Bacon.

Miller, W. R., & Rollnick, S. (1991). *Motivational interviewing: Preparing people to change addictive behavior.* New York, NY: Guilford Press.

Opioid addiction 2016 facts and figures. (n.d.) American Society of Addiction Medicine. Retrieved from https://www.asam.org/docs/default-source/advocacy/opioid-addiction-disease-facts-figures.pdf

Patterson, E. (n.d.). *The "hitting rock bottom" myth.* Retrieved from https://drugabuse.com/library/hitting-rock-bottom-myth/

Prochaska, J. O., & DiClemente, C. C. (1984). *The transtheoretical approach: Towards a systematic eclectic framework.* Homewood, IL.: Dow Jones Irwin.

Roget, N. A., & Fisher, G. L. (2009). *Encyclopedia of substance abuse prevention, treatment, and recovery.* Los Angeles, CA: SAGE Publications, Inc.

Wells, K., Klap, A., Koike, R., & Sherbourne, C. (2001). Ethnic disparities in unmet need for alcoholism, drug abuse, and mental health care. *American Journal of Psychiatry, 158*(12), 2027–2032. doi: 10.1176/appi.ajp.158.12.2027

Zimmermann, P., Wittchen, H., Höfler, M., Pfister, H., Kessler, R. C., & Lieb, R. (2003). Primary anxiety disorders and the development of subsequent alcohol use disorders: A 4-year community study of adolescents and young adults. *Psychological Medicine, 33*(7), 1211–1222. doi:10.1017/S0033291703008158

IMAGE CREDITS

CHAPTER 7

Sexual Addiction

Heather Schroeder, PsyD and Leah Freeman, MA

LEARNING OBJECTIVES

Upon completion of this chapter, readers will be able to

1. understand what sexual addiction is and how it presents itself;

2. identify the etiology of sexual addiction at the societal and individual levels;

3. facilitate conversations about sexual addiction with their congregants; and

4. have resources available for those struggling with sexual addiction.

"The bubbling impulses of puberty befogged and obscured my heart so that it could not see the difference between love's serenity and lust's darkness."
(Augustine, *Confessions*, Section ii(2), AD 397–400)

"My flesh and my heart may fail, but God is the strength of my heart and my portion forever."
(Ps. 73:26, ESV)

THE STORY OF SHAWN

Shawn had owned his private practice as a doctor for the last 30 years. He was dedicated to serving God and serving his congregation. Shawn was also well respected in the community beyond just his church congregation, and he was happily married with two teenage children. He described his relationship with his wife as fulfilling and meaningful. Shawn made time for his two children and rarely missed any of their sporting events. As a family, they made it a priority to have dinner together with no outside distractions at least four times a week. He occasionally experienced mild depression and anxiety, but nothing that he felt needed treatment. Despite his seemingly typical life, Shawn entered treatment because his wife discovered pornography on their home computer.

Shawn disclosed in treatment that he had been looking at pornography since he was 16 years old and had multiple sexual encounters outside of his marriage. In the beginning of treatment, he seemed to struggle with identifying why he was unable to stop viewing pornography and masturbating, and was ashamed of what he called his "sexual indiscretions." Shawn struggled to engage in the recovery process throughout treatment. He often felt that he just needed to pray more and continue to "give it to God." Despite his deep belief that this was the answer, he continued to struggle with porn and had several more sexual encounters outside of his marriage. Treatment for Shawn became a balance of learning to cope with negative emotions and the consequences of his addiction by being challenged to explore why he was resistant to engaging in the recovery process. Shawn was unable to see how the recovery process was actually a program designed to have a deeper and more meaningful relationship with God. His fear of being hurt and/or rejected by others kept him from developing the relationships necessary for successful recovery; this stemmed back to Shawn's childhood experiences of being bullied by his classmates and later constantly trying to please others in his career as a physician. Even though he was consistent in showing up to individual therapy and regular meetings with his pastor, he was still living his life in shame and secrecy. Without a foundation of recovery and sustained sobriety, Shawn was unable to explore his early attachment wounds fully and the connection to his difficulty in regulating emotions. Eventually, Shawn left treatment.

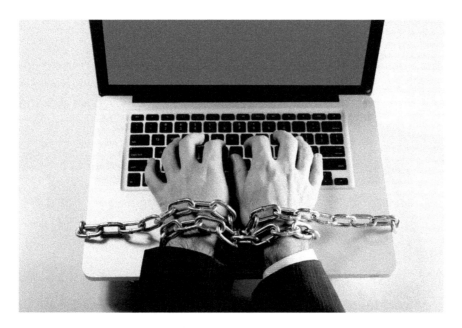

FIGURE 7.1   **Bound by sexual addiction**

WHAT IS SEXUAL ADDICTION AND SEXUALLY COMPULSIVE BEHAVIOR?

Shawn's story is not a new one, but the number of stories similar to his seems to be growing. As pastors continue to face the growing issue of sexually compulsive behavior within our culture, it is evident that this problem is not going away anytime soon. Members of the church come forward to confess compulsive pornography usage. Spouses find out about their partners' chronic infidelity. Parents are worried about their child's exposure to sexually explicit content online. Because of the ever-increasing nature of this issue, this may be one of the most important chapters you will read as a pastoral counselor. This chapter aims to provide you with an overview of some of the most important aspects of sexual addiction so that you will be better equipped to help those who come to you hurting and/or in crisis.

The American Society of Addiction Medicine (2011) defines addiction as

> a primary, chronic disease of brain reward, motivation, memory, and related circuitry. Dysfunction in these circuits leads to characteristic biological, psychological, social, and spiritual manifestations. This is reflected in an individual pathologically pursing reward and/or relief by substance use and other behaviors.
>
> Addiction is characterized by inability to consistently abstain, impairment in behavioral control, craving, diminished recognition of significant problems with one's behaviors and interpersonal relationships, and a dysfunctional emotional response. Like other chronic diseases, addiction often involves cycles of relapse and remission. Without treatment or engagement in recovery activities, addiction is progressive and can result in disability or premature death. (American Society of Addiction Medicine, 2011)

In light of this, **sexual addiction** is a compulsive need to view pornography, masturbate, act out sexually with others, compulsively fantasize, or engage in any other sexually compulsive behavior despite experiencing negative consequences (such as depression, anxiety, guilt, shame, strain on personal relationships, financial consequences, or health problems). On the surface, sexual addiction appears to be merely a matter of personal choice, in sexual preference or character; however, this addiction is an unwanted, progressive disease that often plagues the individual with shame, isolation, depression, and anxiety. These negative consequences are far-reaching and often long-lasting. For example, Shawn had multiple sexual encounters; he experienced depression and anxiety, and he felt shame that he had not been able to rid himself of this behavior since his teen years. While someone who occasionally views pornography or masturbates may feel guilt over his or her behavior, it would not be considered a sexual addiction until it was compulsive, and there were negative consequences. This is important to note, since there are some who would automatically label this behavior as an addiction; however, a focus on intensive recovery may not be appropriate when at this time, he or she might just need additional support, grace, and a listening ear.

Why the Church Needs to Be Informed

Many Christians would say that in either instance, addiction or not, sexually acting out is a moral issue. Every individual is responsible for his or her choices, whether the sexual behavior is compulsive or not. However, for sexual addicts, there are also often reasons under the surface that explain why they make the choices they do. Thankfully, these unseen issues can be addressed, and recovery can be achieved. The power of recovery can change lives, bring people in contact with and deepen their relationship with God, strengthen marriages, and bring personal transformation.

UNDERSTANDING SEXUAL ADDICTION

When people hear of sexual addiction for the first time, there are often two reactions: "Is that even a real thing?" Or, "Well if that's an addiction, then that's the one I wouldn't mind having!" These naïve statements are humorous at best, and at worst, they negate the pain of those struggling with sexually compulsive behavior. This only adds to their shame, which has been present since the Fall.

Sexuality and Shame

God designed us in His image, and we were created to be whole, healthy human beings in perfect communion with our Creator (Gen. 1:27, ESV). In the garden, Adam and Eve had this communion with God without any anxiety or shame (Gen. 2:35, ESV). There was no criticism of each other's bodies because they were so consumed with their Lord and their love for one another. Sex was not a dirty word; God gave them sexuality, and they were not ashamed of it. Up until the serpent began whispering lies to Eve, they had never known evil; all they had known was God's goodness and hope for the world. After their disobedience, the first thing to enter the world was *shame* (Gen. 3:7, ESV). It did not say that their eyes were opened to the reality of their ugliness or imperfection; their perception changed. Their holistic view of themselves and each other was traded for the lie that they should be ashamed of their nakedness and sexuality, which God created.

We can guess that they began to see the person they loved as shameful also. Adam did not object, that we know of, to Eve covering up her body. Eve did not object to Adam covering his body. They did not speak God's truth to one another, but rather covered themselves in complete shame. They did feel **guilt** (the feeling of regret after *making* a mistake), but this **shame** (the feeling of worthlessness that comes from thinking you *are* a mistake) was what promoted their actions of covering up.

Since then, nothing has changed. We are consistently trying to seek after God, while quieting the world's lies. God tells us that we are fearfully and wonderfully made (Ps. 139:14, ESV); the world tells us that we are not good enough. God is our portion (Ps. 73:26, ESV); the world tells us that we should never be satisfied. We are to keep ourselves unstained from the world (James 1:27, ESV); the world tells us to keep ourselves unstained from God or restricting moral codes. As a backlash against the world's lies in sexuality, however, the church has often responded by not talking about sex at all, unless it is the simple message of "just don't have it."

Rather than avoid the topic of sex in the church, we can more fully understand God through a deeper understanding of *our own* bodies and minds. Not surprisingly, pornography and unhealthy sexual behaviors get in the way of this deeper understanding. While sexual addiction can take many forms, such as seeking out multiple sex partners, compulsive masturbation, or constant unwanted sexual fantasies, one of the most common ways of acting out is by engaging with pornography.

Pornography

Pornography is defined as "the depiction of erotic behavior (as in pictures or writing) intended to cause sexual excitement" (Pornography, n.d.). With the rapid growth of pornographic content in print, on television, and on the Internet, pornography has been found to have a significant effect on the brain (Struthers, 2009). Therefore, if we are viewing pornography and engaging our bodies, such as pairing pornography use with masturbation, we are actually getting further away from connecting with God. The content of pornography often promotes a selfish narrative, with objectification at its core. It may be surprising, but, according to one research study, one-third of pornography viewers online are female (Horin, 2007). Problems with pornography is not just an issue for men. Both men and women learn to objectify sex and the human body, as well as internalize messages about themselves and sex from the content they see. We reduce each other and ourselves to nothing but objects to be used; we do not see the image of God in each other. Statistics consistently support this:

- One research study found that out of 304 scenes in popular pornographic videos, 88.2% contained physical aggression (Bridges, 2010).
- As of 2017, the most popular search terms on pornographic websites were often incest- or teen-related (Fight the New Drug, 2018).
- One study found that those who frequently view sexually explicit content online have an increased view that sex is primarily physical, utilitarian, and casual, rather than relational or affectionate (Peter & Valkenburg, 2010).

Exposure to pornography has a significant effect on the brain. Research has found that pornography activates the "reward system" in the pleasure center (ventral tegmental area) of the brain (Struthers, 2009). The **"reward system"** of the brain is responsible for releasing chemicals that make you feel pleasure and awareness that there is something significant occurring. God designed these chemicals to reinforce *healthy* behaviors, such as exercise, laughing, eating, having fun, and sex. Your brain has a built-in mechanism to alert you when you have reached a satisfactory level of "pleasure" chemicals. How amazing that God designed our brains to *enjoy* what is good for us! However, this area of the brain is also activated by drugs and alcohol. Drugs and other mind-altering substances activate this reward center and "hijack" the brain into believing that the individual needs to *keep* consuming the drug. The reward system is unable to feel the effects of being "satisfied" fully, which, in turn, keeps the individual searching for more and more. Pornography, gambling, shopping, fatty foods, and sugar, just to name a few, activate and hijack the brain in the same way as drugs. Neural pathways are formed each time pornographic images are viewed, and these pathways become more and more well-traveled and rooted in the brain. These neural pathways are also accessed when interacting with women, which means that "they have unknowingly created a neurological circuit that imprisons their ability to see women rightly as created in God's image" (Struthers, 2009, p. 85). Eventually, it starts to become much easier to travel down these pathways, which is why Shawn found it so easy to return to pornography, despite negative consequences. This pushes the individual to search out more pornography and/or different types of sexually explicit content to achieve the same level of "pleasure" chemicals, becoming stuck in a prison where the very thing that you are seeking for relief is actually causing more pain.

Because of this increase in tolerance and a change in our brain chemistry, pornography consumption changes our perspective, expectations, and the meaning of sex—we become desensitized. Exposure to pornographic content has been linked to increased sexual dysfunction, sexual aggression, negative views of women, pervasive feelings of shame, and increased feelings of loneliness. These negative consequences of sexual addiction and pornography ultimately erode any space for true intimacy. Mary Ann Layden, a psychological researcher at the University of Pennsylvania, may say it best: "If pornography made us healthy, we would be healthy by now" (Layden, 2004).

Implications for Children and the Family

- In a study of over 500 college students, 93% of boys and 62% of girls were exposed to pornography before the age of 18 (Sabina, Wolak, & Finkelhor, 2008).
- The average age of pornography exposure for boys is 8 to 11 years old (Parents Resource Hub, n.d.).

Children are being exposed to pornography at earlier and earlier ages—some in treatment have reported that they were exposed to it as early as 4 or 5 years old! In fact, a 2007 study by Internet security company McAfee found that there is a 1-in-14 chance of a child accidentally misspelling a URL and stumbling across a porn site (Fight the New Drug, 2017). With how sexually graphic our culture has become, this is affecting how the brain of a child or teenager is being developed, as we saw earlier. In typical development, even from infancy, children begin to explore their bodies and experience their sexuality. For example, babies often touch their genitals during diaper changing out of curiosity, and baby boys can experience erections, much to the concern of some parents! However, these behaviors are a natural part of a person's physical and sexual development (Dowshen, 2014).

Some churches have historically avoided topics related to sexuality, and many people grow up believing "*I am bad* because I have these sexual feelings!" If no one talks to them about these feelings, children grow up believing that they are alone. This isolation is often a major ingredient in the beginning of an addiction as they first get exposed to pornography, and this leads to deep shame. As we have seen, from the very beginning, God never meant for us to be ashamed of our bodies. There is a need for children to have these age-appropriate conversations about healthy sexuality, their bodies, and their brains early on in order to eliminate shame about being created in God's image as sexual beings. If we are to counter all the sexual messages that they are getting from the world around them, we also need to understand what true intimacy means.

Intimacy is created when people are connected by being fully present, vulnerable, authentic, and available. We need intimacy in order to survive. If an individual does not have emotional intimacy from an early age, it is often called a "failure to thrive" (Ward,

Lee, & Lipper, 2000). Researchers found that when infants' physical needs were met, but they were not given the relational/emotional attention they needed, they actually stopped growing. Pornography and sex addiction do not just affect the individual engaging in the behavior, it also affects the family. Loved ones of those engaging in sexually addictive behavior often feel devastated, deeply betrayed, and that their world has been turned upside down (Carnes, 2011). This increases that break of trust in relationship and prevents true intimacy.

KEY TERMS

Sex addiction: a compulsive need to engage in unwanted sexual behavior despite experiencing negative consequences

Guilt: the feeling of regret after making a mistake

Shame: the feeling of worthlessness that comes from thinking you *are* a mistake

Pornography: "the depiction of erotic behavior (as in pictures or writing) intended to cause sexual excitement" (Pornography, n.d.)

Reward system: a part of brain function that is responsible for releasing chemicals that make you feel pleasure.

Intimacy: interpersonal connection by being fully present, vulnerable, authentic, and available

Discussion Questions

1 Have you or someone you know ever struggled with addiction? Why is addiction not just a matter of sin?

2 How can the church help foster a better understanding of sexuality and our relationship with God?

3 How would you help Shawn better understand why he keeps going back to pornography from what you have read so far?

4 How did you learn about your body and your sexuality growing up? How has that influenced your view of sex now?

5 How might you help a parent who is concerned that his or her child has been exposed to pornography?

THE ROOTS OF SEXUAL ADDICTION

While it is necessary to understand how sex addiction and pornography use are detrimental at the societal level, it is equally as imperative to understand it at an individual level. From a clinical standpoint and with recent advances in understanding sex addiction, we must consider attachment theory as a way to conceptualize what has gone wrong. **Attachment theory**, originally articulated by John Bowlby, is the idea that in order to thrive in the world fully, we first need to have a secure attachment to someone (Katehakis, 2016). Typically, this attachment is with our parents. Having a secure attachment then allows us, as infants and children, to explore the world around us and develop our sense of self in our environment. Unfortunately, many people experience less-than-ideal attachments with their parents. Even under the best of circumstances, parents will still fall short of meeting our every need: a product of living in a broken world! Experiencing a less-than-secure attachment then creates either anxiety or avoidance (or a combination of the two), which then leads to difficulty in future relationships.

Kelley (2010) notes that "Bowlby maintains that attachment behavior is an instinctual and constitutive dimension of being human and endures throughout the life span." One never outgrows or develops beyond attachment behavior, but rather it persists, as Bowlby says, "from the cradle to the grave" (Kelley, 2010, p. 55). We know this is true because God created us to connect with Him and others: "We love because He first loved us" (1 Jn. 4:19, ESV). Another way to think about attachment is through the lens of trust. Specifically, Zitzman and Butler (2009) argue that the term "trust" is synonymous with the term "secure attachment." With this trust in the parent-child relationship, a child learns that she can rely on her parent to teach her how to find comfort in a big (and sometimes scary) world. For example, if a child is at a birthday party, and a clown appears, he may start to back away, get wide-eyed, and begin to cry. A mother who has a secure attachment to her child is going to go over to him, kneel down to his level, perhaps wave at the clown, while speaking soft words of comfort that he is safe and that she is right there. This is called **co-regulation.** Parents teach their children ways to cope in the world by showing them how to comfort or soothe themselves. The next time this child is at a birthday party, and his mother is not present, his brain is going to be more likely to remember that he is safe; he may take some deep breaths or wave at the clown and try to calm down as his mother had previously modeled to him. This ability to self-soothe and manage one's emotions is called **self-regulation.** This is even present and significant in infancy! A baby uses his mother's tone of voice, facial expression, mood, and gestures to regulate himself emotionally in the midst of distress (Katehakis, 2016).

A parent-child relationship that does not exhibit a secure attachment may find our previously mentioned parent laughing at her son, pushing him closer, or telling him to "get over it." Or, she may struggle with her own depression or anxiety that is unwittingly preventing her from being attuned to her son's needs. If this behavior happens on a consistent basis, then the child will never learn from his parent how to cope with frightening or stressful situations; he will be left on his own to learn how to self-soothe, and this leaves him at a much higher risk for developing addictive behavior. By relating the notion of trust and emotional regulation to secure attachment, one can better understand the devastating effects of sex addiction (Katehakis, 2016).

If this trust is consistently broken and a parent is not attuned to his or her child, it can open the door to abuse. In fact, 81% of sexual addicts report a history of sexual abuse, 72% report a history of physical abuse, and an overwhelming 97% report some history of ongoing emotional abuse (Carnes, 2016). As we can see, past experiences may include major trauma, such as childhood sexual abuse or a death in the family, but there could also be traumas that are small and repeated (such as bullying, severe stress from school, or parents who do not validate their children's feelings), which can be just as damaging as big traumas. (For a better understanding, see the chapter on trauma). For many individuals who struggle with sexual addiction or compulsive pornography use, they often originally began to use sexual feelings as a way to soothe and cope with uncomfortable and negative feelings. Instead of being able to regulate and tolerate the negative emotions, they cover them up with masturbation, pornography use, acting out sexually with others, or becoming preoccupied with romantic relationships or sex (Katehakis, 2016). For example, we know that Shawn was bullied as a minor and has a stressful job—he eventually turned to pornography to relieve stress at the age of 16. This pattern, or way of coping, often just continues or escalates as one gets older, and the demands of life increase.

Another way trauma can be connected to sexual addiction is when someone is acting out sexually as a means of **trauma reenactment**. For example, a woman might unconsciously search out men who are sexually abusive in an attempt to heal and correct childhood sexual abuse. Alice Miller's classic book *The Drama of the Gifted Child* describes the process of reenactment and why we get pulled into it: The draw to reenact trauma is our desire to right the wrongs that have been done to us. If somehow the woman who was sexually abused could stop the abuse in her current relationship, then perhaps she would finally feel safe in the world (Miller, 2008). This, however, is faulty thinking because the pain of the original wound is still not being fully processed. For this woman, her sense of safety has to be developed within the context of a safe and secure relationship so that she can then feel safe enough to feel the depth of pain of the original wounds. This is often the work of therapy and recovery groups. By working through the original wounds, one can then find freedom. This idea captures the foundation of the principles of therapy and recovery as we will see later.

KEY TERMS

Attachment theory: the idea that in order to fully thrive in the world, we first need to have a secure attachment to someone

Self-regulation: the ability to self-soothe and manage one's own emotions

Co-regulation: when parents (or other attachment figures) teach their children ways to cope in the world by showing them how to comfort or soothe themselves

Trauma reenactment: when an individual unconsciously acts out sexually in a way that reenacts the abuse that was done to him or her

1   In light of Shawn's story, what are some of the reasons that may have led to his development of a sexual addiction?

2   Describe your attachment with your parents. Would you classify it as a secure or insecure attachment? How has this affected you?

3   From a biblical standpoint, what are some thoughts on the roots of addiction? How do justice and grace fit into this issue?

4   If someone from your congregation comes to you and shares about a past trauma or sexual abuse, how might you respond?

PASTORAL RESPONSE

Marnie Ferree (2002) aptly identified pastors and the church, as "first responders" for the communities they serve. When people are hurting and/or in crisis, they often turn to their church and the leaders within. Pastors and church leaders have a unique opportunity to not only help those in need but also to set the tone for how someone proceeds with seeking recovery.

Understanding the Layers of Sexual Addiction

As we have seen, sexual addiction has both a moral and psychobiological component. Having a full scope of both of these elements will be the first step to counseling others well on their path to healing. Many well-intentioned pastors or church leaders may underestimate the complexity of sexual addiction if they are not well informed about the nature of sexually compulsive behavior. There is a component of self-discipline and accountability, but there is also often a relational trauma and/or brain chemistry issue to consider. In the example of Shawn, he was trying to "give it up to God" and pray more, but after continuous relapses, he began to experience frustration and shame. Many sexual addicts feel alone and like failures because they have not been able to "pray it away." Some feel they "must not be a good enough Christian" if God has not healed them yet. Shawn's plan to pray more does hold absolute value and truth, but as we have discovered in this chapter, often there are also deep relational wounds. Dr. Karyn Purvis, author of *The Connected Child*, states that "[we] are harmed in relationship, and [we] will come to experience healing in relationship" (Monroe, n.d.). Addiction thrives when one feels alone and isolated; healing thrives when we are brought into the community that God has provided for us. As a pastoral counselor, you can acknowledge that this is an issue of sin, but to limit yourself to viewing it *only* as a sin limits your ability to use all that we know about addiction and sexuality to help your congregation.

Navigating the Conversation

When a member of the congregation comes to you with an issue of sexual sin, it is important to listen to his or her narrative of what has been happening and the person's concerns. Some report that it can be difficult to listen to someone confess the details of sexual sin and talk about their sexual behavior, but we have to remember that this is likely an issue of great shame for your congregant. In light of what we have learned about attachment, pastoral counselors can keep this in mind when listening and responding to a person's narrative. This individual may have never told anyone about his or her sexual behavior; the person may have been sexually abused as a child, or his or her parents were so uncomfortable talking about sex that they avoided the topic and never told the individual that it was acceptable to ask questions. It could be any number of scenarios, so doing the following will help you understand what exactly might be best for your congregant:

1.   Actively listen. Your congregant will likely be approaching you with much shame and guilt, so being able to make eye contact, show empathy, and suspend judgment or rejection will already be a great start to the person's healing process. Remember, if the individual did not have a secure attachment, then there is likely more shame present, especially regarding his or her coping mechanism and way of self-regulating: the sexually compulsive behavior. You have the opportunity to model healthy regulation and grace in the midst of shame.

2.   Don't assume. It can be easy to rush to assumptions about the person's behavior, especially if you are wanting to get to the "solution" and how to eliminate your congregant's troubling behavior. However, this can be dangerous and can potentially bring about more shame. For example, a woman in your congregation may come to you or someone on your pastoral staff and begin talking about the guilt she feels after having slept with a man she met online. You may assume that he pressured her into sex, or that she was giving him sex in order to feel loved, when, in reality, she may have been the one to instigate the sexual encounter based primarily on her desire for sexual fulfillment. By making the earlier assumption without asking follow-up questions, she may feel even more ashamed, "dirty," or abnormal. This brings us to the next task:

3.   Ask thoughtful questions. After listening to all that your congregant shares, be curious. Ask questions that show empathy as well as clarity: "That was so brave of you to share with me; I know that must not have been easy. How do you feel right now after sharing?" Or, "How often does your behavior typically occur? Are there any patterns in time of day, context of the situation, location, etc.?" Or, even, "I can tell you are frustrated/sad/angry/disappointed, and I appreciate you sharing this with me. What behavior(s) would you like to stop or change?"

4.   Discern. Take the congregant's recovery desire, look at your inventory of resources, and determine what your congregant needs. The individual will be looking to you to point him or her on the path of healing, so take all that you have learned in this chapter and the resources you have in your "tool kit," and guide accordingly. Part of this responsibility should also include a willingness to continue to learn about sexual addiction and engage with new information and resources as they continue to be developed. Further, if you are not sure what this congregant may need, be sure to reach out to a therapist (ideally one who specializes in sexual addiction) who can help you determine the resources that

may be best for your congregant. God never intended for us to do life alone, and it is not only acceptable but also in the best interest of your congregant to reach out for further direction, discernment, and resources from a qualified therapist.

5. Pray. Sexual addiction can be one of the loneliest and shame-filled issues, and it needs to be covered in constant prayer. Some individuals may ask you to pray with them; some may not. Many counselors have found it helpful, in either case, to take a few moments to pray after their congregant has left the room and continuously throughout their journey. The church has the unique ability to help heal the shame that has plagued those who have been struggling with sexually compulsive behavior. They can be assured that they have a pastor and community keeping their recovery and healing process covered in prayer.

Recovery Resources

In order to be prepared for those struggling with sexual addiction who may walk through your door, it is necessary to take an inventory of what resources the church and ministries currently have to help support those who are struggling. This evaluation may include whether conversations are already being had about sexual addiction and pornography within the church. Do the resources, or ways of handling it, increase shame or do they bring hope? By asking yourself these questions, you can better assess what you will be able to offer the church community at large. According to some of the prominent leaders in the field of sex addiction treatment, the best model for successful recovery happens when an individual engages in 12-step work, individual therapy, group therapy, has a community to belong to (such as a church), and engages with his or her Higher Power (from a Christian perspective, this would be God) (Carnes, 1991),

Recovery Groups

Based on addiction research, one of the best tools for recovery are the **12-steps** of Alcoholics Anonymous. In fact, when those being treated for sexual addiction were asked which type of treatment was most helpful, 85% of respondents said their 12-step group (Carnes, 2016). These 12-steps have been adapted to address countless maladaptive behaviors, such as gambling, overeating, codependency, adult children of dysfunctional families, and many more. (You can find resources for different 12-step meetings at the end of this chapter.) There are secular 12-step programs (such as Sex Addicts Anonymous) as well as Christian-based, 12-step programs (such as Celebrate Recovery). Both have their own value. Christians may tend to feel more comfortable in a biblically-based 12-step program. However, there are also benefits of having both options at your church. Since our purpose as believers is to help bring people closer to a relationship with God, then this would be one way of reaching out to the very people who are furthest away. By offering traditional 12-step programs, you may actually be providing a bridge for someone to cross over from believing in a Higher Power to believing in God. Wouldn't it be amazing if every church offered a 12-step program on their campus? Believers and nonbelievers alike would be able to set foot in a place where they should always find healing: the church.

Your congregant may ask follow-up questions, such as if there is a cost for attendance or what to expect in a 12-step program. Fortunately, both secular and Christian-based

12-step programs are self-funded and function by voluntary donations from group members, so there is never a fixed cost required for attendance. Regarding expectations of a meeting, your congregant can expect to be provided with support that is offered through peer accountability and sponsorship. One of the anthems of recovery programs is the idea that meetings are where one can hear and share "experience, strength, and hope." This idea is one of the key ingredients to reducing shame and isolation. For many people who walk into a meeting for the first time, it is the first time that they realize that they are not alone! Not only does a meeting help reduce shame, but it also helps the individual find and build a support network. When you are recommending 12-step programs to congregants, be sure to preface that not all meetings may be helpful or healthy, just like any church or group, so they should try a meeting for a few weeks before they make any final judgments about it. Perhaps if Shawn had tried another 12-step meeting, he would have found one he enjoyed and connected with a sponsor and other men to journey with him in his recovery.

Sometimes, the best way to understand 12-step meetings is for pastoral counselors to work (actually go through) their own 12-step program. This may not necessarily be for sexual addiction, but perhaps for codependency or adult children of dysfunctional families. By working through the 12-steps yourself, you will have an intimate knowledge of what the program is about and will have a better understanding of recovery.

In addition to 12-step programs, there are "integrity" groups. These groups primarily focus on accountability. For those who struggle with the idea of traditional recovery or are resistant to identify as someone who has an addiction, these groups may be a great stepping-stone. This can be a helpful resource for male sexual addicts, but, unfortunately, there are not yet many accountability groups for women who struggle with sexual addiction. Some other factors to consider: often these groups are not enough to sustain long-term recovery, and they can come with costs; there is the cost of specific literature/ workbooks that need to be bought in order to participate or weekend intensives that often carry a hefty price tag. Even if the cost seems minimal, this can be a reason for some to not attend and may even be cost-prohibitive for churches that cannot afford to supplement the group. Yet having one of these groups, which are often facilitated by leaders who are trained for that specific program, can be a great way to introduce sexual addiction treatment options to church leaders who are hesitant to host a 12-step group or individuals who are hesitant to join one. Either way, if hosting a 12-step program or integrity group is not a current option for your church, be sure that you know of local meetings in your area. That way, you will have resources for those in your congregation.

Individual Therapy

In addition to 12-step recovery groups, therapy is an essential component to helping those who struggle with sexual addiction or compulsive pornography use. It is essential to have a relationship with a few therapists in your local area. The idea of finding a therapist, let alone making the phone call, can be an intimidating process, so having names on hand can break down this barrier for those struggling with sexual addiction. It is even better if you can refer to a therapist who specializes in and has specific training and certification in working with sexual addiction. This training is essential in helping clients work through such a specific issue; if there is no training, there is a higher risk for harm or, at the very least, inadequate treatment. As an example, a man (who we'll call Bill) was struggling with sexual addiction and worked with a previous therapist who said he specialized in working with sexual addiction, but had no formal training or certification. Bill sought out a new therapist because he was not able to maintain any sort of sobriety. As he and his new therapist explored why he was not able to maintain sobriety despite being in therapy, they realized that he was still very much living in shame. This shame was keeping him from reaching out to others for support and was leading him to feel even more isolated. What was most heartbreaking was that the first therapist had actually encouraged Bill to stay in the shame as a way to keep him from acting out.

Lastly, it is important to have a handful of therapist referrals on hand. It is a significant amount of work to care for people, and you are likely managing many responsibilities. Having the time to meet the needs of everyone in your church can feel like an impossible burden, and a good therapist will be able to help carry that burden. It is also important to know your limitations in terms of when to refer someone to a therapist. In the case of sexual addiction, it is paramount that they seek individual therapy.

Group Therapy

When money may be an issue, group therapy can be a viable option in place of individual therapy. It could be argued that group therapy may even be better than individual therapy in some ways, and it is also different than 12-step programs. Group therapy is facilitated by a therapist and often involves a fee, which is usually less than individual therapy session costs. Groups are also typically "closed," which means that once a group is formed, no new members can join; groups are often kept between four and eight members. Lastly, group therapy allows for direct feedback from peers in the moment; in contrast, "cross talk" (giving direct feedback or commenting about someone else in the group) in 12-step programs is not allowed. Many times, therapists will offer specific groups for both addicts and their spouses, and even groups for the couple. Groups tend to be more time-limited and focus on specific topics during each session. Again, if you are referring to a therapist that offers group therapy, make sure that he or she has specific training in working with sexual addiction. This will ensure that you are providing your congregant with the best care possible.

KEY TERMS

12-steps: originally created for Alcoholics Anonymous, but adapted for issues such as sexual addiction, gambling, or overeating, these groups provide support in recovery through peer accountability and sponsorship

Integrity groups: accountability-based groups targeting behavioral change

Individual therapy: meeting one-on-one with a trained psychotherapist

Group therapy: meeting as a group with one or two trained psychotherapists as facilitators

1. What resources does your church currently have? If you do not have any, what are the barriers that would keep your church from offering 12-step groups or other on-campus resources?

2. Have you ever attended a 12-step program or do you know someone who has? What was your (or his or her) experience like? If not, what do you imagine it to be like?

3. Do you have a working relationship with a few therapists in your area? If you do, what has been helpful about having this relationship? If not, how could this be a helpful resource?

4. What are your beliefs about therapy? Have you ever done your own therapeutic work?

SPECIFIC CRISIS SCENARIOS

Caring for the Couple in Crisis

It is likely that you will receive a phone call from a spouse who has just discovered his or her partner's sexual acting out in some way. Typically, the spouse will be deeply upset, possibly frantic, feel like his or her life is "upside down," and completely heartbroken. Their reaction is completely normal—the person's world has just been shattered.

In the pair-bond relationship created through marriage, spouses come to depend on one another as their secure base and secure attachment in the world. As discussed earlier, **secure attachment** can be conceptualized as the idea of trust in the context of a pair-bond relationship; it can be viewed as "a belief, confidence, and anticipation that a spouse will be consistently, reliably, and faithfully available, attentive, and responsive—physically, emotionally, and psychologically—to one's needs" (Zitzman & Butler, 2009, p. 213).

Trust is an inherent quality of any pair-bond relationship. In fact, God's commands regarding sexuality and marriage are for our own emotional and relational well-being! As noted by Zitzman and Butler (2009), pornography (and subsequently, sex addiction) disrupts the secure attachment one expects in a pair-bond relationship (p. 213). Further, many partners of sexual addicts actually show symptoms of post-traumatic stress disorder (Carnes, 2011, p. 20). For more information, see the chapter on trauma. While some might believe that the wronged partner is being controlling by obsessively checking the addict's phone or regularly talking about the addict's past actions, research and a better understanding of trauma has shown that these seemingly codependent or controlling behaviors may actually be an attempt to reestablish a sense of safety in his or her world, much like someone who has been severely traumatized (Carnes, 2011).This is because the disruption of a secure attachment leads to a loss of well-being similar to that associated with trauma. This loss of the spouse's secure attachment stems from the "realization that the [sex addiction] and perceived betrayal had been on-going during a time when the [spouse] had assumed they were safe and secure in a trustworthy pair-bond relationship" (Zitzman & Butler, 2009, p. 221). Instead, they have discovered that the addict was "choosing to engage in behavior that inflicted emotional harm or injury ... undermining positive self-esteem, self-concept, body image, and sense of self-in-relationship" (Zitzman & Butler, 2009, p. 225).

The addiction, and the lies and chaos that it often brings, shatters any attachment bond that the couple had (Zitzman & Butler, 2009). The deception surrounding pornography use, according to Zitzman and Butler (2009), leads spouses of sexual addicts to experience a globalized perspective of not being able to rely on their partner as an attachment provider. Because of this, their overall sense of self may be altered as well. Partners of sex addicts experience many negative emotions as a direct consequence of the sex addicts' behaviors.

One way to conceptualize these negative emotions is through the lens of grief. According to Carnes and Tripodi (2011), it is imperative to acknowledge and experience grief before one is able to get through one's pain (p. 48). Furthermore, grief allows the spouse of a sex addict to acknowledge his or her particular pain, losses, and sadness about the reality of sexual addiction in his or her life and relationship. Carnes and Tripodi (2011) argue that the process of grieving gives the spouse the opportunity to find and experience his or her authentic self through the process of examining and making space for the deep feelings from the loss (Carnes, 2011). However, many spouses struggle with this phase of healing because grieving requires them to think about themselves and focus inwardly. Some Christian women are taught to believe that anything self-focused is selfish and un-Christian (Waggoner, 2004), so the church has the opportunity to not only help wives of sex addicts with their particular grief but also to help them redefine and discover who they are in God.

Not only is it important to understand what is going on for both the individual struggling with sexually compulsive behavior and his or her partner, but it is also important to understand your own sexual history, values, pain, and how your sexual experience may affect your view of the addict, spouse, and the couple as a unit. By identifying his or her own values, beliefs, and history, the pastoral counselor can then better separate that from the particular pain of the couple, rather than **projecting** emotions, beliefs, or expectations onto the couple. The act of projection involves seeing one's traits or experiences in other people; one article calls it "cognitive bias" (Baumeister, Dale, & Summer, 1998, p. 1090). By eliminating excessive projection through looking at his own narrative, the pastor can be more present in the couple's pain. This will also provide more space to support both the addict and the partner with what *they* truly need, since those who have never dealt with their own issues regarding sex might be prone to give advice out of their own bias from their marriages or past sexual history. For example, a woman (whom we'll call Mary) is married to her husband, a sexual addict. She had been to two other therapists before she came into her current therapist's office. The first therapist told her that her only choices were to either divorce her husband or deal with his indiscretions. The other therapist told her that she should try being more sexual with her husband as a way to stop his acting out. She left feeling completely misunderstood and even hurt by their words. Neither of these therapists were addressing the real issue—her trauma, pain, *and* the reality of being married to a sexual addict. When an individual has been looking at pornography for as long as Mary's husband had, **mirror neurons** (a set of cells in the inferior frontal gyrus and inferior parietal lobe) are firing constantly. These neurons help the brain understand how something works so it can be repeated (Struthers, 2009, p. 95). As the husband's threshold for sexual excitement got higher and higher, it is clear that it would not help heal his sexual addiction if Mary was simply "more sexual" with him.

In addition to making space for sitting with this particular pain, providing the couple with accurate information about sexual addiction and offering helpful resources can tremendously help in reducing shame. If addiction thrives in darkness, then we want to bring it into the light. Churches have an amazing opportunity to help bring this issue into the conversation so that we can begin to better address this ever-growing addiction.

Caring for the Church in Crisis

According to Kinnaman (2016), a 2016 Barna research study surveyed 432 Christian senior pastors and found that:

- 57% of pastors reported that they had struggled with pornography, either in the past or currently;
- 12% of the pastors surveyed classified themselves as being *currently* addicted to pornography;
- 87% of pastors who currently use pornography feel significant levels of shame about it; and
- 55% of pastors who currently use pornography reported that they are in constant fear of being discovered.

Based on these statistics, over half of Christian senior pastors have struggled with pornography usage, and more than 1 out of 10 pastors are *currently addicted*. While many pastors are shepherding those in their congregation into recovery, a large percentage of them are dealing with their own secret struggle. Often, there is a fear of consequences, so getting treatment can feel impossible; there are questions, such as the following:

- What if I get fired?
- What if my congregation finds out?
- What if my wife wants a divorce?

While these are valid questions, we have seen in this chapter that if sexual addiction does not get resolved, it creates more separation of intimacy in relationships, the tolerance level in the brain is increased, and, typically, more risks are taken, furthering the chance that the person will be found out. If you or someone on your church staff is dealing with a sexual addiction, there is hope. You now have a wealth of information and resources at your disposal, including 12-step groups and individual therapy, among others, where confidentiality is 100% maintained. There have been many pastors who have walked this road of recovery, and they have found renewed hope in their freedom from addiction.

There are also valid questions concerning the congregation, especially if others in the church have been affected by the addiction. Unfortunately, the church is not immune to sexual abuse, and too often, victims have been silenced and left alone to cope with their trauma. Depending on the nature of the sexual addiction, each church has its own system of determining consequences: some pastors have been fired immediately; others have taken an indefinite leave of absence for recovery, and still others have chosen to permanently step down from their position but stay in the church. If others in the congregation have been mistreated or abused, there is the added necessity of making sure the congregation feels safe and heard. Open communication and education about sexual abuse and how to report it will be necessary elements in order to ensure safety of the church. If this has been a silent struggle on behalf of the church leader, with no victims, it may look different. There is not one way to go about this process, but if we are keeping in mind those early attachment wounds, it will be most healing to show grace, take action as needed, and provide support and resources. True healing comes through community.

KEY TERMS

Secure attachment: the belief and expectation that someone will be there to meet one's physical, emotional, and psychological needs

Mirror neurons: a set of cells in the brain that help teach someone how to repeat behavior that is necessary or desired

Projection: seeing one's traits or experiences in others

Discussion Questions

1   If a couple comes to you in crisis, what do you currently do?

2   Describe your own marriage. Talk about a time that you broke your spouse's trust and vice versa. How was it handled?

3   Have you had someone on your church staff disclose that he or she struggles with this issue? How was it handled? If not, what are the current steps that would occur if this issue arose?

4   What does your accountability look like in the church? If you are struggling with an issue, do you feel it is something you can bring to your church staff? Why or why not?

REVIEWING THE CONCEPTS

Learning Objectives

- Understand what sexual addiction is and how it presents itself
  - Sexual addiction is a compulsive need to view pornography, masturbate, act out sexually with others, compulsively fantasize, or engage in any other sexually compulsive behavior despite experiencing negative consequences.
  - Sexual addiction is not just a moral issue—it is an unwanted and progressive disease that often plagues the individual with shame, isolation, depression, and anxiety.
  - When sin entered the world, shame entered the world, and it is the fuel of addiction.

- Identify the etiology of sexual addiction at the societal and individual level
  - Pornography and other sexually compulsive behaviors hijack the brain's "reward system" into wanting more and more stimulation, which perpetuates the addiction.
  - If individuals are insecurely attached and did not grow up with emotional co-regulation, they are at a much higher risk for developing an addiction.

- Facilitate conversations about sexual addiction with their congregants
  - Understand the layers of sexual addiction
  - Actively listen
  - Don't assume
  - Ask thoughtful questions
  - Discern
  - Pray
- Have resources available for those struggling with sexual addiction
  - Recovery groups
  - Individual therapy
  - Group therapy
  - Ongoing education on this issue

Chapter Review Questions

Level 1: Knowledge (True/False)

1. Pornography is becoming less and less of a problem.

2. Masturbation alone cannot be considered a sexual addiction.

3. Women and men use pornography to objectify sex and the human body.

4. Pornography and sexually explicit content do not affect the brain until 25 years old.

5. We need intimacy to survive and thrive.

6. A child with a securely attached parent is often more susceptible to addiction.

7. It is better to seek healing in community rather than in isolation.

8. It is best practice to refer to a professional therapist when needed.

9. All 12-step meetings have the same group dynamic.

10. Church staff are immune to engaging in sexually compulsive behavior.

Level 2: Comprehension

1. Dysfunction in the addicted brain affects an individual
   a. biologically
   b. psychologically
   c. spiritually
   d. all of the above

2. In one study, what percentage of online pornography viewers were female?
   a. One-fifth
   b. One-fourth
   c. One-third
   d. One-half

3. In one study, 88.2% of porn videos contained what?
   a. Physical aggression
   b. Minors
   c. Role-play
   d. Drugs

4. What is the technical term for the pleasure center in the brain?
   a. Prefrontal cortex
   b. Cerebellum
   c. Hippocampus
   d. Ventral tegmental area

5. When do humans begin to explore their bodies and sexuality?
   a. Infancy
   b. Preschool age
   c. School age
   d. Puberty

6. When people are connected by being fully present, vulnerable, authentic, and available, it is called

    a. Dysregulation

    b. Intimacy

    c. Pornography

    d. Anxious attachment

7. Sexual addiction is an issue of

    a. morality

    b. emotional dysregulation

    c. a and b

    d. none of the above

8. The feeling of worthlessness that comes from thinking you *are* a mistake:

    a. Shame

    b. Guilt

    c. Reward system

    d. Intimacy

9. The ability to self-soothe and manage one's emotions is called

    a. co-regulation

    b. intimacy

    c. attachment

    d. self-regulation

10. Which of the following is not one of the pastoral tasks in talking with someone about his or her problematic sexual behavior?

    a. Quickly find a solution

    b. Actively listen

    c. Ask thoughtful questions

    d. Pray

Level 3: Application

1. Has your view of sexual addiction changed after reading this chapter? If so, how?

2. Describe the difference between guilt and shame, including examples of each.

3. A woman comes to you, upset, because she has just discovered that her husband has been compulsively looking at pornography and interacting via webcam with women online. She wants to stay in the marriage, but feels so betrayed and is regularly asking him questions about his behavior and activities; she feels she cannot ever trust him again. How might you help this couple?

4. Write a list of the different resources that your church already has, as well as what it could offer in the future to those struggling with sexual addiction.

5. An associate pastor confides in you that he has been regularly engaging in pornography, masturbation, and sexual fantasies. Using the five tasks of navigating conversations, map out your conversation with him.

ANSWERS

LEVEL 1: KNOWLEDGE

1. F
2. F
3. T
4. F
5. T
6. F
7. T
8. T
9. F
10. F

LEVEL 2: COMPREHENSION

1. d
2. c
3. a
4. d
5. a
6. b
7. c
8. a
9. d
10. a

RESOURCES

12 Step Recovery Programs

- COSA—For anyone whose life has been impacted by compulsive sexual behavior (spouse, partner, parent, child, sibling, etc.)
  - Cosa-recovery.org

- Codependents Anonymous—Addresses codependency
  - Coda.org

- Operation Integrity—A curriculum and model of recovery
  - Operationintegrity.org

- Sexaholics Anonymous
  - Sa.org

- Sex Addicts Anonymous
  - Saa-recovery.org

- Sex and Love Addicts Anonymous
  - Slaws.org

Readings

- *Shattered Vows*—Debra Laaser
- *Out of the Shadows*—Patrick Carnes
- *Facing the Shadows*—Patrick Carnes
- *Don't Call it Love*—Patrick Carnes
- *Addiction and Grace*—Gerald May
- *Healing the Wounds of Sexual Addiction*—Mark Laaser
- *The Pornography Trap*—Ralph Earle and Mark Laaser

CLASSROOM ACTIVITIES

1. Create a time line of your own sexual history, perhaps starting from your earliest memories of having romantic interests, being intrigued by your sexuality, etc., and working your way through school, relationships, adulthood, or marriage. Does anything stand out to you? How do you think this history affects your view of sex in the present?

2. Create a list of what the world and general society might say to a sexual addict; for every item, list a promise or truth from God that we hold as image-bearers.

3. Role-play a scenario—one classmate will be a church member coming in with a confession of a sexual addiction; the other classmate will facilitate the conversation using the five tasks listed in the chapter.

REFERENCES

American Society of Addiction Medicine. (2011, April 19). Retrieved from https://www.asam.org/resources/definition-of-addiction

Augustine. (1992). *Confessions* (Oxford World's Classics) (H. Chadwick, Trans.). Oxford: Oxford University Press. (Original work published AD 397–400).

Baumeister, R. F., Dale, K., & Sommer, K. L. (1998). Freudian defense mechanisms and empirical findings in modern social psychology: Reaction formation, projection, displacement, undoing, isolation, sublimation, and denial. *Journal of Personality, 66*(6), 1081–1124. doi: 10.1111/1467-6494.00043

Bridges, A. J., Wosnitzer, R., Scharrer, E., Sun, C., & Liberman, R. (2010). *Violence Against Women, 16*(10), 1065–1085. Retrieved from http://media.virbcdn.com/files/79/FileItem-273118-AgressionandSexualBehavior2010.pdf.

Carnes, P. J. (2016). Sexual addiction. Normal human sexuality and sexual and gender identity disorders, 1991–2001. Retrieved from https://www.iitap.com/wp-content/uploads/2016/02/ARTICLE_18.4-Sexual-Addiction-Patrick-Carnes.pdf

Carnes, S. (2011). What is Sex Addiction? In *Mending a Shattered Heart* (Second ed., pp. 7–23). Carefree, AZ: Gentle Path Press.

Carnes, S., & Tripodi, C. W. (2011). Is This Going to Get Better? In *Mending a Shattered Heart* (Second ed., pp. 41–62). Carefree, AZ: Gentle Path Press.

Dowshen, S. (Ed.). (2014, October). Understanding early sexual development. Retrieved from https://kidshealth.org/en/parents/development.html

Ferree, M. C. (2002). Sexual addiction and co-addiction: Experiences among women of faith. *Sexual Addiction & Compulsivity, 9*(4), 285–292.

Horin, A. (2007, May 26). One in three porn viewers are women. Retrieved from https://www.smh.com.au/articles/2007/05/25/1179601669066.html

Fight the New Drug. (2017, September 11). How many people are watching porn right now? Retrieved from https://fightthenewdrug.org/by-the-numbers-see-how-many-people-are-watching-porn-today/

Fight the New Drug. (2018, January 16). The most viewed porn categories of 2017 are pretty messed up. Retrieved from https://fightthenewdrug.org/pornhub-reports-most-viewed-porn-of-2017/

Katehakis, A. (2016). *Sex addiction as affect dysregulation: A neurobiologically informed holistic treatment*. New York, NY: W. W. Norton & Company.

Kelley, M. M. (2010). *Grief: Contemporary theory and the practice of ministry*. Minneapolis: Fortress Press.

Kinnaman, D. (2016, February 5). The porn phenomenon. Retrieved from https://www.barna.com/the-porn-phenomenon/#.VqZoN_krldU

Miller, A. (2008). *The drama of the gifted child: The search for the true self*. New York, NY: BasicBooks.

Monroe, M. (n.d.). Healing the wounds of relational trauma. Retrieved from http://empoweredtoconnect.org/healing-the-wounds-of-relational-trauma/

Parents Resource Hub. (n.d.). Retrieved from http://thenovusproject.org/resource-hub/parents

Peter, J., & Valkenburg, P. M. (2010). Processes underlying the effects of adolescents' use of sexually explicit Internet material: The role of perceived realism. *Communication Research, 37*(3), 375–399. doi: 10.1177/0093650210362464

Pornography. (n.d.). In Merriam-Webster's online dictionary (11th ed.). Retrieved from https://www.merriam-webster.com/dictionary/pornography

Sabina, C., Wolak, J., & Finkelhor, D. (2008). The nature and dynamics of Internet pornography exposure for youth. *CyberPsychology & Behavior, 11*(6), 691–693. doi: 10.1089/cpb.2007.0179

Struthers, W. M. (2009). *Wired for intimacy: How pornography hijacks the male brain*. Downers Grove, IL: InterVarsity Press.

Layden, M. A. (2004). Testimony for U.S. Senate Committee on Commerce, Science, and Transportation. Retrieved from http://www.drjudithreisman.com/archives/Senate-Testimony-20041118_Layden.pdf

Waggoner, B. (2004). *The myth of the submissive Christian woman: Walking with God without being stepped on by others*. Colorado Springs, CO: Alive Communications INC.

Ward, M. J., Lee, S. S., & Lipper, E. G. (2000). Failure-to-thrive is associated with disorganized infant-mother attachment and unresolved maternal attachment. *Infant Mental Health Journal, 21*(6), 428–442. doi: 10.1002/1097-0355(200011/12)21:63.0.co;2-b

Zitzman, S. T. & Butler, M. H. (2009). Wives' experience of husbands' pornography use and concomitant deception as an attachment threat in the adult pair-bond relationship. *Sexual Addiction & Compulsivity, 16*(3), 210–240. doi: 10.1080/10720160903202679

IMAGE CREDITS

CHAPTER 8

Eating Disorders

Angela Hanford, PhD

LEARNING OBJECTIVES

Upon completion of this chapter, readers will be able to

1. define the different types of eating disorders;

2. understand the dangers associated with eating disorders;

3. identify risk factors for developing eating disorders; and

4. understand eating disorder treatment.

When your healthy self is strong enough to deal with all that comes your way in life, your eating disorder self will no longer be useful or necessary.

(Costin & Grabb, 2011, p. 38)

TWO STORIES: SARAH AND AARON

Sarah

Sarah is a 16-year-old high school student who enjoys many activities. She is a leader at school, where she serves as the student body vice president. She also loves playing soccer and being a leader in her youth group. Somehow, she still finds time to sing with the church high school worship team. Sarah appears to have everything going for her, including a great family and friends. However, deep down, Sarah feels alone and that if people knew her, truly knew her deepest thoughts and feelings, they would run away. Although part of Sarah knows that she is loved, another part is scared. In order to keep her life together, to cope with her secret pain and the enormous amount of stress, she turns to food as a way to comfort herself. Since she does not want to gain weight, she also finds herself purging the food she consumes. She plans her life in a way that people won't find out, won't discover this secret. She does restrict her eating during the day, but not enough that people make comments. She knows how to play with her food so that it looks like she is eating. She drinks a lot of water so that she does not feel hunger. At night, when no one is around, she turns to her stash of food—what she describes as her relief at the end of the day. But that "relief" is momentary; then comes the waves of shame and guilt,

FIGURE 8.1   **Exploring people's relationship with food**

followed by throwing up, and then more shame and guilt. Part of her likes how she feels when she throws up because it is a way to punish herself, and then, afterward, she feels relief. Again, the relief does not last long before the cycle begins again. Sarah has cried out to God, but she feels as though He is not listening. Sarah wonders if maybe God is too mad at her and won't help her because of her eating behaviors. She knows that she is unhappy, but she does not know where to turn.

Aaron

Aaron is 25 and has struggled with insecurities for most of his life. Although he has friends and regularly goes to church, there is an emptiness deep inside. He works excessively to try to escape the overwhelming feelings of hollowness. Aaron believes that if he could attain the perfect physique, he would finally feel loved and acceptable to others. However, his hours and hours at the gym are not bringing the results he wants. Next, he decides to try to eat healthier, increasingly restricting his diet. All of this effort is cutting into his time with friends and making him more isolated. None of his friends know his secret or the immense load of guilt and shame that he carries every day, which is why he feels utterly alone and not worthy of being loved. He does not know where he can turn for help.

Like these two case studies, many people struggle with hidden hurts, including people in church congregations. To begin to help those who struggle with eating disorders, it is important to understand the difference between eating disorders and eating disorder behaviors. Eating disorder behaviors may be present, but they do not necessarily meet diagnostic criteria for a full-blown eating disorder. It is also important to empathize with the intense lonely and shameful experiences that accompany these conditions. The Academy for Eating Disorders (AFED) (2017) reported the prevalence of anorexia nervosa (AN) as 0.3% to 1% in young adult females. Bulimia nervosa (BN) appears even more common at 1% to 3% of young adult females (AFED, 2017). When examining unhealthy dieting behaviors, binge eating, and purging, as opposed to full eating disorders, those numbers jump to 4% to 20% (AFED, 2017). National surveys conducted in the United State have revealed that approximately 20 million woman and 10 million men will develop an eating disorder during their lifetime (Wade, Keski-Rahkonen, & Hudson, 2011). Furthermore, AN has one of the highest mortality rates of any psychiatric disorder (AFED, 2017).

These statistics indicate a strong likelihood that there are people suffering from eating disorders in your congregation. As the body of Christ, we can be there to show God's love and comfort to others who are in pain (John 13:13). We all have struggles and have sought comfort in unhealthy ways as well. The goal is to understand the unique needs of those suffering with eating disorders and to be able to share where God wants to meet them and comfort them in their pain. In 2 Corinthians 1:4, Paul writes, "Praise be to the God and Father of our Lord Jesus Christ, the Father of compassion and the God of all comfort, who comforts us in all our troubles, so that we can comfort those in any trouble with the comfort we ourselves receive form God" (New International Version).

AN OVERVIEW OF EATING DISORDERS

Eating disorders and eating disorder behaviors are prevalent in today's society. In fact, most people probably know someone who struggles with some type of disordered eating or body image concerns. Disordered eating and unhealthy body image do not have to meet clinical criteria for an eating disorder in order to have a significant negative effect on a person's life. For example, an individual may go from diet to diet, never actually meeting criteria for an eating disorder but still struggle with deep feelings of shame and low self-worth. Another person may restrict food and exercise frequently without enjoyment, not to the point of a diagnosable disorder, but still not content with themselves. Rather, this person is controlled by a need to attain a certain body size in hopes of feeling better emotionally. Neither person feels free or has a healthy relationship with food or exercise. However, hope lies in the fact that they could become free to live the lives that God intended if they are willing to learn how to deal with their pain in a productive manner.

As you may have noticed in these examples, eating disorders are not simply about food or appearance; rather, they have deep roots in feelings, such as inadequacy, shame, and emptiness. No matter how thin someone with AN becomes, it is never enough to feel satisfied with who he or she is. Restriction of food, purging, or other compensatory behaviors can actually be a way for the person to cope with the intense emotions that he or she does not know how to manage otherwise. Although treatment for eating disorders does require professional help, people in the church can support them as well by showing a desire to truly know them, especially in their pain. This is one way of demonstrating God's unconditional love to them. Furthermore, it is not just the individual who is diagnosed with an eating disorder who is affected. This illness can also have devastating effects on the lives of his or her family and friends. Again, this is where people in the church can step in and show love and support. For example, small groups can be a great place for people to feel emotionally supported. Mentors also offer useful spiritual guidance and support.

In order to truly come alongside someone with an eating disorder, it is vital to have an understanding of what eating disorders are, including the dangers, risk factors, and treatment approaches. Education is crucial and could save lives.

Diagnostic and Statistical Manual of Mental Disorders, 5th Edition Diagnoses

The *Diagnostic and Statistical Manual of Mental Disorders, Fifth Edition* (*DSM-5*) placed eating disorders under the category of feeding and eating disorders (FED). The diagnoses that fall in this category all have behavior that is related to eating, which leads to problems with food absorption or consumption, and results in significant impairment. The diagnoses included in FED are pica, rumination disorder, avoidant/restrictive food intake disorder, AN, BN, binge-eating disorder (BED), other specified feeding or eating disorder (OSFED), and unspecified feeding or eating disorder (American Psychiatric Association, 2013).

The purpose of this chapter is to focus on the more common problems that you will likely encounter at some point in your congregation, based on my experience as a clinician and the statistical prevalence as reported in the *DSM-5*. These include AN, BN, BED, and OSFED. We will briefly review all the diagnoses under FED, but give more attention to those diagnoses traditionally associated with eating disorders. All criteria mentioned in this section are provided by the *DSM-5*, unless otherwise stated.

1. **Pica:** Pica is a diagnosis given when an individual continually eats nonfood items that have no nutritional value, taking into consideration the person's developmental level. The *DSM-5* notes that the eating behaviors should also not be part of any normal practice of a given culture or social group in order for a diagnosis of pica to be given. Examples of types of food that might be consumed by someone displaying symptoms of pica are paper or dirt.

2. **Rumination disorder:** Rumination disorder occurs when someone frequently regurgitates his or her food. This food may then be rechewed, spit out, or reswallowed. However, these behaviors must not be related to a medical condition for a diagnosis of rumination disorder to be given. Rumination disorder is associated more frequently with certain groups, such as those with intellectual disabilities (American Psychiatric Association, 2013).

3. **Avoidant/restrictive food intake disorder:** Avoidant/restrictive food intake disorder (ARFID) is diagnosed when an individual avoids or restricts his or her intake of food, which then results in not meeting nutritional/energy needs (e.g., significant loss of weight). For this diagnosis to be given, the lack of food intake is not associated with not having access to food or other culture-specific practices, and it must not be caused by any other medical condition. Unlike AN or BN, ARFID is not associated with body image concerns. Examples of ARFID include a child refusing food because of sensory issues or an adult not eating because of a fear of choking or vomiting. For example, a child with sensitivity to texture may refuse to eat lettuce because it is "slimy" or chicken because it "feels weird." Again, AFRID is only diagnosed if the avoidance of food has significant consequences.

4. **Anorexia nervosa:** AN is characterized by an individual restricting food, which results in very low body weight. When defining what is considered low body weight, one must take into account a variety of factors, such as age and sex. For children and teens, this may be failing to develop at a normal rate and/or attain expected weight gain. The individual must also experience significant fear about gaining weight or engage in behaviors that prevent weight gain. Some behaviors that are used to prevent weight gain include excessive exercise, vomiting, diuretic use, and laxative use. Finally, an individual with AN experiences at least one of the following: distortion in how a person perceives

his or her body shape/weight, denial of the seriousness of his or her low body weight, or places a high degree of emphasis on body shape/weight in evaluating him or herself.

Once a diagnosis is made, a clinician will specify whether the type of AN is restricting type or binge-eating/purging type. The clinician can also specify that the disorder is in partial remission or in full remission, depending on symptom remittance. The severity of the disorder is then noted as mild, moderate, severe, and extreme.

According to the *DSM-5*, AN usually begins during the adolescent or young adult years and a stressor often precedes its onset. Although AN is reported more frequently in females, males also struggle with the disorder.

5. **Bulimia nervosa:** BN is diagnosed when an individual engages in frequent binge eating, followed by some type of behavior to prevent weight gain. For an eating episode to be considered a binge, the behavior must meet two criteria: (1) the eating must be in one distinct time period and a larger amount of food than most people would consume in a similar time frame and circumstance, and (2) the individual must experience a feeling of not being in control over the eating. In addition, to be classified as BN, the individual must also recurrently engage in unhealthy behaviors that compensate for eating in order to avoid weight gain (e.g., vomiting, diuretics, laxatives, excessive exercise). Finally, weight and body shape also play major roles in how the individual with BN evaluates him or herself. With a diagnosis of BN, a clinical can specify if the person is in partial remission or in full remission and a severity of mild to extreme.

Shame over eating behaviors is very common in people who are diagnosed with BN. Therefore, eating is typically done in secret (American Psychiatric Association, 2013). After the binge, an individual typically feels upset with what he or she has done, which can perpetuate a cycle of unhealthy coping. According to the *DSM-5* authors, the most common precursor to a binge is feeling negative emotions, although there can be a variety of other triggers (e.g., dieting, relational problems, stress). Compensatory behaviors, such as vomiting, can also be a way of coping with feelings. Throwing up may at first be a way to feel relief from a binge episode, but often, it turns into a binge-purge cycle (i.e., eat so one can vomit) (American Psychiatric Association, 2013; Fairburn & Brownell, 2002). It may be that the individual receives momentary relief from negative feelings by purging, as seen in self-harm behaviors, or uses purging as a form of self-punishment.

The onset of BN is typically during the adolescent or young adult years, and it is diagnosed more in females than males (American Psychiatric Association, 2013). According to the authors of the *DSM-5*, a precursor of a binge is often dieting, but could also be other life stressors. People who are diagnosed with BN typically have weights between normal and overweight (American Psychiatric Association, 2013).

6. **Binge-eating disorder:** BED is new with fifth edition of the *DSM*. In order to receive a diagnosis of BED, an individual must engage in recurring periods of binge eating. In addition, the binge behavior must have at least three out of five characteristics: eating quicker than normal, continuing to eat until feeling discomfort, eating a lot of food despite not feeling hungry, solitary eating because of feeling embarrassed, and feeling very upset (e.g., guilty) with oneself after the binge. The individual must also feel a significant amount of distress about the binge eating. Unlike BN, someone with BED does not engage in any behaviors to prevent weight gain.

   As with BN, an individual with BED also typically feels shame regarding his or her eating and, therefore, attempts to hide the eating disorder behavior. Similar to BN, a binge is most often preceded by negative emotions, but also could be triggered by other stressors (American Psychiatric Association, 2013). Those diagnosed with BED are typically normal to overweight to obese. The *DSM-5* authors noted that most people who are obese do not regularly binge.

   Although BED can begin in adulthood, it appears that BED often starts during the adolescent or young adult years (American Psychiatric Association, 2013). Dieting often occurs after the development of binge eating (American Psychiatric Association, 2013).

7. **Other specified feeding or eating disorder:** Most people who experience significant eating disorder symptoms do not meet diagnostic criteria for AN or BN (Hoek & Van Hoeken, 2003), and this is where the category of OSFED comes in. OSFED is used when eating disorder symptoms cause significant distress or impairment, but there are not enough symptoms to diagnose another specific eating disorder. Some examples of this diagnosis include

   - when all criteria is met for AN except for weight;
   - when behaviors associated with BN do not occur at the specified frequency; and
   - **night eating syndrome:** NES occurs when an individual engages in recurrent night eating after either waking up from sleep or after dinner. The person with NES is aware of the eating behavior and can remember eating. In order to be considered NES, the individual must experience distress or impairment.

8. **Purging disorder** (PD): PD occurs when an individual purges in an attempt to change weight and/or shape, but without binging.

9. **Unspecified feeding or eating disorder:** This category is very similar to the OSFED category. The difference here is that the clinician does not specify why the client does not meet criteria for another eating disorder diagnosis, or there is not enough information to solidify another diagnosis (American Psychiatric Association, 2013).

Body Dysmorphic Disorder

Body dysmorphic disorder (BDD) is not classified under the FED category, but rather under obsessive-compulsive and related disorders in the *DSM-5*. BDD is diagnosed when an individual is preoccupied with what he or she views as defects in his or her appearance. The defects are either very small or not seen by others. Also, the person either engages in "mental acts" (e.g., making comparisons) or behaviors that are repetitive in nature (e.g., checking in the mirror or picking at skin) (American Psychiatric Association, 2013). Lastly, the individual must experience significant impairment or distress because of the preoccupation.

Orthorexia

Orthorexia is a newer term, first proposed in 1997, and is not included in the *DSM-5*. Bratman and Knight (2000, pg. 9) defined orthorexia as "a fixation on eating healthy food" in an attempt to improve one's health and/or prevent disease. This "fixation" is obsessive and can result in nutritional deficits and medical complications. It should be noted that orthorexia is not simply eating healthy, but it is overly rigid and results in negative consequences. More research is needed on orthorexia.

Comorbid and Co-occurring Diagnoses

Comorbid diagnoses occur when there are two *DSM-5* diagnoses occurring at the same time. For example, an individual may be diagnosed with AN and major depressive disorder. This is in contrast to a **co-occurring diagnosis** (also called dual diagnosis), which means a substance use disorder and another psychiatric disorder. Alcohol use disorder and major depressive disorder would be considered co-occurring diagnoses.

Diagnoses that are frequently comorbid with AN include depressive disorders, anxiety disorders, and bipolar disorders. Obsessive-compulsive disorder is sometimes reported in individuals diagnosed with AN, especially those with restricting type. Substance use disorders, including alcohol, are also frequently reported with AN, especially those endorsing symptoms of the binge-eating/purging type (American Psychiatric Association, 2013; Fairburn & Brownell, 2002).

The *DSM-5* indicates that people with BN often experience another psychiatric disorder in tandem with BN symptoms. For example, there is an association between BN and depressive disorders, bipolar disorders, and anxiety disorders. Substance use, especially alcohol and stimulants, is estimated to be as high as 30% in patients with BN (American Psychiatric Association, 2013). Personality disorders, especially borderline personality disorder, have also been associated with BN.

According to the *DSM-5* authors, BED has similar comorbidity rates as AN and BN. It appears the most common diagnoses that occur with BED are depressive disorders, anxiety disorders, and bipolar disorders (American Psychiatric Association, 2013). Substance use disorders also can co-occur, but less so than with AN and BN.

Medical Complications

Medical complications for eating disorders can be severe and life threatening, which is why appropriate treatment is vital. Here is a brief overview of possible complications;

however, many more can also occur. To begin, patients diagnosed with AN are at risk for heart problems (e.g., bradycardia), blood pressure concerns, hypothermia, or organ problems. Amenorrhea also is a concern. This is when a woman stops having her period because of the restriction of caloric intake. In prepubescent females it can be a delay in menarche. Some people with AN develop lanugo, which is "a fine downy body hair" (American Psychiatric Association, 2013). Loss of bone mineral density, which may or may not be reversible, can also occur. Lastly, starvation can also result in symptoms of depression (American Psychiatric Association, 2013).

With AN purging type and BN, vomiting and other methods of purging (e.g., laxatives, diuretics, and enemas) may result in abnormalities in lab tests (e.g., electrolyte imbalances). Vomiting can cause esophageal ruptures and scarring, along with enlarged salivary glands and erosion of teeth. Marks on the hand can also be present due to inducing vomiting. Laxative use can result in serious problems with bowel movements. Irregular periods and amenorrhea can also occur with BN. Intestinal problems, including ruptures, can be the result of binging and purging behaviors. As with AN, heart and organ problems can also be a consequence of BN behaviors (American Psychiatric Association, 2013).

Medical complications can also occur with BED. Besides intestinal problems, including ruptures, heart disease and high blood pressure are other possible consequences.

Suicide Risk

Individuals who are diagnosed with AN and BN have an increased risk of suicide (American Psychiatric Association, 2013; Pompili, Girardi, Tatarelli, Ruberto, & Tatarelli, 2006). Birmingham, Su, Hlynsky, Goldner, and Gao (2005) found that, in their sample of participants, the most common cause of death from AN was suicide. In addition, depressive disorders, of which suicide is a symptom, can be comorbid with eating disorders. Therefore, a suicide risk assessment should always be conducted when treating someone with an eating disorder.

Whenever there is suicidal thinking present, it is important to seek professional help. If an individual is actively suicidal, he or she should immediately call 911 or go to the local emergency room. When assessing for suicide, clinicians look for suicidal thinking (called "ideation"), a plan, means, and intent. For example, a clinician will ask a client directly if he or she is having suicidal thoughts, following up with questions about any specific plans that he or she may have made. Please refer to Chapter 2 for further information on suicide warning signs.

A Pastor's Response

Because eating disorders can be a life or death issue, it is important for pastors to understand the signs of eating disorders in congregation members in order to make the appropriate referral to a professional. It might be helpful to have an eating disorder expert train church staff, particularly youth workers, on how to spot and respond to those who may be struggling with an eating disorder. Furthermore, it would be beneficial to have a referral list of competent Christian therapists who specialize in treating eating disorders. It is ideal to have the church and professional work together to promote hope and healing as the individual strives to become the person that God created him or her to be.

KEY TERMS

Pica: frequently eating nonfood items that have no nutritional value

Rumination disorder: frequent regurgitation of food

Avoidant/restrictive food intake disorder: avoidance or restriction of food, not associated with body image concerns

Anorexia nervosa: restriction of food, resulting in very low body weight and body image disturbance

Bulimia nervosa: frequent binge eating, followed by some type of behavior to prevent weight gain

Binge-eating disorder: recurring binge episodes without compensatory behavior

Other specified feeding or eating disorder: significant eating disorder symptoms that do not meet diagnostic criteria for AN or BN

Night eating syndrome: recurrent night eating, which results in significant distress or impairment

Unspecified feeding or eating disorder: significant eating disorder symptoms, but no specification of symptoms or there is not enough information to solidify another diagnosis

Body dysmorphic disorder: under the category of obsessive-compulsive and related disorders, the preoccupation with perceived deficits in appearance

Orthorexia: obsession with healthy eating/nutrition that becomes clinically significant

Comorbid diagnoses: two or more diagnoses occurring at the same time

Co-occurring diagnosis (dual diagnosis): a substance use disorder and another psychiatric disorder

Discussion Questions

1   What diagnoses appear to relate to Sarah's and Aaron's symptom presentations?

2   Why are eating disorders so dangerous?

3   What eating disorder behaviors have you seen firsthand in someone you know, and what made you notice?

RISK FACTORS AND OTHER CONSIDERATIONS

Risk Factors

A **risk factor** is a variable that increases the chance of a problem occurring. In this case, it is important to be familiar with the issues that make someone vulnerable to developing an eating disorder. In examining risk factors, it is important to understand that a risk factor does not necessarily imply causation.

Furthermore, it is important to understand that eating disorders are complex and multifaceted. Research has not determined one single risk factor or cause that creates an eating disorder, but rather that there are many factors that contribute to someone developing a problem. The good news is that not everyone who displays risk factors will go on to experience an eating disorder. That being said, we will review some factors that have been associated with the appearance of an eating disorder.

Biological

A variety of researchers have noted a tendency for increased family transmission of AN, BN, and BED (e.g., Fowler & Bulik, 1997; Strober, Freeman, Lampert, Diamond, & Kaye, 2000, 2001). According to the American Psychiatric Association (2013), research has demonstrated that there is an increased risk for developing an eating disorder when an individual has a first-degree relative (e.g., parent or sister) who has been diagnosed with an eating disorder or other mental illness (e.g., bipolar and depression).

However, it remains unclear as to precisely how the genetic piece factors into the equation. It has been hypothesized that genes may provide an individual with a genetic predisposition to a specific disorder that is then expressed when triggered by other risk factors. In addition, some researchers have suggested that hormonal and other neuro-logical factors may contribute to eating disorder behavior (e.g., Fairburn & Brownell, 2002). Further research is needed to clarify the genetic and biological connection to eating disorders.

In terms of gender, there is a higher incidence of eating disorders in women compared to men (American Psychiatric Association, 2013). There may be many explanations for this difference, including research methodology and participant recruiting. Regardless, it does appear as though women are reporting more eating disorders (American Psychiatric Association, 2013).

Family/Environmental

The AFED (Le Grange, et al., 2010) published a position paper regarding the role that the family plays in the development and treatment of eating disorders. In this paper, the authors stated that although "family factors can play a role in the genesis and maintenance of eating disorders, current knowledge refutes that idea that they are either the exclusive or even primary mechanism that underlie risk" (Le Grange, Lock, Loeb, & Nicholls, 2010). Therefore, it is important to not focus on placing the blame on family members as being the sole cause for why an eating disorder developed. Nevertheless, there can be dynamics in a family that contribute to or help maintain eating disorder behavior. Some family dynamics that have been associated with eating disorders include the following (e.g., Tozzi, Sullivan, Fear, McKenzie, & Bulik, 2003):

- Lack of emotional expression: an atmosphere that discourages emotional expression can be associated with eating disorder behavior. Therefore, it is important for family members to learn how to express and cope with emotions in a healthy manner
- Disconnected family
- A chaotic family environment
- Rigid or unclear emotional and physical boundaries (Fairburn & Brownell, 2002): *Boundaries are important in families. They help us to develop identity apart from another and also give safety as children and teens begin to explore the world. Having too few boundaries or too rigid of boundaries can become problematic to emotional and social development.*
- An overemphasis on the importance of physical appearance
- An overly critical family environment where perfection is the goal
- Emotional disorders, such as substance abuse (American Psychiatric Association, 2013)

It should also be noted that family dynamics may be a function of having someone in the family unit who is struggling with the eating disorder. For example, having someone in the family with an eating disorder may increase conflict in the family, as parents disagree on the severity or treatment options.

The good news is that although certain family dynamics are associated with eating disorders, the family can play an important role in an individual's recovery from an eating disorder (La Grange & Eisler, 2009. Especially for children and teenagers, family therapy can help each family member learn how to support the person who is in recovery and learn healthy ways of interacting with each other. In addition, family members can help instill a positive body image and teach healthy coping skills.

Cultural and Societal

One needs only to turn on the television, peruse social media, or browse a magazine stand to see that Americans live in a society where the perfect body is idealized. In Western culture, for women, it is the thin ideal that is prevalent. Cultural pressure also occurs with men. Although the American Psychiatric Association (2013) reported that AN occurs across cultures, research has indicated that it is "most prevalent in post-industrialized, high income countries." Since not all people in Western culture have an eating disorder, it has been hypothesized that other factors, including a possible genetic predisposition, are involved in developing an eating disorder. According to the National Eating Disorders Association (2018), research has demonstrated that exposure to a perceived ideal body type (e.g., thinness) is associated with an increase in body dissatisfaction. Body dissatisfaction, in turn, is a risk factor of eating disorders.

Polivy and Herman (2004) explain the **sociocultural model** of eating disorders. In this model, it is proposed that individuals are exposed to an ideal body image through media; the ideal image is then internalized; the individual begins to view herself or himself as being undesirable, which leads to changes in eating and behavior in an attempt to attain that ideal body image. All of this possibly leads to an eating disorder. Supporting this notion, the American Psychiatric Association (2013) reported that when the thin ideal body image is internalized, there is an increased risk for the individual to develop concerns about his or her weight. This, in turn, leads to increased risk for developing BN.

In addition to exposure to an ideal body type, experiencing bullying about weight and/or other size/weight prejudices can also be contributing risk factors to someone developing an eating disorder. You can see this influence not only occurring during the teen years but also throughout adulthood in the work and social environments

Although eating disorders occur across cultures, more research is needed within and outside of Western culture in order to truly understand how eating disorders may or may not appear on a global scale.

Trauma

Experiencing trauma or any life event that feels especially overwhelming may also precede the onset of an eating disorder. For example, researchers have found an association between emotional, physical, and sexual abuse and eating disorders (Brewerton, 2007; Kong & Bernstein, 2009). Not only do many abuse victims often suffer from shame and body image concerns, but when life becomes overwhelming, eating disorder behavior can provide the individual with perceived control over his or her life and/or a way to cope with overwhelming feelings.

Psychological Characteristics/Temperament

There are psychological traits and temperament factors that have been associated with increased risk for eating disorders. However, one's personality does not necessarily cause an eating disorder, as many people with similar characteristics do not develop eating disorders. Common psychological and/or temperament characteristics that have been associated with eating disorders include the following:

- Perfectionism: **Perfectionism**, which can be defined as having a much higher exception for performance than is warranted by the situation, is associated with the development of eating disorders, especially AN restricting type (Fairburn & Brownell, 2002). Those who are perfectionistic tend to set unrealistic standards for themselves.
- Feeling a lack of control in life: Eating disorder behavior can be a way for the individual to feel like he or she is taking back control when life feels chaotic.
- Tendency toward being highly self-critical: With high self-criticism, which is often accompanied by perfectionistic traits, one can develop an overall negative view of oneself, depression, or other types of emotional struggles.
- Emotional disorders (e.g., depression, anxiety, substance abuse): The American Psychiatric Association (2013) stated that people who have other psychiatric disorders, such as anxiety, have an increased risk for AN. Furthermore, it was also noted that an increased risk for BN was associated with symptoms of depression and anxiety.

- Obsessive and compulsive traits: **Obsessions** are recurrent thoughts or images. **Compulsions** are recurrent urges. Those with a diagnosis of AN also often display obsessive and compulsive traits (American Psychiatric Association, 2013). For example, they tend to obsess about food, even going to the extent of planning and cooking elaborate meals. Researchers have discovered that AN restricting type is associated with a personality style that is more obsessive (Fairburn and Brownell, 2002).
- Low self-esteem: Low self-esteem has been associated with eating disorders (e.g., Gual et al., 2002; Peck & Lightsey, 2008).
- Difficulty expressing emotions: Sometimes this is due to a family dynamic where emotional expression is avoided, or it can simply be an aspect of one's own psychological makeup. Regardless, many people who have eating disorders feel as though they are wearing a mask, needing to act happy and "together" in order to be accepted by others.
- Difficulty coping with emotions: Eating disorder behaviors, such as purging, food restriction, excessive exercise, or binging become a way for an individual to cope with emotions that he or she does not feel able to handle in a healthier manner (American Psychiatric Association, 2013).

Dieting

Although dieting alone does not necessarily cause an eating disorder, dieting has often been associated with the development of eating disorders, especially BN (Fairburn & Brownell, 2002). Furthermore, most people who diet do not go on to develop full-blown eating disorders. It is true that the diet industry promotes achieving an ideal body shape and weight as success. This exposure to the ideal body may lead to greater body dissatisfaction in those who do not meet that ideal. Rather than focusing on health and eating intuitively and mindfully, the dieting industry typically promotes restriction and achieving a certain body type. Another reason for this association may be that someone who has a genetic predisposition to eating disorders may go on to develop an eating disorder because of dieting (Fairburn & Brownell, 2002). In addition, dieting often increases obsession with and shame surrounding weight and food, which may also contribute to eating disorder behavior. Dieting becomes a cycle, where restriction and hope in change lead to shame when the results do not last, or weight loss is not achieved (Ekern, 2012). This could then lead to more dieting behavior. Furthermore, when foods are restricted and certain foods are labeled as "bad," this may increase the chance for binging (Fairburn & Brownell, 2002). Regardless of the reason for a connection with eating disorders, dieting often promotes an unhealthy relationship with food and one's body.

Sports and Career Factors

Certain athletic activities, such as dance, gymnastics, running, swimming, and wrestling, that focus on an individual maintaining a certain size and/or weight have been associated with eating disorder development (Fairburn & Brownell, 2002). Similarly, professions that require a specific size, such as modeling, have also been associated with eating disorders.

Special Populations

Men

Even though a large percentage of individuals who suffer from eating disorders are female, there are many males who also have eating disorders. Because of many factors, including the stereotype that eating disorders are a female problem, there can be added shame and reluctance to seek help. However, eating disorders are no less dangerous in men. There is a phenomenon called "**reverse anorexia nervosa**" or "**muscle dysmorphia**" that occurs mostly in males (Fairburn & Brownell, 2002). Reverse anorexia occurs when an individual perceives himself or herself as being very thin, but he or she is actually very muscular. This person becomes obsessed with gaining muscle and, to that end, engages in muscle building and diets. As Fairburn and Brownell state (2002), reverse anorexia is sometimes connected to steroid use. As with females, males who have eating disorders are at risk for severe medical complications

Childhood Eating Disorders

Although the highest level of onset for eating disorders is in adolescence and young adulthood, this does not rule out the onset of eating disorders during childhood. Furthermore, eating disorder behavior and concern about body shape and weight may sometimes begin in childhood. For example, a child may feel dissatisfied with his or her body and begin to take measures to lose weight. This might be a good time for intervention rather than waiting for a full-blown eating disorder. It should be noted that, although less frequently, children do develop diagnosable eating disorders.

Eating Disorders and the Internet

The Internet has many helpful resources for understanding eating disorders and where and how to seek treatment. For example, the AFED has resources for patients and caregivers on eating disorder education. However, there are other sites, such as pro-anorexia sites, that promote eating disorders and ways to "improve" and hide eating disorder behaviors. Social media, such as Instagram and Snapchat, are filled with images that promote the ideal body image and offer dieting and weight loss tips. Therefore, it is important to be careful with the Internet content that is being viewed.

A Pastor's Response

As a pastor, it is important to be aware of risk factors for eating disorders and who may be at risk or is suffering from one or more. A pastor is also in a position to help guide family and friends who suspect someone has an eating disorder. Furthermore, youth ministry is a great place for addressing the topic of identity. This could include ideas such as finding our identity apart from culture or maintaining a certain ideal. If these conversations are happening, then the youth pastor has an opportunity to teach about finding our identity in God. Developing a relationship and trust are primary when we have an opportunity to speak into someone's life. In light of a good relationship, we can overcome shame and encourage someone to develop his or her relationship with God.

In this case, it is important to understand what God's design is for us in our relationship with food and our bodies.

KEY TERMS

Risk factor: a variable that increases the chance of something occurring

Sociocultural model: a model for how eating disorders develop after being exposed to the ideal body image

Reverse anorexia nervosa/muscle dysmorphia: the perception of being very thin when, in fact, the person is muscular

Perfectionism: having a much higher exception for performance than is warranted by the situation

Obsessions: recurrent thoughts or images

Compulsions: recurrent urges

Discussion Questions

1   What are some risk factors for eating disorders?

2   Why does a risk factor not equal causation?

3   What risk factors have you noticed in people you know who struggle with eating disorder behavior?

4   How might you approach someone who you are concerned is exhibiting eating disorder behavior?

5   What is your reaction to eating disorders in boys and men?

6   What are the benefits and risks associated with the Internet, particularly in regard to eating disorders?

TREATMENT

A Multidisciplinary Team Approach

Because of the seriousness of these illnesses, eating disorder treatment is usually structured with a team approach. The team would consist of the patient, a physician, a psychiatrist, a registered dietitian, a psychotherapist, and other treatment professionals (e.g., equine therapist, case manager).

1. **Medical doctor:** Because of the medical complications that can occur with eating disorders, it is important to have a comprehensive medical evaluation by someone who works with eating disorders. A certified eating disorders specialist (CEDS) is a physician (or therapist) who has been certified through the International Association of Eating Disorders Professionals Foundation (IADEP). IADEP certified professionals have demonstrated the required education, skills, and experience in the treatment of eating disorders, as well as continuing education units in the area of eating disorders.

2. **Psychiatrist:** A psychiatrist is a medical doctor who specializes in treating patients who have mental illness and prescribe psychotropic medication. A psychiatric evaluation can help to determine if medication could be helpful in an individual's treatment, especially when someone has a comorbid diagnosis. The psychiatrist should be someone who works with patients who have been diagnosed with eating disorders

3. **Registered dietitian:** A registered dietitian is someone who has received the appropriate training from an accredited university (bachelor's or master's degree) and has completed all the requirements (including supervision and examination) for registration as a dietitian. The dietitian should have experience working with eating disorder patients. A certified eating disorders registered dietitian is a registered dietitian who has been certified through IADEP.

4. **Licensed psychotherapist:** A licensed psychotherapist could be a psychologist, a licensed marriage and family therapist, a licensed clinical social worker, or other counseling professional who is licensed to provide psychotherapy. As with the other treatment professionals, it is important to find someone who has experience treating patients with eating disorders. A CEDS is a therapist who has been certified through IADEP.

Level of Care

Eating disorders may be treated in a variety of settings, depending on severity of the problem and any medical or nutritional complications. The American Psychiatric Association publishes guidelines for determining which level of care is appropriate. The options for treatment settings include inpatient hospitalization, residential treatment center, partial hospitalization, intensive outpatient treatment, and outpatient treatment. The American Psychiatric Association guidelines (2010) include factors to consider when determining level of care, such as medical concerns, level of suicidality, weight, motivation for treatment/cooperativeness, control of obsessive thoughts, severity of co-occurring disorders, other psychiatric disorders that need hospitalization, whether a structured environment is needed for progress, purging behaviors and severity/level of control, environmental stressors (e.g., level of support), and if supervision is needed for meals and/or bathroom use.

1. **Inpatient hospitalization:** Inpatient hospitalization is considered the most restrictive or "highest" level of care. This setting is reserved for individuals who are not medically stable, acutely suicidal, or have other factors that require

hospitalization (e.g., very uncooperative with treatment or severe purging that has been unresponsive to outpatient treatment).

2. **Residential treatment:** Residential treatment is when the client lives at a treatment center for a specified amount of time in order to receive eating disorder treatment. Examples of clients who may need more support include those with poor motivation, those who have spent a significant amount of time battling intrusive thoughts, or those who require supervision at meals (American Psychiatric Association, 2010). Residential programs typically have nutritional counseling, psychotherapy (individual, group, family), medical oversight, and possibly other types of therapy (e.g., occupational, expressive arts, yoga).

3. **Partial hospitalization program:** A partial hospitalization program (PHP) is when the patient spends the day at the eating disorder program, but returns home at night. The client typically has medical monitoring (e.g., for medications), nutrition sessions, group therapy, individual therapy, and meals/snacks.

4. **Intensive outpatient program:** An intensive outpatient program (IOP) is when the patient lives at home, but treatment is usually 3 to 5 days a week from 3 to 4 hours each day. Patients typically have nutritional counseling, group therapy, individual therapy, and some meals/snacks. Family therapy may also be a part of an IOP program.

5. **Outpatient treatment:** Outpatient treatment is typically on a weekly or twice a week basis, depending on client need. Group therapy is also an option on an outpatient basis. During outpatient treatment, the client continues to see a registered dietitian and is monitored by a physician.

Stepping Down

When a patient is in a higher level of care, he or she often "steps down" to a lower level of care when ready. For example, someone who is hospitalized may go to a PHP, or someone in residential treatment may go to an intensive outpatient program. It can be difficult for an individual to go from one highly structured setting into the "real world," which is why a step-down approach can be helpful.

Recovery Groups

Recovery groups can be especially helpful for clients with co-occurring disorders. Groups such as Alcoholics Anonymous, Al Anon, and Narcotics Anonymous are examples of groups for those with co-occurring disorders. There are recovery groups that target eating behaviors, including Christian recovery groups. However, 12 step programs are not recommended as a first line of treatment. These types of groups should be explored with caution, and it is important that any group is not a weight loss group or a group that triggers eating disorder thoughts and/or behaviors. The reason that these precautions need to be considered is that when treating someone with an eating disorder, we want to encourage him or her not to focus on counting calories or working toward a specific body size. If the group focuses on weight loss, for example, this would go against the goal of learning to eat in an intuitive manner. Some recovery programs (e.g., residential and intensive outpatient) offer support groups for people who are in eating disorder recovery and their families. These may be safer since they are sponsored by eating disorder programs and often lead by therapists. There may be a Christian-based eating disorder treatment center in your area that has support groups.

Therapy Approaches

There are many different approaches to psychotherapy that can be used when treating someone who has an eating disorder. Here are several of these approaches.

Acceptance and commitment therapy (ACT): ACT focuses on changing one's behaviors based on one's values. Part of ACT is learning to accept feelings and to learn to respond to feelings (versus reacting) in a healthier manner. Mindfulness is used in ACT so that an individual can learn to live in the moment.

Cognitive-behavioral therapy (CBT): As the name implies, CBT examines, among other things, distortions in thinking (i.e., cognitions). In CBT, the goal is to challenge the distorted thinking, leading to a positive change in emotions and behavior.

Dialectical behavioral therapy (DBT): DBT is considered a cognitive-behavioral treatment. In DBT, there is an emphasis in skill building in such areas as distress tolerance, emotional regulation, and interpersonal relationships. There is also a focus on learning to accept dialectics in life. For example, one dialectic is the dilemma of acceptance versus change. Mindfulness is also a large component of DBT. DBT has individual therapy and group therapy components.

Family therapy: As implied in the name, this type of therapy involves the client and his or her family. There are many different types of family therapy approaches, such as behavioral family therapy, family systems, and the Maudsley Approach.

Interpersonal psychotherapy (IP): IP is a shorter-term therapy approach that examines interpersonal contributors to symptoms.

Psychodynamic psychotherapy: Psychodynamic therapy is a longer term therapy that explores internal conflicts and motives, family of origin dynamics that affect current functioning, and other unconscious drives to behavior.

A Pastor's Response

A person's relationship with God is very important in the healing of emotional wounds, including recovering from an eating disorder. Spiritual direction can be one area where pastors can help someone struggling with an eating disorder to explore his or her relationship with God. How we view God is tainted by our own traumas and past experiences. Offering spiritual mentors who understand eating disorders and respect the treatment process could also be an area where the church could aid in treatment. Ultimately, it is God who heals, but we (i.e., treatment professionals and pastoral staff/volunteers) can come alongside someone who struggles with an eating disorder as a unified team that provides support and encouragement. Working together is so important, as everyone has a unique role that he or she can play in coming alongside individuals who are struggling with eating disorders.

KEY TERMS

Inpatient hospitalization: the most restrictive or "highest" level of care, especially for medically compromised individuals

Residential treatment: the client lives at a treatment center and receives eating disorder treatment

Partial hospitalization program: the client spends the day at the eating disorder program, but returns home at night

Intensive outpatient program: the patient lives at home, but treatment is usually 3 to 5 days a week from 3 to 4 hours each

Outpatient: typically on a weekly or twice a week basis

Acceptance and commitment therapy: focuses on changing one's behaviors, based on one's values

Cognitive-behavioral therapy: examines distortions in thinking, leading to change in emotions and behaviors

Dialectical behavioral therapy: an emphasis in skill building in such areas as mindfulness, distress tolerance, emotional regulation, and interpersonal relationships. Dialectical dilemmas are also examined

Family therapy: therapy with the client and his or her family. Examples of types of family therapy include behavioral family therapy, family systems, and the Maudsley Approach

Interpersonal psychotherapy: examines interpersonal contributors to symptoms

Psychodynamic psychotherapy: explores internal conflicts and motives, family of origin dynamics that affect current functioning, and other unconscious drives to behavior

Discussion Questions

1. What do you see as the potential pros and cons of each level of care?

2. Why is "stepping down" important?

3. What are the benefits and dangers of support groups?

REVIEWING THE CONCEPTS

Learning Objectives

- Define the different types of eating disorders
  - Pica is characterized by frequent eating of nonfood items that have no nutritional value.
  - Rumination disorder occurs when someone frequently regurgitates food.
  - ARFID is the avoidance or restriction of food, but it is not associated with body image concerns.
  - AN is restriction of food, resulting in very low body weight, along with the presence of body image disturbance.
  - BN is characterized by frequent binge eating, followed by some type of behavior to prevent weight gain.
  - BED is recurrent binge episodes, without compensatory behavior.
  - OSFED is diagnosed when someone has significant eating disorder symptoms that do not meet diagnostic criteria for AN or BN.
  - NES, which is under the diagnosis of OSFED, is recurrent night eating, which results in significant distress or impairment.
  - Unspecified feeding or eating disorder is diagnosed when a person exhibits significant eating disorder symptoms, but the clinician does not specify symptoms or there is not enough information to solidify another diagnosis.
  - BDD is under the category of obsessive-compulsive and related disorders, and is characterized by the preoccupation with perceived deficits in appearance.
  - Orthorexia, which is not in the *DSM-5*, is an obsession with healthy eating/nutrition that becomes clinically significant.

- Understand the dangers associated of eating disorders
  - Medical complications can be severe and life threatening.
  - Examples of medical complications include heart problems, blood pressure concerns, hypothermia, organ problems, amenorrhea/irregular periods or delay in menarche (in females), bone density loss, depression, abnormal labs (e.g., electrolyte imbalances, esophageal ruptures, enlarged salivary glands, erosion of teeth, and problems with bowel movements).
  - Suicide should always be assessed, as those with AN and BN have an increased risk of suicide.

- Identify risk factors for developing eating disorders
  - A risk factor does not necessarily mean causation
  - Biological family/environmental
  - Cultural and societal
  - Trauma
  - Psychological characteristics/temperament

- Examples: perfectionism, feeling a lack of control, highly self-critical, emotional disorders, obsessive and compulsive traits, low self-esteem, difficulty expressing emotions, difficulty coping with emotions
    - Dieting
    - Sports and career factors
- Understand eating disorder treatment
    - A multidisciplinary approach
        - Medical doctor
        - Psychiatrist
        - Registered dietitian
        - Licensed psychotherapist
    - Level of care
        - Inpatient
        - Residential treatment
        - PHP
        - IOP
        - Outpatient

Chapter Review Questions

Level 1: Knowledge (True/False)

1. Eating disorders are primarily rooted in food and appearance.

2. Research has demonstrated that eating disorders have clear causes.

3. Orthorexia occurs when someone is fixed on healthy eating/nutrition, which results in nutritional deficits and medical complications.

4. Suicide is not common in people with eating disorders.

5. There is an increased risk for developing an eating disorder if a first-degree relative has been diagnosed with an eating disorder.

6. One primary cause of eating disorders is a chaotic family environment.

7. Women have higher reported rates of eating disorders than do men.

8. Reverse AN is when someone perceives himself or herself as very thin when, in fact, the person is muscular.

9. A PHP is when the patient lives at home, but treatment is usually 3 to 5 days a week from 3 to 4 hours each day.

10. The treatment of choice for AN is DBT.

Level 2: Comprehension

1. Which diagnosis is NOT in the *DSM-5's* category of FED:

   a. AN

   b. Pica

   c. BDD

   d. Avoidant/restrictive food intake disorder

2. If an individual frequently binges and then engages in a type of compensatory behavior as to not gain weight, then he or she would most likely be diagnosed with

   a. rumination disorder

   b. BN

   c. AN

   d. BED

3. OSFED is used when

   a. there is not enough information to solidify another diagnosis

   b. the clinician is unable to specify why the criteria is met

   c. the disorder is clinically significant, but does not meet criteria for an eating disorder

   d. a and c

4. NES is diagnosed when the individual

   a. recurrently eats at night

   b. the amount eating is larger than would be considered normal in a typical situation

   c. the person must not be aware of the eating behavior

   d. both b and c

5. What are common types of purging methods?

   a. Vomiting

   b. Cutting

   c. Laxative use

   d. a and b

   e. a and c

6. Which are co-occurring diagnoses?

   a. Major depression and alcohol use disorder

   b. Major depression and attention deficit hyperactivity disorder

   c. Major depression and heart disease

   d. Major depression and schizophrenia

7. Which are possible risk factors for eating disorders (could be more than one)?
    a. Genetic predisposition
    b. Bullying
    c. Major depression
    d. Family dynamics

8. Which is the "highest" level of care?
    a. Outpatient treatment
    b. Residential treatment
    c. PHP
    d. IOP

9. Which type of care is necessary for a patient who is medically compromised?
    a. Inpatient hospitalization
    b. Residential treatment
    c. PHP
    d. Outpatient treatment

10. What are therapy approaches that are used for treating eating disorder?
    a. DBT
    b. Family therapy
    c. Systematic conversion therapy
    d. a and b

Level 3: Application

1. A teenage girl reports that another youth member has been purging every day. What is your initial response? How would you follow up?

2. How would you react if someone came to you saying that he or she wanted to die? What steps would you take to assess the person, and what referrals might you make?

3. Describe the sociocultural model of eating disorders. What role could the church take in protecting teens from the cultural influences on body image?

4. Why is a multidisciplinary team approach needed for treating eating disorders? What role could a pastor or other church leaders play on the team?

5. What is a pastor's role in treating eating disorders? What scriptures do you see that show us who we are in Jesus?

ANSWERS

LEVEL 1: KNOWLEDGE

1. F
2. F
3. T
4. F
5. T
6. F
7. T
8. T
9. F
10. F

LEVEL 2: COMPREHENSION

1. c
2. b
3. d
4. a
5. d
6. a
7. a, b, c, d
8. b
9. a
10. d

RESOURCES

Online Resources

- National Eating Disorders Association—nationaleatingdisorders.org
- Academy for Eating Disorders—aedweb.org
- International Association of Eating Disorders Professionals—iadep.com
- National Alliance on Mental Illness—nami.org

- National Institute of Mental Health—nimh.hih.gov/index.shtml
- National Suicide Prevention Lifeline—suicidepreentionlifeline.org
- Timberline Knolls Residential Treatment Center—timberlineknolls.com
- The Meadows Ranch—meadowsranch.com

Readings

- *Life Without Ed: How One Woman Declared Independence from Her Eating Disorder and How You Can Too* (2003)—Jenni Schaefer
- *Goodbye Ed, Hello Me: Recover from Your Eating Disorder and Fall in Love with Life* (2009)—Jenni Schaefer
- *The Eating Disorder Sourcebook: A Comprehensive Guide to the Causes, Treatments, and Prevention of Eating Disorders* (2006)—Carolyn Costin
- *The Treatment of Eating Disorders: A Clinical Handbook* (2011)—Carlos M. Grilo and James E. Mitchell

Crisis Hotlines

- National Suicide Prevention Lifeline: 800-273-TALK
- Suicide Prevention Crisis Hotline: 877-7CRISIS
- National Hopeline Network: 800-SUICIDE
- Cutting Yourself?: 800-DONTCUT

CLASSROOM ACTIVITIES

1. Role-play counseling someone whose family member is concerned about his or her loved one having an eating disorder.
2. Role-play talking with a teenager about an eating disorder.
3. Brainstorm ways in which the church can be more active in education and care for those who struggle with an eating disorder and their loved ones.
4. Explore personal reflections on your own struggle with food or body image.

REFERENCES

Academy for Eating Disorders. (2017). Fast facts on eating disorders: How common are eating disorders. Retrieved from https://www.aedweb.org/learn/resources/fast-facts#8

American Psychiatric Association (2010). Practice guideline for the treatment of patients with eating disorders (3rd ed.). Retrieved from https://psychiatryonline.org/pb/assets/raw/sitewide/practice_guidelines/guidelineeatingdisorders.pdf

American Psychiatric Association. (2013). *Diagnostic and statistical manual of mental disorders* (5th ed.). Washington, DC: Author.

Brewerton, T. D. (2007). Eating disorders, trauma, and comorbidity: Focus on PTSD. *Eating Disorders*, 15 (4), 285–304.

Birmingham, C. L., Su, J., Hlynsky, J.A, Goldner, E.M., & Gao, M. (2005). The mortality rate from anorexia nervosa. *International Journal of Eating Disorders, 38(2)*, 143–146.

Bratman S., Knight, D. (2000). *Health food junkies. Orthorexia nervosa—overcoming the obsession with healthful eating*. New York, NY: Broadway.

Costin, C., & Grabb, G. S. (2011). *8 keys to recovery from an eating disorder: Effective strategies form therapeutic practice and personal experience*. New York, NY: W.W. Norton & Company, Inc.

Ekern, J. (reviewed) (2012). Dieting and eating disorders. Retrieved from https://www.eatingdisorderhope.com/treatment-for-eating-disorders/specialissues/dieting

Fairburn, C. G., & Brownell, K. D. (2002). *Eating disorders and obesity (2nd ed.): A comprehensive handbook*. New York, NY: Gulford Press.

Fowler, S. J., & Bulik, C. M. (1997). Family environment and psychiatric history in women with binge-eating disorder and obese controls. *Behavior Change, 14* (2),106–112.

Gual, P., Pérez-Gaspar, M., Martínez-González, M. A., Lahortiga, F., Irala-Estévez, J.D, & Cervera-Enguix, S. (2002). Self-esteem, personality, and eating disorders: Baseline assessment of a prospective population-based cohort. *International Journal of Eating Disorders, 31 (3)*, 261–273.

Hoek, H.W., & Van Hoeken, D. (2003). Review of the prevalence and incidence of eating disorders. *International Journal of Eating Disorders, 34 (4)*, 383–396.

Kong, S., & Bernstein, K. (2009). Childhood trauma as a predictor of eating psychopathology and its mediating variables in patients with eating disorders. *Journal of Clinical Nursing, 18(13)*, 1897–1907.

Le Grange, & Eisler, I. (2009). Family interventions in adolescent anorexia nervosa. *Child and Adolescent Psychiatric Clinics of North America*, 18(1), 159–173.

Le Grange D., Lock, J., Loeb, K., & Nicholls, D. (2010). Academy for eating disorders position paper: The role of the family in eating disorders. *International Journal of Eating Disorders, 43* (1), 1–5.

National Eating Disorders Association (2018). Body image. Retrieved from https://www.nationaleatingdisorders.org/body-image-0

Peck, L. D. and Lightsey, O. R. (2008). The eating disorders continuum, self-esteem, and perfectionism. *Journal of Counseling & Development, 86* (2), 184–192.

Polivy, J., & Herman, C. P. (2004). Sociocultural idealization of thin female body shapes: An introduction to the special issue on Boyd image and eating disorders. *Journal of Social and Clinical Psychology, 23* (1), 1–6.

Pompili, M., Girardi, P., Tatarelli, G., Ruberto, A., & Tatarelli, R. (2006). Suicide and attempted suicide in eating disorders, obesity and weight-image concern eating behaviors, *Eating Behaviors, 7*(4), 384–394.

Strober, M., Freeman, R., Lampert, C., Diamond, J., & Kaye, W. (2000). Controlled family study of anorexia nervosa and bulimia nervosa: Evidence of shared liability and transmission of partial syndromes. *American Journal of Psychiatry, 157*(3), 393–401.

Strober, M., Freeman, R., Lampert, C., Diamond, J., & Kaye, W. (2001). Males with anorexia nervosa: A controlled study of eating disorders in first-degree relatives. *The International Journal of Eating Disorders*, *29*(3), 263–269.

Tozzi, F. Sullivan, P. F., Fear, J. L., McKenzie, J., & Buik, C. M. (2003). Causes and recovery in anorexia nervosa: The patient's perspective. *International Journal of Eating Disorders*, *33*(2), 143–154.

Wade, T. D., Keski-Rahkonen, A., & Hudson, J. (2011). Epidemiology of eating disorders. In M. Tsuang and M. Tohen (Eds.), *Textbook in psychiatric epidemiology* (3rd ed., pp. 343–360). New York, NY: Wiley.

IMAGE CREDITS

CHAPTER 9

Severe Mental Illness

Lauren Richardson, PhD

LEARNING OBJECTIVES

Upon completion of this chapter, readers will be able to

1. broadly define and provide examples of severe mental illness;

2. understand key features and symptoms of schizophrenia;

3. be familiar with typical treatment for severe mental illness and what to consider when referring;

4. identify several key areas of impairment for individuals with severe mental illness;

5. learn specific ways to interact with individuals who suffer from a severe mental illness, including issues of safety and homelessness; and

6. understand the support necessary for family members of individuals with severe mental illness.

"No great mind has ever existed without some touch of madness."
—Aristotle

INTRODUCTION TO SEVERE MENTAL ILLNESS

Caleb and His Family

Melony and Chris requested to meet with their pastor in order to seek counsel regarding their son, Caleb, and his mental health issues. Caleb was 19 years old when his parents first noticed something was off with him. They described that he seemed more aloof, became increasingly isolated, and struggled with his college courses. They made attempts to support him and inquire about what might be occurring, but these efforts to connect were not reciprocated by Caleb.

FIGURE 9.1   Journey With Severe Mental Illness

His parents shared that Caleb's situation became much worse about a year later. They noticed that Caleb rarely left his room to attend class or to go to work. In addition, he was not eating regular meals. Melony shared that during that same window of marked decline, in Caleb's room, she found what she described as candle wax art. Several abstract candle wax structures were spread around his room and affixed to pieces of furniture. When Melony asked her son about the wax, she learned that Caleb had also been consuming it and thought that he needed to do so to "ward off evil." Chris shared that he tried to reason with Caleb and "talk some sense into him." However, instead of helping his son, this agitated Caleb to the point of engaging in a physical altercation with his father. Melony called the police during this traumatic experience, and the police determined that Caleb needed to go to the hospital.

They shared that Caleb was hospitalized for 7 days. During that time, medical and mental health professionals shared more with them regarding the nature of Caleb's symptoms. Caleb also believed that he was a part of a special group that needed to wear a specific clothes patch to "ward off evil people." He had shared that he regularly heard a voice tell him that he needed to protect himself with the patch. Mental health professionals had described this as auditory hallucinations and explained that Caleb was regularly focusing on his need to have this patch to protect himself. Melony and Chris were further provided education on Caleb's diagnosis of schizophrenia. They were also directed by the social worker at the hospital to seek further treatment for Caleb.

Melony and Chris explained to their pastor that they are struggling with sadness and grief over their son's diagnosis. Caleb is currently attending an outpatient treatment program through the hospital and regularly meeting with a psychiatrist. He was resistant to this at first but mental health professionals, along with his parents, helped Caleb realize that attending treatment would help him return to work, which was a hope of Caleb's. His parents find it challenging to understand that Caleb still focuses on his need to keep evil people away; he discusses this frequently. However, he is no longer consuming wax or wearing his clothes patch. They struggle to connect with him and to discern the best way to support him. They worry about what this means for their family and seem to be looking for support from their church.

Depending on the church setting, pastors and ministry workers are likely to encounter individuals who suffer from severe mental health issues. Churches serving a population of lower socioeconomic status individuals—that is, a person's economic and social position as defined by level of education, income, and occupation—will likely have a higher chance of needing to address and support individuals and families with severe mental illness (Hudson, 2005). Several key issues should be understood and addressed in these situations. In this chapter, I will provide a brief definition of severe mental illness, a description of schizophrenia, cover the potential issues related to severe mental illness within the church community, and, finally, offer some considerations for supporting individuals and families.

Definition

One specific definition of severe mental illness is not agreed upon among professionals in the mental health community; however, a few key features are often included when describing severe mental illness. **Severe mental illness** is typically characterized as a mental health disorder that is persistent, includes a severe level of pathology/symptomology (e.g., psychosis, mania), and a significant degree of functional impairment (e.g., Gregoire, 2000; Mental Illness, 2017).

These key features have a significant level of interplay with each other. Persistence includes a *consistent* presence of severe symptoms and functional impairment. This is compared to acute conditions, such as a drastic, immediate response to trauma that diminishes a short time after the traumatic event (within 6 months). The next key feature involves the severity of the illness. Mental health issues are considered severe when there is a high degree of symptoms and the symptoms are recurring. For example, an individual with a *mild* form of major depressive disorder might feel hopeless, have decreased appetite, and low motivation. Despite these symptoms, this individual is most likely still able to maintain employment. However, an individual with a *severe* form of major depressive disorder will have several symptoms, including suicidal thoughts, and will have significant difficulties maintaining employment and social connections.

The last significant marker of severe mental illness is **functional impairment,** which includes significant difficulties engaging in and managing key components of daily living. Functional impairment in individuals with severe mental health issues is often global, meaning multiple areas are affected, such as the occupational, social, and psychological aspects of their lives. This will be discussed further in subsequent sections.

Prevalence and Related Factors

The National Institute of Mental Illness estimated that 10.4 million, 4.2% of the population, suffered from a severe mental illness in 2016 (Mental Illness, 2017). Examples of severe mental health disorders include the following:

- Bipolar 1 disorder
- Schizophrenia
- Severe major depressive disorder
- Severe form of an anxiety disorder that affects several levels of daily functioning
- Any other disorder that *significantly* affects several levels of daily functioning

Individuals with severe mental health issues often have a family history of severe mental health as well. For example, with schizophrenia, various researchers have found a high concordance rate of schizophrenia among identical twins (53%) versus a lower rate (15%) among fraternal twins (Tsuang, Glatt, & Faraone, 2011). Because of the 100% genetic similarity of identical twins, researchers have concluded that there is a high genetic component for schizophrenia. However, research also shows that the experience of early life stress or trauma in addition to a genetic predisposition is a significant risk factor for developing a severe mental health disorder in adulthood. A correlation between schizophrenia and childhood relational/interpersonal trauma (e.g., abuse or highly conflictual relationship with parents) has been identified (Read & Ross, 2003; Shattock, Berry, Degnan, & Edge, 2017).

Severe mental health issues often co-occur with addiction issues. Researchers have estimated that 50% of individuals diagnosed with schizophrenia have some type of substance use disorder (Green, Drake, Brunette, & Noordsy, 2007). Typically, the presence of a co-occurring addiction issue relates to a combination of biological and environmental factors, as well as using substances to cope with symptoms. Ministry workers will want to be aware of this co-occurrence and familiarize themselves with addiction issues as well (see Chapter 6).

A common experience for individuals with severe mental health issues is recurrent hospitalization. Hospitalization becomes necessary when the individual is a danger to him/herself or others. Some examples of this include suicidal/homicidal ideation and/or an inability to care for oneself such that it becomes life threatening. For example, an individual with schizophrenia might need to be hospitalized if he or she is no longer drinking water or eating food and is regularly consuming a nonedible product. Hospitalization is likely to recur when the individual ceases his or her medication, resulting in an increase in symptoms.

KEY TERMS

Severe mental illness: mental health disorder that is persistent, includes a severe level of pathology/symptomology, and a significant degree of functional impairment

Functional impairment: significant difficulties engaging in and managing key components of daily living, such as psychological, social, and occupational abilities

Discussion Questions

1 Reflect on your previous understanding of severe mental illness. Based on the earlier information, how has it changed, if at all?

2 What are some challenges that individuals and families might face with recurrent hospitalization for mental health issues?

3 Sometimes, it is not apparent that an individual is suffering from a severe mental health issue. How might you be aware of and sensitive to this issue within your church community?

PSYCHOTIC DISORDERS AND SCHIZOPHRENIA

Symptoms of Schizophrenia

Psychotic disorders are characterized by several symptoms that greatly affect the functioning of the individual, much like Caleb's experience earlier. The symptoms include delusions, hallucinations, disorganized motor functioning, disorganized thinking or speech, and a cluster of behaviors called negative symptoms (American Psychiatric Association, 2013). These will be delineated next. The type and degree of symptoms will vary between people experiencing psychosis; thus, there is a spectrum of psychotic disorders, with schizophrenia being one of the more severe disorders. Not all people who experience psychotic symptoms are diagnosed with schizophrenia. It is important to keep in mind the range of severity so that sweeping generalizations regarding psychosis are not made and reasonable expectations are held regarding prognosis. For example, an individual might experience a brief episode of psychotic symptoms as a result of drug use. Typically, symptoms subside after a significant period of sobriety and marked improvement is observed (American Psychiatric Association, 2013). However, in the case of Caleb, symptoms are pervasive and will remain even with medication use. In this section, the various psychotic symptoms will be described briefly.

Delusions are defined as beliefs about oneself or others that are not likely to be changed despite alternative evidence. Caleb experienced a delusion in the form of believing that he could ward off evil people by consuming candle wax. His delusion remained despite significant efforts by his family to reason with him. Some delusions might be bizarre in this way; however, some delusions might seem highly plausible but are still discernable as not true. For example, an individual might have a delusion that an ex-boyfriend is stalking him, but there is no evidence to indicate that this is true. This type of delusion would not be considered bizarre (American Psychiatric Association, 2013). Also, common types of delusions are ones that center on religious/spiritual content, which can make it challenging for pastors to discern (Tsuang et al., 2011).

Hallucinations are the occurrence of perceptual experiences despite the absence of an external stimulus. Hallucinations generally are clear and vivid for the individual and are experienced as a typical perception. Also, hallucinations can be in the form of any sensory modality (e.g., tactile); however, auditory hallucinations are the most common. Caleb experienced auditory hallucinations when he heard his friend talk to him about the evil people (American Psychiatric Association, 2013).

The presence of hallucinations and delusions might contribute to an experience of **paranoia** by the individual. Paranoia is the preoccupation with delusions, hallucinations, thoughts, and/or experiences that center on feelings of persecution or grandiosity. For example, Caleb was focused on protecting himself from evil people that might harm him. Individuals who experience the symptom of paranoia might also present as hostile, aggressive, or violent (Tsuang et al., 2011).

Disorganized thinking, speech, and motor behavior are also key symptoms of psychotic disorders. **Disorganized thinking or speech** is characterized by one of the following: loose associations, tangential thoughts, or incoherent communication. These symptoms significantly affect the person's ability to communicate and interact with others. **Disorganized motor behavior** is defined as the presence of some type of abnormal behavior that typically affects daily functioning. Some examples include increased levels of or excessive motor agitation, rigid posture, significant lack of verbal or motor behaviors, and repetitive movements. Both disorganized thinking/speech and motor behaviors have a significant effect on the individual's ability to interact and meaningfully connect with others, which might contribute to an experience of isolation and lack of social support (American Psychiatric Association, 2013).

A cluster of symptoms called **negative symptoms** are a key feature of schizophrenia and are sometimes present within other psychotic disorders. This group of symptoms is characterized by an absence of typical emotional and relational behaviors. Some examples include decreased emotional expression (especially in body language and facial expression), decreased motivation for self-directed activities (avolition), decreased verbal expression, decreased experience of pleasure, and decreased interest in social interactions (American Psychiatric Association, 2013).

An individual diagnosed with **schizophrenia** will exhibit at least two of the earlier symptoms of psychosis. The person's functioning in at least one domain will be significantly impaired (e.g., occupational). In addition, the disturbance of functioning and symptoms are present for at least 6 months. This disorder is typically considered one of the most severe psychotic disorders (American Psychiatric Association, 2013). The National Institute of Mental Health reported that approximately 0.25% to 0.64% of the U.S. population suffers from some type of psychotic disorder, including schizophrenia (Schizophrenia, 2018). However, despite lower prevalence rates, the National Institute of Mental Health also reports that schizophrenia is ranked in the top 15 of leading disabilities in the United States.

How to Interact With Someone Experiencing Psychosis
Given the earlier symptoms, one might find it difficult to discern a helpful way to interact with someone who presents with psychotic symptoms. Because of the often bizarre and significant pervasiveness of the symptoms, ministry workers might feel unsure, tentative, or anxious about interacting in a supportive way with an individual

experiencing psychosis. Because of this discomfort, a common response is to seek to reground the individual in reality, especially when interacting with someone who has active hallucinations and/or delusions. This was the case with Caleb's father, Chris. Although well intentioned, this type of approach will not be helpful and is likely to foster more resistance and defensiveness from the individual and in some cases physical aggression. The best approach is to engage the individual as you would another person, unless there is an issue of safety. (Safety issues will be discussed next.) For example, Caleb's father might ask him about his candle wax art and its purpose. The reason for this approach is to gather more information regarding the seriousness of the situation. Post-treatment, Caleb's parents will want to foster a connection with Caleb, such as showing an interest in his daily activities and goals. Although there are many barriers to interacting with someone who has psychotic symptoms, the core of the interaction should include establishing a supportive relationship with the individual.

Various components should be considered when seeking to refer someone to treatment for psychotic symptoms. Often, individuals in the throes of psychotic symptoms become a danger to themselves or others. When this is the case, the individual needs to be taken to the hospital, or the police need to be contacted. If the individual is not a danger to him/herself or others, it would be best to consider referring the individual to a psychiatrist or a medical/mental health professional, especially one connected to a hospital. It is best to get the family involved, when appropriate, since the individual is not likely to communicate the issues lucidly because of the pervasive effect of the psychotic symptoms. If an individual with psychotic symptoms is resistant to seeking professional help, which is often the case because of a lack of insight into the issue, you can help the individual identify a motivating factor for seeking help. For example, Caleb wanted to return to work and had some awareness that he was not able to do so. His family helped him realize that by regularly attending treatment, he would get help with being able to take steps toward identifying and accomplishing his vocational goals.

In summary, here are some key ideas to keep in mind when interacting with someone with psychotic symptoms:

- Establish a supportive connection with the individual by acknowledging his or her experience, while remembering that it is not based in reality. Reflecting back the person's words or phrases, for example, can be helpful.
- Ask questions about the individual's interests and goals.
- Limit attempts to ground the individual in reality or to confront odd thoughts.
- Put safety first and consider whether there is a need for referral. If you are consistently uncomfortable in the individual's presence, or feel anxiety or worry about encountering him or her, it might be an indication to consult with a mental health professional about a referral.

These suggestions do not address all situations, of course, but are helpful as general guidelines.

KEY TERMS

Psychotic disorders: mental health disorder characterized by symptoms of delusions, hallucinations, impairments in motor functioning, disorganized thinking or speech, and negative symptoms

Delusion: belief that is not likely to be changed despite alternative evidence

Hallucination: presence of perceptual experience despite the absence of an external stimulus

Paranoia: preoccupation with delusions, hallucinations, thoughts, and experiences that are centered on feelings of persecution or grandiosity

Disorganized speech: the presence of loose associations, tangential thoughts, or incoherent communication that further affect the individual's ability to communicate effectively

Disorganized motor behavior: abnormal behavior that typically affects daily functioning

Negative symptoms: psychotic symptoms characterized by an absence of typical emotional and relational behaviors

Schizophrenia: the presence of two or more psychotic symptoms and significant impairment in functioning for at least 6 months

Discussion Questions

1 Reflect on your personal comfortability in interacting with someone with psychotic symptoms. How might you interact with an individual with psychosis given what you just read? What support might you need?

2 How does your background and culture inform your understanding and perception of schizophrenia? How has this perception shifted, if at all, given what you have read thus far?

TREATMENT AND ASSESSING NEED FOR REFERRAL

Typical Treatment

Treatment for individuals with severe mental health issues includes several key components to address the global functional impairments and severe symptoms. The initial goal of treatment is stabilization. Often, the first step toward reaching this goal is seeking medical treatment (Tsuang et al., 2011). Psychiatry is typically the best way for these services to be obtained. The psychiatrist will conduct a thorough evaluation of the patient, provide a diagnosis, and prescribe medication. **Psychotropic medications** will specifically reduce mental health symptoms, thus resulting in the stabilization of functioning. For example, hallucinations, delusions, manic behaviors, or panic attacks are likely to significantly reduce, allowing the individual to progress toward improvements in daily functioning (see chapter on psychiatric interventions).

Once stabilization is obtained and symptoms are reduced, the role of the psychiatrist is to work with the individual and family to maintain **medication compliance**, consistently taking medication as prescribed by a medical professional (Tsuang et al., 2011). To prevent the recurrence of severe symptoms and significant decline in functioning, compliance with medical treatment is a key component of long-term care for individuals with severe mental illness. A common barrier to medication compliance is the individual's resistance to or limited understanding of the necessity of medication (Tsuang et al., 2011). An individual diagnosed with bipolar 1 disorder might discontinue medication because he or she misses the feeling of mania. An individual with schizophrenia might cease medication because he or she does not have insight into the importance of it or perceives that the medication is causing harm (e.g., delusions are present around the purpose of the medication). Another barrier to medication compliance can be the experience of adverse side effects (Tsuang et al., 2011). For example, an individual taking a medication to treat psychotic symptoms might experience psychomotor agitation, a common side effect, that causes significant discomfort physically and socially. The psychiatrist can provide psychoeducation to the family and individual so that they can watch out for early signs of adverse side effects. If the problems are noticed and addressed early, the psychiatrist will be able to make adjustments so that medication compliance is maintained. Thus, the psychiatrist will work with the individual regularly to continue to identify motivation for continued medication compliance and provide the family or support system with psychoeducation regarding the purpose and side effects of the prescribed medication. Given this goal of treatment, ministry workers will want to encourage families of individuals with severe mental illness to attend or be involved in their loved one's psychiatric appointments on a regular basis.

In addition to psychiatric treatment, it is typically best for individuals to participate in an outpatient program (Lim et al., 2016). Medical professionals generally recommend that individuals enroll in some type of outpatient treatment after leaving the hospital or participate in conjunction with initial outpatient psychiatry treatment. This type of mental health service is often provided through one's county mental health department, local psychiatric hospital, or privately owned treatment facility. Interventions typically provided in outpatient treatment include individual/group therapy for the purpose of changing thoughts, moods, and behaviors; social skills training; family therapy; vocational skills training; and case management. The idea behind having an individual engage in this holistic treatment program is to develop a foundation for the individual to thrive and integrate into society.

Legal issues will also need to be addressed throughout the course of treatment. A situation might arise where the family or treatment professionals realize that the individual is no longer able to effectively care for him or herself, thus posing a significant danger to him or herself. The court can then determine that the individual is **gravely disabled** and unable to meet his or her basic needs because of a mental illness, further requiring mental health services. (Note: Laws regarding grave disability vary by state.) In this case, the family might decide to pursue **conservatorship**, when one person has the legal right to make decisions for another adult as determined by the court (Being Prepared for a Crisis, n.d.). This legal process often occurs for individuals with schizophrenia. In addition to conservatorship, individuals with severe mental health issues who are not able to maintain employment will also want to consider seeking county or state financial services. For example, the state of California has state disability services that provide financial support for individuals with severe mental health issues. Typically, a case manager through a treatment program or a family member can assist the individual in gaining access to these services.

Historically, the long-term goal of treating individuals with severe mental health issues has been "stabilization and acute care" (Rouse, Mutschler, McShane, & Habal-Brosek, 2017, p. 139). However, in recent decades, medical and mental health professionals have changed the focus to include interventions and programs that support individuals with severe mental illness in reaching their personal goals and successfully participating in their communities (Hamm, Buck, Leonhardt, Luther, & Lysaker, 2018; Rouse et al., 2017). This is a reorientation from surviving to thriving. Several key components of treatment programs have been identified to assist individuals in achieving and maintaining this long-term goal. Researchers have found that reduction of stigma, fostering a sense of purpose and agency, viewing oneself as worthy of an improved lifestyle, engaging in social relationships, and engaging in self-directed treatment contribute to success in treatment (Hamm et al., 2018; Rouse et al., 2017). As a result, ministry workers will need to remember these long-term goals and motivating factors. It will be important to keep in mind that the long-term goal is not to eliminate or "cure" the symptoms fully. Rather, ministry workers can come alongside individuals with severe mental health issues and assist them in viewing themselves as valuable contributing members of the church community.

Assessing the Need for Referral

As mentioned in the earlier discussion, the initial assessment of the necessity for referral is the individual's safety to him or herself and others. Beyond safety concerns, ministry workers can engage in a discussion with the individual and his or her family regarding functional impairment. If the individual significantly struggles to maintain employment, attend school, care for daily needs (e.g., hygiene, meals), or regularly interact with others, and these issues have persisted despite changes in external circumstances, then a referral to psychiatry and/or outpatient treatment should be considered. The best place to direct the family to access mental health services initially is through county programs. Your county's National Alliance of Mental Health's website will provide addresses and telephone numbers to county mental health clinics (see the "Resources" section). The family can also be directed to contact their insurance provider to obtain a list of covered psychiatrists and severe mental health programs.

KEY TERMS

Psychotropic medications: medications that specifically reduce mental health symptoms

Medication compliance: a possible goal of treatment to ensure an individual is consistently taking medication as prescribed by a medical professional

Gravely disabled: legal status determined by the court when an individual is unable to meet his or her basic needs because of a mental illness

Conservatorship: a legal relationship that allows one individual to hold the legal rights to make decisions for another adult as determined by the court

Discussion Questions

1   Reflect on your thoughts and reactions regarding the idea that severe mental health issues are typically not "cured" through treatment.

2   Why might it be important for individuals with severe mental health issues to integrate into their communities (e.g., church community)?

FUNCTIONAL IMPAIRMENT AND COMMON ISSUES WITHIN THE CHURCH COMMUNITY

Depending on locale, some churches may be affected by issues related to severe mental health. Often, these issues are centralized on the core areas of functional impairment experienced by the individual. Next, each type of functional impairment with the related community issues will be discussed.

Psychological Functioning

Various impairments in psychological and cognitive functioning might be experienced by individuals with severe mental health issues. Examples of cognitive impairments include hallucinations and delusions. The individual might not have a clear concept of reality as a result of such symptoms. Thus, reasoning with and interacting with the individual can become difficult. Psychological impairments might include suicidal thoughts that affect the individual's ability and motivation to engage in daily activities, such as personal hygiene or eating regular meals (American Psychiatric Association, 2013).

Delusions and Spirituality

A common way in which church communities might experience the challenges of psychological impairment is through the displayed symptom of delusions or hallucinations.

As mentioned earlier, delusions can be spiritual or religious in nature, so it would be expected that individuals might seek relief within a church community. Pastoral staff should be aware of these potential psychiatric issues to best meet the specific needs of the individual, or they may run the danger of further exacerbating the person in distress. For example, Caleb believed that he needed to protect himself from evil people and that the only way to do this was to wear his patch and make candle wax art. A well-intentioned pastor might try to direct Caleb toward other biblically based protections from evil. However, Caleb might experience an increase in distress because his erroneous belief in the patch as protective is being challenged. He probably would require professional help to be prepared to give up this belief. Pastors and ministry workers will want to engage in a process of discernment in such situations.

Although there is a significant overlap and interaction between psychological and spiritual issues, some key features indicate a need for mental health support in addition to spiritual support. For example, it is helpful to determine whether the person is displaying intensity and lacking openness as opposed to being willing to take steps toward spiritual health and healing. Also, when it is difficult to talk rationally, such as when the individual presents bizarre ideas, you will want to consider referral to a mental health professional. In addition to simultaneous medical services, referral to spiritual healing ministries might be considered, which will allow both the psychological and spiritual needs of the individual to be addressed. However, a level of openness will likely need to be demonstrated when referring the individual to spiritual healing ministries. Furthermore, discussing the issue with other pastors and engaging in a process of prayer will be important components of the discernment process.

Social Functioning

A person with mental health impairments often has a limited or no social support network. The individual might have limited ability or knowledge of how to access support or how to identify when support is necessary. Or, it might even be possible that the individual chooses to remain in solitude, much like Caleb did before treatment. This impairment can lead to isolation and exacerbation of other symptoms (American Psychiatric Association, 2013).

Violence and Aggression

In some cases, potential for an individual to exhibit violence and aggression can be evident. This type of social interaction also has significant overlap with psychological impairments. For example, an individual who is experiencing delusions or hallucinations might perceive that it is necessary to defend him or herself physically as the result of the pervasive presence of a perceived threat. Or, an individual experiencing mania might exhibit intense anger leading to aggressive behaviors. Often, individuals who exhibit this type of social behavior will need to be approached in a specific way. Because of the overlap with psychological impairment, de-escalation is not likely to be achieved through reasoning with the individual and asking him or her to "calm down." It is typically best to find a way to remove the individual from the current situation and redirect the individual away from the person or situation that is causing distress/aggression. Ministry workers and church staff will want to have a plan in place prior to the occurrence of this type of event. Staff members will want to set up a protocol for how to handle violent or aggressive individuals. Such plans might include a procedure for how and when police will become involved and which staff members will be notified immediately to provide support and protection for the church community.

Occupational Functioning

Occupational impairment is common with untreated severe mental health issues. The illness can create significant challenges in maintaining employment (American Psychiatric Association, 2013). Some reasons for this impairment include the inability to maintain basic needs (e.g., hygiene, meals), social isolation, and untreated symptoms (e.g., delusions, hallucinations) that make it very difficult to complete work tasks. Oftentimes, individuals will require financial support from family or government programs, or they will become homeless.

Homelessness

As you might imagine, an individual who has severe symptoms, limited social support, and is unable to maintain employment has a very high chance of become homeless. As a result, accessing services might be equally challenging. Although difficult to determine, the National Coalition for the Homeless estimates that 30% of homeless individuals suffer from severe mental health issues (Admin, 2018). Church communities, likely in urban and suburban settings, might consider establishing a ministry program that supports individuals who are homeless in the area. Such services might include access to resources such as food, clothing and personal hygiene items. In addition, ministry leaders might also connect individuals who are homeless to local programs and services. It will be important for ministry workers to keep in mind the possibility that they are serving those with severe mental health issues and/or addiction. This awareness will help you support the individual's core needs rather than only address the issue of homelessness.

KEY TERMS

Psychological impairment: significant cognitive and emotional symptoms that effect daily functioning

Social impairment: significant difficulty accessing and maintaining social connections as the result of mental health symptoms

Occupational impairment: significant difficulty obtaining and maintaining employment because of mental health symptoms

1 What steps might you take to discern the needs of someone presenting with spiritual oppression? What resources might you access to assist you in the discernment of mental health issues?

2 Does your church have a safety plan in place for addressing aggressive and violent individuals? What procedures might you put in place having read about the possibility of individuals with severe mental health exhibiting these behaviors? How might you educate your staff regarding this issue?

3 Reflect on how your interactions with a homeless individual might be different given the correlation between homelessness and severe mental health.

THE SUPPORT OF THE CHURCH

Both the individual with severe mental health issues and his or her family will need a community that uniquely supports them through the challenges of finding stability and flourishing. Some general recommendations are discussed next. Beyond these ideas, ministry workers will want to remember that each individual has his or her unique needs and experiences. As with anyone suffering, a posture of seeking to understand and come alongside should be taken prior to offering support.

Support for the Individual

As discussed earlier, individuals with severe mental health issues (e.g., individuals with schizophrenia) are likely to have a difficult time regularly seeking support and will often isolate. While others who want help will experience barriers to this process, such as fear of judgment, feeling shame, or feeling very different from the rest of the community. In addition, a stigma has existed, both historically and presently, concerning individuals with severe mental health issues (Linhorst, 2006). Often, people will be treated as different, less than, or incapable as a result of their mental illness. Ministry workers will want to be mindful of these barriers when seeking to support people with severe mental health issues. Thankfully, the church community is a stable support presence for suffering individuals to access. Above all else, ministry workers will want to hold a posture of Christ's love and grace. All people are welcome in Christ's family, even those who experience significant brokenness in body and mind. In the gospels, we see clear examples of the various barriers that Christ breaks through to bring salvation to the most broken and isolated individuals. Jesus Christ tears down barriers of culture, ethnicity, and gender to proclaim who he is and to bring new life. For example, Jesus's interactions with the woman in the crowd who touches his garment demonstrates the restoration of an individual who is an outcast in her society (Luke 8:43–48). No matter how broken an individual might be, Christ offers his love and grace to all. It is essential that ministry workers hold this central as they seek to support individuals with severe mental health issues.

An important component of this posture of Christ's love is honoring the person-hood of the individual (e.g., the woman at the well in John 4). This key component can sometimes get lost in the relational dynamic or supportive process when an individual is presenting with very abnormal behaviors. Unfortunately, in our sinful nature, it is sometimes easy to label someone as an "other" when he or she is engaging in very bizarre behaviors during a manic episode (e.g., running down the middle of the street) or while experiencing hallucinations or delusions. If this is the case, one will want to re-center their perceptions and posture toward the individual, focusing on the idea that all humans are created in the image of God despite how broken one is. In Genesis 2, we see that God created both women and men in his image. This proceeds the bro-kenness of human nature. Thus, it is key that we hold central the **personhood** of the individual despite brokenness and significant challenges in functioning. An individual with schizophrenia deserves to be treated as a person of God's family and kingdom. Mental health professionals often focus on how the individual with severe mental illness can be empowered (Linhorst, 2006). This empowerment includes having some sense of agency, control, and influence over one's day-to-day experiences. Empowering individuals with severe mental health issues to participate in God's kingdom is likely to be an experience that supports healing and hope.

Support for Families

In some situations, ministry workers might find themselves with the opportunity to support family members of individuals with severe mental health issues. Research shows that family members often move through a few key experiences while supporting their loved one (Tsuang et al., 2011; von Kardorff, Soltaninejad, Kamali, & Eslami Shahrbabaki, 2016). Hopelessness and helplessness are often primary emotions experienced on the journey. Sometimes, family members feel blame or shame for the condition of their loved one. Parents might feel stuck or lost in how to help their adult child. In addition, parents might also grieve the loss of the typical developmental milestones that are experienced by most (e.g., one's adult child getting married, loss of the opportunity to have grandchildren). Sadness and high levels of stress are also common as family members adjust to a new normal of caring for their loved one's well-being. In addition, family members might experience depression, anxiety, or burnout as a result of their role as caregivers.

The church community can be a place for family members to access needed support. Whether it is directly meeting with a ministry worker or within a small group, family members will need a place to share their suffering, grieve, be understood, and supported. This can happen in a variety of structured or non-structured ways. Support offered might be in the form of tangible resources, such as providing referrals for services, bringing over meals, or financial support. Socioemotional support can include offering an empathic listening ear, giving space for them to share their suffering, praying for the family, and imparting hope.

KEY TERMS

Personhood: the idea that all people are created in the image of God and should be treated as such

Discussion Questions

1   Reflect on your automatic perceptions of someone who displays bizarre behavior (e.g., psychotic behaviors). What steps might you take to re-center or continue to remain in the idea that all people are created in the image of God?

2   What steps might your church take to provide support for individuals and families experiencing severe mental health issues?

REVIEWING THE CONCEPTS

Learning Objectives

- Broadly define and provide examples of severe mental illness
  - Severe mental illness is characterized by persistent and severe symptoms.
  - Individuals with severe mental illness demonstrate functional impairments.
  - Examples include bipolar I disorder, schizophrenia, severe anxiety disorders, and severe major depressive disorder.

- Understand key features and symptoms of schizophrenia
  - Key features include delusions, hallucinations, and paranoia
  - Other symptoms include disorganized speech and motor behavior, as well as negative symptoms.

- Be familiar with typical treatment for severe mental illness and what to consider when referring
  - The initial goal of treatment is stabilization, which often includes psychiatric treatment through hospitalization and/or medication.
  - Ongoing treatment will focus on medication compliance and/or outpatient treatment.
  - Legal issues such as grave disability and conservatorship should also be considered when the individual is not able to care for him or herself.
  - Long-term care typically focuses on successful integration within the community rather than a "cure."

- Identify several key areas of impairment for individuals with severe mental illness
  - Psychological impairment, including delusions and hallucinations, might affect an individual's openness to the spiritual direction of a pastor.
  - Social impairment will limit an individual's access to support.
  - Individuals with limited ability to engage socially might also engage in violent or aggressive behaviors.
  - Occupational impairments can also lead to the experience of homelessness by the individual.

- Learn specific ways to interact with individuals who suffer from a severe mental illness, including issues of safety
  - Establishing a supportive connection and showing interest in the person should be primary ways of interacting.
  - Holding in mind the personhood and value of the individual to God's kingdom will allow for a supportive stance.
  - Attempts to ground the individual in reality should be limited due to a potential response of defensiveness.
  - Safety issues, such as harm to self or others, should be assessed in the initial interaction with the person.

- Understand the support necessary for family members of individuals with severe mental illness
  - The church community can support family members as they navigate a wide variety of experiences, such as hopelessness, shame, and grief.
  - Tangible resources and socioemotional support can be offered to the family members.

Chapter Review Questions

Level 1: Knowledge (True/False)

1. Severe mental illness includes mild symptoms and short-term treatment.
2. Individuals with severe mental health issues often experience recurrent hospitalization.
3. Mild major depressive disorder is an example of a severe mental illness.
4. The presence of severe mental health issues does not typically occur with other mental health issues, such as addiction.
5. Schizophrenia includes symptoms of delusions and hallucinations.
6. Treatment for severe mental health issues often include psychiatry and medication compliance.
7. Individuals with occupational impairment are at a lower risk of homelessness.
8. Legal issues and financial support are often key components of long-term care for individuals with severe mental health issues.

9. Long-term support for individuals with severe mental health issues should focus on successful integration into the community.

10. Family members will only need support in the initial stages of learning that their loved one suffers with severe mental health issues.

Level 2: Comprehension

1. Which of the following is correlated with severe mental health?

   a. Recurrent hospitalization

   b. Addiction issues

   c. Genetic predisposition

   d. All of the above

2. Psychosis includes the following symptoms except

   a. delusions

   b. depression

   c. disorganized speech

   d. paranoia

3. Severe mental illness is characterized by which of the following?

   a. Severe level of symptoms

   b. Persistent symptoms

   c. Significant functional impairment

   d. All of the above

4. It is best to interact with an individual with psychosis in the following way:

   a. Reason with the individual to reground him or her in reality.

   b. Engage in learning about his or her interests and goals.

   c. Disregard issues of safety.

   d. Ignore the individual.

5. The initial stages of treatment are likely to focus on

   a. integration into the community

   b. support for the family

   c. finding the person a job

   d. stabilization through psychiatry

6. Long-term goals of treatment are likely to include

   a. integration into the community

   b. support for the family

   c. addressing legal issues

   d. all of the above

7. Functional impairment within severe mental health includes the following domains except

   a. social

   b. psychological

   c. physical

   d. occupational

8. Individuals with severe mental illness will likely need support in the following areas:

   a. Addressing issues of stigma

   b. Being an active participant in the community

   c. Experiencing a sense of empowerment

   d. All of the above

9. Family members of individuals with severe mental health issues are likely to need support in which area?

   a. Finding a job

   b. Grief and hopelessness

   c. Delusions

   d. Aggression

10. Support can be offered to family members through which of the following ways?

    a. Offer a listening ear

    b. Provide the family with referrals to services

    c. Offer to pray with the family

    d. All of the above

Level 3: Application

1. You have been made aware that Caleb, who has interest in candle wax and clothes patches to ward off evil, is a new member at your church. Identify and describe three ways that you might connect with and support Caleb within your church community.

2. Describe how you might interact with homeless individuals given the possible presence of severe mental health issues. Identify and describe key concepts from this chapter that you want to hold in mind in this situation.

3. Describe a potential ministry program for family members of individuals with severe mental health. What components would you include in this program based on what you have read?

4. From your personal Christian worldview, discuss the potential importance of viewing individuals with severe mental health issues as being created in the image of God.

5. Identify three symptoms of psychosis/schizophrenia. For each symptom, discuss how the symptoms might limit the person's ability to participate successfully within your church community. Also, for each, provide a recommendation of how these symptoms/limitations can be addressed.

ANSWERS

LEVEL 1: KNOWLEDGE

1. F
2. T
3. F
4. F
5. T
6. T
7. F
8. T
9. T
10. F

LEVEL 2: COMPREHENSION

1. d
2. b
3. d
4. b
5. d
6. d
7. c
8. d
9. b
10. d

RESOURCES

Online Resources

- National Alliance on Mental Illness—https://www.nami.org
- Supporting a Family Member With a Serious Mental Illness—http://www.apa.org/helpcenter/improving-care.aspx
- The Campaign to Change Direction—https://www.changedirection.org/
- The National Coalition for the Homeless—http://www.nationalhomeless.org/
- National Institute of Mental Health—https://www.nimh.nih.gov

Readings

- *A Balanced Life: 9 Strategies for Coping with the Mental Health Problems of a Loved One*—Tom Smith
- *I Am Not Sick, I Don't Need Help! How to Help Someone with Mental Illness Accept Treatment*—Xavier Amador
- *Empowering People with Severe Mental Illness: A Practical Guide*—Donald Linhorst
- *Me, Myself and Them: A Firsthand Account of One Young Person's Experience with Schizophrenia*—Kurt Snyder with Raquel Gur, MD, PhD and Linda Andrews

CLASSROOM ACTIVITIES

1. Reflect on your perceptions of individuals with severe mental health issues. How have your perceptions changed since reading this chapter? Share your reflections with someone in the class.

2. Role-play a counseling session with Caleb's parents.

3. Role-play a counseling session with Caleb after he has reached stabilization through treatment.

REFERENCES

Admin. (2018, May 17). #TBT—In celebration of mental health month. Retrieved from http://nationalhomeless.org/tbt-celebration-mental-health-month/

American Psychiatric Association. (2013). *Diagnostic and statistical manual of mental disorders* (5th ed.). Arlington, VA: Author.

Being Prepared for a Crisis. (n.d.). National Alliance on Mental Illness. Retrieved from https://www.nami.org/Find-Support/Family-Members-and-Caregivers/Being-Prepared-for-a-Crisis

Green, A. I., Drake, R. E., Brunette, M. F., & Noordsy, D. L. (2007). Schizophrenia and co-occurring substance use disorder. *American Journal of Psychiatry, 164*(3), 402–408. doi: 10.1176/appi.ajp.164.3.402

Gregoire, A., & United Nations International Year of Older, P. (2000). *Adult severe mental illness*. London, England: Cambridge University Press.

Hamm, J. A., Buck, K. D., Leonhardt, B. L., Luther, L., & Lysaker, P. H. (2018). Self-directed recovery in schizophrenia: Attending to clients' agendas in psychotherapy. *Journal of Psychotherapy Integration, 28*(2), 18–201. doi: 10.1037/int0000070

Hudson, C. G. (2005). Socioeconomic status and mental illness: Tests of the social causation and selection hypothesis. *American Journal of Orthopsychiatry, 75*(1), 3–18. doi: 10.1037/0002-9432.75.1.3

Lim, C., Barrio, C., Hernandez, M., Barragán, A., Yamada, A., & Brekke, J. S. (2016). Remission of symptoms in community-based psychosocial rehabilitation services for individuals with schizophrenia. *Psychiatric Rehabilitation Journal, 39*(1), 42–46. doi: 10.1037/prj0000154

Linhorst, D. M. (2006). *Empowering people with severe mental illness: A practical guide*. New York, NY, US: Oxford University Press.

Mental Illness. (November 2017). National Institute of Mental Health. Retrieved from https://www.nimh.nih.gov/health/statistics/mental-illness.shtml#part_154784

Read, J., & Ross, C. A. (2003). Psychological trauma and psychosis: Another reason why people diagnosed schizophrenic must be offered psychological therapies. *Journal of the American Academy of Psychoanalysis, 31*(1), 247–268.

Rouse, J., Mutschler, C., McShane, K., & Habal-Brosek, C. (2017). Qualitative participatory evaluation of a psychosocial rehabilitation program for individuals with severe mental illness. *International Journal of Mental Health, 46*(2), 139–156. doi: 10.1080/00207411.2017.1278964

Schizophrenia. (May 2018). National Institute of Mental Health. Retrieved from https://www.nimh.nih.gov/health/statistics/schizophrenia.shtml#part_154880

Shattock, L., Berry, K., Degnan, A., & Edge, D. (2017). Therapeutic alliance in psychological therapy for people with schizophrenia and related psychoses: A systematic review. *Clinical Psychology & Psychotherapy, 25*(1), e60–e85. doi: 10.1002/cpp.2135

Tsuang, M. T., Glatt, S. J., & Faraone, S. V. (2011). *Schizophrenia*. Oxford, United Kingdom: Oxford University Press.

von Kardorff, E., Soltaninejad, A., Kamali, M., & Eslami Shahrbabaki, M. (2016). Family caregiver burden in mental illnesses: The case of affective disorders and schizophrenia—a qualitative exploratory study. *Nordic Journal of Psychiatry, 70*(4), 248–254.

IMAGE CREDITS

CHAPTER 10

Mental Health Issues Specific to Children and Adolescents

Laura Niebaum, MA Theology, MFT

LEARNING OBJECTIVES

Upon completion of this chapter, readers will be able to

1. develop insight into how mental health disorders manifest in children and adolescents, and properly identify symptoms specific to a few common disorders;

2. understand basic brain development in an effort to understand children and adolescents better;

3. identify possible steps to treatment for disorders common to children and adolescents; and

4. provide effective pastoral care and spiritual development to children and adolescents in pain.

"Don't let anyone look down on you because you are young, but set an example for the believers in speech, in conduct, in love, in faith and in purity."
(1 Timothy 4:12, New International Version (NIV))

"Since you cannot do good to all, you are to pay special attention to those who, by the accidents of time, or place, or circumstances, are brought into closer connection with you."
(Augustine, *On Christian Teaching*)

AN INTRODUCTION TO COMMON DISORDERS IN CHILDREN AND ADOLESCENTS

Case Study: The Fletcher Family

The Fletchers are a nuclear family who are well known in their small beach community. The mother, Lydia, manages the home and is also a waitress at the family restaurant. The father, Brian, spends most of his time managing the family restaurant. Lydia and Brian have three children, Tonya age 13, Greg age 11, and Lacy age 9. Recently, Lydia and Brian

FIGURE 10.1 **Caring for our youth**

have noticed some emotional and behavioral changes in the children, and Lydia has been in contact with the children's school counselor, Mr. Palm, to seek some advice.

The Fletcher family struggle together to run the restaurant while balancing the other aspects of daily life. For the children, this is especially difficult. The amount of stress has affected each child differently, and Tonya, Greg, and Lacy are all exhibiting atypical behaviors that are concerning to their parents. In addition, when Brian spoke with the children's youth pastor, she confirmed a change in the children and reassured Brian that she is available for additional support.

Lydia and Brian became concerned when noticing Tonya's strange coping mechanisms. They noticed that when Tonya, age 13, is in distress, she commonly speaks with a slowed speech pattern, groans, and lies face down on the floor. She displays odd behaviors with boys at school, is constantly worried about fitting in, and hates speaking when in public. For more than 2 weeks, several people have noticed that Tonya is sad most of the day; she's irritable, and very slow to get moving at school. She has recently expressed to her school counselor, Mr. Palm, that she has feelings of worthlessness and constant guilt for no reason. Mr. Palm has also noticed that Tonya is no longer interested in activities she once loved at school and likes to spend most days at home or in the family restaurant. After a few assessment sessions with Mr. Palm at Barkley Intermediate School, Tonya also reported that she is having suicidal thoughts. Mr. Palm immediately contacted Tonya's parents, who have also reported this to her youth pastor at church.

In addition to Tonya's concerning behaviors, her brother Greg is also beginning to behave differently, as observed by both his parents and teachers. Greg, the middle child, is 11 years old' he is the musician of the family and loves practical jokes. He is bright, quirky, and loves to laugh with his family, especially his dad, Brian. Greg is energetic, talkative, and has been easily distracted for as long as people can remember. Lydia first became concerned when she noticed that Greg was having difficulty falling asleep at night. Greg's youth pastor reported that when he is at church, he is loud, sometimes misbehaves, and can be a distraction for others, but he is well liked. After Greg's behavioral concerns at home and hearing complaints from his teachers, Brian and Lydia feel confused, anxious, and unsure about what to do for Greg.

The youngest child, Lacy, age 9, may arguably have the biggest personality of the family. She is known around town by the playful dog tail she wears every day. Although it is normal for a young child to dress up, her need to wear her tail at all times has begun to concern her family. It has become more evident that she carries a lot of fear and insecurity.

People around Lacy commonly make comments about her worrying, which seems out of her control. She is irritable, tense, and often stays up late at night with her brother Greg planning pranks. After noticing these behaviors going on for more than half a year, Brian and Lydia have recently become very concerned. They decided to send Lacy to the school counselor and encouraged her to talk to her small group leader at church about her worries. After a few meetings, Mr. Palm suggested that Lacy be assessed by a therapist for a possible anxiety disorder because her level of worry is starting to interfere with her daily life.

How to Identify the Complex Signs: Childhood and Adolescent Depression, Anxiety, and Attention Deficit Hyperactivity Disorder

Unfortunately, it seems that common disorders such as **depression** and **anxiety** are steadily increasing (John Hopkins University and John Hopkins Medicine, 2018), especially in children and adolescents. According to the National Institute of Mental Health, 20% of youth ages 13–18 live with a mental health condition (2018). With great potential for this statistic to rise as demands on young people also increase, most pastors and educators I speak with have also developed concern that they are not equipped to properly evaluate the signs of these disorders. Furthermore, they are unsure of how to intervene even when they are able to identify the signs. One purpose of this chapter is to help caregivers properly identify these common disorders and to know what steps to take to help children and adolescents.

It is impossible to cover all disorders that children and adolescents may face throughout their emotional development. In my experience, most caregivers seek help for depression, anxiety, and attention deficit hyperactivity disorder (ADHD) in their children and adolescents. We will cover these three disorders, with the expectation that this discussion may also apply to other disorders or concerns faced in childhood and adolescence.

Identifying concerning signs in young people is not an easy task. They are in a season of rapid physical and emotional development, which makes it more complicated than with most adults. Chap Clark, a well-known youth ministry practitioner, describes this complexity in his book *Hurt 2.0*: "These fragile young people are not pretending to be callous; rather, they are wearing their toughness as a shield to protect them from further disappointment" (Clark, 2011, p. 54). Clark speaks to a **defense mechanism** that hurting youth feel they may need to use to protect themselves, which makes it hard for adults to identify the emotions under the surface. Children and adolescents can fear disappointment so deeply that they become callous, unable and unwilling to express emotion. These hidden emotions make it hard to notice the signs of mental health problems and therefore provide help.

Lacy, from our case study, is an excellent example. She exhibits a tough exterior and uses humor to push people away. From the outside, it would be easy to miss that she is highly anxious and simply hiding this condition very well. When she is in youth group, most staff would see her as a quirky, funny girl with no filter. This would be the natural conclusion without any knowledge about the true signs of anxiety. Although Lacy is very good at hiding, church will most likely become the first place she finds an adult she can trust and finally share her hurts.

Childhood and Adolescent Major Depression Disorder

Clinton and Clark (2010), define **depression** as

> feelings of dejection and hopelessness that last for more than two weeks. While everyone has a bad day from time to time, individuals struggling with depression often experience changes in eating and sleeping habits, as well as agitation, irritability, and restlessness. Depressed people generally lack energy and find little pleasure in activities they once enjoyed, such as playing sports or hanging out with friends. (p. 92)

Unlike adults, young people with depression commonly appear irritated and/or agitated. Although these behaviors are not commonly associated with depression in adults, they are very common in young people.

For example, a small group leader who has a student like Tonya may commonly report, "I think one of the students in my small group may be depressed, and I am worried she may be suicidal. I don't want to make it worse, so what do I do?" This is an important question, and it addresses four significant issues. First, how does a youth worker know if the student is actually depressed? Second, and even deeper, is the student a danger to him or herself? Third, how does the youth worker manage his or her own worry about the issue. Finally, what do you do next?

According to the *Diagnostic and Statistical Manual of Mental Disorders, 5th Edition* (*DSM-5*; American Psychiatric Association, 2013), when looking for depression in children and adolescents, there must be for five or more of the following symptoms that interfere with daily life:

- Young person reports, as well as others notice, a depressed mood (sad, empty, hopeless, teary) most of the day, nearly every day
- Different from adults, depressed mood may present as irritability in young people
- Young person reports, as well as others notice, he or she is no longer interested in activities he or she many have once loved (sports, friends, school, etc.)
- Significant weight loss or gain
- Not sleeping or sleeping too much nearly every day
- Restlessness or moving slowly
- Fatigue or loss of energy nearly every day
- Feeling worthless or excessively guilty every day
- Can no longer think or concentrate, indecisive
- Recurrent thoughts of death, recurrent suicidal thoughts without a plan, or a suicide attempt or a specific plan for committing suicide
- Unlike adult depression, children and adolescents may also have the following symptoms in addition to *DSM* criteria:
  - Irritable mood
  - Frequent vague physical complaints
  - Frequent absences from school and/or poor performance
  - Boredom
  - Alcohol or substance abuse
  - Anger or hostility
  - Reckless behavior

In our case study, Tonya would fit the criteria for depression based on the following signs: depressed mood, irritability, slow moving, worthless and guilty feelings, and no longer interested in activities she once loved. Also, Tonya has reported to her small group leader that she is having suicidal thoughts. All of these issues should catch the attention of a youth worker and be addressed immediately. Later in the chapter, we will fully cover crisis intervention.

Pastor's Initial Response to Depression

Here are some suggestions of what actions need to be taken when concerned with possible depression in young people:

- Approach the young person with empathy and listen to his or her feelings.
- Ask a few clarifying questions, such as how long has he or she felt depressed, and what is the level of seriousness either from mild depression to feeling suicidal.
- Assess the proper initial intervention.
  - For example, do you need to involve family, seek additional support at church, or call a professional for an opinion?
- Decide on a plan *with the student* and possibly involve the young person's family.
- Ask permission to pray for the student.

Childhood and Adolescent Anxiety Disorder

An **anxiety disorder** can be defined as "debilitating feelings of fear, which may be exhibited in a number of different ways, including generalized anxiety disorder, panic disorder, obsessive-compulsive disorder, post-traumatic stress disorder and phobias of all kinds" (Clinton and Clark, 2010, p. 42). According to our case study, Lacy has some symptoms of an anxiety disorder. She is irritable, tense, and can be characterized by extreme worry.

Lacy's small group leader may notice she comes to youth group constantly worried and seems excessively anxious. The leader may ask others, including the youth pastor, if this is normal behavior. Although some seasons of life can cause more worry than others, according to the *DSM-5* (American Psychiatric Association, 2013), if a young person fits the following symptoms for more than 6 months, then he or she may have higher levels of anxiety than is considered normal:

- Generalized anxiety disorder:
- Extreme worry that is difficult to control, occurring most days for at least 6 months
- Must cause distress and interfere with daily functioning
- Worries are associated with three (or more) of the following six symptoms:
  - Note: Only one item is required in young people
  - Restlessness, on edge
  - Becoming sleepy easily
  - Trouble concentrating or mind going blank
  - Irritable
  - Tense muscles
  - Difficulty falling or staying asleep

It can sometimes be difficult to identify normal levels of anxiety, especially in young people. This is because anxiety has a healthy place in everyone's emotional life. Humans are designed to use anxiety to survive and protect themselves. We all have a common **flight-fight-freeze response** when faced with stressful and/or dangerous situations. This response prepares our bodies to react and respond, and anxiety is designed to help us function. But it can become debilitating when out of control.

To help form an accurate perception of normal anxiety in children and adolescents, it is important to know what fears are normal for these age groups. First, consider the context, development, and temperament of the individual child. Typical fears for children are separation, dogs, spiders, monsters, costumes, death, and darkness. In early childhood, children are still learning how to resolve what is real and not real (Muris, 2007). Common fears are different for adolescents and may include social acceptance, identity, belonging, moral issues, future, and public speaking (Muris, 2007).

Identifying symptoms can feel difficult because many children and adolescents may exhibit these signs simply because of developmental or hormonal changes. As a result, knowing how to talk effectively with young people when you have a concern is an important aspect of your role in youth ministry. Later in the chapter, we will discuss how to listen and promote healthy conversations concerning these sensitive topics.

For Lacy's parents, her anxiety became a concern after they noticed that her extreme worrying had lasted more than 6 months. In addition, the school counselor suggested that she be assessed for an anxiety disorder. She was described as insecure, irritable, tense, often staying up late at night, and having uncontrollable worry that causes her distress. Based on what we know of Lacy, she's meets the criteria for a childhood anxiety disorder. Her symptoms have presented within the 6 months or more time line; she is in distress, irritable, tense, not sleeping, and her worry is excessive. Lacy will need intervention to help her understand, cope with, and overcome her anxieties.

Pastor's Initial Response to Anxiety

Similar to depression, here are some common first steps when concerned with possible clinical levels of anxiety in youth:

- Approach the young person with empathy and listen to his or her feelings.
- Ask some clarifying questions, such as when did the anxiety begin, and how severe is it either from some mild episodes to full panic attacks.
- Assess the proper initial intervention.
  - For example, are there ways you can help the youth cope at church (allow him or her to step out when needed, sit out of large group activities, or sit in a specific spot)
- Decide on a plan with the student and, when possible, involve the family.
- Ask permission to pray for the youth.

Childhood Attention Deficit Hyperactivity Disorder

The last disorder, typically beginning in childhood, is **attention deficit hyperactivity disorder** (ADHD). We will pay special attention to this disorder because it is most prevalent in children; whereas the other disorders focused on thus far, depression and anxiety, tend to develop in adolescents or early adulthood (Berger, 2014). In addition, ADHD is one of the most "common and yet misunderstood childhood disorders" (Clinton and Clark, 2010, p. 50). The American Psychiatric Association estimates that between 3% and 7% of children suffer from ADHD, and many other children are still affected by several symptoms, although not diagnosable as ADHD (2013).

Many youth workers meet children who seem consistently distracted, cannot focus, and commonly cause disruption. It is important to keep in mind that some of these behaviors could be considered typical in children. So, a simple question for youth workers to ask may be, "What does ADHD actually look like?" Many children and adolescents are incorrectly labeled with ADHD when in fact they may not meet the necessary criteria to be diagnosed with the disorder. To minimize mislabeling someone as having ADHD, it may be helpful to explore the diagnostic symptoms of the disorder.

ADHD is defined by a noticeable reoccurrence of inattention and/or hyperactivity that interferes with daily life or development for at least 6 months. In addition, young people must "exhibit impaired functioning in multiple environments such as school, work, and friendships. Also, we need to see difficulty in not just one but three main areas: impulsiveness, hyperactivity, and inattention. Individuals with ADHD often act without thinking, have a hard time sitting still and/or being quiet, and are easily distracted from the task at hand" (Clinton and Clark, 2010, p. 50). Those who struggle with ADHD would fit into one of two types: inattentive and/or hyperactive-impulsive.

According to the *DSM-5* (American Psychiatric Association, 2013), the **inattentive type** of ADHD is typically defined as exhibiting five or more of the following behaviors:

- Failure to notice details
- Making careless mistakes
- Having difficulty paying attention to tasks or play
- Unable to listen when spoken to one-on-one
- Inability to follow instructions
- Failing often to finish schoolwork or chores
- Trouble organizing (messy, poor time management, turns things in late)
- Avoidant of tasks that require mental effort
- Loses necessary things
- Easily distracted or overstimulated
- Forgetful in daily activities

Perhaps one reason it may be hard to identify ADHD properly is because of the amount of symptomology and the fact that most children exhibit some of these behaviors during different times of normal development. The key is to pay attention to the *amount* of behavior children display. As referenced earlier, a child or adolescent needs five or more of the aforementioned symptoms occurring at the same time for at least 6 months.

In addition, according to the *DSM-5* (American Psychiatric Association, 2013), the **hyperactive-impulsive type** of ADHD is typically defined as exhibiting five or more of the following behaviors:

- Frequently fidgets with hands
- Squirms in seat
- Leaves seat when expected to remain seated
- Unable to remain quiet
- Often "on the go," as if powered by a motor
- Excessive talking
- Blurts out answers or cannot wait for turn in conversation or activities
- Interrupts or intrudes on others

Children with **combined type** of ADHD display both inattentive *and* hyperactive-impulsive symptoms (American Psychiatric Association, 2013). There will be a variety of mixed symptomology, but they must meet criteria for both types. These behaviors must be present before the age of 12, appear in two or more settings (school, home, friends, activities), and must cause distress for the child.

There is a lot of symptomology when discussing ADHD that can be confusing. While it's important to skim and have a basic understanding of what to look for, it is not a youth workers responsibility to diagnosis a young person. You simply need to know enough to report a possible concern and then know how to help meet the needs of the individual struggling with ADHD.

Thinking back on the earlier case study, would Greg be identified as a child with ADHD? He is described as being energetic, talkative, and easily distracted for as long as people can remember. The case study also mentions that he is having trouble falling asleep at night. When he is at church, he is loud, sometimes misbehaves, and can be a distraction for others. Are his behaviors concerning enough, and does he meet the criteria for ADHD?

Greg's behaviors do not meet the criteria to diagnosis him with ADHD because he does not have enough of the symptoms at this time. Greg certainly does have some behavioral issues causing difficultly for him and those who care for him. However, he may need these behaviors to be further assessed by a professional. Furthermore, his actions may simply be explained as normal development, or they could be connected to other emotional difficulties. Similar to Greg, some children may display disruptive symptoms that would be considered normal for a child who is experiencing a significant transition, death, divorce, learning disability, anxiety, depression, difficulties with discipline, or poor nutrition.

It is very important to note that there may also be some risks for those suffering with ADHD. Some children with ADHD "tend to develop methods of **coping** to deal with any impairments of normal functioning the disorder causes. However, for some, many aspects of daily life can be very difficult" (Clinton and Clark, 2010, p. 51). Having ADHD may cause behavioral issues, including defiance, anger, and disrespect. This is why treating

ADHD is imperative. If left unaddressed, ADHD can affect the growth and development of children. According to Clinton and Clark,

> Often teens with this disorder are not involved in after-school or recreational activities. Their parents are half as likely to say that their ADHD teens have a lot of good friends and more than twice as likely to report that their teenagers are picked on at school or have trouble getting along with peers. These social problems can put teens at increased risk for anxiety, behavior or mood disorders, substance abuse and teen delinquency. (Clinton & Clark, 2010, p. 51)

Conclusion and Treatment

The *International Journal of Special Education* (Reiber & McLaughlin, 2004) speaks to the need for a wide variety of treatments for ADHD. It reports, "A recent comprehensive review found that there are currently three treatments for ADHD that can be considered supported by research: (1) psychostimulant medications, (2) behavior intervention, and (3) a combination of these two" (Busch, 1993; Pelham, Wheeler, & Chronis, 1998; Waschbush & Hill, 2001). It is important to assess and implement behavioral interventions for ADHD continually throughout childhood and adolescence. The American Academy of Pediatrics (AAP) recommends that initial treatment of ADHD be educational and behavioral (Wolraich et al., 2011). For example, the first line of treatment for school-aged children should be parent/teacher-administered behavior therapy. After some success with behavioral therapy, the AAP recommends the possibility of U.S. Department of Agriculture–approved medications for ADHD, but medication should never be used as an isolated treatment (Wolraich et al., 2011). Evidence-based literature regarding classroom behaviors of children with ADHD also supports the idea that behavioral interventions should accompany any medication management of symptoms (Wolraich et al., 2011). A primary care clinician should **titrate**, or adjust the amount of a drug consumed, doses of medication to achieve maximum benefit with minimum adverse effects (Wolraich et al., 2011).

Pastor's Initial Response to Attention Deficit Hyperactivity Disorder

Responding to possible ADHD symptoms in a child or adolescent may include the following steps:

- Discuss with the family that you are noticing some inattentive and/or hyperactive behaviors
- Consult with teachers if possible or appropriate
- Recommend that the young person get further assessment through his or her school psychologist or a psychologist who specializes in ADHD assessment
- Adapt some of the youth group activities to meet the young person's needs: sit the child up front, give him or her extra jobs, allow the child to stand when needed, etc.

KEY TERMS

Depression: feelings of dejection and hopelessness that last for more than 2 weeks

Anxiety: extreme worry that is difficult to control, occurring most days for at least 6 months

Attention deficient hyperactivity disorder: a noticeable reoccurrence of inattention and/or hyperactivity that interferes with daily life or development for at least 6 months in multiple environments

Defense mechanism: defense mechanisms are psychological strategies that are unconsciously used to protect a person from anxiety arising from unacceptable thoughts or feelings

Flight-fight-freeze response: physiological response that prepares the body to react and respond to actual or perceived threat

Coping: skills or strategies to help reduce psychological stress

Titrate: to adjust the amount of a drug consumed until the desired effects are achieved

Discussion Questions

1 What does "normal" anxiety look like in young people?

2 What are a few factors that make it difficult to identify signs of depression in young people?

3 How is ADHD different (give at least five signs) from normal development?

4 Why is the amount of time the symptoms are present important when identifying depression, anxiety, and ADHD? How long must you notice signs with each disorder?

BRAIN DEVELOPMENT COMMON IN CHILDREN AND ADOLESCENTS

Magnetic resonance image (MRI) studies show that it takes at least 10 years, between the ages of 10 to 24 years old, for the brain to arrive at full physiological adulthood (Arian et al., 2013). In general, a young person's brain is still in the process of reaching full capacity until age 24, sometimes later. As a result, a young person will not be able to think or behave to his or her full potential until reaching his or her early 20s. We will explore the child and adolescent brain to gain a deeper understanding of the way a young person thinks, feels, and relates to others.

The Child Brain

In childhood, the most important parts of the brain have not yet fully developed—namely, the prefrontal cortex. This is the part of the brain that develops social understanding and is involved in complex decision making (Berger, 2014).

The psychological term for the operations carried out by the prefrontal cortex is **executive functioning**. Executive functioning is the ability to differentiate among conflicting thoughts, think about future consequences of current activities, work toward a defined goal, predict outcomes, and establish expectations based on actions and social control (Berger, 2014). This is an important part of the brain because it gives humans the ability to suppress urges that could otherwise lead to socially unacceptable outcomes (Berger, 2014). This function is not fully available to children, which explains why a child may suddenly blurt out in class that he or she needs to go to the bathroom.

Another important function of the prefrontal cortex is **emotional regulation**. According to Berger (2014), this is the part of the brain that upon maturity allows for the appropriate expression as well as control of emotions. Between the ages of 2–6 years, the prominent psychosocial task is to learn to moderate emotion as the limbic system connects to the developing prefrontal cortex. As the child's brain matures, he or she becomes better at evaluating emotion, particularly by the age of 24 (Berger, 2014).

The primary way to promote healthy brain development is through relational play (Berger, 2014). Play helps children develop physically and teaches emotional regulation, empathy, and cultural understanding. It is normal for a child to be **egocentric,** which is a child's tendency to think about the world entirely from his or her own perspective. But, as the brain develops, early relationships prove foundational for expanding a child's limited perspective and improving overall physical and emotional health (Berger, 2014).

Siegel and Bryson (2011) emphasize the essential need for **brain integration**, especially in childhood. "Integration takes the distinct parts of your brain and helps them work together as a whole" (p. 6). They describe the left brain as logical, literal, linguistic, and loves lists. Whereas the right brain is described as holistic, nonverbal, sends and receives signals, establishes meaning and feeling of experience, and stores emotions, images, and personal memories. While it's essential for all people to integrate both sides of the brain, Siegel and Bryson (2011) believe the process of successful integration begins in childhood.

Siegel further suggests that empathy, creating positive mental models of relationships, families enjoying each other, and learning how to connect through conflict all significantly support brain integration (Siegel and Bryson, 2011). Ideally, adults should view conflict as an opportunity to teach essential relationship skills to children, as it allows for seeing another's perspective, reading nonverbal cues, and making amends. When children are taught both insight into the self and empathy for another, they are able to begin to develop a healthy integrated brain.

The Adolescent Brain

As we may know, adolescents generally have a reputation for being difficult to understand. Aside from the challenges that changing hormones bring, the brain is also still developing. The developing adolescent brain may create a few complex problems of its own that need to be understood to best minister to this age group.

To begin, the timing of the developing limbic system, which includes the emotion-regulating amygdala, can be problematic. The issue here is that the limbic system matures before the prefrontal cortex, which is the planning and impulse control center. Full functioning in the prefrontal cortex only happens after the teenage years. The instinctual and emotional areas of the adolescent brain develop ahead of the reflective, analytic areas (Berger, 2014). The fact that the prefrontal cortex is the last to mature may explain why many adolescents seem so driven by the thrill of new experiences and sensations, but they may momentarily forget the cautions that adults have tried to instill in them.

In addition, an adolescent needs proper space and understanding, along with age-appropriate boundaries. Similar to the child brain, if adolescents are not given the freedom to self-explore, they will also not develop a strong sense of self-esteem or empathy for another (Siegel, 2013). At this stage in adolescent development, the balance between structure from parents, teachers, coaches, pastors, etc., and self-exploration is crucial for a healthy identity formation. It is difficult for many parents to shift from raising a younger child who needs parental boundaries to parenting an adolescent who needs to begin to set his or her own boundaries.

Another potential problem arises for adolescents as it relates to peer relationships. At the neural level, it is shown that adolescents perceive social rejection as a threat to existence. Brain scans show reaction to peer exclusion is similar to a threat to physical health or food supply (Berger, 2014). Adolescents move away from an identity rooted in family to an identity rooted in peer relationships. This allows for more independent thinking and behavioral exploration but may cause confusion in the family. For a period of time, adolescents tend to become more concerned with peers and the desire to become absent from family commitments. This can be frustrating for both parents and adolescents alike.

Attachment in Children and Teenagers

As mentioned in the first chapter, **attachment theory** comes from observing the quality of one's relationship with one's primary caregiver(s). Relationships begin shaping us at birth and continue to do so through the life span. As children, we learn fundamental ways to connect to others that support a healthy mind and promote integration in our brains that can guide positive or negative relationship with ourselves and others throughout our lifetimes (Siegel, 2013). The relationships we form throughout childhood and adolescence have a lasting effect on the people we become, and it all begins with how we attach to our primary attachment figure after birth.

Siegel believes, "Our brains are capable of maintaining several different models of attachment, one for each relationship to given attachment figure" (Siegel, 2013, p. 149). As we know, secure attachments form the healthiest perception of the world, ourselves, and others. But when secure attachment is not available, we adapt through avoidance, ambivalence, and disorganization (Siegel, 2013). Children cannot control how they attach; furthermore, they have no ability to reflect on their attachment relationships (Siegel, 2013). It is in adolescence when we usually start to get a sense of how a person connects with others.

In his book *Brainstorm*, Siegel (2013) emphasizes the importance of beginning to reflect on our attachment relationship as soon as adolescence. Siegel reports, "Fantastic news that if you can make sense of your childhood experiences—especially your relationships with your parents [primary care givers]—you can transform your attachment models toward security" (Siegel, 2013). We find hope in that no matter our background, we can have healthier relationships with friends, partners, coworkers, children, etc.

As children grow into adolescents and begin exploring interests, beliefs, and relationships, we see how many complications can arise. With challenges in changing bodies, developing brains, and possible poor attachment models, it is easy to see why this time in life is so difficult for families.

Part of youth ministry is the privilege of providing secure attachment figures for young people to navigate this formative time in life. Adolescents need a safe person and/or place to begin to understand their experiences so that they know how to continue or begin forming healthy relationships as adults (Siegel, 2013). This means a secure parent, coach, friend, or youth worker.

KEY TERMS

Executive functioning: relates to abilities to differentiate among conflicting thoughts, comparative thinking, thinking about future consequences of current activities, working toward a defined goal, predicting outcomes, and establishing expectations based on actions and social "control"

Emotional regulation: effective control and expression of the emotions in the limbic system

Egocentric: child or adolescent tendency to think about the world entirely from his or her own personal perspective

Brain integration: the ability of the distinct parts of the brain to work together as a whole

Attachment theory: the primary attachment relationship acts as a prototype for future relationships. If an attachment has not developed securely, then the child will suffer from emotional and developmental consequences

Discussion Questions

1   Why is it important to understand the basics of brain development in children and adolescents?

2   Why is empathy important for the brain?

3   Is it important for an adult to reflect on early attachment experiences? Why or why not?

4   Can your work with young people effect their brain health?

KEY COMPONENTS IN PASTORAL CARE FOR CHILDREN AND ADOLESCENTS

To best respond to young people with mental health needs, it is helpful to understand empathy, good listening skills, and knowledge regarding crisis intervention, along with a familiarity with treatment. The following approaches to pastoral care for children and adolescents may provide a good starting point and produce better results toward genuine connection and care for young people.

Empathy

Working with youth can feel very complex at times, but providing plenty of empathy for young people can help. Children and adolescents need to know they are supported and understood in all their life circumstances. There are times when empathizing can be a difficult task, like when they make poor choices or act impulsively. But it is still a necessary ingredient to successful youth ministry.

Typically, adults are quick to correct or teach before offering empathy. However, I suggest offering empathy as a first step to communicate your genuine care and understanding. Young people want help from the adults in their lives, but they need empathy before receiving teaching or correcting. Most youth I meet suffer from deep levels of pain because they don't feel seen, heard, or understood. They often feel misunderstood by adults who tend to be too quick to correct without offering empathy first. This is where a pastor can be an additional support to the family by offering an adult perspective from a neutral, empathetic point of view.

As their pastor, it helps if they know that you're there for them, fully and unconditionally. Holding back from asking too many questions gives them room to think. Be gentle but persistent in moving toward them to help. But don't be discouraged if a young person shuts you out at first, because opening up to talk about feelings can be very tough for them.

Listening Skills

Listening is actually a skill that people develop with practice. Good listening includes remaining open-minded while interacting with a young person. Feeling grateful that a young person is communicating with you goes a long way with them. Research shows that just talking about pain can begin to alleviate the aspects of the pain experience (Kaufman, n.d.). Talking is a form of **externalization,** the process of transforming our thoughts into some sort of external form. This is helpful because it puts the issue outside a person and becomes something that can be solved as opposed to becoming a part of his or her identity. Typically, by writing or speaking, we can improve our emotional health by converting the internal thoughts into an expressed communication (Kaufman, n.d.). When emotions are shared or externalized with an empathic listener, the person begins to feel less emotional pain.

Empathetic listening may sound easier than it is. For some it may not come naturally and needs to be developed through practice. If you want to improve these skills, I suggest you consider the following list of empathetic listening skills (Davenport, 2015):

- *Listen with a nonjudgmental, inviting posture*
  - Even if you disagree with what the person is saying, hear him or her out completely first before responding.

- *Summarize what you heard*
  - "What I heard you say was ..."

- *Ask for clarification*
  - "Can you tell me more about what your worried about?"

- *Empathize and normalize*
  - Again, even if you think they may end up in potential trouble you can say, "I can see why you would feel that way ..."
  - "Lots of kids are afraid of ..."

- *Validate*
  - Do not try to talk youth out of how they are feeling, even if it seems irrational.
  - Acknowledge the pain and sadness, and take it seriously.

- *Tell a short story related to when you were around their age*
  - Be careful not to take the attention away from the young person.
  - "I remember when I was your age and my grandpa died ..."

- *Listen to how you are feeling while talking to the young person*
  - Be honest with yourself about your own feelings.

- *After practicing these listening skills, you can ask if the young person wants your guidance or help*
  - Collaborate for solutions.

Crisis Intervention

When a young person confides in you, sometimes a crisis may arise. If the child or adolescent feels safe, he or she may share information that concerns you. For example, the young person may report that he or she is a harm to him or herself, like cutting or having suicidal thoughts. The child or adolescent may even tell you someone else is harming him or her. Understandably, this information can create anxiety and fear regarding how to best handle these types of situations. So, it is important to know exactly what steps to take when a crisis arises.

First, it is best not to make a promise to a young person that you cannot keep. A young person may come seeking help and ask you to promise you'll never tell anyone. Clarify that you take his or her **confidentiality** very seriously, but if the young person or anyone else is in danger of harm, you need to do everything in your power to keep people safe.

Second, in a crisis, do not be afraid to talk and ask questions. For example, if a young person tells you he or she is having suicidal thoughts, you should feel confident enough to ask direct questions, such as, "Are you thinking about killing yourself?" Or, "Do you have a plan?" In fact, these are the best questions to ask. This can feel awkward or counterproductive, but studies show that asking at-risk individuals if they are suicidal does not increase suicides or suicidal thoughts (Suicide Prevention Lifeline, n.d.). If the young person has a plan for suicide, seek professional help immediately. If the threat is serious and/or immediate, you need to involve the family and/or may need to call 911.

A third step is to do your best to keep the young person safe, and when possible, see the process through with him or her. Reducing a suicidal person's access to highly lethal items or places is also an important part of suicide prevention. While this is not always easy, asking if the at-risk person has a plan and removing or disabling the lethal means can make a difference. Also, listen carefully and learn what the individual is thinking and feeling. Research suggests, acknowledging and talking about suicide may in fact reduce rather than increase suicidal thoughts (Suicide Prevention Lifeline, n.d.).

Fourth, it is important to guide young people toward connecting with others who can also help. One way to do this may be to save the National Suicide Prevention Lifeline's phone number so that it's available when you need it: 1-800-273-TALK (8255). You may want to call with the young person and/or give him or her the number as a precautionary measure. Staying in touch after the crisis or hospitalization can also make a difference. Studies have shown that the number of suicide deaths goes down when someone follows up with the at-risk person (Suicide Prevention Lifeline, n.d.).

Finally, refer the at-risk person out to a trusted psychotherapist. When a life is threatened, professional care along with the support of the youth pastor is the best course of action. A therapist can assess and properly treat the young person and his or her family as needed. Asking the family how you as the youth pastor can support this process is often appreciated and very helpful.

Holistic Collaboration and Treatment

As briefly mentioned earlier, it may also be helpful to collaborate with a young person and his or her family, friends, medical professionals, teachers, etc. This shows the person how much you care and that you are taking him or her seriously. However, sometimes family members or friends are not necessarily safe for the young person to share confidences with them. This is when offering your support can make a big difference to a child or adolescent. If a young person is struggling with mental health issues, collaborating with people who have a long history with the child or adolescent can help his or her **prognosis** or likely outcome of treatment. As a youth worker, your best contribution is as a caring relationship and spiritual support. In some cases, this spiritual support may be sufficient for the individual to make progress, but in other cases, they may need additional professional support.

We'll turn back to our case study to give an example of what collaboration and treatment may look like for Tonya, who is struggling with depression. In review, Tonya meets the criteria based on her depressed mood, irritability, slow moving, worthless and guilty feelings, no longer interested in activities she once loved, and suicidal thoughts reported to a small group leader. Ideally, the steps in her treatment would look as follows:

1. Tonya reports suicidal thoughts to a small group leader one night at youth group. Along with suicidal thoughts, Tonya's leader has also noticed some signs of depression.

2. The small group leader has an empathetic conversation and assesses for suicide immediately (see the "Crisis Intervention" section).

3. The small group leader rules out any threat of suicide and collaborates with Tonya on the next steps. For example, Tonya and her leader decide to call her parents together and tell them that Tonya is feeling depressed and needs help.

4. Tonya and her group leader pray at the end of the conversation.

5. Tonya and her group leader decide that she is safe to go home, and her parents will follow up with more conversation.

6. The leader also assures Tonya that she will follow up with her the following day.

7. Tonya's parents continue the conversation when Tonya arrives home from church, and they all decide to call her medical doctor and to find a therapist to get Tonya professional intervention.

8. Tonya begins psychotherapy with a therapist who works with adolescents and depression.

9. Tonya remains in therapy until everyone agrees she is ready to finish.

10. In addition to her therapy, Tonya's leaders at church, her parents/siblings, and friends check in with her and give her support throughout the process.

KEY TERMS

Externalization: the process of transforming our thoughts into some sort of external form, typically by writing or speaking

Confidentiality: keeping private

Prognosis: likely outcome of treatment

Suicidal ideation: suicidal thought or preoccupation with suicide, may not lead to the threat of suicide

Discussion Questions

1. What does empathetic listening look like? Give three specific skills.

2. Why is it important not to promise a young person that you will keep his or her secrets?

3. What are some differences between suicidal thoughts and the threat of suicide?

4. What actions should you take if you believe someone is suicidal?

5. Aside from youth workers, who should collaborate in a young person's treatment and why?

HOW MENTAL HEALTH ISSUES CAN INTERFERE WITH SPIRITUAL DEVELOPMENT IN YOUTH

Why Do Adolescents Commonly Leave the Church in Young Adulthood?

There are many books written about the common struggles young people face in the church (see the end of the chapter for some suggested readings). As young people navigate this very complex time of identity formation, they sometimes place their faith on hold. Kara Powell and Chap Clark (2011), of Fuller Youth Institute, describe it this way,

> Several of the students interviewed by the Fuller Youth Institute acknowledged that they put their faith on hold when they entered college so that they could "enjoy the college life." Translated, that means party. And yet when asked about shelving their faith, a couple of them noted the inconsistency of it all. "I know it doesn't make sense. If I kick God to the curb for four years just so I can have fun, then why would I pick him up again? Obviously, I don't think he's worthwhile, or I wouldn't dog him in the first place. I mean, we are talking about God, right?" (Powell & Clark, 2011, p. 54)

Most youth pastors, including myself, notice a change in faith commitment for adolescents as they begin to enter into young adulthood. I remember several conversations with our youth staff and volunteers on why upper classmen were not attending youth group, camp, small groups, etc. We commonly thought it was something we were doing wrong, and it may have been, but it also may have to do with adolescent development. It helps for pastors to remember "that identity and **faith formation** is a messy process of 'two steps forward, one step back'" (Powell and Clark, 2011, p. 55). This is when youth pastors desire to guide young people in discovering their own personal relationship with God. This may be disheartening for parents and youth workers alike but it's normal and even healthy for young people to wrestle with their faith as they develop their own sense of identity.

Unfortunately, young people who are deeply hurting may have an even higher probability of leaving the church for good. If a child or adolescent is in pain and possibly struggling with a mental health disorder, he or she needs empathy and intervention. When this does not get noticed by the adults in their lives, their spiritual development can suffer greatly. Sadly, sometimes they hold this against God and struggle with faith for a lifetime. For example, imagine a young person in your church with serious anxiety who has not received professional intervention. He or she may struggle to find ways to manage the anxiety through **maladaptive coping mechanisms**, which are methods that may relieve symptoms temporarily but do not address the root cause of emotional stress. This often leads to unhealthy behaviors to self-medicate or distract from the pain. If they risk sharing this significant problem with their youth pastor, they will need prayer as well as someone who recognizes their need for intervention. Having someone take them seriously can be a profound example of how God cares for them.

Without intervention, some young people begin to believe that either they aren't praying correctly, praying hard enough, or possibly that God doesn't care about them because the pain never goes away. As a result, some adolescents leave their faith and turn to other coping mechanisms that seem to have more immediate results (i.e., drugs, sex, alcohol, etc.).

Young people who use substances or other means instead of God to deal with their pain get delayed in their spiritual maturing process. Fortunately, we know God is able to reach that child or adolescent in spite of circumstances.

Theology of Pain

One approach to addressing this **disillusionment**, or the realization that the church may disappoint because it is different than what they thought it was, is to have conversations about the theology of pain. Consider the following verses and how a child or adolescent may relate to the emotions expressed in each context:

- "When anxiety was great within me, your consolation brought joy to my soul" (Ps. 94:19, NIV).
- "Therefore, do not worry about tomorrow, for tomorrow will worry about itself. Each day has enough trouble of its own" (Matt. 6:34, NIV).
- "Cast all your anxiety on him because he cares for you" (1 Pet. 5:7, NIV).
- "I have told you these things, so that in me you may have peace. In this world you will have trouble. But take heart! I have overcome the world" (John 16:33, NIV).
- "Why are you downcast, O my soul? Why so disturbed within me? Put your hope in God, for I will yet praise him, my Savior and my God" (Ps. 42:11, NIV)

As we reflect on these scriptures, God's Word warns us that there will be pain. It also assures us that God will bring comfort. Oftentimes, turning to scriptures like these and/or prayer is exactly what a person needs. However, there are situations when a young person needs additional intervention. Young people who have symptoms beyond the normal troubles that arrive in childhood and adolescence need spiritual *and* psychology intervention. Youth workers can be equipped to guide young people toward finding God in the pain as well as provide practical direction when needed.

Prayer for the Hurting

Your role of praying into a young person's life is essential. When this is done well, the youth worker is listening with empathy *and* praying into the pain. If the leader does not listen with empathy, prayer alone can feel **dismissive** of young person's pain—that is, making the person feel uncared for or that his or her pain is unimportant. It may feel like the leader doesn't want to hear about the young person's experience and simple wants to pray it away.

Let us look at the practical example of David in Psalm 69. He begins the Psalm by crying out his feelings to God:

> *Save me, O God,*
> *for the waters have come up to my neck.*
> *²I sink in the miry depths,*
> *where there is no foothold. (Ps. 69:1–2, NIV)*

David then immediately asks for help, and gives the reader the picture of his drowning, sinking, in the depths of the water. Perhaps he is overwhelmed. He also tells God that he is tired of calling out; he feels like God isn't there. Perhaps he is angry and afraid.

David then admits his own sin and imperfection: "You know my folly, O God; my guilt is not hidden from you" (Ps. 69:5, NIV). He then asks God for mercy:

> [16]*Answer me, O LORD, out of the goodness of your love;*
> *in your great mercy turn to me.* (Ps. 69:16, NIV)

He pleads for mercy and rescue from his circumstances. Davis appeals to the God of mercy, goodness, and love to help him. David then ends his song with praise:

> [30]*I will praise God's name in song*
> *and glorify him with thanksgiving.* (Ps. 69:30, NIV)

As we look at Psalm 69, we see David lay out the elements of prayer for a person who is hurting. Aside from the first element, the order is not necessarily important:

1. Always address feelings first
2. Ask for help
3. Admit imperfection/sin
4. Ask for mercy/guidance
5. Praise God

The following is an example of a Psalm 69 prayer for our case study, Lacy, who is deeply anxious:

> Lord, Lacy is feeling so worried by life, overwhelmed by pain and confusion. It all feels so hard and like too much at times (address the feelings). She needs you now, Lord (ask for help). We know we are not perfect and that's why we need You so badly in this moment (admit imperfection). Please God, help calm her heart and give her the next steps toward feeling whole again, we need Your wisdom (ask for mercy/guidance). We know You are good, loving and the ultimate healer of hearts. Thank You for all You have done in Lacy's life and for giving her courage to share her struggles. We thank You in advance for all You will continue to do in Lacy's heart. Amen.

KEY TERMS

Maladaptive coping mechanisms: coping that may relieve symptoms temporarily but does not address the root cause of emotional stress

Dismissive: making the person feel uncared for or that his or her pain is unimportant

Faith formation: desire to guide young people in discovering their own personal relationship with God

Disillusionment: realization that the church may disappoint because it is different than what they thought it was

Discussion Questions

1 How does scripture form the way you think about pain and suffering?

2 Why is the integration of spiritual and psychological intervention important in some cases?

3 Why are hurting people leaving the church?

4 How is David a good example of honesty and prayer?

REVIEWING THE CONCEPTS

Learning Objectives

- Develop insight into how disorders manifest in children and adolescents, and properly identify symptoms specific to a few common disorders
  - Discussion and review of criteria of depression
  - Discussion and review of criteria for anxiety versus normal anxiety
  - Discussion and review of criteria of ADHD

- Understand the basic developmental processes currently used to understand children and adolescents
  - Child brain development
    - Preoperational brain
    - Primary attachment figure
  - Adolescent brain development
    - Attachment

- Identify possible steps to treatment for disorders common to children and adolescents
  - Identifying need for further intervention beyond basic support
  - Holistic collaboration: parents, teachers, friends, youth leaders, and, possibly, therapists
  - Psychotherapy

- Provide pastoral care and spiritual development to those in pain
  - Empathetic listening skills
  - Crisis intervention
  - Prayer that acknowledges pain

Chapter Review Questions

Level 1: Knowledge (True/False)

1. Depression commonly presents as irritation and/or agitation in young people.

2. A common initial response to depression is advising a young person on what action to take.

3. A common symptom of anxiety is weight loss/weight gain.

4. Fight-flight is a normal response related to survival and protection.

5. ADHD is a noticeable reoccurrence of inattention and/or hyperactivity that interferers with daily life for at least 3 months.

6. Brain integration promotes self-understanding, which leads to better relational skills.

7. Young people need teaching and correction before empathy and spiritual direction.

8. Validation is an important empathetic listening skill.

9. Lack of professional intervention for some psychological disorders may be a reason some young people leave the church.

10. It is essential for a youth pastor to take care of others before prioritizing self-care.

Level 2: Comprehension

1. Which of the following is not a symptom of inattentive type ADHD?

    a. Inability to follow instructions

    b. Not finishing schoolwork

    c. Unable to remain quiet

    d. Trouble organizing

2. Relational play promotes

    a. egocentrism

    b. emotional regulation

    c. attachment

    d. anxiety

3. According to Erikson, adolescents face the following conflict:

    a. Trust versus mistrust

    b. Ego integrity versus despair

    c. Identity versus role confusion

    d. Initiative versus guilt

4. Anxiety symptoms must be present every day for

    a. 2 weeks

    b. 6 months

    c. 1 week

    d. 1 year

5. The following are ways to practice self-care:

    a. Boundaries

    b. Seeking wisdom

    c. Quiet and rest

    d. All of the above

6. What is the best first step in praying for someone who is hurting?

    a. Ask for guidance

    b. Admit sin

    c. Address feelings

    d. Ask for mercy

7. What is the best question to ask a young person who has expressed that he or she is having suicidal thoughts?

    a. "Do you have a plan?"

    b. "Why would you kill yourself?"

    c. "Do you know anyone who has killed themselves?"

    d. "What do you think God would say?"

8. According to the adolescent brain, young people must live in a world run by

    a. sports

    b. family

    c. peers

    d. adrenaline

9. The child's brain intelligence can be described as

    a. immature

    b. preoperational

    c. emotional

    d. disordered

10. Typical fears for children include

    a. identity and acceptance

    b. morality

    c. separation and darkness

    d. none of the above

Level 3: Application

1. Name all the symptoms of anxiety. How would you approach a young person who you notice is worrying a lot? What would be some possible next steps if you're worried that he or she may need professional intervention?

2. How would you teach young people about their own mental health? Write a 5-minute lesson and five small group questions.

3. First, a young person approaches you after youth group and asks for help/prayer. He asks you not to tell anyone what he shares with you. What do you say? Then he shares that he is suicidal. What are four empathetic listening skills you may practice during this crisis?

4. According to the chapter and your personal experience, how may common mental health disorders interfere with spiritual development?

5. What are five steps you can take toward effective self-care?

ANSWERS

LEVEL 1: KNOWLEDGE

1. T
2. F
3. F
4. T
5. F
6. T
7. F
8. T
9. T
10. F

LEVEL 2: COMPREHENSION

1. c
2. b
3. c
4. b
5. d
6. c
7. a
8. c
9. b
10. c

RESOURCES

Online Resources

- Fuller Youth Institute—https://fulleryouthinstitute.org/
- National Suicide Prevention Lifeline—https://suicidepreventionlifeline.org/
- Youth Workers—https://www.youthworker.com/
- National Alliance on Mental Illness (NAMI)—https://www.nami.org
- National Institute of Mental Illness (NIMH)—https://www.nimh.nih.gov
- Psychology Today—https://www.psychologytoday.com
- Barna Group—https://www.barna.com/

Readings

- *The Whole-Brain Child*—Dan Siegel
- *Brainstorm*—Dan Siegel
- *Growing Young*—Kara Powell, Jake Mulder and Brad Griffin
- *God Attachment*—Dr. Tim Clinton and Dr. Joshua Straub
- *Boundaries: When to say yes, when to say no to take control of your life*—Dr. Henry Cloud and Dr. John Townsend

Video Resources

- *Mindfulness and Neural Integration: Dr. Daniel Siegel, TEDxStudioCityED*— https://www.youtube.com/watch?v=LiyaSr5aeho
- *3 Stages of Adolescence, Dr. Chap Clark*—https://www.youtube.com/watch?v=Nx5oCFHDGlc
- *Bobs Burgers* (2011): 20th Century Fox—Comedy commentary on young people
- *Lady Bird* (2017): A24—R-rated, coming of age story

> ## CLASSROOM ACTIVITIES

1. Interview a young person: Make a list of 10–15 intentional questions (i.e., how he or she feels about God, what does he or she worry about, what does he or she know about mental health/self-care, etc.) and spend some time with a child or adolescent. Make it casual/comfortable. Take the young person for an ice cream or coffee and just be interested in how he or she thinks and feels. It may help to record the conversation rather than taking notes during the interview.

CLASSROOM ACTIVITIES—CONTINUED

2. Role-play empathetic listening and counseling a young person: Use any of the listening skills provided in this chapter to role-play with a colleague in class. For example, have one person share an issue that he or she is currently experiencing and the other person practice using empathy, summarization, and validation as he or she listens. Then reverse roles.

3. Personal attachment exploration paper: Explore your own attachment style through reflection and reading course-assigned texts. Write a three- to five-page reflection paper on your perception of your personal attachment style.

4. Classroom discussion: Allow for classroom discussion in groups or dyads during class time. Discussion will always help encourage self-reflection and tangible learning.

REFERENCES

American Psychiatric Association. (2013). *Diagnostic and statistical manual of mental disorders* (5th ed.). Arlington, VA: Author.

Arian, M., Haque, M., Johal, L., Mathur, P., Nel, W., Rais, A., ... Sharma, S. (2013, April 3). Maturation of adolescent brain. Neuropsychiatric Disease and Treatment, *9*, 449–461. Retrieved from https://www.ncbi.nlm.nih.gov/pmc/articles/PMC3621648/

Berger, K. (2014). *The developing person through the life span* (9th ed.). New York, NY: Worth Publishers.

Busch, B. (1993). Attention deficits: Current concepts, controversies, management, and approaches to classroom instruction. *Annals of Dyslexia*, 43, 5–25.

Clark, C. (2011). *Hurt 2.0*. Grand Rapids, MI: Baker Academic.

Clinton, C. & Straub, J. (2010). *God attachment*. New York: Howard Books.

Clinton, T., Clark, C. (2010). *The quick reference guide to counseling teenagers*. Grand Rapids. MI: Baker Books.

Davenport, B. (2015). Empathic listening: 8 strategies for compassionate communication. Retrieved from https://liveboldandbloom.com/06/self-improvement/empathic-listening

John Hopkins University and John Hopkins Medicine. (2018). *The rise of teen depression*. Retrieved from http://www.johnshopkinshealthreview.com/issues/fall-winter-2017/articles/the-rise-of-teen-depression

Kaufman, J. (n.d.). What is externalization? Retrieved from https://personalmba.com/externalization/

Muris, P. (2007). *Normal and abnormal fear and anxiety in children and adolescents*. London, England: Elseveier.

National Alliance on Mental Illness. (2018). Mental health facts children and teens. Retrieved from https://www.nami.org/learn-more/mental-health-by-the-numbers

Pelham, W. E., Wheeler, T., & Chronis, A. (1998). Empirically supported psychosocial treatment for attention deficit hyperactivity disorder. *Journal of Clinical Child Psychology, 27(2)*, 190–205.

Powell, K. & Mulder J. & Griffin B., (2016). *Growing young*. Grand Rapids, MI: Baker Books.

Powell, K., Clark, C. (2011). *Sticky faith*. Grand Rapids, MI: Zondervan.

Reiber, C. & McLaughlin T. F. (2004). Classroom interventions: Methods to improve academic performance and classroom behavior for students with attention-deficit/hyperactivity disorder. *International Journal of Special Education, 19(1),* 1–19.

Siegel, D. (2013). *Brainstorm*. New York, NY: Penguin Random House LLC.

Siegel, D. & Bryson T. (2011). *The whole brained child*. New York, NY: Bantam Books.

Suicide Prevention Lifeline (n.d.). We can all prevent suicide. Retrieved from https://suicidepreventionlifeline.org/how-we-can-all-prevent-suicide/

Waschbush, D. A., & Hill, G. P. (2001). Alternative treatments for children with attention-deficit/hyperactivity disorder: What does the research say? *The Behavior Therapist, 24(8),* 161–171.

Wolraich, M., Brown, L., Brown, RT., DuPaul, G., Earls, M., Feldman, H. M., ... Visser, S. (2011). ADHD: Clinical practical guideline for diagnosis, evaluation, and treatment of attention-deficit/hyperactivity disorder in children and adolescents. *American Association of Pediatrics, 128*(5), 10007–10027. Retrieved from http://pediatrics.aappublications.org/content/pediatrics/early/2011/10/14/peds.2011-2654.full.pdf

IMAGE CREDITS

Fig. 10.1: Source: https://commons.wikimedia.org/wiki/File:The-Early-Days-of-Timothy-xx-Henry-Le-Jeune.JPG.

CHAPTER 11

Spectrum Disorders

Colleen Harrington, MFT

LEARNING OBJECTIVES

Upon completion of this chapter, readers will be able to

1. understand the nature of autism spectrum disorder;

2. differentiate between individuals on different ends of the spectrum;

3. recognize the varying difficulties related to life on the spectrum;

4. distinguish between the needs of individuals on the spectrum and family members of those on the spectrum; and

5. understand ways in which pastors/churches can respond to afflicted members of their congregation.

Do not be conformed to this world, but be transformed by the renewal of your mind, that by testing you may discern what is the will of God, what is good and acceptable and perfect.
—Romans 12:2

CASE STUDY: LIFE ON THE SPECTRUM

Craig and Lauren had been married for 6 years when their second child, Dylan, was born. From day one, Dylan was a little different from other kids. His older brother, Christopher, had slept, eaten, and generally followed a typical developmental path, while everything about Dylan seemed a little less predictable. He cried a lot, slept little, and was extremely picky about food. When he learned to walk, he did so on his tiptoes. At his 2-year checkup with the pediatrician, Lauren shared her concerns about his hearing. Dylan was frequently nonresponsive when she called to him, and he screamed more than he spoke. His vocabulary was very limited, but he did seem to have his own language, made up of consistent babbling. The family found it endearing and had even learned to interpret some of the phrases that Dylan regularly used. Dylan's pediatrician recommended speech therapy to boost his language skills, and Lauren began taking him for regular sessions soon after.

FIGURE 11.1   **When a person experiences the world differently**

By the age of 5, Dylan was diagnosed with autism spectrum disorder (ASD). Speech therapy was helpful, but as he grew older, it became evident that Dylan also struggled with social interaction. He would play quietly *next* to other kids, but rarely played *with* them. He was fascinated with cars, but didn't want to push them around or race them like the other kids did. Instead, he would hold the cars close to his eyes and spin the wheels rapidly. He had very rigid routines and did not tolerate changes well. When interrupted, Dylan would often shriek and throw things. Meltdowns and tantrums were common, and sometimes, they even seemed to appear out of nowhere. Dylan's preschool-aged peers were mostly accepting of him, leaving him be and seeming to understand that this was "just how Dylan is." The parents, however, were another story. Craig and Lauren quickly learned that many grownups were far less accepting of Dylan's differences. Party invitations were withheld, playdates were declined, and even parental interaction was limited. Lauren suffered contemptuous looks and even the occasional lecture from others, who seemed to believe that Dylan's behavior was the result of poor discipline.

After Dylan had experienced a particularly rough morning in Sunday school, Craig and Lauren asked to meet with their pastor. They discussed their struggles with Dylan, including at church, in the classroom, and at home. They shared feeling distant from others at church and noted that it was extremely difficult for them to join small groups because of their unique needs for childcare. The stress of navigating this road with Dylan had put a strain on Craig and Lauren's marriage, and it was negatively affecting their older son, Christopher, who seemed to have fallen a bit off of his parents' radar. Lauren showed signs of depression, and the financial effect of Dylan's needs was also becoming evident. Seeing their difficult situation, the pastor referred the family to a local counseling center for help. In addition, the pastor was able discuss some potential strategies to make Sunday school and childcare services at the church more hospitable environments for Dylan.

The family's struggles with Dylan illuminated a need for support within their church community, not only for families affected by ASDs but also for all of those who live "outside of the lines."

AN INTRODUCTION TO AUTISM SPECTRUM DISORDERS

With the prevalence of autism continuing to rise, it is increasingly likely that those involved in pastoral care will be called upon to help families who are affected by this disorder. The needs of each family will vary according to the severity of their autistic member, as well as by the presence of external support systems, their financial situation, and their individual capacities for the inevitable stressors that accompany this diagnosis. Research from the Centers for Disease Control and Prevention (CDC) shows that autism now affects 1 in 68 individuals nationwide, becoming more prominent because of an increased awareness of the disorder and for reasons that remain unknown. The CDC also reports that boys are 4.5 times more likely to be diagnosed than girls and that the majority of cases are not diagnosed until after 4 years of age (CDC, 2014). While autism is most often diagnosed during childhood, it is a lifelong condition with no known cure. As such, pastoral care providers are encouraged to consider the needs not only of the parents of autistic children or the children themselves but also the adult autistic individual.

One of the unique aspects of autism is that our understanding of it is still rapidly evolving. The first clinical identification of it was in 1943 by Dr. Leo Kanner (Grandin & Panek, 2013), and it has changed shape in many ways since that time. As of 2013, the fifth edition of the *Diagnostic and Statistical Manual of Mental Disorders* (*DSM-5*) defined ASD as "an umbrella diagnosis enveloping a cluster of previously categorized Pervasive Developmental Disorders (PDD)" (American Psychiatric Association, 2013). It encompasses prior diagnoses of autistic disorder, Asperger's disorder, Rett's syndrome, childhood disintegrative disorder, and pervasive developmental disorders-not otherwise specified. Per the *DSM-5*, this new classification requires the presence of the following for a diagnosis of ASD:

- Persistent deficits in social communication and social interaction, both verbally and nonverbally. This could be observed as
  - awkward conversational skills
  - not appearing to "hear" or be interested in the speaker
  - little to no eye contact
  - difficulty reading or using body language
  - trouble understanding imaginative language or play
  - difficulty forming or maintaining relationships

- Restricted, repetitive patterns of behavior, interests, or activities, such as
  - repetitive motor movements, as in lining up objects
  - inflexibility to change or difficulty with transitions
  - intensely focused on certain interests
  - hyper- or hyposensitive to environment

The *DSM-5* also notes that symptoms must be present in the early developmental period, but may become more noticeable with age. The symptoms must also cause significant impairment in social, occupational, or other important areas of functioning to meet the requirements for a diagnosis. It is important to note the requirement for clinicians to specify the severity of the individual when diagnosing ASD. This **specifier** is meant to clarify and direct the appropriate supports for those on the spectrum, emphasizing their diverse needs. Dr. Stephen Shore, a renowned advocate for those with autism who was himself diagnosed at the age of 4, aptly stated, *"If you've met one person with autism, you've met one person with autism"* (Me, 2009). His words remind us that that caring for someone on the spectrum is not a one-size-fits-all proposition. The "**spectrum**" nature of this condition describes the wide-ranging appearance of autism, which varies greatly from any one point to another. Understanding the potential for vast differences between individuals with a diagnosis of ASD can help us to not only recognize it but also to feel the confusion and frustration that often accompany this disorder. With an empathic understanding of life on the spectrum, pastors can better attend to affected members of their congregation.

KEY TERMS

Autism: a developmental disability significantly affecting verbal and nonverbal communication and social interaction

Spectrum: wide-ranging appearance or presentation, varying greatly from one point to another

Specifier: clarifies and directs supports according to diversity of needs

Discussion Questions

1   Craig and Lauren have come to you, their pastor, with concerns over their son's difficulties in the Sunday school classroom. What would be an appropriate response to their situation?

2   How might Dylan's difficulties be affecting others?

3   Why is Craig and Lauren's scenario a very likely one for parishioners to encounter?

COGNITION AND COMMUNICATION

Cognitive capability is just one variable characteristic of an autism diagnosis and helps to illuminate the wide range of functioning for individuals on the spectrum. According to statistics, approximately 30% of children with ASD show **intellectual disability** (CDC, 2014), presenting significant challenges in both cognitive functioning and in adaptive behavior. Individuals on the higher functioning end of the autism spectrum may demonstrate normal to high levels of intelligence, with an estimated 10% possessing **savant skills**, or superior aptitudes within certain subject matters, such as math, music, or memorization (U.S. Department of Health and Human Services, 2016).

Speech and language abilities may vary as well, but significant communication impairment is evident in any spectrum diagnosis. Often, delayed speech is the first indication of autism in early childhood. Some children are verbally expressive, but may babble or "speak their own language" instead of picking up the one spoken in their homes. A consistent feature of ASD, however, is an overall deficit in the understanding and employment of communication skills required for typical interaction. Spectrum individuals often have difficulty reading body language and social cues. **Echolalia** is a symptom of ASD in which the individual "echoes" or repeats phrases he or she has just heard. It is also referred to as "parroting" and is sometimes viewed as a normal stage of language development in children, but may carry on into adulthood in those with autism (Lewis, 2013). **Scripting** is another linguistic tool that is symptomatic of autism. Just as it sounds, ASD individuals will use lines from movies or other media influences to communicate, even mimicking the script's original inflection or intonation in their delivery. Scripting is sometimes witnessed when an autistic is rehearsing for a conversation he or she is anticipating, or while reflecting on one he os she has already had. These practices, while atypical to the outside viewer, can be quite helpful for the autistic individual, as they can provide socially appropriate words and phrases that are otherwise difficult to find. **Pragmatics**, the unspoken "rules" for communication, are difficult for those with ASD. Understanding the role of turn-taking in conversation, vocal pitch, and whether the intended audience is listening are all skills that can be difficult for spectrum individuals. Body language is often foreign to them, and they tend to avoid making direct eye contact with others, so unspoken communication is sometimes lost entirely. The hand gesture of waving a person over, if even recognized in the first place, is often misunderstood or ignored. This inability to read others' actions inhibits the communication of others' with them, while their own mannerisms or attempts to communicate nonverbally will likely appear awkward, or even robotic. Without the unspoken language of facial expressions, hand motions, or postures, the words or intentions of others are easily misinterpreted. Introduce the added linguistic elements of voice inflection, sarcasm, or idioms, and confusion is virtually inevitable for the ASD individual (Hutten, 2015).

The preceding features of ASD are frequently used to designate an individual as either "high-functioning autistic" or "low-functioning autistic," and both terms are used with underlying connotations of a person's capabilities. While these descriptors may be accurate, they are often perceived as offensive by those in the ASD community. The term **"high-functioning autistic"** generally indicates milder symptoms and a lesser need for accommodations, but seems to carry with it a suggestion of intellectual superiority, while **"low-functioning autistic,"** indicating a more noticeable presentation of symptoms, implies significant deficits. There is, sadly, an element of degradation inherent in the term "low functioning" that reflects an unfair judgment of aptitude and shows insensitivity to autistic individuals. Conversely, the removal of the diagnosis of **Asperger's syndrome**, often used interchangeably with high-functioning autistic, was met with resistance by some in the "high-functioning" ASD community. The diagnosis of

Asperger's syndrome contained within it an inaccurate, but preconceived notion of an odd, but perhaps brilliant individual. While the diagnosis of Asperger's syndrome has been removed from the *DSM-5*, the term is still often used by those in the community to garner a degree of respect. For the most part, the ASD community is supportive of the new criteria because of its previous inaccuracies and in hopes of further research to define this broader diagnostic category (Parsloe & Babrow, 2015). The spectrum is not entirely linear, but a range of traits, individual to each person. Autistic individuals who have no language whatsoever might have the ability to compose incredible symphonies or to create brilliantly detailed works of art. It is noteworthy to consider the importance of this small, but critical example of each and every individual's need to be revered. Alan Turing, creator of the first computer used to break codes during WWII and the subject of the film *The Imitation Game*, stated, "Sometimes it is the people no one can imagine anything of who do the things no one can imagine" (Nicholson, Goclowska, & Nolan, 2018). His words remind us, as caring professionals and fellow humans, that we all need to feel valued and considered for what we *are*, rather than defined by what we *are not*.

KEY TERMS

Intellectual disability: presenting significant challenges in both cognitive functioning and in adaptive behavior

Savant skills: superior aptitudes within certain subject matters such as math, music, or memorization

Echolalia: a symptom of ASD in which the individual "echoes" or repeats phrases he or she has heard

Scripting: a linguistic tool in which individuals will use lines from movies or other media influences to communicate

Pragmatics: the unspoken "rules of communication," including body language, expression, and eye contact, among other elements

Discussion Questions

1. Discuss the differences between the terms "high functioning," "low functioning," and Asperger's syndrome. What might we discern from someone's use of the terms "high functioning" or "Asperger's syndrome" in a description of an autistic individual? Consider the clinical and emotional implications of these terms in your answer.

2. Discuss the significance of removing the diagnosis of Asperger's syndrome from the most recent edition of the *DSM*.

3. How might communicative impairments affect those afflicted with ASD?

SENSORY INTEGRATION

Sensory integration is another prominent feature of ASD and may be one of the first indications of the disorder, even if it is not recognized. Sensory integration is the process by which we receive, interpret, and use information acquired through our five senses. Difficulties with sensory integration may affect three primary systems: tactile, vestibular, and proprioceptive. **Tactile** sensitivities are the easiest to observe, and it is likely that this hypersensitivity to the physical surroundings will be the reason for the initial call to pastoral care. For those with ASD, the world is often too bright, too loud, too rough, and too crowded. Imagine having the worst headache possible, add in the skin sensitivity that occurs with the flu, while wearing a hot, itchy, wool sweater with the inside tags still attached, walking through the mall on the biggest shopping day of the year. This paints a picture of the discomfort experienced by ASD individuals every day. Things that are pleasurable to others may be tortuous to them. Backrubs, back scratches, massages, haircuts, and even hugs are among a myriad of uncomfortable, if not painful, experiences for the autistic. **Vestibular** integration difficulties affect a person's sense of balance and feeling of safety, especially during movements such as climbing or jumping. **Proprioception** involves a person's motor movements and awareness of body postures. Impairment in this area can cause delays in motor skills, such as crawling, manipulating objects, and writing. It is easier to empathize with this aspect of the autistic experience if we imagine what it is like to feel the world the way they do, and it is not difficult to imagine the desire to withdraw from such a distressing place. Sensory overload, which is common for ASD individuals, can significantly reduce their tolerance to external stimuli, leading to tantrums, meltdowns, or even isolation (Hatch-Rasmussen, 2018).

To alleviate the discomfort of this overwhelming world, ASD individuals may exhibit abnormal physical responses to help them cope. **Repetitive or restricted behaviors or movements** are another primary symptom of ASD and are often called "stims," short for "self-stimulation." These include motor activities, such as hand flapping, spinning, head-banging and repeatedly making a sound or a noise, to deliberately increase sensory input when needed. Heightened sensory input can induce an overall feeling of pleasure by releasing beta-endorphins into the body, thereby reducing external pain or discomfort (Siri & Lyons, 2012). Stims are often triggered by stress, fear, or anxiety and can serve to reduce present emotional distress. When these behaviors continue beyond the presence of a stressor, they become **perseverations** and can be difficult to regulate. Perseverations may include, among other things, a preoccupation with a specific subject that borders on or becomes obsessive in nature. Autistics may line things up or find specific ways of ordering them, or insist on routine, ritualistic ways of manipulating objects. It is important to be aware of whether the stim is affecting an individual's normal functioning level or whether it is, in fact, a coping mechanism. Identification of the external stressor can help to reduce the need for stimming, and interventions such as extended physical activity can be used when the need for self-regulation is present (Carter & Van Andel, 2011).

FIGURE 11.2   **Stacking or Lining Up Objects Is a Common Perseverative Behavior of Autistic Children**

KEY TERMS

Sensory integration: the process by which we receive, interpret, and use information acquired through our five senses

Tactile: of or connected to the sense of physical touch

Vestibular: of or relating to body position, sense of movement, and balance

Proprioceptive: movement, equilibrium, and spatial orientation of the body

Stims: short for "self-stimulating," these are repetitive or restricted movements used when sensory input is needed

Perseverations: a preoccupation with a specific subject, focus, or behavior that borders on or becomes obsessive in nature

Discussion Questions

1   Describe a scenario in which an ASD individual might experience sensory overload.

2   What are some possible stims or perseverate behaviors that we might witness in an ASD individual?

3   How should we attend to the presence of stimming or perseverations in an autistic individual?

SOCIAL STRUGGLES AND RELATED DIFFICULTIES

The sensory integration issues and communication deficits of ASD bleed easily into educational and social difficulties. A maladaptive capacity to tolerate a loud, busy environment combined with inadequate communication skills severely limits the ASD individual's ability to learn effectively and to form relationships. Parties of any kind, field trips, and even playdates can become extremely difficult endeavors. Perceived as awkward, intellectually disabled, or even deaf, the ASD child may quickly realize that he or she is different. While younger children are generally more accepting, they are also more apt to vocalize their curiosities and perceptions. It is in the best interest of the child to implement accommodations within the school setting. Parents should be encouraged to meet with school counselors, teachers, and outside clinicians to develop an **Individualized Educational Plan** (IEP) for their student. Public schools are required to assess and implement IEPs for all students who qualify for services, which may include different forms of therapy, behavioral modifications, and other special accommodations that should benefit the child (Wright & Wright, 2018). Often, parents are reluctant to address the need for services. Awareness of their potential sensitivity on this issue is extremely important, as this may be the first conversation they will have about the concrete determination of their child's disabilities. Rejection of the suggestion is quite common, out of fear that their child will be "labeled" or viewed negatively by others. It can be helpful to empathize with their concerns while allowing them time to educate themselves on the process and to weigh the outcomes versus consequences of interventions for their child.

By fourth grade, most children are entering puberty, and self-image becomes a central focus. This is the gateway to years of potential social struggles for the autistic person. Ostracizing behavior—deliberate or otherwise—is common, as is very intentional bullying. Reports show that people with autism are three times as likely to be bullied as the general population (Sarris, 2018). For some on the spectrum, their lack of social awareness can actually be viewed as a gift during these years, providing a form of naïve insulation from the cruelness of their peers. For others, these years can be the most difficult to endure. Cognizant of their differences, but able to participate fully in a standard school setting, these autistic teenagers must navigate the typical trials of middle school and high school while having little to no connection with others.

The social isolation and feelings of inferiority that accompany ASD have the potential to generate several comorbid mental disorders. Studies on depression have found it to be three times as likely in the autistic population than in the general population, with the incidence of suicide being five times higher than average (Sarris, 2018). Difficulties with communication and the identification of emotions, combined with atypical displays of depression may be partly responsible for this increased incidence and missed diagnoses (Sarris, 2018). Features that would typically describe a depressed person—flat affect, withdrawal, introversion—may be confused with an autistic's natural appearance. Symptoms such as aggression or emotional outbursts may be viewed as behavioral issues rather than an alternative expression of a depressed state.

ASD individuals are also at an increased risk for developing **obsessive-compulsive disorder** (OCD) or other related anxiety disorders (Mazzone, Ruta, & Reale, 2012). One study showed that 40% of ASD individuals are diagnosed with anxiety, with 30% of those diagnoses being specific phobias and the 17% being OCD (Meier et al., 2015). **Social anxiety** is especially prevalent, and the presence of both depression and anxiety can quickly become a downward spiral. The autistic person's tendency toward introversion fuels a desire to avoid social situations, which leads to increased depression and isolation. The fear of social situations continues to grow, alienating the individual even more, and reinforcing their disconnection from others. When the symptoms of depression and anxiety begin to impair an individual's functioning, it is prudent to encourage a psychiatric evaluation and possible medications. Functional impairment would include a decreased ability to participate or succeed in areas where the person was previously capable, such as academically, socially, or vocationally. It could also be indicated by a disruption in the person's ability to maintain healthy self-care routines or habits, such as eating, sleeping, exercise, or hygiene (Meier et al., 2015).

Pastors can encourage parents to seek out social skills support groups, individual therapy, and ASD communities to promote healthy responses to these difficult years. Having a network of referrals to provide in these situations can be extremely beneficial. The prevalence of autism and the activism of spectrum families has created a wealth of opportunities for connection with others, including organized meetings and activities for every interest under the sun. Despite the appearance of a preference for solitude, ASD individuals benefit greatly, as all people do, from relationships with others. An attuned pastor can be of great value in guiding these families to helpful outside resources, especially in moments of crisis. Often, families come to their pastor or church leaders when they feel lost, and having a network of available resources can provide these families with the direction they need.

KEY TERMS

Individualized Educational Plan: designed by schools to include different forms of therapy, behavioral modifications, and other special accommodations to meet the varying needs of students with disabilities

Obsessive-compulsive disorder: an anxiety disorder involving unwanted and repeated thoughts, feelings, images, and sensations, and engagement in behaviors or mental acts in response to these thoughts or obsessions

Depression: feelings of sadness, loss of interest in things once enjoyed

Social anxiety: a fear of social situations that may involve interaction with others

Discussion Questions

1 What difficulties might arise for an ASD individual in a school setting?

2 Discuss why adolescence might be a particularly challenging time for children on the autistic spectrum.

3 Why is depression more common in autistic individuals than in the general population?

4 What are some signs that might indicate an ASD individual is struggling with other mental health issues?

UNDERSTANDING THE IMPACT OF AUTISM ON THE FAMILY

The vignette at the start of this chapter tells just one story of autism's impact on a family. As you are likely learning, the effects on an individual, married couple, or a family are broad and vary according to the afflicted person's place on the spectrum. In more severe cases of autism, the affect will likely be greater, while in milder cases, the needs for support may be less. Severity is not the only factor in need, however, so we must attend to each case with a clear picture of the family's situation.

A conscientious understanding of relationships within the family, including marital, sibling, and extended family members, is highly recommended. Roles and expectations within the family should be discussed, with the pastor expressing curiosity and not judgment. An important goal of this conversation is to understand the family's system better, including which members hold what responsibilities, to identify areas of conflict and potential need. During this discussion, it could be helpful to hear from each member individually in an effort to ascertain the presence of unspoken concerns for each other, for their autistic family member, or for themselves. Feelings of grief are common, with one or both parents struggling to accept that their hopes for their child's future may be unrealized. Their own dreams of future retirement from the responsibilities of parenthood may be challenged by the knowledge that their child's needs will likely continue beyond their years. Siblings may experience a wide range of emotions about their impaired sibling, including embarrassment, shame over their embarrassment, protectiveness, and even increased feelings of rivalry. It is likely that the autistic sibling will require more attention and may be held to lower expectations by the parents, causing feelings of unfairness in the typical siblings. Resentment and acting out by the typical children may occur, often resulting in increased frustration for the parents. Extended family members may bring other emotions to the table, varying on their own understanding of autism. Empathic relatives can be a tremendous support to the family, while less accepting ones can easily increase the areas of existing conflict.

Particular attention to the mother of an autistic individual is advised. As a child's first and primary attachment figure, she is especially vulnerable to **caregiver depression** (Often associated with end-of-life illnesses, caregivers can begin to exhibit typical symptoms of depression, as the demands of caring for the diagnosed individual begin to drain their physical and psychological resources.) The needs of an autistic child can test the limits of even the strongest parent, and their attempts to meet those needs may feel futile. In our chapter vignette, Lauren struggled to comfort a child who was not easily comforted. It is feasible that she would experience fatigue, frustration, and feelings of rejection in her efforts to care for Dylan. Her attempts to show love and care for a distressed child appear to have no effect on him, so she may be left feeling useless and ineffective. In her weakest moments, she may feel like a bad mother. It is a feeling shared by many mothers of autistic children and is especially difficult to rationalize prior to an actual diagnosis of ASD, which may not come until years later.

Regrettably, there is historical relevance to Lauren's story. Beginning with Leo Kanner's diagnosis of autism in 1943, mothers of autistic children were blamed for their child's condition (Grandin & Panek, 2013). Kanner described a "lack of maternal warmth," and later, in 1967, Bruno Bettelheim coined the term "refrigerator mother" to describe the mothers of autistic children, whose coldness was presumed to be the cause of their children's emotional dysregulation. Both clinicians failed to note the existence of unimpaired siblings, who were well adjusted, nonautistic, and, apparently, raised in the same homes by the same mothers. Vast and significant research has debunked the "refrigerator mother" theory, with Bettelheim himself finally being exposed as a fraudulent child psychologist (Grandin & Panek, 2013). Nonetheless, mothers of ASD children often feel blamed for their children's behavior. Assuming the role of counselor for these caregivers requires an understanding of their experience, so the pastor is urged to empathize with the feelings of criticism and misunderstood frustration that are all too familiar to these women.

Attachment theory, which provides a lens through which we can view relationships based on early interaction with caregivers, challenges our previous assumptions about child-parent bonding in ASD individuals. Research shows that autistic children are capable of attachment to their caregivers and that approximately 50% of infants demonstrate secure attachment styles with their caregivers (Filippello, Pina & Flavia, Marino & Chilà, P & Sorrenti, Luana. 2015). While this statistic is lower than the secure attachment rate in neurotypical children, it is significant enough to dispel the notion that autistic individuals are incapable of relational attachment. Mary Ainsworth's original "**Strange Situation**" experiment identified different attachment styles in different children. By observing several children and their responses to their mothers' versus strangers' entrances and exits from a room, Ainsworth was able to define three primary attachment styles (McLeod, 2014). When replicated with autistic children, their attachment styles were found to correspond with unaffected children, with relatively similar numbers of autistic children exhibiting secure attachment as compared to typical children (Takahashi, Tamaki, & Yamawaki, 2013).

Cognitive ability did appear to affect the results, however, implying that future attachment research should consider cognition as a factor in attachment. Attachment studies also suggest that reciprocity is an important piece of attachment, with sensory-disordered individuals showing some resistance to physical affection, such as hugging. There is also research supporting the idea that autistic infants may not make the connection between their distressed cries and the mother's appearance to comfort them (Esposito & Scattoni, 2017). Their distress is new each and every time, and mom's appearance is also new each and every time. One can imagine how this would create a feeling of isolation, where the child's needs are not easily understood to be met by others, regardless of a caregiver's presence. Autistic individuals often prefer a solitary, unchanging world. They are comforted by routine and are averse to the chaos of ordinary life, but this does not negate their need, or even their desire, for relationships. The challenge is how to care for them, addressing their preference for solitude, while encouraging and providing healthy relationships with those around them. It is important to note the common misconceptions that autistic people are not empathic or capable of close relationships with others. While their mannerisms and sensitivities may present as resistance to physical closeness, this does not mean that they desire it any less. Similarly, while communication deficits may impair an autistic person's ability to convey emotions, this is not indicative of an inability to feel deeply or to recognize deep feelings in others. Relationships may be more challenging for those with autism, but are no less essential or significant. Openly addressing an ASD individual's desire for relationship can be an effective way of implementing change. Often, autistic individuals have a very blunt manner, void of nuance or innuendo, and thus may appreciate directness when offered to them. Simply asking an ASD individual, "Do you want to make some friends?" could lead to opportunities for connection with others. A pastor who is comfortable being this direct might find a way to arrange small groups befitting these individuals.

KEY TERMS

Attachment theory: the establishment of a relational style based on a child's early interaction with caregivers

"Strange Situation": Mary Ainsworth's experiment and research into three primary attachment styles

Discussion Questions

1   How might autism affect a child's attachment to his or her primary caregiver?

2   Why is it important for a pastor and fellow church members to understand the relational aspects of autism?

3   Discuss at least three different and noteworthy dynamics possible within the family system of an ASD individual.

4   Describe some areas of a family's structure to which a pastor should pay special attention.

A FAITH-BASED VIEW OF AUTISM

From Mark 9:17–29, New International Version (NIV):

[17] A man in the crowd answered, "Teacher, I brought you my son, who is possessed by a spirit that has robbed him of speech. [18] Whenever it seizes him, it throws him to the ground. He foams at the mouth, gnashes his teeth and becomes rigid. I asked your disciples to drive out the spirit, but they could not."

[19] "You unbelieving generation," Jesus replied, "how long shall I stay with you? How long shall I put up with you? Bring the boy to me."

[20] So they brought him. When the spirit saw Jesus, it immediately threw the boy into a convulsion. He fell to the ground and rolled around, foaming at the mouth.

[21] Jesus asked the boy's father, "How long has he been like this?"

"From childhood," he answered. [22] "It has often thrown him into fire or water to kill him. But if you can do anything, take pity on us and help us."

[23] "'If you can'?" said Jesus. "Everything is possible for one who believes."

[24] Immediately the boy's father exclaimed, "I do believe; help me overcome my unbelief!"

[25] When Jesus saw that a crowd was running to the scene, he rebuked the impure spirit. "You deaf and mute spirit," he said, "I command you, come out of him and never enter him again." [26] The spirit shrieked, convulsed him violently and came out. The boy looked so much like a corpse that many said, "He's dead." [27] But Jesus took him by the hand and lifted him to his feet, and he stood up.

[28] After Jesus had gone indoors, his disciples asked him privately, "Why couldn't we drive it out?"

[29] He replied, "This kind can come out only by prayer."[a]

While this account from the Bible portrays a boy being exorcised of a "demon," it could be argued that his features are somewhat symptomatic of autism. Especially in childhood, seizures are consistent with an ASD diagnosis, and the words "mute," "deaf," and "dumb" all imply a communication disorder. We must consider, however, the negative implication that autism is "possession" by a demon, and that faith and prayer might be enough to cure it. Many historical citing's of demonic possession are now viewed as mental disorders, with clinicians understanding that what appears to be "demonic possession" may have underlying neurological and emotional causes. It can be helpful to cast a wide net over the root causes of autism to help those afflicted to understand God's plan in this. Evidence points us in many different directions, but they all leave the lingering questions of *how* and *why*, which may remain unanswered. Calling upon all of our resources to address our inherent need for explanation is vital, especially when we are faced with such unanswerable questions. Prayers for peace and understanding should accompany our search for scientific knowledge, as both may help to illuminate the road ahead.

Life on the autism spectrum presents many challenges—vocational, emotional, and relational. Frustration during the more difficult times may be inevitable, but scripture directs us to have faith beyond our understanding: "Now faith is the substance of things hoped for, the evidence of things not seen" (Heb. 11:1 King James Bible). It may be helpful to view autism less like an affliction and more like an aspect of a personality. By defining it negatively, autism becomes an obstacle to be overcome rather than part of a whole. This stigmatization can limit our view of the future, lowering expectations and even masking the potential gifts of autism. Scripture instructs us that "everything is possible for one who believes" (Mark 9:23 NIV). "Everything" is not limited to exorcism, or to the miraculous disappearance of autism, nor is "one who believes" reserved for the unafflicted. It is simply that *everything is possible for one who believes.* As challenges are encountered, we are called to meet them with faith in God's promise of endless possibilities.

Pastors can demonstrate this truth by doing God's good work of supporting those who are struggling and by providing every opportunity for their success. In Mark 9:22, the afflicted boy's father pleas, "But if you can do anything, take pity on us and help us." This is a very poignant verse in this account, which could be considered a call to the caring person. Jesus models precisely how to answer it: "But Jesus took him by the hand and lifted him to his feet, and he stood up" (Mark 9:27). Jesus reminds the people of the power of prayer and once again demonstrates that faith removes all limitations. For autistic individuals and their families, those limitations may appear in various forms. The helping pastor can provide care and relief when he or she is able and can be a bridge to outside supports when they are needed. First and foremost, the pastor should respond with empathy to the family. The initial call for help may be in a time of crisis, and it is likely that the family feels lost and possibly outcast. As the head of their church family, the pastor's response should reflect acceptance and care. Simply sitting with them and letting them know that the church is there to help can be incredibly comforting as the family comes to grips with the diagnosis. The family may have many questions, and the pastor can direct them to the proper resources as they arise. A referral for couples' or family counseling can be beneficial to help them process the different emotional responses that come up, and encouragement to pursue academic assistance is advisable. Because of the spectrum nature of autism, there is a wide range of accommodations for the church to consider. It would be most beneficial to check in with the family periodically to determine what assistance can be provided. For instance, additional aides on hand in the Sunday school classrooms may be necessary to accommodate the needs of an autistic child. If the classroom environment is presenting sensory integration difficulties, an extra helper on hand could alleviate stress for the entire class. Assistance with motor-skill-related classwork or even relief from the noise or lights in the room could be provided by an additional volunteer. Again, checking in with the parents and meeting the autistic child's needs as they arise would likely be a most welcome response, indicating a desire to help and a consistent effort to care for them as part of the church family.

Discussion Questions

1. How can a pastor address the questions of "why" an individual has been afflicted with autism?

2. How does Jesus model our response to an individual who might be struggling to live a life with autism?

3. How can pastors and churches support the needs of families or people on the autism spectrum?

REVIEWING THE CONCEPTS

Learning Objectives

- Describe the "spectrum" nature of ASD
  - High-functioning autism
  - Asperger's syndrome
  - Low-functioning autism

- Identify and describe the symptoms of ASD
  - Communication difficulties
  - Social impairment
  - Restricted, repetitive behaviors or interests

- Identify areas in need of support for ASD individuals and their families
  - Educational
  - Social
  - Environmental

- Understand how to attend to affected individuals and members of their family
  - Varying perceptions and experiences of the ASD individual
  - Roles of different family members
  - Attention to the needs of the primary caregiver

- Understand ways is which pastors and churches can respond to afflicted members of their congregation
  - Empathy for afflicted members and their families
  - Referral to outside supports
  - Accommodations within the church as needed

Chapter Review Questions

Level 1: Knowledge (True/False)

1. Autism is primarily recognized as a cognitive impairment.

2. High-functioning autism and Asperger's syndrome are often used interchangeably.

3. Stimming and other repetitive behaviors are nonfunctional symptoms of ASD.

4. The social deficits of autism sometimes act as a natural barrier to social anxiety.

5. Research has shown that autistic children demonstrate extremely different attachment styles than neurotypical children.

6. Mothers of autistic children are at an increased risk for depression.

7. Autistic individuals are incapable of establishing close relationships with others.

8. Sensitivity to bright lights is symptomatic of the sensory integration difficulties in autistic individuals.

9. Schools are required by law to provide IEPs for students who meet the requirements for accommodations.

10. In the Book of Mark, Chapter 9, Jesus reminds us that everything is possible for one who believes.

Level 2: Comprehension

1. According to the *DSM-5*, which of the following are diagnoses of autism?
    a. High-functioning autism
    b. Low-functioning autism
    c. Asperger's syndrome
    d. None of the above

2. Which of the following is often the first indication of autism?
    a. Absence of crying as an infant
    b. Poor motor skills, such as jumping or climbing
    c. Delayed speech development
    d. Hand flapping

3. Sensory integration affects the following systems:
    a. Tactile
    b. Vestibular
    c. Proprioceptive
    d. All of the above

4. Sensory overload can cause
    a. meltdowns
    b. tantrums
    c. isolation
    d. all of the above

5. The purpose of "stimming" is to

    a. increase feelings of pleasure

    b. reduce feelings of discomfort

    c. relieve feelings of stress

    d. all of the above

6. Comorbid disorders related to autism include

    a. OCD

    b. Tourette syndrome

    c. oppositional defiant disorder

    d. none of the above

7. Young siblings of autistic individuals may exhibit which of the following?

    a. Increased expressions of rivalry

    b. Embarrassment

    c. Protectiveness

    d. All of the above

8. Research on attachment in autism shows that

    a. the secure attachment rate is equivalent to that of typical children

    b. cognitive ability is a factor in attachment

    c. cold "refrigerator mothers" are often to blame for autistic children

    d. ASD individuals do not desire close relationships with others

9. The increased prevalence of autism is most likely due to which of the following?

    a. Early immunizations

    b. An overall increase in the male population

    c. Increased awareness of autism

    d. All of the above

10. Pastors can help autistic individuals by providing which of the following?

    a. Empathy

    b. Supportive resources

    c. Accommodations

    d. All of the above

Level 3: Application

1. Write a short sermon about Jesus's words to us about the connection between faith, prayer, and possibilities as they might pertain to church members with impairments such as autism.

2. How might you distinguish between the typical symptoms of autism and a presentation of depression or anxiety?

3. Imagine that a volunteer from children's ministries meets with you to discuss ongoing difficulties with an autistic child in his or her Sunday school class. How might you address this volunteer and his or her concerns?

4. Upon meeting with the parents of a 6-year-old boy, you suspect that their frustrations with his behavior—both at school and at church—may be indicative of ASD. After some discussion, they share that his schoolteacher has mentioned a possible diagnosis of autism, but they strongly disagree with her. How might you attend to these parents?

5. Write a short essay describing the way you would like to approach ASD church members. Think and write about the types of accommodations, trainings, or structural elements that you could implement in your church to support these individuals.

ANSWERS

LEVEL 1: KNOWLEDGE

1. F
2. T
3. F
4. T
5. F
6. T
7. F
8. T
9. T
10. T

LEVEL 2: COMPREHENSION

1. d
2. c
3. d
4. d
5. d
6. a
7. d
8. b
9. c
10. d

RESOURCES

Online Resources

- Autism Speaks—www.autismspeaks.org
- Autism Society—www.autism-society.org

Readings

- *1001 Great Ideas for Teaching and Raising Children with Autism or Asperger's*—Ellen Notbohm and Veronica Zysk
- *The Autistic Brain: Helping Different Kinds of Minds Succeed*—Temple Grandin and Richard Panek
- *The Complete Guide to Asperger's Syndrome*—Tony Attwood
- *The Loving Push: How Parents and Professionals Can Help Spectrum Kids Become Successful Adults*—Temple Grandin, PhD and Debra Moore, PhD

CLASSROOM ACTIVITIES

1. Imagine that a childcare worker from the church approaches you for advice on how to manage a disruptive child with autism who is attending Sunday school classes. How would you handle this situation?

2. Role-play a conversation between yourself and the parents of an autistic child, who have come to you to share their distress over recently learning of their child's diagnosis.

REFERENCES

American Psychiatric Association. (2013). *Diagnostic and statistical manual of mental disorders* (5th ed.). Arlington, VA: Author.

Carter, M. & Van Andel, G. (2011). *Therapeutic recreation: A practical approach.* Long Grove, IL: Waveland Press, Inc.

Centers for Disease Control and Prevention. (2014). Autism and developmental disabilities monitoring (ADDM) network. Retrieved from https://www.cdc.gov/ncbddd/autism/addm.html

Esposito, G., Hiroi, N., & Scattoni, M. L. (2017). Cry, baby, cry: Expression of distress as a biomarker and modulator in autism spectrum disorder. *International Journal of Neuropsychopharmacology, 20*(6), 498–503. http://doi.org/10.1093/ijnp/pyx014

Filippello, Pina & Flavia, Marino & Chilà, P & Sorrenti, Luana. (2015). Attachment and social behavior in children's autistic disorders. *Life Span and Disability.* 18. 101–118.

Grandin, T. & Panek, R. (2013). *The autistic brain: Helping different kinds of minds succeed.* New York, NY: Houghton Mifflin Harcourt Publishing Company.

Hatch-Rasmussen, C. (2018). Sensory integration. Retrieved from https://www.autism.com/symptoms_sensory_overview

Hutten, M. (2015). Pragmatic language impairment in Asperger's and high-functioning autism. Retrieved from http://www.myaspergerschild.com/2015/04/pragmatic-language-impairment-in.html

Lewis, M. (2013). Echolalia. In F. R. Volkmar (Ed.), *Encyclopedia of autism spectrum disorders.* New York, NY: Springer.

Mazzone, L., Ruta, L., & Reale, L. (2012). Psychiatric comorbidities in Asperger syndrome and high functioning autism: Diagnostic challenges. *Annals of General Psychiatry, 11(1),* 16. http://doi.org/10.1186/1744-859X-11-16

McLeod, S. A. (2014). Mary Ainsworth. Retrieved from www.simplypsychology.org/mary-ainsworth.html

Meier, S. M., Petersen, L., Schendel, D. E., Mattheisen, M., Mortensen, P. B., & Mors, O. (2015). Obsessive-compulsive disorder and autism spectrum disorders: Longitudinal and offspring risk. *PLoS ONE, 10*(11), e0141703. http://doi.org/10.1371/journal.pone.0141703

Me, M. (2009). Autism awareness month: Interview with Stephen Shore [Interview transcript]. Retrieved from https://www.healthcentral.com/article/autism-awareness-month-interview-with-stephen-shore

Nicholson, A., Goclowska, A. & Nolan, S. (2018). STEMsational figures. Retrieved from http://stemsational-figures.co.uk/?page_id=125

Parsloe, S. & Babrow, A. (2015) Removal of Asperger's syndrome from the *DSM V*: Community response to uncertainty. *Health Communication,* 31(4), 485–494. doi: 10.1080/10410236.2014.968828

Sarris, M. (2018). Diagnosing depression in autism. Retrieved from https://www.iancommunity.org/diagnosing-depression-autism

Siri, K. & Lyons, T. (2012). *Cutting edge therapies for autism.* New York, NY: Skyhorse Publishing.

Takahashi, J., Tamaki, K. & Yamawaki, N. (2013). Autism spectrum, attachment styles, and social skills in university students. *Science Research: Creative Education,* 4(8)514–520. http://dx.doi.org/10.4236/ce.2013.48075

U.S. Department of Health and Human Services. (2016) Autism spectrum disorder: Communication problems in children [Data File]. Retrieved from https://www.nidcd.nih.gov/sites/default/files/Documents/publications/pubs/AutismSpectrumDisorder-508.pdf

Wright, P.W.D. & Wright, P. D. (2018). Individualized education programs. Retrieved from http://www.wrightslaw.com/info/iep.index.htm

IMAGE CREDITS

Understanding Psychopharmacology

Thomas Okamoto, MD

LEARNING OBJECTIVES

Upon completion of this chapter, readers will be to

1. understand the pervasiveness of mental health needs in the community, including church congregations, and be able to cite frequencies of mental disorders likely to be seen in the church population;

2. define the term "psychopharmacology" and describe its role in the treatment of mental illnesses;

3. describe the theory of how psychiatric medications treating mental illness restore the brain's ability to function normally, regulating human perceptual, cognitive, and emotional experiences and functions; and

4. describe ways mental illnesses and their psychopharmacologic treatments affect the spiritual experience.

All the most acute, most powerful, and most deadly diseases,
and those which are most difficult to be understood
by the inexperienced, fall upon the brain.
(Hippocrates 400 BCE)

For You formed my inward parts;
You covered me in my mother's womb.
I will praise You, for I am fearfully and wonderfully made;
Marvelous are Your works,
And that my soul knows very well.
(Ps. 139:13–14, New King James Version)

THE STORY OF BRIAN

Brian, a 42-year-old married, successful businessman visits the pastor "for one last try" at getting help from the church. He had been drinking too often, sleeping too little, is angry too much, and is having an affair almost "in front" of his wife, as if there is a part of him that wants to get caught to stop the chaos. He is fearful that he will be caught, that his wife will divorce him, and that his grade-school children will see him as a bad father. He knows the "right" thing to do. He is depressed, anxious, and progressively angry for no reason. He feels that he needs to "turn to God." He was raised in a home with an alcoholic and physically abusive father. His father was a womanizer, but his wife (Brian's mother) was withdrawn and often cried. Upon further questioning, Brian discloses that he had been to therapy and had taken medications for mood problems, but as with many times before, he decided to stop both to pursue more "spiritual resources."

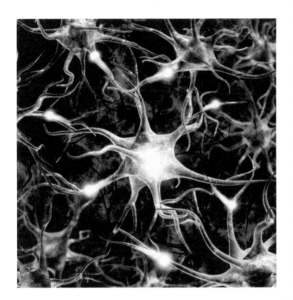

FIGURE 12.1 **Neurons**

There are many moments of personal crises that force church leadership to demonstrate the church's heart. The choice in this case is between engaging Brian and his needs or turning him away for lack of "the right resources." The choice to connect includes encouraging and referring him back to counseling and psychiatric care, offering prayer with competent support ministries and ongoing church fellowship with follow-up. The church could provide relationships to walk alongside Brian through his struggles to make good choices, with the church investing in his life. Avoiding Brian's needs brings up Matthew 25:42–45: *"For I was hungry, and you gave Me nothing to eat; I was thirsty, and you gave Me nothing to drink; I was a stranger, and you did not invite Me in; naked, and you did not clothe Me; sick, and in prison, and you did not visit Me' ... 'Truly I say to you, to the extent that you did not do it to one of the least of these, you did not do it to Me'"* (New American Standard Bible). Brian, if turned away, could choose to search for another church or be discouraged one last time, leaving the church to move toward self-destruction and spiritual disaster. The added awareness of psychopharmacology can equip today's church and, in this case, can alert the leadership to Brian's need to return to professional care. If engaged and assisted by the church toward professional care, personal support, and spiritual direction, the church could be a part of Brian's life transformation and spiritual victory.

INTRODUCTION TO PSYCHOPHARMACOLOGY

Throughout history, mental illness has been present, and philosophers, physicians, and more recently psychiatrists have tried to understand these conditions now seen as the most disabling illnesses known in medicine. From Hippocrates, the father of medicine, to the father of American psychiatry, **Benjamin Rush**, famous physicians (most of whom were originally neurologists, and many were of the Christian faith) were studying mental illnesses to discover treatments to relieve suffering. Even Sigmund Freud, originally a neurologist, predicted that psychological symptoms that in his time could only be treated by psychoanalysis, would be treated in the future with hormones or chemical substances (Freud, 1964). There have been many scientific "treatments," including bloodletting, seizure induction, and lobotomy. Now they are seen as primitive and ineffective, but were motivated by compassion to relieve the extreme suffering of mental illness.

Modern science has led to better treatments, with hope for continued progress for future psychiatric care. Currently, a major area of psychiatry is the field of **psychopharmacology** (from Greek ψῦχή, *psȳkhē*, "breath, life, soul"; φάρμακον, *pharmakon*, "drug"; and -λογία, *-logia*) (Meyer & Quenzer, 2005). Psychopharmacology is defined as the scientific study of the use of medications in treating mental disorders (American Society of Clinical Psychopharmacology, 2018). Recently, the public health and medical communities have realized the scope of disability that mental illnesses cause (Lynskey & Strang, 2013). The huge global impact of mental illness and the significant benefits of modern psychopharmacology are now being recognized throughout the medical world.

This chapter will introduce church leaders to the psychiatric specialty of psychopharmacology, an established part of modern medicine. It will explore basic fears and inform the sometimes outdated beliefs of those who serve in the Christian church toward those who suffer from mental illnesses. With successful treatment of these medical illnesses, spiritual growth and transformation can be enhanced for afflicted individuals. The restoration of mental health can promote a clearer God-created identity, healthier relationships, and growth in the family and in the church for those afflicted and for those involved with their care and support. This chapter is not intended to be a complete reference for all the names, uses, and science of psychiatric medications. Current and more comprehensive resources off and online will be listed at the end of the chapter.

The purpose of this chapter is to further develop bridge building between the modern Christian church and those who are being prescribed psychiatric medication, both in the congregation and in the unchurched. Leadership either in the pulpit or at the greeting tables will be equipped with a basic understanding and knowledge of psychopharmacologic treatments of common mental illnesses. The hope of this chapter is to promote more grace and mercy for those who are afflicted, equipping the church to further love one another (John 13:34) and to be the hands and feet of Christ.

MYTHS AND REALITIES OF PSYCHIATRIC MEDICATION TREATMENT

Myth 1: My Church Congregation Has No Mental Health Problems (So We Can Ignore Issues of Mental Illness and Mental Health Care)

The World Health Organization (WHO), the Harvard School of Public Health, and the World Bank published the **Global Burden of Disease Study** (Lynskey & Strang, 2013), which surveyed all diseases on the globe to prepare for health needs in future decades. The study results shocked the public health world, finding that most of the worst disabling diseases were mental health diagnoses. In 2017, WHO declared major depression as the most disabling illness worldwide (World Health Organization, 2018).

Numbers quoted by the National Alliance on Mental Illness (NAMI) cite 1 in 5 in the United States experiences mental illness in a year, 1 in 5 adolescents between the ages of 13 and 18 experience a severe mental disorder during their lifetimes (National Alliance on Mental Illness, 2018b). Furthermore, NAMI data suggests that 1.1% in the United States live with schizophrenia, 2.6% live with bipolar disorder, and 6.9% of adults experience at least one major depressive episode in a year, while 18.1% experience some form of anxiety disorder. The numbers are no different for Christians and non-Christians. In 2014, Lifeway Research published a survey (Lifeway Research, 2014), supported by Focus on the Family and the family of a person who suffered with schizophrenia. The study surveyed 1,000 Protestant pastors, 120,000 Protestant individuals with major mental illness, and family members of those with acute mental illness, using experts in Christian mental health for analysis and discussion. They found that people with mental illness often turn to the church first for help. A majority of pastors (59%) have counseled one or more people who were eventually diagnosed with an acute mental illness. Surprisingly, 23% of the pastors surveyed indicated that they personally struggled with mental illness of some kind.

There has never been a time when the church had "no mental health problems."

An example of possible depression can be seen in Elijah (1 Kings 19), who was in fear for his life because of threats from Jezebel. Elijah retreated to Beersheba in Judah and withdrew into the wilderness, wanting to die. He left his servant and wanted to isolate away from God. God provided relationship, along with touch, food, and rest through an angel. When Elijah was restored physically and emotionally, God again spoke to him, giving him purpose with his next mission and a relationship with helper and protector Elisha. God restored Elijah from a depression that had threatened to defeat him even when Jezebel could not.

Many prominent American Christians who personally experienced mental illness or had family members who were afflicted advocated for mental health care and were discussed in the book titled *Madness: American Protestant Responses to Mental Illness* (Vacek, 2015). God's will and purpose are sovereign despite illness.

The history of mental illnesses extends back to hundreds of years BC, and as in other areas of medicine, there have been many diagnostic systems used over the centuries. Prior to the 19th century, it was commonly believed that mental illness represented demonic possession, and this became a reference for mental illness. Jesus's ministry of healing was significant in healing those with "demon possession" likely including the experience of mental illness.

Mental health care and the accompanying discussions about psychiatric medications are now part of missionary care, prayer requests, pastoral counseling, church staff issues, and hospital visits. The church can choose to be a credible, physical, and spiritual resource for these suffering individuals and families looking for direction and support.

Myth 2: The Mental Health Field Is "Anti-Christian" and Influenced Mainly by Freud

Freud is cited as the genius who developed the concept of the unconscious. As with other scientists, Freud's own humanity and psychological issues were expressed in his writings and unscientifically steered his perspectives. He devalued spirituality and belief in God, as did other scientists of his time, as part of the modern age of a godless scientism. In contrast, there were other scientists who were devout Christians who also influenced scientific discovery. This was true in the field of psychoanalysis. Many men and women of faith developed historic mental health theories in ways that supported biblical truth. A regular correspondent with Freud in the early 1900s, Oskar Pfister, was a Swiss Lutheran pastor who advocated and practiced psychoanalysis. He also encouraged a return to the fundamental teachings of Jesus Christ while founding the Swiss Society for Psychoanalysis (Roazen, 1993). Pfister bears the name of the American Psychiatric Association's yearly award for contributions to the field of religion and psychiatry. Other Christians in the field of psychiatry who advanced psychological and psychiatric care of the mentally ill included Benjamin Rush, a physician and one of the signers of the Declaration of Independence, known as the father of American psychiatry. D. W. Winnicott, a Christian pediatrician and child psychoanalyst, developed a major theoretical school of psychoanalysis. The Tavistock Clinic, a historic British psychoanalytic clinic, included influential Christian psychoanalysts (Hoffman, 2011).

Recent psychiatric research has dismissed Freud's blanket devaluation of religion and has embraced healthy spirituality as a positive component of mental health. Newer studies document the benefits of religious commitment, including improved outcomes in mental health treatments, reduced suicide rates, and protection against returning depression (Verghese, 2008).

Physicians and psychiatrists are now encouraged to perform a spirituality assessment as part of a medical evaluation and to partner with faith-based supports, clergy, church supports, and recovery groups.

The American Psychiatric Association has recently recognized and encouraged the positive relationship between the mental health care field and the faith communities. In 2014, the American Psychiatric Association started "The Mental Health and Faith Community Partnership" (American Psychiatric Association, 2018), a collaboration between psychiatrists and clergy aimed at fostering a dialogue between the two fields, reducing stigma, and accounting for medical and spiritual dimensions as people seek care. The American Psychiatric Association, the American Psychiatric Association Foundation, and the Interfaith Disability Advocacy Coalition committed to promote a spirituality and psychiatry partnership.

Myth 3: Mental Illness Is the Result of a Spiritual Problem That Has to Be Resolved Spiritually

The Lifeway Research study (2014) found that labeling mental illness as only a spiritual issue is not helpful and can be detrimental. Strong faith alone was found to be ineffective in resolving mental illness.

Although the Lifeway Research study (2014) found that pastors, individuals affected, and families of the ill all felt that a Christian with an acute mental illness can thrive spiritually regardless of whether the illness was stabilized, the study also found that 28% of individuals with acute mental illness agreed that their mental illness hindered their ability to live like a Christian. In most cases, the experts participating in the study felt the illness needed to be treated and stabilized before spiritual growth could take place.

To deny medical treatment to encourage a spiritual trial prevents available healing from illness, which is not loving or Godly. The withholding of medical care in other conditions, such as cancer or heart disease would be both unethical and cruel. Withholding psychiatric care from one suffering from mental illness would be equally cruel.

KEY TERMS

Psychopharmacology: the scientific study of the use of medications in treating mental disorders

Global Burden of Disease Study: first published in 2005, a major worldwide public health research project documenting 6 out of the top 10 medical causes of disability were mental health issues

Benjamin Rush: early U.S. signer of the Declaration of Independence, legislator, and psychiatrist in the 17th century who championed mental health care, founded the first U.S. psychiatric hospital in Philadelphia, and was a Christian.

Discussion Questions

1   Discuss the frequency of mental disorders in the general population and estimate how many in the church suffer from them.

2   Does God intend mental illness to be healed?

3   Is psychopharmacology consistent with Christian principles?

THE MORALITY OF PSYCHOPHARMACOLOGY

Arguments Against Psychopharmacology

There are many questionable arguments against psychiatric medication use, despite acceptance in the medical and public health fields.

One strong factor for accepting the concept of mental illness and participating in psychopharmacologic treatment is that of denial. It is challenging for most individuals to accept and rise above the personal denial of a "mental disturbance" in oneself. Denial and pride are powerful forces that block self-awareness of illness, preventing restoration. It is frightening to accept a diagnosis of mental illness, which can be humbling and like accepting a loss of personal control, as with other illnesses. In addition, the effects of shame and stigma in mental illness discourage seeking help.

Other arguments against psychopharmacology include the challenge of who is qualified to define what are "symptoms" of illness and who defines a "treatable disease?" Who decides what is a "normal temperament?" Some of these issues were highlighted by Peter Kramer, MD in *Listening to Prozac: A Psychiatrist Explores Antidepressant Drugs and the Remaking of the Self* (1993). In this book, Prozac introduced the capability to "improve" traits once thought to be a stable part of temperament and character, including shyness, jealousy, and aggressiveness. The widening of depression's treatable "symptoms" challenges what a person's "identity" and "character" really are and questions what medications can do. Is psychopharmacologic treatment ethical for self "enhancement?" Are certain character traits really treatable symptoms of illness? The physician and patient ultimately choose these fluid boundaries of healing and illness.

There are also nonmedical arguments against the concept of "mental illness." Thomas Szasz argued in the 1960s that there is no such thing as "mental illness" (1974). He published the opinion that mental illness was a myth used by industry and society, that symptoms could not be scientifically quantified, and that the mentally ill were not suffering. He wrote that "mental illness" was only a social metaphor. The philosopher Michael Foucault (2006) similarly argued that beginning in the middle ages, treatment and diagnosing of the mentally ill were motivated by the wish to cast out a class of people from regular society, confining them away because they were "undesirable." He saw treatment as relieving them of their rights to their symptoms.

Reductionism (a prescription-only approach to psychiatry) is an error in the practice of and participation in psychiatry—a mistake for both the psychopharmacologist and the patient, not an intended part of appropriate care. The term "psychiatry" was originally translated as the "medical treatment of the soul." The term was coined in 1808 by Johann Christian Reil, a German physician and neurologist (Marneros, 2008). He wanted to establish the breadth and depth of the practice of psychiatric medicine to include philosophy, theology, internal medicine, and psychotherapy. Psychiatry was meant to be practiced while considering all of these areas of knowledge, appreciating the complexity of a relational and spiritual human being, not a simple binary formula altering chemical levels in the brain.

Critics against drug therapy argue that they are used for "covering up" and "masking" reality. This is considered misapplied psychopharmacology. The goal of treatment is to enable healthy emotional function, not to control behavior through side effects or secondary treatment effects. The true medical goal is to restore health, which restores normal perception and function in reality. Healing encourages unique identity and expression of the true self, and opposes suppressing humanity for external control of behavior and thought.

Some arguments against psychopharmacology in society are motivated by proprietary interest and are not based in a concern for better mental health care. One visible voice is the Church of Scientology and its Citizen's Commission on Human Rights. Desai (2005) reports that the founder of Scientology, L. Ron Hubbard, was dedicated to the "eradication of psychiatry from the face of the earth," and the Citizen's Commission on Human Rights was formed to "expose the evils of psychiatry."

Philosophic and theoretical arguments may debate about mental illness and argue the question about personal freedom, but they do not address the pain and suffering of the afflicted individuals and their families caused by the illnesses themselves. The need for release from the bondage and slavery of mental illness is the argument for psychiatric healing, as illness prevents the free expression of the unique self in identity and community.

Arguments for Psychopharmacology

The Lifeway study (2014) demonstrated that 94% of the individuals with acute mental illness had been prescribed medications, and 78% of the family members reported medications had been effective. In addition, 54% of individuals with mental illness and 40% of pastors in the study felt medications should be used anytime they can ease symptoms of acute mental illness.

The biggest support of psychopharmacology comes from medical research, establishing treatment of illness as the standard of care. To treat illness and relieve physical and mental suffering is a moral action when the illness is validated. To continually affirm the validity of psychiatric illness categories, psychiatry organizes work groups of expert professionals to inform and shape the latest index of mental disturbances named the ***Diagnostic and Statistical Manual of Mental Disorders*** or *DSM*, published by the American Psychiatric Association (American Psychiatric Association, 2013). It is integrated into medicine's similar index called the International Classification of Diseases produced by WHO. These classification systems include symptoms of inner feelings and outward behaviors, organizing illnesses according to severity as well as their effects on daily functioning. It is an index only, as mental illnesses are not yet completely understood, as is the case with other medical diseases.

Spiritual benefits of treatment include allowing the restoration of a God-created self by removing the illness and facilitating a possible release from the bondage of dysfunction and pain. Depressive disorders, mood disorders, anxiety disorders, psychotic disorders, and autism and attentional disorders are examples of illnesses that work against other-directedness. They, like other medical illnesses, cause the sufferer to withdraw into him or herself either by the illness' symptoms or the search for relief from the pain. With less pain, illness, and suffering, it is easier to be more present spiritually, as well as more relational. Treatment allows more clarity of perceptions, emotional appropriateness, and cognitive abilities that clarify choices in the struggle between flesh and spirit.

Another level of pain and suffering caused by these illnesses is that experienced by the spouse and family. For a parent, child, or significant other of one afflicted by mental illness, the pain is shared. Relief from symptoms of mental illness can aid in the spiritual development of an entire family.

Morality and Legality of Treatment and Nontreatment

Western society is moving toward medical care as a social responsibility (Resnik, 2007). National parity laws require large employers to provide access to mental health care

(U.S. Centers for Medicare & Medicaid Services, 2018). Psychiatric care, including psychopharmacologic treatment, is now seen as a compassionate and responsible action. For parents or family members of one afflicted by mental illness, it is considered responsible behavior to encourage mental health treatment for the afflicted family member (Mental Health America, 2018).

There is still debate, however, over legal rights and personal freedom to choose or refuse psychiatric care as a person afflicted with mental illness. Illness-caused misperceptions of reality can lead to tragic choices in the same way as someone who suffers from other neurologic diseases, such as dementia. Those with acute psychosis, depression, or mania at times can make impulsive or irrational choices, including the choice to obtain and comply with treatment. This can become a legal battle between advocates of personal freedom and loving families of the afflicted. Those with mental illness who refuse psychopharmacologic treatment can quickly cause themselves emotional, relational, and financial ruin. Even worse, untreated illness can progress to self or other-directed harm, including suicide and homicide. **Legal competence** is a complex concept argued in the courts and involves determining one's mental capacity to evaluate reality and choose and accept responsibility for personal, financial, relational, and medical choices (Buchanan, 2004).

Psychopharmacology has exposed new depth to the redemptive self and its vulnerability to illness. Society is reevaluating the role that mental illness plays in all spheres of identity and community. The church needs to participate and lead in this reevaluation.

KEY TERMS

Reductionism: oversimplifying mental illness as simply a biological switch needing medications only, ignoring the relational and spiritual dimensions of mental illness

Legal competence: a complex legal concept influenced by mental capacity to appropriately assess, legally choose and accept responsibility for a specific choice

Diagnostic and Statistical Manual of Mental Disorders: the diagnostic manual classifying mental disorders based on scientific evidence and expert consensus, published by the American Psychiatric Association

Discussion Questions

1   Is it moral to treat mental illness as a disease?

2   Is it consistent with Christian and biblical truth to treat mental illness as a disease?

3   Is facilitating relief from pain and suffering part of Christian duty?

PSYCHOPHARMACOLOGY

The relatively new science of psychopharmacology studies a profound frontier in medicine. It combines chemical technology with neurology to treat illness that affects mental and emotional experience. While this new technology stimulates philosophic, spiritual, and moral debate on the concepts of identity and self, its profound benefits to relieve human suffering and disability expands the scope of medicine and its ability to improve the human condition.

Brief History

Psychopharmacology began in the 1840s with the use of nitrous oxide, ether, and chloroform for anesthesia (Lehmann, 1993). From anesthesia, treatments for insomnia developed and then medicines for mental illnesses were discovered beginning in the 1950s, including lithium, antipsychotic medications, antidepressants, and treatments for anxiety. Before modern psychopharmacology, naturally occurring and other manufactured substances were used for therapeutic as well as recreational use. Alcohol, cannabinoids, herbals, opiates, amphetamines, hallucinogens, and anesthetics, among others, have been used to relieve emotional pain, treat unrecognized illness, or "enhance" human experience, at the risk of addiction or hazardous use. Psychopharmacology attempts to understand these practices and define their boundaries of safety and utility.

The Theory of Neurotransmission (How It Works)

The discovery of the nerve synapse in 1906 outlined a system of nerve connections throughout the brain and body communicating through "electrical signals," like wires connecting electricity in a home. In the 1950s, researchers recognized that nerves transmit these signals through different chemicals named "**neurotransmitters**." The theory of neurotransmission became the model of how chemicals, including psychopharmacologic medicines, could improve symptoms and restore damaged functions of the brain. The figure below illustrates the structure of nerves and their function.

In Figure 12.2, the initial nerve (beyond the top of the picture) sends an electrical signal down the axon to communicate with the lower nerve cell. The top nerve's signal is transmitted through a release of a packet of chemicals, "neurotransmitters," that travel through the space of the synapse to reach a "receptor" on the surface of the lower nerve (picture insert.) The chemical, through its own physical shape and other properties, "fits" the physical shape and properties of the "receptor" on the lower nerve surface. Once connected into the receptor, the lower cell is switched "on" to perform actions that can signal the next nerve cell in the circuit, and in coordination with other neurons, signals the brain to perceive sensation, feel emotions, think, or act. Once the neurotransmitter has signaled the next nerve cell, it is released out of the receptor back into the synapse, and the chemical is pumped back into the original neuron through a "**reuptake pump**" and saved for future use. The neurotransmitter can also be destroyed by enzymes in the synapse. The "reuptake pump" and these destructive enzymes are both blocked by different types of antidepressants. Both antidepressant classes lead to higher levels of neurotransmitters. This higher level of chemical is known as an early step in brain repair where normal nerve function is restored, and symptoms are relieved. In psychotic disorders, the opposite is helpful, as symptoms improve with a reduction in neurotransmitters (dopamine).

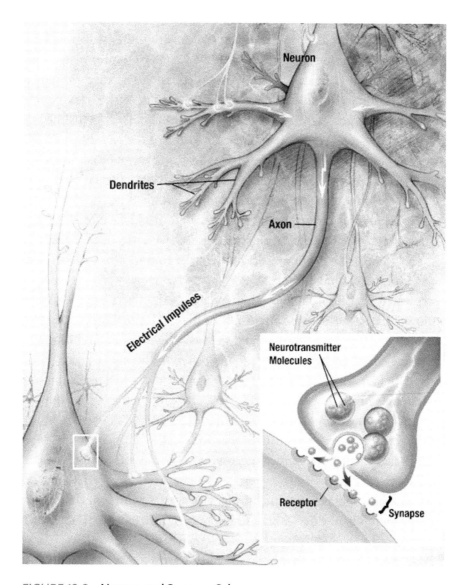

FIGURE 12.2 **Neuron and Synapse Schema**

This "neurotransmitter theory" is the basis for understanding how psychiatric medications change the levels of neurotransmitters to restore brain function. The effects that occur after neurotransmitter levels change are not yet fully known. Current theory suggests that medications ultimately repair damaged brain cells and structures that are damaged from stress and other negative influences on the brain that have caused symptoms. Medications may also protect neurons from future damage (Andrade & Rao, 2010; Forlenza, De-Paula, & Diniz, 2014). Many aspects of this complex neural process are not fully understood. The hope in psychopharmacology is to discover new treatments that will result in safer and more effective healing.

Risks, Side Effects, and General Concepts

As in general medicine, psychopharmacologic medicines have risks and possible side effects. This can be misunderstood, leading to the refusal of treatment when individuals think that treatments always have side effects. It is important to affirm that possible side effects occur only occasionally, and if these negative effects happened too often, the medication would not be approved by the Food and Drug Administration (FDA). In medical care, treatment is determined by weighing possible risks and side effects against likely benefits relative to that treatment. This is referred to as the "**risk-benefit ratio**."

Patients need to be medically "informed" to balance the risks versus the benefits and alternatives to taking medicines. That discussion informs the patient about whether the medication will be a good or bad choice. This education cannot be completely thorough, as a medical education cannot be transferred in minutes. Also, the patient is experiencing an illness that may affect perfect judgment and reasoning. Since there are no currently validated scan technologies or laboratory tests to determine ideal medicines and doses, symptom improvement is balanced against side effects, which leads to changing medicine. It is common to adjust medications as treatment continues. This can be frustrating, as changing treatments can take time.

Newer treatments recently developed have reduced side effects and risks. New research has also shown that suffering from an untreated mental illness is severe. Because of that research, there is reason for aggressive and early treatment of mental illness.

Common side effects of medications can be related to the medications' intended neurologic action, but with effects on other parts of the body as well. For example, selective serotonin reuptake inhibiting (SSRI) antidepressants work in the brain to block uptake of serotonin back into the neurons, which improves depression. There are many other types of serotonin receptors, which have different actions in the brain and body. Most of them are in the digestive tract, which explains occasional SSRI side effects of nausea or diarrhea. Serotonin also affects functions in sleep, hunger, sexual function, anxiety, and other areas.

Neurons have multiple nerve connections that use other neurotransmitters. This is why dopamine, norepinephrine, gamma-aminobutyric acid (GABA), and many hormones may affect serotonin receptors and depression treatment. This explains how one medicine can have multiple effects on other areas of the body, and why the list of side effects can be long.

Other possible negative effects can come from an incorrect diagnosis. For example, this can occur in the treatment of depression. Despite a seemingly accurate diagnosis, patients may have underlying risks, or they can forget symptoms that might suggest a diagnosis of bipolar depression. Antidepressant treatment could result in worsening symptoms, "switching" the mood to mania. This is an unintended negative effect, not a side effect.

Side effects can also be unexplainable, sometimes including rare, negative reactions, such as allergies.

Medications Used by Categories and More Specifics

This section is only a brief survey of common medications prescribed to patients with mental disorders. More complete references are listed at the end of the chapter.

Bipolar Medications (Mood Stabilizers)

Mood stabilizers may function through glutamate, serotonin, GABA, or arachidonic acid (Schloesser, Martinowich, & Manji, 2012).They include lithium, antiseizure medications, and antipsychotic medications. Psychopharmacologists do not yet have a full explanation guiding the development of new medications for bipolar disorder. There are multiple theories currently used to explain mood "swings" and the symptoms of mood instability or dysregulation. The metaphor of mood stability can be likened to temperature regulation in a home, regulated by a thermostat. Normal mood and anxiety functions, along with energy, concentration, sleep, and anger are the result of the brain's ability to provide regulation for many of these functions (like a thermostat) so that emotions and body rhythms can be appropriate, steady, and consistent. The brain needs to produce consistent emotional reactions. Small events should result in small emotional reactions, and big events should cause bigger emotional reactions. Healthy emotional function helps us know how we feel about inner and external events, feelings within ourselves, and in relationships. Feelings help us understand our emotional responses. Emotions define our God-created identity, revealing our character and our unique giftedness. In mood dysregulation and mood swings, the brain doesn't perform normal emotional regulation. Perceptions of and responses to events can be random, confusing, and meaningless. This can impair our ability to understand ourselves, others, and God, thus disorganizing our emotional experience of God and others, confusing our spiritual growth.

Mood stabilizing medications include lithium, antiseizure medications, and antipsychotic medications. There are other medications and nonmedication interventions that benefit bipolar disorder, including medications that have not obtained FDA approval for this use. These interventions include cardiovascular, thyroid medications, antiparkinson, stimulant medications, fatty acid supplements, light therapy, electroconvulsive therapy (ECT), and others.

Lithium

Lithium is the "gold standard" for treatment of mania in bipolar disorder, and prevents future mood swings for future mood stability. It is proven to be the most effective medication in preventing suicide. Despite possible side effects recently reevaluated (Gitlin, 2016), lithium continues as one of the most important medications of the 20th century. Through clinical observations, research, and clinical trials, lithium became the major treatment for bipolar mania replacing ECT and barbiturate treatments by the 1960s (Shorter, 2009). Lithium is known to promote nerve repair and protects nerve cells from damage (Machado-Vieira, Manji, & Zarate, 2009).

Side effects for lithium are related to its similarity to sodium: involved in the body's fluid balance, affected by water intake and kidney function. Medications and diet can affect lithium side effects. Toxicity from too much lithium can be serious. Lithium can be hard on the kidneys and thyroid gland over time. Because of these risks, physicians order regular laboratory tests to monitor for these risks. Common side effects can include nausea, diarrhea, tremor, and weight gain.

Antiseizure Medications

Depakote, or Divalproex (generic), is an older epilepsy treatment found to be very effective in treating acute mania and preventing recurrences of mania. It is often combined with other medications to treat bipolar disorder. Common side effects include fatigue and weight gain. Lamictal (lamotrigine) is an epilepsy medication that is used in the prevention of the return of depression in bipolar illness. This is often used in combination with antimanic medications and is monitored for the rare development of severe rash. Beyond this, Lamictal has relatively fewer side effects and risks than other medications.

Tegretol (carbamazepine) is an older epilepsy treatment with mood stabilizing properties. Its chemical "cousin," Trileptal (oxcarbazepine), is not FDA approved for use in bipolar disorder, but its lower risks and the lack of side effects of weight gain or sedation have led to more use. Tegretol does have risks of suppressing blood cells, so blood tests are performed.

Topamax (topiramate) is another epilepsy medication that has been used in the treatment of bipolar disorder, but it has not been approved for this by the FDA. It is used for appetite reduction and mood regulation, and has been used in alcohol recovery as well. Common side effects can include cognitive and memory difficulties.

Antipsychotic (neuroleptic) medications are commonly used as mood stabilizers for bipolar disorder and depression applications alone and in combination with other medications, and will be discussed in the "antipsychotics" section that follows.

Antidepressants

Depression symptoms dull the perception of joy, hope, and strength. Depression can disable one's physical, emotional, cognitive, and spiritual life, leading to despair. Depression can disable positive emotions, including hope and joy, and cements a person into uncharacteristic darkness, irrational pessimism, and catastrophic fear. It is irrational and can be psychotic. Spiritually destructive, it blocks the reality of any positive experience, eliminating an experience of God's or others' actions such as grace, forgiveness, and love. The world of depression is torment and torture, including repeated self-critical condemnation and absence of any loving input or comfort. Again, research confirms it as the most disabling illness in the world.

Antidepressant medications target the neurotransmitters serotonin, norepinephrine, and, to a lesser degree, dopamine and glutamate. The levels of these chemicals in the brain synapse increase by use of antidepressants. The increases of these neurotransmitters are believed to stimulate the brain's growth factors, which enhance nerve growth and repair. This is thought to repair neuronal damage that leads to symptoms of depression. This repair restores the ability to sleep, relax, be motivated, relate, think sharply, remember, hope and feel joy, grace, and love.

Side effects of antidepressants can include withdrawal or "discontinuation" experienced within a few days of dropping doses too quickly. Although these symptoms are not medically serious, they can be uncomfortable, including nausea, dizziness, headaches, and body aches. Activation is another possible side effect, developing within hours of starting treatment or after increasing doses. Activation consists of nervousness, anxiety, and insomnia. A similar but more serious side effect is called "switching," usually occurring later in treatment but is seen as triggering hypomania or mania in someone with an underlying risk of bipolar disorder. Other common side effects include weight gain, sedation, and sexual dysfunction.

Monoamine Oxidase Inhibitors

These medications were originally discovered in the 1950s and derived from the medication Iproniazid. Besides its antituberculosis effect, it was found to be helpful for depression symptoms. With further research, monoamine oxidase inhibitors (MAOIs) were developed specifically for depression. They include the brand names Marplan (isocarboxazid-generic), Nardil (phenelzine), and Parnate (tranylcypromine), as well as a patch called Emsam (selegeline). They work by blocking the enzyme responsible for the destruction of neurotransmitters (monoamines) in the nerve synapse. Neurotransmitters in the body as well as other areas of the brain are also increased by MAOIs, prohibiting certain medications and foods that can also increase levels of monoamines and can cause excessively high levels of neurotransmitters. This can produce a hypertensive crisis (extremely high blood pressure), which can be life threatening. Although MAOIs do not have side effects of weight gain or sedation and can be very effective, the added dietary and medication restrictions make these medications more difficult to use and are now rarely prescribed. Side effects for these medications can also include low blood pressure.

Tricyclics

This group of older antidepressant medications originated in the 1950s. Imipramine was first used as an antihistamine and tranquilizer for the treatment of schizophrenia. It was noted to have an antidepressant effect, which stimulated the development of other antidepressants. This older antidepressant group includes Tofranil (imipramine—generic), Elavil (amitriptyline), Norpramin (desipramine), and Anafranil (clomipramine), among others. These medicines are rarely prescribed now, as other newer medicines are effective and risk fewer side effects. Elavil, Norpramin, and Tofranil are now used more for pain and sleep treatments than as antidepressants, and Anafranil is used in the treatment of obsessive-compulsive disorder. These medications' side effects include dry mouth, constipation, blurry vision, dizziness, sedation, and weight gain.

Newer Antidepressants

The advancements of the late 1980s heralded the beginning of a "new age" of antidepressants. Peter Kramer (1993) noted this improvement. Dr. Kramer described the medication's new effectiveness as elevating expectations to a higher level, not just in treating mental illness but also in transforming "stable" personality and life experience for some patients. It showed psychopharmacology as capable of enhancing identity and the experience of "self." Prozac was the first of the SSRI medications designed to block the serotonin reuptake pump that clears neurotransmitter from the synapse. These medications include Prozac (fluoxetine—generic), Paxil (paroxetine), Zoloft (sertraline), Luvox (fluvoxamine), Celexa (citalopram), Lexapro (escitalopram), and newer SSRIs, including Viibryd (vilazodone) and Trintellix (vortioxetine). Typical side effects include possible weight gain, sexual side effects, and sedation.

Another class of new antidepressant is the serotonin-norepinephrine reuptake inhibitors (SNRIs). These medications block reuptake of serotonin as with SSRIs, but also block reuptake of norepinephrine from the synapse. This group includes Effexor (venlafaxine), Pristiq (desvenlafaxine), Cymbalta (duloxetine), and Fetzima (levomilnacipran).

Other antidepressants include Wellbutrin (bupropion), Remeron (mirtazapine), and Serzone (nefazodone).

Antipsychotic Medications (Neuroleptics)

Antipsychotic medications were considered "miracle" drugs, developed in the 1950s, with the introduction of chlorpromazine (Carpenter & Koenig, 2008). This was a chemical with antihistamine properties, but was effective in reducing psychosis. It functioned by blocking the neurotransmitter dopamine. Prior to chlorpromazine, psychosis was treated by such interventions as lifetime institutionalization, insulin shock therapy, ECT, seizure therapy, cold sheet therapy, and lobotomy. Antipsychotic medications are based on the theory of "dopamine blockade," that excessive dopamine activity causes psychosis.

Psychosis distorts the ability to perceive reality, replacing reality with paranoid fear or sounds, smells or sights that are not occurring in reality. It destroys identity and relationship, and requires treatment for restoration of normal brain function to return the person to this world. Spiritually, the inability to perceive reality transforms the world, without the ability to feel and relate to others or God. Spiritual experience can become a paranoid threat or grandiose delusion, sometimes progressing to losing self and others in unreality.

Treatment reduces dopamine receptor signals to the more primitive area of the brain, the limbic system, decreasing agitation, delusions, and hallucinations, and restoring the person toward reality. In addition, the effects of elevating serotonin levels by newer antipsychotic medications can improve social interactions and emotionality of those afflicted with schizophrenia.

First-Generation (Typical) Antipsychotics

Beginning in the 1950s, Thorazine (chlorpromazine—generic) was a major advance in the treatment of schizophrenia. This class of medicines allowed the release of thousands of chronically ill patients with psychotic symptoms to live outside of hospitals with the hope of living independently as outpatients. Mellaril (thioridazine), Haldol (haloperidol), Navane (thiothixene), and Prolixin (fluphenazine) were used for decades with significant life-changing benefits. The effectiveness of these medications was balanced against side effects that could be severe, including extrapyramidal, anticholinergic, antiadrenergic symptoms, tardive dyskinesia, and others. More common side effects included weight gain, sedation, light-headedness, dryness, urinary and sexual symptoms, dystonias (experienced as tightening muscles), akathisia (a physical restlessness and painful agitation), and Parkinson's-"like" symptoms (tremor, shuffling, stiffness, decreased emotional expression). Harsher risks included tardive dyskinesia (a neurologic movement disorder) and a rare medical life-threatening reaction called neuroleptic malignant syndrome (NMS) (fever, confusion, and muscle rigidity).

Second Generation (Atypical) Antipsychotics

This newer group of medications demonstrated major improvements in side effects compared to the first-generation medications. They also improved mood regulation. This is likely related to their action on serotonin receptors. These medications are useful in bipolar disorder and depression, both with and without psychotic symptoms, in addition to their effectiveness in schizophrenia. This category of medications includes Clozaril (clozapine), Zyprexa (olanzapine), Risperdal (risperidone), Seroquel (quetiapine), Geodon (ziprasidone), Abilify (aripiprazole), Saphris (asenapine), Latuda (lurasidone), Rexulti (brexpiprazole), and Vraylar (cariprazine). Side effects in this newer group of medications are similar to those in the group of first-generation antipsychotics, but they occur less frequently.

Attention Deficit Hyperactivity Disorder Medications

Medications used in the treatment of attention deficit hyperactivity disorder (ADHD), including stimulants and nonstimulants, act by enhancing the brain's dopamine and norepinephrine neurotransmitter systems. These medications help the brain filter out distractions. The ability to focus and concentrate allows us to think and feel deeply. It is required for integrating and storing memory, helping us in relationships and groups to express who we are. Milder forms of ADHD can impair a person's ability to follow conversations, and instead of being "part of," those with ADHD can feel outside of social relationships.

ADHD can be spiritually destructive, blocking a person's experience to think through and carefully expressing their God-given identity. They can appear disobedient and unable to listen despite good intentions. Impulsive actions and forgotten conversations caused by distractibility look like insensitivity and aloofness, leading to rejection. Treatment can restore depth and breadth of thinking, feeling, and choosing, normalizing relationships and allowing intelligence to be expressed. As attention and focus improve, others can respond positively, and love and grace can replace condemnation by self and others. This can significantly enhance spiritual growth.

Treating ADHD can improve academic and career function, but more profound changes occur in identity, relationships, and spiritual growth.

Stimulants

Stimulants are the FDA's first-line recommended treatments; they are effective and safe in the treatment of ADHD. Studies have been done to compare intensive behavioral interventions against stimulant treatments, with stimulants being found to be most effective (De Sousa & Kalra, 2012; National Institute of Mental Health, 2009). Ritalin (methylphenidate—generic) and its long-acting forms (including Focalin XR and Concerta) and Adderall (mixed amphetamine salts) and its long acting forms (including Vyvanse (lisdexamfetamine), Adzenys, Evekeo, and Adderal XR) are commonly prescribed. Side effects of stimulants include nausea, appetite suppression, abdominal pain, and mood switches. Stimulant use is regarded as a low risk, with a lower likelihood of addictive disorders (Wilens, Faraone, Biederman, & Gunawardene, 2003), (Quinn et al., 2017) in treated ADHD.

Alpha-2 Adrenergic Agonists

Catapress (Clonidine) and Intuniv (guanfacine) affect norepinephrine-related neurotransmitter systems. The mechanism of how these medicines improve ADHD symptoms is still not settled. Side effects can be dizziness, light-headedness, stomach ache, low blood pressure, nausea, and headache.

Antidepressants used in the treatment of ADHD

Strattera (atomoxetine), Wellbutrin (bupropion), and Effexor (venlafaxine) are used in the treatment of ADHD. They are believed to be effective due to their effects on norepinephrine-related neurons. Side effects are discussed in earlier sections.

Antianxiety Medications

Anxiety disorders are the most common of the psychiatric disorders, cited by NAMI at 18% of adults in the United States and 8% of children and adolescents (National Alliance on Mental Illness, 2018a). Most anxiety disorders occur before the age of 21. Emotional and physical symptoms are listed in the *DSM-5* (American Psychiatric Association, 2013). These symptoms can be very disabling.

In anxiety disorders, doubt and fear are excessive, preventing the experience of God's peace and rest, and preventing comfort from God and His people. Treating an anxiety disorder and restoring normal function of the brain's anxiety systems can allow God's peace to finally be an emotional reality, not a spiritual failure.

In the past, various chemicals were used to treat anxiety, including antihistamines, anesthetics, and barbiturates, but most recently, medications used in anxiety treatments block synaptic receptors that use the neurotransmitter GABA. GABA receptors inhibit other neurons in the brain and have a calming effect.

Benzodiazepines

These medications are named benzodiazepines due to their chemical structure. This list includes Xanax (alprazolam—generic), Ativan (lorazepam), Serax (oxazepam), and Klonopin (clonazepam). They are more effective with lower side effects than the medications they replaced (barbiturates). They still have significant risks, including addiction, physical dependence, sedation, slowing, and a risk of memory loss with extended use. Because of these risks, this group of medications is prescribed cautiously with warnings against combining use with other sedatives, pain medications, and alcohol, and prohibition from operating heavy machinery with use. This risk is balanced against the disability and suffering that occurs from acute anxiety disorders.

Nonbenzodiazepines

Buspar (buspirone) is a nonaddictive, nonmemory-impairing, nonsedating medication for chronic anxiety whose mechanism of action targets serotonin receptors. It is also prescribed for treatment in depression. Side effects of buspirone are usually mild.

Antidepressants used in the treatment of anxiety

Both SSRI and SNRI antidepressants are approved for the treatment of anxiety. Side effects of these medications were mentioned earlier in the "Antidepressants" section, but do not include addictive risks or memory risks as do the benzodiazepines.

KEY TERMS

Neurotransmitters: chemicals used by neurons released to the synapse, signaling the neighboring nerve to activate and transmitting the nerve signal to the next nerve for active function

Reuptake pump: the function of a neuron that takes back the neurotransmitter from the synapse back into the neuron for future use. Antidepressants block this

pump, which increases neurotransmitter levels

Risk-benefit ratio: the balance the physician and patient weigh between possible positive treatment benefits against its possible risks and side effects

Discussion Questions

1   How can mental illness hide a person's true character, spiritual gifts, and identity?

2   How can mental illnesses affect relationships?

3   How do mental illnesses affect spiritual growth?

4   Can psychotropic medication enhance spiritual growth?

CONCLUSION

People represented by Brian present the church with an opportunity to provide spiritual and practical help to a hurting soul. As Brian returns to the church in pain, an informed church leader can address his mental health as part of his spiritual needs rather than react with fear and avoidance. He can be supported to return to professional care and other resources, including church and community recovery groups with fellowship and spiritual counsel in the body of believers. Psychopharmacologic medicine and treatments can be encouraged, aiding in the healing of the illness of the brain as the church nourishes the soul. Not only could Brian, his spouse, and children grow and heal but also the church and its community grow and heal through the church's active care as the church embodies Christ on earth.

REVIEWING THE CONCEPTS

Learning Objectives

- Understand the pervasiveness of mental health needs in the community, including church congregations, and be able to cite frequencies of mental disorders likely to be seen in the church population

- As reported by NAMI, 1 in 5 experience a mental illness in one year, 1.1% in the United States live with schizophrenia, 2.6% live with bipolar disorder, 6.9% of adults experience at least one major depressive episode in a year, and 18.1% experience an anxiety disorder.
- As per the Lifeway Research study, 59% of pastors have counseled one or more people who were eventually diagnosed with an acute mental illness, including 23% of the pastors personally struggling with mental illness of some kind.

- Able to define the term "psychopharmacology" and describe its role in the treatment of mental illnesses
  - The term "psychiatry" was defined by Christopher Reil as medical soul care.
  - Psychopharmacology is defined as the scientific study of the use of medications in treating mental illness, for the relief of pain and suffering, and for the restoration of mental health.
  - Psychopharmacology was meant to be prescribed by psychiatrists and other medical providers not as a binary algorithm of drug prescribing, but within a consideration of psychological, philosophical, and relational dynamics, and in a patient of Christian belief, healing within a Christian theological framework.

- Able to describe the theory of how psychiatric medications treating mental illness restore the brain's ability to function normally by regulating human perceptual, cognitive, and emotional experiences and functions.
  - Psychopharmacology and medications used to treat mental illnesses are standard medical treatments that are thought to restore the brain's normal functions of emotions, thoughts, and perceptions, and to relieve suffering and pain.
  - Mental illnesses disturb the ability to feel, think, and perceive realities of self and others, as well as distort the ability to have relationships and practice spirituality.
  - The predominant theory explaining the actions of current medicines and steering development of new medicines is the "neurotransmitter theory."
  - This theory describes brain neurophysiology as dependent on the transmission of neural signals through the transfer of many neurotransmitters from nerve to nerve using specific neurotransmitters for specific nerves.
  - These nerves express specific functions in the brain, and in mental illness, these neurons are unable to function normally.
  - Psychiatric medicines treating mental illness can repair and restore normal functions by altering the levels of neurotransmitters either up or down to produce healing effects restoring normal perception, thinking, and feeling to perform tasks, perceive feelings, and participate in relationships in healthy ways.

- Able to describe ways mental illnesses and their psychopharmacologic treatments affect spiritual experience
  - Restoring mood regulation through mood stabilizers can enable individuals to better understand and identify their feelings, as they are normally intended to be consistent emotional preferences and reactions to external and inner events.

- The clearer and more consistent these feelings are, the easier it is to identify God's created identity in us.
- We can better identify our feelings in relationships, teaching us how biblical principles apply in relationship to others and God.
- If moods are unstable and random, these lessons are difficult to experience, delaying spiritual growth.
- Depression limits emotional experience toward all negative and critical condemnation, which is spiritually destructive, preventing others' and God's love and grace from being experienced.
- The relief that treatment can provide can restore the experience of love and grace that is the message of Christ.
- In anxiety disorders, doubt and fear are excessively driven by the brain, preventing the experience of God's peace and rest, and preventing comfort.
- Treating an anxiety disorder and restoring the function of the brain's anxiety systems can allow God's peace to finally be an emotional reality, not a spiritual failure.
- Psychosis is a condition that distorts the perception of reality and disturbs not only humanity but also relational reality, replacing reality with misperceived threat or intent in an isolated universe.
- Psychosis destroys identity and relationship, and requires medical treatment for restoration of normal brain function to return the person to this real world of God and people.
- ADHD can be deceptively destructive in hiding a person's true ability to fully experience, think, and choose to express his or her God-created identity.
- Without the function of sustained, deliberate attention and concentration, the ability to filter out extraneous distractions diverts true expression of one's wishes and can be disrupted by impulsive, premature actions, while missing conversations and events because of one's distractibility.
- Relationships suffer, and personal defeat is assumed, with impulsivity replacing obedience and distraction replacing emotional caring, leading to disastrous misperceptions by self and others.
- Treatment can restore depth and breadth of thinking, feeling, and choosing, changing relational and life capabilities, including deepening spiritual growth.

Chapter Review Questions

Level 1: Knowledge (True/False)

1. Lithium is the most effective anti-suicide medication.
2. Depression is the most disabling illness according to WHO.
3. The American Psychiatric Association endorses the use of brain scans for current psychiatric clinical care and diagnosis.
4. Treating ADHD with stimulants reduces the risk of substance abuse.

5. Antipsychotic medications also treat mood disorders, but only if there are psychotic symptoms.

6. In the Lifeway study, over three-fourths of people on medications felt the medicines were effective.

7. The American Psychiatric Association discourages discussion of spiritual practice and faith in the practice of psychiatric medicine.

8. The father of American psychiatry was a follower of the Christian faith.

9. Christians have a lower incidence of mental illness than the general population.

10. Antidepressants were discovered from medications used in treating leprosy.

Level 2: Comprehension

1. Neurotransmitters involved in the treatment of depression do not include

   a. serotonin

   b. norepinephrine

   c. acetylcholine

   d. glutamate

   e. dopamine

2. Mood stabilizing medications do not include the following:

   a. Antiseizure medicines

   b. Lithium

   c. Adderall

   d. Antipsychotic medicines

3. Common side effects of antidepressant medicines do not include

   a. activation

   b. sedation

   c. addiction

   d. weight gain

4. The class of psychiatric medication that does not involve increasing neurotransmitter levels:

   a. Antidepressant medications

   b. Antianxiety medications

   c. ADHD medications

   d. First-generation antipsychotic medications

5. The most disabling illness in the world:

   a. Heart attack

   b. Cancer

   c. Diabetes

   d. Depression

6. The most common mental illness:

   a. Bipolar disorder

   b. Obsessive compulsive disorder

   c. Depression

   d. Anxiety disorders

   e. ADHD

7. Physicians prescribe treatments based on the concept of

   a. "do no harm"

   b. risk versus benefit ratio

   c. amount of possible side effects

   d. patient preference

8. The historic medication that allowed the discharge of tens of thousands of people with mental illnesses to leave lifetime in-hospital care was

   a. Lithium

   b. Chlorpromazine

   c. Prozac

   d. Anafranil

   e. Zyprexa

9. A philosophical approach that denies the complexity of mental illness that simplifies human psychiatric care to binary algorithms:

   a. Reductionism

   b. Scientology

   c. Psychopharmacology

   d. Reilism

10. This psychoanalytic figure was an accepted early psychoanalyst, friend of Freud, and Lutheran pastor who promoted Christ and felt psychoanalysis was compatible with faith.

    a. D. W. Winnicott

    b. Benjamin Rush

    c. Philippe Pinel

    d. Oskar Pfister

Level 3: Application

1. Discuss your personal experience, either professional or personal, with someone with mental illness and if you witnessed the person's symptoms before and after treatment with psychiatric medicines. Explore your experience as it informed you on the role of medications in mental illness.

2. Discuss your own personal or theological biases about psychopharmacologic interventions. You may include morality, philosophy, and theology of personal self-hood and the vulnerability of this concept in the face of treatable mental illnesses. Is the concept of the self's vulnerability to illness spiritually destructive or helpful?

3. Consider the role of the church as an access point in the delivery of mental health care. Create two models, one for a small church of less than 300 members and another for a large church of over 1,000 members. Describe the pastoral position, programs, ministries, and referral functions of these two sizes of churches and the church's perspective regarding psychiatric medication treatment.

4. Explore the possible challenges to and opportunities for spiritual counseling from the leadership of a church, especially regarding the approach to afflicted people and their psychiatric medication needs and refusal of professional care.

5. Discuss possible spiritual benefits of a church's mental health ministry, for the church as a whole and individuals afflicted, including counseling those with psychopharmacologic treatments. How are some of the ways effective medications can further spiritual growth? Address possible personal, relational, and spiritual benefits in one diagnostic category of illness.

ANSWERS

LEVEL 1: KNOWLEDGE

1. T
2. T
3. F
4. T
5. F
6. T
7. F
8. T
9. F
10. F

LEVEL 2: COMPREHENSION

1. c
2. c
3. c
4. d
5. d
6. c
7. b
8. b
9. a
10. d

RESOURCES

Online Resources

- American Psychiatric Association (2018): *Mental health and faith community partnership*—https://www.psychiatry.org/psychiatrists/cultural-competency/faith-community-partnership
- American Psychiatric Association (2018): *Information for Patients and Families*—https://www.psychiatry.org/patients-families
- National Alliance on Mental Illness—https://www.nami.org/
- NAMI Minnesota (2018). *Fact sheet: Commonly prescribed psychotropic medications*—http://www.namihelps.org/assets/PDFs/fact-sheets/Medications/Commonly-Psyc-Medications.pdf
- Depression Bipolar Alliance—www.dbsalliance.org/site/PageServer
- National Institute of Mental Health—www.nimh.nih.gov/index.shtmlNIH.GOV
- The National Institute of Mental Health Information Resource Center (October 2016). *Mental Health Medications*—https://www.nimh.nih.gov/health/topics/mental-health-medications/index.shtml#part_149856
- American Academy of Child and Adolescent Psychiatry—https://www.aacap.org
- Less Darkly—https://lessdarkly.com
- U.S. Food and Drug Administration. (Nov 29, 2017). *Dietary supplements*—https://www.fda.gov/Food/DietarySupplements/

Readings

- *Handbook of Clinical Psychopharmacology for Therapists: 8th Edition*—John D. Preston, John H. O'Neal, and Mary C. Talaga

- *The Psychotherapist's Guide to Psychopharmacology: 2nd Edition*—Michael J. Gitlin
- *Philosophy of Psychopharmacology: Smart Pills, Happy Pills, and Pep Pills*—Dan J. Stein
- *Madness: American Protestant Responses to Mental Illness*—Heather H. Vacek

Video Resources

- National Institute of Mental Health, videos on mental illness—https://www.youtube.com/user/NIMHgov/videos
- *Frontline: The Medicated Child (Psychotropic Medications in Children)*—http://www.pbs.org/video/frontline-the-medicated-child/
- *Frontline: Inside a Mental Health Court*—https://www.pbs.org/wgbh/pages/frontline/released/inside/
- *Frontline: Supplements and Safety*—https://www.pbs.org/wgbh/frontline/film/supplements-and-safety/

CLASSROOM ACTIVITIES

1. Discuss pros and cons of psychopharmacology and its approach to mental health treatment.

2. Discuss spiritual pros and cons of the psychopharmacologic treatment of mental illness.

    a. Discuss the necessity for the church leaderships' role in promoting psychopharmacology as spiritually positive.

3. Discuss the approach of planning psychopharmacology education for adults and youth as part of a mental health ministry. Include the differences between programs of a small church and large church, with respect to resources, programs, referral functions, and integrating the mental health ministry into the main programs of the church.

    a. Discuss the possible challenges with resources and peoples, and difficulties of promoting medical treatment of mental illness within the church and within the community.

    b. Discuss the possible benefits to the congregation and ministry, and of medical treatment of mental illness, including community benefits as well as individual spiritual benefits.

4. Explore, investigate, and map available local private and public mental health resources for adults and youth, including psychopharmacologic treatment availabilities. Experience connecting with a community resource, including support groups such as NAMI, Depression and Bipolar Support Alliance (DBSA,) codependency, boundary, Al-Anon, and Alcoholics Anonymous 12-step groups.

5. Investigate a church based mental health ministry, such as Stephen Ministries and Celebrate Recovery Ministries, and share your findings with classmates.

REFERENCES

American Psychiatric Association. (2013). *Diagnostic and statistical manual of mental disorders* (5th ed.). Arlington, VA: Author.

American Psychiatric Association. (2018). *Mental health and faith community partnership.* Retrieved from https://www. psychiatry.org/psychiatrists/cultural-competency/faith-community-partnership

American Society of Clinical Psychopharmacology. (2018). *What is psychopharmacology?* Retrieved from https://www. ascpp.org/resources/information-for-patients/what-is-psychopharmacology/

Andrade, C., Rao, N.S.K. (2010). How antidepressant drugs act: A primer on neuroplasticity as the eventual mediator of antidepressant efficacy. *Indian Journal of Psychiatry, 52*(4), 378–386. http://doi.org/10.4103/0019-5545.74318

Buchanan, A. (2004). Mental capacity, legal competence and consent to treatment. *Journal of the Royal Society of Medicine, 97*(9), 415–420.

Carpenter, W. T., & Koenig, J. I. (2008). The Evolution of drug development in schizophrenia: Past issues and future opportunities. *Neuropsychopharmacology: Official Publication of the American College of Neuropsychopharmacology, 33*(9), 2061–2079. http://doi.org/10.1038/sj.npp.1301639

De Sousa, A., Kalra, G. (2012). Drug therapy of attention deficit hyperactivity disorder: Current trends. *Mens Sana Monographs, 10*(1), 45–69. http://doi.org/10.4103/0973-1229.87261

Desai, N. G. (2005). Antipsychiatry: Meeting the challenge. *Indian Journal of Psychiatry, 47*(4), 185–187. Retrieved from http://doi.org/10.4103/0019-5545.43048

Forlenza, O. V., De-Paula, V.J.R., Diniz, B.S.O. (2014). Neuroprotective effects of lithium: Implications for the treatment of Alzheimer's disease and related neurodegenerative disorders. *ACS Chemical Neuroscience, 5*(6), 443–450. http://doi.org/10.1021/cn5000309

Foucault M. (2006). *History of madness* (J. Khalfa, Ed., trans., & J. Murphy, trans). New York, NY: Routledge.

Freud, S. (1964). *An Outline of Psychoanalysis. Standard Edition,* Vol. 23, p. 182. London, England: Hogarth Press.

Gitlin, M. J. (2016). Lithium side effects and toxicity: Prevalence and management strategies. *International Journal of Bipolar Disorders, 4*(1), 27.

Hippocrates. (400 BCE). *On the sacred disease.* (Francis Adams, trans.). Retrieved from http://classics.mit.edu/Hippocrates/sacred.html

Hoffman, M. T. (2011). *Relational perspective book series: Vol. 48. Toward mutual recognition: Relational psychoanalysis and the Christian narrative.* New York, NY: Routledge/Taylor & Francis Group.

Kramer, P. D. (1993). *Listening to Prozac: A psychiatrist explores antidepressant drugs and the remaking of the self.* New York, NY: Viking.

Lehmann, H. E. (1993). Before they called it psychopharmacology. *Neuropsychopharmacology, 8*(4), 291–303. doi: 10.1038/npp.1993.69

Lifeway Research. (2014). *Study of acute mental illness and Christian faith: Research report.* Retrieved from http://lifewayresearch.com/wp-content/uploads/2014/09/Acute-Mental-Illness-and-Christian-Faith-Research-Report-1.pdf

Lynskey, M. T., & Strang, J. (2013). The global burden of drug use and mental disorders. *The Lancet, 382*(9904), 9–15, 1540–1542.

Machado-Vieira, R., Manji, H. K., & Zarate, C. A. (2009). The role of lithium in the treatment of bipolar disorder: Convergent evidence for neurotrophic effects as a unifying hypothesis. *Bipolar Disorders, 11*(Suppl 2), 92–109. http://doi.org/10.1111/j.1399-5618.2009.00714.x

Marneros, J. (2008). Psychiatry's 200th birthday. *British Journal of Psychiatry, 193*(1), 1–3.

Mental Health America. (2018). *Who we are.* Retrieved from http://www.mentalhealthamerica.net/who-we-are

Meyer, J. S., Quenzer, L. F. (2005). *Psychopharmacology: Drugs, the brain, and behavior.* Sunderland, MA: Sinauer Associates.

National Alliance on Mental Illness. (2018a). Anxiety disorders. Retrieved from https://www.nami.org/Learn-More/Mental-Health-Conditions/Anxiety-Disorders

National Alliance on Mental Illness. (2018b). Mental health by the numbers. Retrieved from https://www.nami.org/Learn-More/Mental-Health-By-the-Numbers

National Institute of Mental Health. (2009). *Multimodal treatment of attention deficit hyperactivity disorder (MTA) study.* Retrieved from https://www.nimh.nih.gov/funding/clinical-research/practical/mta/multimodal-treatment-of-attention-deficit-hyperactivity-disorder-mta-study.shtml

Quinn, P. D., Chang, Z., Hur, K., Gibbons, R. D., Lahey, B. B.,. Rickert, M. E., ... D'Onofrio, B. M. (2017, September). ADHD medication and substance-related problems. *American Journal of Psychiatry, 174*(9), 877–885. https://doi.org/10.1176/appi.ajp.2017.16060686

Resnik, D. B. (2007). Responsibility for health: Personal, social, and environmental. *Journal of Medical Ethics, 33*(8), 444–445. http://doi.org/10.1136/jme.2006.017574

Roazen, P. (1993). Introductory note to Pfister, the illusion of a future: A friendly disagreement with Prof. Sigmund Freud. *International Journal of Psycho-Analysis, 74*, 557–558.

Schloesser, R. J., Martinowich, K., Manji, H. K. (2012). Mood-stabilizing drugs: Mechanisms of action. *Trends in Neurosciences*, 35(1), 36–46. doi: https://doi.org/10.1016/j.tins.2011.11.009

Shorter, E. (2009). The history of lithium therapy. *Bipolar Disorders, 11*(Suppl 2), 4–9. Retrieved from http://doi.org/10.1111/j.1399-5618.2009.00706.x

Szasz, T. (1974). *The myth of mental illness: Foundations of a theory of personal conduct.* New York, NY: Harper & Row.

U.S. Centers for Medicare & Medicaid Services. (2018). The mental health parity and addiction equity act (MHPAEA). Retrieved from https://www.cms.gov/cciio/programs-and-initiatives/other-insurance-protections/mhpaea_factsheet.html

Vacek, H. H. (2015). *Madness: American Protestant Responses to Mental Illness.* Waco, TX: Baylor University Press.

Verghese, A. (2008). Spirituality and mental health. *Indian Journal of Psychiatry, 50*(4), 233-237. http://doi.org/10.4103/0019-5545.44742

Wilens, T. E., Faraone, S. V., Biederman, J., Gunawardene, S. (2003). Does stimulant therapy of attention-deficit/hyperactivity disorder beget later substance abuse? A meta-analytic review of the literature. *Pediatrics*, 111(1) 179–185. doi: 10.1542/peds.111.1.179

World Health Organization. (2018). *Depression: Fact sheet.* Retrieved from http:// www.who.int/mediacentre/factsheets/fs369/en/

IMAGE CREDITS

Fig. 12.1: Copyright © 2015 Depositphotos/100502500.

Fig. 12.2: Source: https://commons.wikimedia.org/w/index.php?title=File:Chemical_synapse_schema_cropped.jpg&oldid=270111938.

CHAPTER 13

Personality Disorders

Robyn Bettenhausen Geis, PsyD

LEARNING OBJECTIVES

Upon completion of this chapter, readers will be able to

1. identify and define the various personality disorders pastors may encounter;

2. differentiate the three clusters into which the 10 personality disorders are divided;

3. identity pastoral response strategies for all of the personality disorders;

4. compare personality disorders to other possible diagnoses; and

5. be familiar with resources available for those suffering with personality disorders.

"I'm selfish, impatient and a little insecure. I make mistakes, I am out of control and at times hard to handle. But if you can't handle me at my worst, then you sure as hell don't deserve me at my best."
—Marilyn Monroe

INTRODUCTION TO PERSONALITY DISORDERS

Having congregants or staff members who struggle with a personality disorder can make a pastor's job interesting at best, or at worst make the job much more challenging. Whether it be church members, fellow staff, or even family members, individual personalities can sometimes make or break a church community. The fact that we all have different personalities, some more intense than others, can make life interesting, but on the other hand it can make relationships very painful. Learning about these extreme character profiles will be both enlightening to better understand your congregants and possibly personally challenging in gaining better insight into yourself. It may be helpful to keep in mind that a person does not need to fully meet the requirements for diagnosis to occasionally demonstrate some of these personality disorder behaviors or attitudes.

FIGURE 13.1   **Seeing past the exterior**

My hope is that this chapter will help you develop a compassion for those suffering from a personality disorder, in spite of their difficult demeanor. Millon, Grossman, Millon, Meagher, & Ramnath (2004) write, "Today, personality is seen as a complex pattern of deeply embedded psychological characteristics that are expressed automatically in almost every area of psychological functioning. That is, personality is viewed as the patterning of characteristics across the entire matrix of the person" (p. 2). My goal is that you too will appreciate the complexity of individuals and increase your understanding of how people become who they are.

Screening Test

Here is a brief screening test and a summary of the 10 *Diagnostic and Statistical Manual, 5th Edition (DSM-5)* personality disorders. Keep in mind, a person can only be diagnosed when he or she meets several more criteria and is experiencing impairment in functioning because of these traits.

1.   Do you find it very hard to trust anyone? Instead you most often believe others will likely take advantage of you?

2.   Do you feel relationships are more trouble than they are worth and therefore believe being alone is better?

3.   Do you behave in ways that others find odd, like believing you have special powers—for example, reading other people's minds?

4.   Do you get bored easily, behave dangerously, and/or hurt others and don't feel bad about it?

5.   Do you fear abandonment, often have unstable emotions, and have trouble keeping relationships?

6. Do you need to be the center of attention, like being dramatic, and need other people's constant approval?

7. Do you believe you are better than others, yet get upset when they do not see your worth?

8. Do you avoid other people because you fear their rejection or disapproval of you?

9. Do you prefer others to make decisions for you because you believe they are more capable than you?

10. Are you very orderly and controlling and set unreasonably high standards for yourself and others?

Corresponding Potential Personality Disorder:

1. Paranoid Personality Disorder
2. Schizoid Personality Disorder
3. Schizotypal Personality Disorder
4. Antisocial Personality Disorder
5. Borderline Personality Disorder
6. Histrionic Personality Disorder
7. Narcissistic Personality Disorder
8. Avoidant Personality Disorder
9. Dependent Personality Disorder
10. Obsessive-Compulsive Personality Disorder

(American Psychiatric Association, 2013)

Were any of these familiar to you? The fact is that all of us demonstrate a few of these traits to some degree or another. Having these characteristics may not really be problematic until they become too rigid, interfere with relationships, and/or create some impairment in an individual's life. This is when a person with a personality disorder, or someone in close relationship with him or her, will be knocking on your door asking for help.

Hallmarks of Personality Disorders

According to the *DSM-5*, the definition of a **personality disorder** is when a person consistently demonstrates unsound personality traits, such as distorted thinking or unhealthy emotional reactions. It must be evident long term, and the individual will demonstrate some rigidity in self-evaluation. Generally, a person would not be given a personality disorder diagnosis until after adolescence. Most importantly, it is considered diagnosable when the personality issues create distress for the individual or marked impairment in functioning. Two important criteria that must be met for diagnosis are **pervasiveness** and **significant impairment** in relationships with others (American Psychiatric Association, 2013). We will discuss each of these points in more detail.

First, the personality problem has to be **pervasive,** evident in multiple areas of one's life, and over a long period of time. If you begin to suspect someone may have some personality issues, it must be taken into account how long he or she has manifested these problems and in what context. If the person is enduring a temporary hardship resulting in some momentary personality change, this does not qualify. For example, bereavement may cause someone to be shorter tempered than usual. Or the individual may have some medical condition, which can include the consumption of drugs, thus creating a change in his or her personality expression. In this case, the symptoms may be accounted for by these medical causes.

Many people experience radical shifts in personality during their teen years, which is why we wait until adulthood to diagnose anyone. Unfortunately, the *DSM-5* does not give specific time frames during which the symptoms must be manifested to identify a personality disorder. However, we do know that it has to be enduring over time.

Further, we take into account how individuals' problems are creating stress and are **relationally impairing**, meaning their connections with others are diminished in some way. If you notice their interpersonal skills are lacking and are significantly interfering with their functioning, like not being able to keep a job, it is reasonable to consider whether there is a personality issue at play. You will likely notice that erratic emotional responses to others appear to be causing serious difficulty in their relationships, which is what motivates them and/or their significant others to seek help.

Another difficulty regarding personality disorders is the presence of **rigidity,** which is a lack of flexibility or willingness to change. This particular characteristic is likely what will catch your attention about the individual you are helping. What you will notice in talking with someone who suffers from a personality disorder is that he or she seems to have some distorted perceptions compared to others. It can be extremely difficult to persuade the person to consider that his or her perspective may not be correct (American Psychological Association, 2004). For example, you may meet people who tell you that they believe others are intentionally and repeatedly offending them. They may not be able to offer a reason why, but they honestly believe that there is something different about them that causes others to not like them and treat them poorly as a result. *If* you try to help them consider that there may be alternative perspectives, they will likely get offended by you as well. Do not get discouraged yet as we will discuss several ways to increase effectiveness in helping this type of individual.

Causes of Personality Disorders

Charlotte Huff (2004) suggests that there are several possible causes for someone to develop a personality issue. Here are a few potential sources from her list: childhood trauma, genetics, experiencing verbal abuse, high sensitivity to stimuli, lack of positive relationships, and emotional neglect. Any combination of these increases the likelihood of a personality disorder. However, it is important to remember that not all people with the aforementioned experiences necessarily develop personality problems.

Alan Shore's (2000) work on attachment and right brain regulation helps us understand how childhood trauma affects people. He suggests that there is a link between one's upbringing and the development of the brain. In turn, this may help explain how one might incur a personality disorder. As you have seen in other chapters, **attachment** is how well we connect to others based on early parent-child/caretaker relationships. It also seems that **neural networks**, a group of connected neurons in the brain, may be influenced by the quality of one's attachment experience. "Developmental neuro-psychologists are demonstrating that neglect and lack of attachment during early child-hood may lead to the lack of the cortical organization needed for self-soothing and self-regulation" (Shapiro, 2001).

In his book *Neurological Foundations for EMDR Practice*, Uri Bergmann (2012) also makes a case for the biological predisposition to develop psychological disorders. He points to hormonal hereditary traits passed down from one generation to the next in traumatized people. Bergmann states that traumatized offspring may develop increased levels of cortisol, which in turn create significant physical problems in the immune system and possible lack of affect regulation. This could create a predisposition to personality disorders as well.

Elaine Aron (1996) argues that some people in the population are much more sensitive to stimuli than others. She calls this individual a highly sensitive person (HSP). They experience visual, auditory, tactile, taste, and smell to a greater degree than others. It is further hypothesized that these same individuals could experience emotions to a greater degree as well. Therefore, if an HSP endures abuse, neglect, or any other form of pain, it may be more difficult for him or her to emotionally manage than someone not as influenced by stimuli. This could leave the individual more susceptible to incurring a psychological disorder as well.

In my book, *The Relational Brain: A Path to Heal Broken Relationships* (Bettenhausen, 2017), I explain how relationships and emotional neglect affect the brain. I give a structure for understanding the brain and why the individual with a personality disorder behaves logically at times but in other moments may seem very unreasonable. Briefly stated, the quality of one's attachment experience literally affects the brain in how well the prefrontal cortex (logical part) and the amygdala (emotional part) communicate with each other. This lack of communication within the brain negatively affects how a person experiences him or herself and others. One moment the person can seem reasonable but in the next instance he or she can become so emotional that the person is unable to problem solve or handle difficult situations. Fortunately, the scientific majority consensus is that our brain is able to grow new neural pathways through insight and understanding, which can improve the communication between these parts in our brain. The individual's new expanded capacity to evaluate circumstances promotes safety within him or herself and with others. I see this potential as God's grace to suffering people and that humans are not determined by circumstances.

No matter our disposition, we know that through good decisions we can change circumstances for the better. Many people who come from disadvantaged situations are able to improve their lives. It is interesting to compare this with Numbers 14:18 where we are told, "The Lord is slow to anger and abundant in lovingkindness, for-giving iniquity and transgression; but He will by no means clear the guilty, visiting the iniquity of the fathers on the children to the third and fourth generations." We understand that maladaptive behaviors, such as alcoholism, are passed down in families. However, we also know God is gracious and I Corinthians 10:13 tells us that God "always provides a way out." No one is determined by his or her past. Good decisions affect the future for ourselves and our descendants (Ps. 112:1–2, Prov. 20:7, Prov. 14:26, Jer. 32:39, Jer. 4:40).

Personality Disorder Facts

The rate of occurrence for any personality disorder in the general population is about 1 out of 10 people (Lenzenweger, 2008). Therefore, the chances of you meeting someone affected by a personality issue are high, so being familiar with these disorders can be useful for understanding and providing correct direction. The most common personality disorders are obsessive-compulsive (9.6%), narcissistic (7%), and borderline (7%) (Gawda & Kararzyna, 2017). However, this can vary depending on your congregation demographics, such as sex, education, marital status, and age. For example, Cluster A personality disorders are more common in men who never marry. Cluster B personality disorders may be more likely in young men who do not finish high school (Samuels et al., 2002). As a pastor, you will want to be familiar with these disorders to know how to manage the relevant issues, how they may affect your church, and how to help those suffering.

Because there are several personality types, and many have similar characteristics or overlapping qualities, the 10 disorders have been classified into three groupings to make conceptualization easier. The three main clusters are (A) odd, bizarre, and eccentric, (B) dramatic and erratic, and (C) anxious and fearful. To really simplify them, some have described these three groupings, respectively, as weird, wild, and worried (Li, 2018). In addition, people may be diagnosed with more than one disorder within a cluster or across groups.

Treatment

The structure of this chapter includes a definition for each disorder, a case example, differential diagnosis, and recommended pastoral responses for each disorder. It is assumed that if you assess the individual is presenting with severe symptoms that you would refer them to a professional therapist. Generally speaking, it is recommended that personality disorders are treated with either some form of relational and/or cognitive therapy. The former teaches them how to best interact with themselves and others, while the latter is used to identify faulty thinking patterns and offer adaptive alternatives. Sometimes, people suffering from a personality disorder also have depression, anxiety, and/or an addiction. In these cases, it is best to refer to a therapist or psychiatrist for evaluation.

As stated, each disorder has a section offering pastoral responses. As believers, we know that God uses circumstances to draw people to Himself. Our goal in helping others is to find where God is already working in that individual's life and to come alongside them. We want to ask the Lord for discernment as to what the Holy Spirit wants to speak into the other's life. A general rule of thumb is to be a really good listener first. Because personality disorders can be difficult, my suggestion is to be prayerful regarding when or how one or more of these interventions should be applied.

KEY TERMS

Personality disorder: when a person consistently demonstrates unsound personality traits, like distorted thinking or unhealthy emotional reactions. It must be evident long term, and the individual will demonstrate some rigidity in self-evaluation

Pervasive: evident in multiple areas of one's life and over a long period of time

Rigidity: lack of flexibility or willingness to change

Relational impairment: connections with others are diminished or weakened in some way

Attachment: how well we connect to others based on early parent-child/care-taker relationships

Neural networks: a group of connected neurons in the brain

Discussion Questions

1   What thoughts and reactions did you have after taking the initial screening test for the 10 personality disorders?

2   Discuss the differences between the three hallmarks of personality disorders.

3   If someone were to ask you to explain from a Biblical perspective why people may have personality disorders, what would you say?

4   Define one of the characteristics required for a personality disorder and provide an example.

THE *DIAGNOSTIC AND STATISTICAL MANUAL, 5TH EDITION* PERSONALITY DISORDERS: CLUSTER A: THE ODD, BIZARRE, AND ECCENTRIC CATEGORY, WHICH INCLUDES PARANOID, SCHIZOID, AND SCHIZOTYPAL PERSONALITY DISORDERS

You may find the names of these first three personality disorders intimidating. Paranoid, schizoid, or schizotypal personality disorders are not referring to **schizophrenia,** which, according to the *DSM-5*, is the mental illness marked by having a thought disorder.

This would be an auditory or visual **hallucination**, which is seeing or hearing something that is not there and/or having a **delusion**, which is a rigid belief that is not considered to be reality or rational, but the person maintains the belief despite evidence to the contrary (American Psychiatric Association, 2013). The paranoid, schizoid, and schizotypal personalities types are less severe than someone with a thought disorder and would more likely be described as socially awkward than disturbing.

Paranoid Personality Disorder

Paranoid personality disorder, as defined by the *DSM-5*,

- Is marked by a significant suspiciousness and mistrust of others above and beyond what society would consider normal guardedness
- Is a strong belief they need to be self-protective when around other people, in order to not be taken advantage of or mistreated
- And, the behavior would have to be present for a long time not just following a recent trauma (American Psychiatric Association, 2013)

If someone just experienced being robbed at gunpoint, and the person become paranoid when strangers approach him or her, this would not necessarily be problematic. That would be considered a **post-traumatic stress response**, a normal fight or flight response to a traumatic or very stressful event. The paranoid personality expresses a more pervasive and long-term attitude of not trusting others, in spite of no apparent evidence there is an actual current threat to them.

In the church, you would most likely see this personality type evidenced in someone who really struggles to trust others. This creates isolation for the person, and he or she is often angry at the church or with specific pastors or people. In spite of pastors or congregants trying to help, the paranoid personality individual will persist in believing others are against him or her. This may happen because the person tends to see hidden negative meaning in most of his or her interactions with others. For example, Pastor Matt spent several days trying to help move the belongings of a homeless individual, who had paranoid personality disorder, into his new accommodations. In spite of Matt's efforts on behalf of this person, the relationship ended when the man accused Matt of wanting to steal some of his clothing. This type of negative thinking makes it very difficult to have consistent and healthy relationships with a person with this type of personality disorder.

John 4:4–42 tells us the story of a Samaritan woman who regularly visits the town well at a time of day when nobody else is there. She had reason to believe others would reject her because of her promiscuous lifestyle. We do not have enough information to tell if she would meet the criteria for paranoid personality disorder, but we do see similarities in her mistrust of others and taking measures to avoid people. However, through Jesus's intervention in her life, she finds herself free of her concerns regarding others and instead she becomes bold in sharing her good experience of Jesus.

Differential Diagnosis

There is a paranoid subtype within the diagnosis of schizophrenia, which can seem similar to the paranoid personality disorder. However, a person with paranoid personality disorder will be able to talk rationally and make sense even though you may disagree with their beliefs. The schizophrenic will have hallucinations and delusions and will not necessarily produce coherent thoughts.

Case Example

Andrea is seeking help because her marriage is struggling. She reports to Pastor Eric that she and her husband fight constantly, but according to her, he is unwilling to come in with her to talk with any pastor. When asked for details regarding their marital problems, she says she believes her husband is having an affair, but he will not admit it. Andrea shared that when she discusses this with her friends, they have not been very supportive of her concerns but rather told her she may need to get some help. Further, she reports that she checks her husband's phone repeatedly, has spent days following him to and from work, and has gone as far as hiring a detective to find evidence to prove her suspicions. None of these inquiries have produced any solid evidence; however, she explains that is because her husband is clever and able to hide any proof there may be. She reports that he calls her paranoid and says she needs to get help, or he will leave her. This, of course, is proof to her that she is correct in the first place; otherwise, he would not make such a threat.

Pastoral Response

It is useful for the pastor to keep in mind the rigidity of the paranoid personality belief system and the deeply embedded mistrust of others. This will be a good reminder to not assume that the other person feels safe just because you are trying to help him or her. The best intervention is to build a supportive relationship with this person by validating his or her experience of whatever issue brought the person to you. Focusing just on the individual's current issue and problem solving may be the best course of action as well. We do not want to escalate the paranoia by asking too many questions about the person's history. Because of the individual's suspiciousness, it is advisable to not dig too deeply into his or her past, unless the person brings it up as relevant to his or her current concerns (Bressert, 2017b).

Schizoid Personality Disorder

The *DSM-5* tells us that **schizoid personality disorder** is as follows:

- An uncommon condition in which people avoid social activities and consistently shy away from interaction with others
- A demonstration of a limited range of emotional expression
- A presentation of being a loner, dismissive of others, and appearing to lack the desire or skill to form close personal relationships
- A pattern of diminished emotional expression, which gives the impression they don't care about others (American Psychiatric Association, 2013)

You may be working alongside people with this disorder and not even know it. They can be great at their jobs, especially with goal-oriented projects or working alone. In their personal lives, they prefer not to be around people or any situations that force them to interact with others outside of task-oriented activities like work.

We do not know for sure what the cause is of this disorder, but if the parent was neglectful and/or emotionally distant, then someone could be at risk for this disorder. Because of the marked reclusiveness, this person is not likely to seek help.

Differential Diagnosis

Triebwasser, Chemerinski, Roussous, and Siever (2012) suggest that schizoid personality disorder may not be a valid or reliable personality disorder on its own. They define the two key features of this personality disorder as **affect constriction,** which is when a person has limited emotional capacity, and **seclusiveness,** a desire to be alone rather than with people the majority, if not all, of the time. Their argument is that someone with affect constriction might better be diagnosed as having a schizotypal personality, and if seclusiveness is predominant, the person may better fit the avoidant personality disorder. For now, if the emphasis is on the individual's affect constriction *and* reclusiveness, schizoid may be the most accurate.

Even though schizoid sounds like schizophrenia, and they are both considered to be a demonstration of strange behavior, they are different in distinct ways. The schizoid person is in touch with reality, and his or her speech will be cohesive and make sense. The person with schizophrenia will likely not carry on a normal conversation, unless he or she is on medication. Lastly, because of the person's isolation, this individual may also have **depression**, which is having sadness along with other severe symptoms, such as significant loss of interest in activities and social interactions.

Case Example

Bower is well liked in his office, but this is mostly because he does not create any drama, and he just keeps to himself. He gets his job done and is considered reliable when it comes to finishing projects. His colleagues would say that they do not know him very well because he avoids conversations and any general interaction with people. When his coworkers invite him out for happy hour after work, he always has an excuse not to go, or he just does not show up. His office mates describe Bower as very shy. However, they started to wonder if there was a bigger problem when they noticed he would not even attend the funeral of one of their beloved fellow employees, with whom Bower worked closely.

Pastoral Response

Schizoid individuals are going to be very difficult to help. Most likely they will not reach out for support because they are more comfortable alone than risking connection with others. If they are seeking help, focusing on building skills to feel safe and comfortable in social situations is the best course. This can be done through discussion and role-playing. While trying to support schizoid persons, it is helpful to keep in mind that they function well with task-oriented, goal-directed, or intellectual pursuits as opposed to emotional or relational activities.

Schizotypal Personality Disorder

A *DSM-5* definition summary of **schizotypal personality disorder** is as follows:

- A consistent pattern of unusual thinking
- Discomfort with people
- A lack of skill in relating to others
- A non-conventional way of thinking
- Distrust in others
- Limited capacity for emotions
- Holding some odd beliefs
- Socially awkward and anxious (American Psychiatric Association, 2013)

An example of an odd belief would be maintaining that they have special powers like knowing what other people are thinking. Another unique perspective is they may have **body illusions**, which are a belief that something is wrong with them physically in spite of evidence to the contrary. An example of this is the belief that they do not have control over their tongue.

Differential Diagnosis

Some consider schizotypal personality disorder to be on the spectrum with schizophrenia (Walsh, 2016). Most likely this person would be viewed as very odd and could get mistaken for those who meet the criteria for schizophrenia. The main difference is that a schizotypal personality disorder will have more grounding in reality than a schizophrenic. A person with schizotypal personality disorder will be able to communicate coherently, and his or her sentences will make sense, even if they sound a little bizarre in content. Schizotypal differs from schizoid in that the focus in schizoid is the withdrawal from people, while the schizotypal person will leave the impression as having odd beliefs and/ or a strange appearance.

Case Example

Clarissa comes to you seeking advice on how to get a job. In your interview with her, she shares that she was adopted by her grandmother because her birth mother is mentally challenged and was unable to raise her. Since her grandmother was in her early 70s and was preoccupied with several medical issues while raising her, Clarissa says she did not get much meaningful interpersonal interaction with her caretaker. In conversation, you notice that she appears to lack normal social cues. While sharing her history of being raised by an elderly grandparent and the painful challenges that went along with that, you observe that she demonstrates no emotional expression. When it would have been appropriate to be sad or angry, she merely appeared emotionless about it. Further, she reports to you that when she was applying for a job, she seemed convinced that she knew exactly what her job interviewers were thinking and why they did not hire her. Clarissa strongly believes that she could tell they were rejecting her because she is adopted. When you inquire about how they knew she was adopted, she reports that the subject did not come up in her interviews but rather that she just knows they were thinking that. Lastly, even though she reports not having any friends, you notice that does not seem to concern her as much as getting employment.

Pastoral Response

If persons with this type of personality disorder seek help, building rapport with them will be very important. Giving them an opportunity to evaluate their odd beliefs in a trusting relationship may be helpful. Because this disorder is associated with the biological and cognitive deficits that schizophrenics share, you will most likely be referring these individuals for professional help. However, many therapists are confident that psychosocial interventions may help (Walsh, 2016). If the person seems open to some insight, **psychodynamic therapy,** which is therapy that focuses on a person's internal thought processes, may be helpful. This approach can bring what is not necessarily conscious into the person's awareness and give him or her the opportunity to see relationships with others differently. The second possible treatment would be **cognitive-behavioral therapy**, which emphasizes unhealthy thought patterns and teaches the client alternate viewpoints.

KEY TERMS

Hallucinations: seeing something that is not there

Delusions: a rigid belief that is not considered to be reality or rational, but the person maintains the belief despite evidence to the contrary

Paranoid personality disorder: a mental illness demonstrated in significant suspiciousness and mistrust of others above and beyond what society would consider normal guardedness

Schizoid personality disorder: a mental illness in which people avoid social activities, consistently shy away from interaction with others, and demonstrate a limited range of emotional expression

Schizotypal personality disorder: a mental illness where there is a consistent pattern of unusual thinking, discomfort with people, and lack of skill in relating to others

Schizophrenic: the mental illness marked by having a thought disorder, which includes hallucinations and delusions

Psychodynamic therapy: a therapy that focuses on a person's internal thought processes and gaining insight

Cognitive-behavioral therapy: a treatment that emphasizes discovering unhealthy thought patterns and teaching the person alternate viewpoints

1   Make an argument for or against this statement: All three of the "odd and eccentric" personality disorders may be described as guarded.

2   Someone in your congregation came to you for advice because he or she just experienced a home robbery. The person explains that he or she is fearful of anyone who comes to his or her door and is not sure if getting a home security system and maybe a gun will make him or her feel safer. What would you say to this person, and how can you tell if this is a situation-specific problem or paranoid personality disorder?

3   Does the schizoid personality disorder individual experience emotions more deeply than others? Explain your answer.

4   Is schizotypal personality disorder a mild form of schizophrenia, explain your answer?

THE DIAGNOSTIC AND STATISTICAL MANUAL OF MENTAL DISORDERS, 5TH EDITION PERSONALITY DISORDERS: CLUSTER B: DRAMATIC, EMOTIONAL, AND OVERLY UNPREDICTABLE BEHAVIOR, WHICH INCLUDES ANTISOCIAL, BORDERLINE, HISTRIONIC, AND NARCISSISTIC PERSONALITY DISORDERS

This "wild" cluster of personality disorders are people with whom it is generally very hard to be in a relationship with. At times, it can feel like they are actively pushing people away, even though for most of them that is probably the last thing they would want. Like anyone in the helping profession, pastors may feel overtaxed by these individuals, while also seeing their genuine cry for help.

Antisocial Personality Disorder

Antisocial personality disorder is considered when a person is found to regularly dismiss the rights or needs of others without conscience. They appear to have no remorse in hurting others for their own gain or pleasure. This individual's attitudes and behaviors will suggest that he or she does have any concern for the well-being of others.

This may be one of the most interesting and intimidating types of people you could encounter. They do not usually seek any intervention, so most likely you will be approached by the person who is suffering in a relationship with them. They are egocentric and only seem to care about their own needs, while having little to no regard for others.

Here is a summary of the *DSM-5* criteria that must be met for this diagnosis:

- A pattern of behavior that would go back to starting about age 15
- Engaging in criminal behavior and having a lack of respect for the law
- Lying and mistreating others just for fun would be typical behavior for them

- Often their actions are impulsive, and sometimes they engage in aggressive acts toward others
- They appear fearless regarding themselves and others
- There is also a pattern of consistent irresponsibility
- Most importantly, they do not see that hurting others for their own personal gain is wrong (American Psychiatric Association, 2013)

Differential Diagnosis

Some people may question if there is much difference between narcissistic and antisocial personality disorder because of the extreme selfish disposition. The main distinction is antisocial personality disorder is an active and aggressive stance toward others for personal gain. The narcissistic personality disorder disposition is more passive and entitled, believing one is deserving of special treatment, even at the expense of others.

Case Example

House (Attanasio, 2004) was a television show about a genius medical doctor who was very obnoxious in the interpersonal interactions he had. His character may fit more than one of the personality disorders, but we will focus on his dislike for people and disregard for their well-being. Dr. House seemed to intentionally act in such a way as to push all people away from him. He thought only of his own desires and advancement, even risking his own and other's lives to achieve his end. He constantly lied, even to those with whom he worked closely, for his own personal gain. Drug addiction was one of his many vices. Most importantly, he never seemed to care how his behavior had negative effects on others. Perhaps the writers of this show used the *DSM-5* antisocial personality description to develop this main character.

Pastoral Response

Because people with antisocial personality disorder would not normally seek any kind of treatment, they will not likely be asking for any help from a pastor. Rather, people in relationships with individuals with an antisocial personality disorder may approach you for support. Helping them set boundaries as needed or being with them to grieve the pain in their relationships would be very valuable. It may be useful to know that the antisocial personality disorder is often correlated with a diagnosis of conduct disorder, which is antisocial behavior first evident in childhood. This may help the friend or family member better understand why the person behaves the way he or she does. The hope for someone dealing with a person who has antisocial personality disorder is that this diagnosis does seem to show some improvement with age, being married, and maintaining a job (Black, 2015). One of the problems is there likely will be a **comorbid** presentation. This means the person has a second diagnosis (e.g., drug addiction) in addition to the original diagnosis. If the person with antisocial personality disorder is willing to take some advice, his or her aggression can be addressed through anger management courses or therapy. If there is an addiction problem, both the individual and friends or family members would benefit from 12 step, Al-Anon, or Celebrate Recovery type programs. For a thorough understanding of and treatment for antisocial personality disorder consider this book: *Antisocial Personality Disorder: The NICE Guidelines on Treatment, Management, and Prevention (National Clinical Practice Guideline)* (National Collaborating Center for Mental Health, 2009).

Borderline Personality Disorder

The *DSM-5* **describes borderline personality disorder** (BPD) as a consistent pattern of instability in relationships and emotions (American Psychiatric Association, 2013). This is arguably one of the most well-known personality disorders and definitely one you will encounter as a pastor. Mason and Kreger (2010) quote an individual who suffers from BPD: "While others might feel manipulative, I feel powerless. Sometimes I just hurt so bad from the mean things that people do to me, real or perceived, or I'm so desperately feeling abandoned, that I withdraw and pout and go silent. At some point people get pissed off and fed up with that crap and they go away and then I'm left with nothing all over again." This quote provides some insight into their internal experience of constantly reading deeply into their interactions with others with negative conclusions. They likely learned to be this hypervigilant early in their lives to try to avoid emotional pain.

BPD individuals have a reputation in the psychology world of being very challenging clients because of their initial extreme **idealizing**, seeing the other as perfect and able to meet all of one's needs and then **devaluing** them through a complete rejection of the other and finding no worth in them in spite of past kind efforts. This pattern will also happen in relationship with any pastor who is trying to help them. They feel their emotions very intensely, and they seem to not be aware, or do not care, how that affects others. They have such a strong need to be known and to not be abandoned that they may even go to extremes sometimes to express themselves. This is often demonstrated in self-harm or suicidal thinking when they are very distressed. Their experience of emotions seems to be heightened compared to others. For example, what one person may label as a 3 on a distress scale of 0–10, for the same event, the BPD might rate it as a 9. Knowing this helps us to appreciate their subjective experiences as being very different from our own. There are a number of descriptors that are important to cover because of your likely chances of meeting a BPD. The following are a synopsis of the *DSM-5* qualifiers:

- A long history of significant relationship problems will bring them to seek help
- They struggle to feel a solid concept of self and will engage in extreme behaviors to try to make themselves feel better like being promiscuous, overspending, or engaging in addictive behaviors
- Self-harm is a significant concern because they often use this as a tangible method to express their inner pain
- They may also **dissociate**, this is when a person feels disconnected or detached from themselves (American Psychiatric Association, 2013)(National Institute of Mental Health, 2016)

Differential Diagnosis

It is usually difficult to tell the difference between BPD and bipolar disorder, which is a mental illness marked by behavior alternating between a state of mania, excessive, and frantic energy and a state of depression with hopelessness and despondency. Bipolar is marked by extreme mood swings from high energy behaviors, such as excessive spending, and then to experiencing serious lows. You will likely need a professional to be able to diagnose the differences. Very generally speaking, the emphasis with BPD individuals are a history of erratic relationships and possible self-harm behaviors. Whereas the bipolar individual cycles more in his or her moods and may have evident frequent sleep disturbances (American Psychiatric Association, 2013).

Dissociative identity disorder (formerly multiple personality disorder) may also appear to have some overlap with BPD. **Dissociation** happens when a person experiences a shift in consciousness and is temporarily not aware of him or herself or his or her surroundings (American Psychiatric Association, 2013). In addition, a person may be diagnosed with both BPD and dissociation.

Case Example

Maude finds Pastor Jim in the church lobby and asks for advice on men. She reports that she has a history of dating several men who seemed to be her ideal mates when she first met them. However, not too long into her relationships, she would eventually get very hurt by them. She tells Pastor Jim when she tries to communicate to her significant other what she perceived to be his problem, he never seemed to understand what he had done wrong. Instead, he would tell her she seemed fine one moment, and then the next moment he could not understand what set her off into an emotional tirade. It seemed like the little mistakes became really big offenses to her. Most of her relationships ended very messy, with Maude feeling abandoned. She reports the ex-boyfriends would complain that her extreme mood swings were more than they could handle, and they did not like that she would be angry most of the time. To deal with these breakups, Maude reported that she usually would go to bars to pick up men. She explains that it comforted her to know that somebody else did want her after the rejection she experienced with her latest boyfriend. When Pastor Jim tries to help Maude by finding a female pastor to meet with her, she gets very angry, telling Pastor Jim he is abandoning her just like all the other men.

Pastoral Response

The first thing to be aware of is that borderline individuals will likely be very frustrating. They will love you one minute and hate you the next. Whatever it is you feel with them, they are likely feeling the same but worse because they experience their emotions very intensely and do not know how to calm themselves. Realizing this will help you have compassion for them.

Although BPD has historically been thought of as hard to treat, there are new interventions, such as **dialectical behavior therapy** (DBT) developed by Marsha M. Linehan that has been proven to be very effective. This cognitive-based treatment focuses on personality disorders and helps increase emotion management. One aspect is the identification of **triggers**, which can be anything that sets off a memory and makes the person feel as though he or she is re-experiencing something painful from his or her past.

My approach to helping those with BPD focuses on understanding how our brains develop in relationships and how applying this understanding can increase safety in relational experiences. The brain-based relational method can be very helpful for both the person with BPD and his or her support system to better understand how the person's early attachment experiences have affected brain development. This awareness enables all involved to feel a sense of understanding and hope for change. Through insight and exercises, the BPD person can learn to regulate his or her emotions and lead a more emotionally balanced life. The best way to help the BPD person is to focus on **emotion regulation,** which is the ability to identify one's feelings and to have a socially appropriate plan to get one's needs met (Bettenhausen, 2016).

Histrionic Personality Disorder

Histrionic personality disorder (HPD) is associated individuals who are very dramatic. There is a lot of exaggeration in their communication style in order to garner attention from others. Individuals with HPD likely did not get recognized enough early in life, so they feel they must overstate their needs or experiences in order to get a response from others.

A summary of the *DSM-5* key descriptors for HPD is as follows:

- They can be very flirtatious and provocative and described as good actors because of their exaggerated way of communicating
- This would be the person who is friends with many people but not really known by or close to anyone
- When not getting enough attention, they can be prone to depression
- Their desire to be seen by others can make them vulnerable to suggestion
- They also tend to be sensitive to criticism due to their desire for constant approval (American Psychiatric Association, 2013)

Differential Diagnosis

Because of the significant amount of energy this person invests socially, as well as his or her tendency toward depression when alone, HPD may be mistaken as having **bipolar disorder**. The main difference is that while someone with HPD may rapidly shift in his or her emotions, the person does not necessarily feel in extremes like bipolar disorder. Further, the HPD likely has a shallower experience of his or her emotions (American Psychiatric Association, 2013).

Case Example

Cadd is the life of the party, according to all his friends. The conversation is never dull when he is around, and he always has a funny story to tell. He was voted prom king in high school and continues to be very well known on his college campus. Somehow, he has time to be involved in many activities and always knows someone wherever he is. It would also be hard to keep track of how many different women he has dated. In spite of knowing so many people, he does not really have any really close friends. None of the people who Cadd calls his friends would claim to know him very well. Because he appears to love attention so much, his friends would be surprised to hear that he is extremely afraid of getting hurt by others and often suffers from depression.

Pastoral Response

Keep in mind that the histrionic personality person's exaggerated way of communicating is likely because early on in life, he or she did not get much validation for his or her thoughts and emotions. Having a consistently confirming experience with someone can really help him or her **de-escalate**, which is to decrease the intensity of the emotion the person is having. Usually, failed relationships bring the HPD person to ask for help. If the person's partner is willing, couples counseling may be suggested to learn each other's communication style.

Narcissistic Personality Disorder

This will be a familiar term, as it has become a normal part of our lexicon for people who think too much of themselves. **Narcissistic personality disorder**, as defined by the *DSM-5*, is a regular pattern of grandiosity and a need to impress, along with a deficit of compassion for others (American Psychiatric Association, 2013). It is ironic that narcissists give the impression that they think they are better than others, because in fact, they probably have very low self-esteem. Their "puffed up" presentation is likely an attempt to hide weaknesses and vulnerabilities.

The *DSM-5* shows us the hallmarks of NPD as summarized here:

- They demonstrate **grandiosity**, a pretentious belief that one is very unique and therefore better than others
- Their excessive desire for admiration may cause them to give the impression they do not care about others
- They will seem self-serving and portray an all-consuming need for validation
- There is a strong sense of **entitlement,** which is believing they have a right to special privileges

If anyone raises a concern about the narcissist's behavior or attitude, his or her inflated beliefs about themselves may cause them to conclude that others are likely jealous of them, and therefore they will dismiss any criticisms as invalid (American Psychiatric Association, 2013). For example, a narcissist would feel no qualms about cutting to the front of a long line of people for his or her own interest. It would not cross the person's mind to consider how the others in line would feel. In fact, the narcissist often feels entitled to special treatment because of what he or she perceives to be exceptional accomplishments or character traits regarding him or herself.

I am reminded of several of the Old Testament kings while considering the qualifications for narcissistic personality disorder. In 1 Kings, we have Jeroboam as one example. He was given a great opportunity by God to rule the Northern Kingdom of Israel, and all he had to do was be obedient to God. Instead, he cared more about keeping his important position, even at the expense of his people, so he disobeyed God and set up his own place of worship using idols. He thought so much of himself that he believed he could get away with sinning against God.

Differential Diagnosis

Histrionic, borderline, and antisocial personality disorders have similar traits to narcissistic personality disorder, such as they all can demonstrate some form of exaggerated presentation. The key difference for narcissistic personality disorder is the emphasis on grandiose thinking and excessive need for admiration from others (American Psychiatric Association, 2013).

Case Example

Jin is a very entertaining party guest. When she is around, you know the conversation will never wane. She seems to have endless detailed stories of her adventures either from college, travels, or several jobs she has held. Usually, her monologues are very long, sometimes lasting longer than 20 minutes at a time. Jin hates to be interrupted when sharing a tale and will quickly redirect the conversation back to her subject. In fact, usually, there is no break for questions or comments from her listener. She prefers to be listened to rather than engaged as she shares every last detail. It would appear that she is not aware that the others around her have not spoken much or at all. Jin enjoys the attention she garners from her audiences, but she shows no effort in asking others about themselves.

Pastoral Response

The challenge with narcissists is that they use their inflated sense of self to cover or mask a deeper insecurity; therefore, it can take some time to build trust in their relationships. This requires the pastor to see beyond their off-putting attitudes and have patience in the process. This stance will create a safe relationship for them, so they can explore how their perspective is affecting their relationships. It may also help for them to gain insight into how their background shaped them. For example, the person's parents may have only rewarded their child when he or she accomplished something; therefore, the individual develops a belief that he or she is only accepted while impressing others.

KEY TERMS

Antisocial personality disorder: a mental illness indicated for a person who regularly dismisses the rights or needs of others without conscience and will have no remorse in causing others pain for their own gain or pleasure

Comorbid presentation: when a person has a second diagnosis in addition to the original diagnosis

Idealizing: seeing the other as perfect and able to meet all of one's needs

Devaluing: complete rejection of the other and finding no worth in him or her in spite of past positive experiences with them previously

Dissociate: an experience of feeling disconnected or detached from oneself

Bipolar: behavior alternating between the states of mania and depression

Dialectical behavior therapy: cognitive psychological treatment developed by Marsha M. Linehan that focuses on personality disorders and helps increase emotion management

Triggers: anything that sets off a memory and makes a person feel as though he or she is re-experiencing something painful from the past

Emotion regulation: the ability to identify one's feelings and to have a socially appropriate plan to get one's needs met

Histrionic personality disorder: a mental illness marked by a very dramatic and exaggerated communication style in order to garner attention from others

De-escalate: to decrease the intensity of the experienced emotion

Grandiosity: a pretentious belief that one is very unique and therefore better than others

Borderline personality disorder: a mental illness defined by a consistent pattern of instability in relationships and in emotions

Narcissistic personality disorder: a mental illness involving a regular pattern of grandiosity and a need to impress along with a deficit of compassion for others

Discussion Questions

1. Name two of the characteristics that define antisocial personality disorder and provide an example of this disorder.

2. How is BPD distinguished from bipolar disorder?

3. You have a church member who is great at telling exaggerated but funny stories. This person knows almost everyone in the church and seems to have endless energy. The individual is usually found with a crowd of people around him or her and seems to never get enough attention from others. What possible personality disorders could this person have and how do you know when it becomes problematic?

4. Develop a detailed plan on how to approach a person with narcissistic personality disorder to help him or her with a troubled relationship.

THE DIAGNOSTIC AND STATISTICAL MANUAL OF MENTAL DISORDERS, 5TH EDITION PERSONALITY DISORDERS: CLUSTER C: "ANXIOUS AND FEARFUL," WHICH INCLUDE AVOIDANT, DEPENDENT, AND OBSESSIVE-COMPULSIVE PERSONALITY DISORDERS

This "worried" category of personality disorders is marked by extreme and excessive anxiety. It can be frustrating and sometimes feel hopeless trying to help very anxious people because they often are very persistent in their nervousness. Although the anxiety they experience is causing them significant distress, at times, they almost seem resistant to intervention. Anxiety, however, is treatable, but intervention needs to be personalized based on the individual's history, present circumstances, and support available.

Avoidant Personality Disorder

The **avoidant personality disorder** is defined by the *DSM-5* as follows:

- Withdrawal from social interaction due to extreme shyness and fear of rejection
- Panic over potential spurning from others, and this anxiety has a significant effect on their daily functioning
- Avoiding work or social activities and likely remaining distant in their personal relationships. This could hinder their professional growth as well as contribute to depression if untreated
- A tendency to obsess about their own shortcomings, therefore feeling "less than" other people
- Having an inner critical voice that is so strong they are not able to tolerate disapproval and therefore limit their exposure to the scrutiny of others
- Feeling imprisoned by their own harsh internal judge but externally it appears they are shy or removed (American Psychiatric Association, 2013)

Avoidant personality disorder may develop as the result of parental neglect, both physical and emotional. This leads a person to believe that his or her needs are unimportant to others, and therefore the individual does not expect to receive care (Eikenaes, Egeland, Hummelen, & Wilberg, 2015). Assuming that they will not receive care makes it understandable why they sometimes **catastrophize**, which is to make something out to be much worse than it is in reality. Expecting the worst can feel like a protection from disappointment, but in actuality, it leads to more withdrawal and pain. Even though they may report being lonely most of the time, they still prefer loneliness over risking not receiving acceptance and love from others.

Jesus's parable of the talents comes to mind when I think of avoidant personality disorder. In Matthew 25:14–30, Jesus taught us about three servants who each were allotted a certain amount of money from their master. The emphasis is on the third servant, who took his share of money and buried it in the ground instead of investing it like the other two servants. His excuse was that he was fearful his boss would get mad, so he did not want to risk losing anything. He did not believe in himself or in the relationship with his master. He hid his own talent in order to avoid rejection.

Differential Diagnosis

Schizoid personality disorder is also marked by shyness and avoiding social situations. However, schizoid people do not necessarily desire the company of other people, whereas the person with avoidant personality disorder may want relationships, but they are very afraid of rejection. Also, generalized anxiety disorder occurs when someone is very fearful as well, but that anxiety can come and go depending on circumstances. Avoidant personality disorder is considered to be more severe, consistent over time, and centered more on the personality (American Psychiatric Association, 2013).

Case Example

Mackie has known his group of friends since high school. He was always known to be shy, but it seems to have been increasing in severity the older he gets. His friends and family do not see much of Mackie because he is usually working a lot or has some other reason to decline invitations. His friends are very frustrated with him because they feel he does not care to be around them. When he does attend one of their get-togethers he does not stay very long. Mackie's demeanor may look calm on the outside but inside he is extremely anxious. He fears people may find out how troubled he feels and reject him because they think he is weird.

Pastoral Response

Since it will be a big deal for people with this personality disorder to work up the courage to talk with you, assessing how anxious they feel will determine your next steps. Teaching them relaxation exercises can help. For example, have them put both feet on the floor and put their hands on their belly; then they can breathe in and out slowly and feel their hands lift as their chest expands and contracts with the air. Sometimes I refer them to YouTube relaxation videos to find what works best for them. There are lots of resources available to deal with anxiety. *Mind Over Mood Workbook* by Greenberger, Padesky and Beck has lots of worksheets and ideas on how to address anxiety. Further, I try to find out how open they are to talking about God because low self-esteem issues need to be attended to as well. If they are open to spiritual things, then you can provide verses, Biblical stories, or other resources that demonstrate how much God values people. **Systematic desensitization** is another helpful tool but should likely be done by a professional. This is when you slowly introduce an anxiety-provoking situation and build tolerance as the person learns to calm down through new coping skills. For instance, a shy person may begin by having lunch with one friend to build confidence before trying to attend a dinner party with multiple friends.

Dependent Personality Disorder

According to the *DSM-5*, those suffering from **dependent personality disorder** are as follows:

- Very needy and dependent, believing they must completely rely on others to the point of losing self-agency
- Not likely to speak their own mind for fear of offending someone and losing connection with others

- Pleasing others as a top priority because they are fearful of **abandonment**, which is the fear of having one's significant others leave or withdraw from relationship
- Often believing they are incapable of caring for themselves, which makes it very scary for them to be or feel alone (American Psychiatric Association, 2013)

It can be very frustrating to be in relationships with people who have dependent personality disorder because they are very passive and do not like to make decisions. They seem to prefer to have someone else make most decisions for them. It would appear that they are avoiding adult responsibilities and choosing a more helpless disposition. Sadly, dependent personality individuals are more likely to get in abusive relationships with people who enjoy controlling others. Their naiveté and neediness make them susceptible to this type of dynamic in relationships.

Differential Diagnosis

The *DSM-5* suggests that there are overlapping features between dependent, borderline, and HPD (American Psychiatric Association, 2013). In this case, you would be considering whether problematic dependency on others is the primary presenting issue.

Case Example

Alia has been married three times. Her first husband was an alcoholic and abusive to her. In spite of his repeated physical aggression toward her, she did not leave him. He divorced her and told her she had to move out of their house. Her ex-husband then proceeded to move Alia's best friend in to live with him. She did not fight him for the house or alimony. Alia's second husband was similar to the first, but this time she was forced to leave him because child protective services said she could either stay with him or lose her children. In spite of this warning, she continued to see her second husband until he went to jail for hitting someone while driving drunk. He divorced her as well. The third husband is not an addict, but he is very controlling of her every move. She has to let him know where she is at all times. He tells her how to dress, who she can hang out with, and what activities she is allowed to do. Even though she complains about how controlling her current husband is, she is not taking any steps to confront his behavior for fear that he will get angry and leave her.

Pastoral Response

Low self-esteem makes it challenging to confront people who have dependent personality disorder. They are very sensitive to criticism, although they might agree with you just to gain approval and avoid argument. The best way to help your dependent personality congregants is insight and exercises for cognitive change. A conversation about past relationships that may have modeled this type of behavior can be enlightening. Support them in owning the helpless identity they have taken on and what the pros and cons are to such a position. If the person is a believer and open to God, I commonly discuss the topic of stewardship with him or her—how we are all only accountable for ourselves. It is also useful to identify negative self-talk with people in this group, like believing they are not capable of caring for themselves. Becoming aware of negative thinking enables them to realize that they can choose more affirming thoughts, such as verses that affirm how God sees them (Bornstein, 2007).

Obsessive-Compulsive Personality Disorder

According to the *DSM-5*, we identify **obsessive-compulsive personality disorder** (OCPD) when the following occurs:

- There is such a rigid personality that they are unable to be influenced by others or adapt to new circumstances
- Individuals are very obstinate in their viewpoints and lack flexibility in their attitudes
- The individual really likes structure and gets agitated when expected to deviate from it
- Someone gets so focused on the task at hand that it becomes to the exclusion of a balanced life (American Psychiatric Association, 2013)

Differential Diagnosis

OCPD is not to be confused with obsessive-compulsive disorder (OCD), which is a separate yet related mental disorder. A person will be labeled OCD when he or she suffers from **obsessions**, intrusive repeated thoughts that occupy a person's mind to the point of distress, and **compulsions**, behaviors that are constantly repeated, usually in an attempt to relieve some anxiety (American Psychiatric Association, 2013). The typical example of OCD is the person who compulsively locks his or her door, excessively washes his or hand hands, or experiences intrusive obsessive thoughts. The difference between these two is that the person with OCD will have insight that his or her thoughts are unhealthy, whereas the person with OCPD will not experience their behavior and unusual (Van Noppen, 2010).

Case Example

Carmen was in charge of the church volunteer team to help collect tickets at a concert. Barney's wife coerced him to come along with her to give a hand and help their church with this event. Carmen gathered her team just before the doors opened and explained how they were to take the tickets from the attendees. When she was done training her group, Barney spoke up with what he explained was a much more efficient way to collect the tickets. Carmen thanked him but asked the group to continue with the process she taught them. Barney began to argue with her in front of the other volunteers that his method was much better. After quite some time of Barney continuing to insist on his plan, it became uncomfortable for everyone. To avoid the conflict, Carmen gave in to Barney's method. Barney's wife later apologized to Carmen for Barney's behavior. She further stated that Barney tends to be overly insistent when he believes he is correct about something.

Pastoral Response

When engaging people with OCPD, it helps to understand that they tend to **intellectualize,** that is to respond with the rational and logical part of their brain, while not being in touch with their feelings. There is a feeling chart you can find online that you may use to help the person add emotion words to his or her stressful situation. Here is where to find one example: https://edgeofmyknowledge.wordpress.com/2012/12/12/20-primary-and-secondary-emotions/ I also like to remind people that God demonstrated emotions throughout scripture. John 11:35, "Jesus wept," is one of many examples. Often, this individual has not had an experience of someone being interested in how he or she feels, so the person has little to no practice with identifying feelings. This black or white thinking can be frustrating, so be prepared to show the person grace and patience when you get criticized by him or her (Bressert, 2017a).

KEY TERMS

Avoidant personality disorder: a mental illness marked by withdrawal from social interaction due to extreme shyness and fear of rejection

Catastrophize: making something out to be much worse than it is in reality

Systematic desensitization: when you slowly introduce an anxiety provoking situation and build tolerance as the person is learning to calm themselves with new coping skills

Dependent personality disorder: a mental illness demonstrated in excessive neediness and dependency, believing one must completely rely on others to the point of losing self-agency

Abandonment: fear of having one's significant others leave or withdraw from relationship

Obsessive-compulsive personality disorder: a mental illness demonstrated in a rigid personality and an inability to be influenced by others or adapt to new circumstances

Obsessions: intrusive repeated thoughts that occupy a person's mind to the point of distress

Compulsions: behaviors that are constantly repeated, usually in an attempt to relieve some anxiety

Intellectualize: respond with the rational and logical part of the brain, while not being in touch with feelings

Discussion Questions

1. How is anxiety expressed differently in each of the three Cluster C personality disorders?

2. How can you tell if someone is just extremely shy or he or she has avoidant personality disorder?

3. Make a Biblical argument for or against dependent personality disorder.

4. What would a Christian suffers from obsessive-compulsive personality possibly look like?

REVIEWING THE CONCEPTS

Learning Objectives

- Identify and define the various personality disorders pastors may encounter, depending on their congregation demographics
  - Paranoid personality disorder: a mental illness as seen in a significant suspiciousness and mistrust of others above and beyond what society would consider normal guardedness
  - Schizoid personality disorder: a mental illness in which people avoid social activities, consistently shy away from interaction with others, and demonstrate a limited range of emotional expression
  - Schizotypal personality disorder: a mental illness showing a consistent pattern of unusual thinking, discomfort with people, and lack of skill in relating to others
  - BPD: a mental illness demonstrated in a consistent pattern of instability in relationships and in emotions
  - Narcissistic personality disorder: a mental illness involving a regular pattern of grandiosity and need to impress others along with a deficit in compassion
  - HPD: a mental illness where the individual is very dramatic and uses exaggeration in his or her communication style in order to garner attention from others
  - Antisocial personality disorder: a mental illness describing people who regularly dismisses the rights or needs of others without conscience
  - Avoidant personality disorder: a mental illness marked by withdrawal from social interaction because of extreme shyness and fear of rejection
  - OCPD: a mental illness where there appears to be a rigid personality, and the person is unable to be influenced by others or adapt to new circumstances
  - Dependent personality disorder: a mental illness defined as a person who is very needy and dependent, believing he or she must completely rely on others to the point of losing self-agency

- Identify the three clusters into which the 10 personality disorders are divided.
  - Cluster A: the odd and eccentric group, which includes paranoid, schizoid, and schizotypal personality disorders
  - Cluster B: the dramatic, emotional, and unpredictable group, which includes antisocial, histrionic, narcissistic, and borderline personality disorders
  - Cluster C: the anxious and fearful group, which includes avoidant, dependent, and obsessive-compulsive personality disorders

- Identity pastoral response strategies for all of the personality disorders.
- Compare personality disorders to other possible diagnoses.

Chapter Review Questions

Level 1: Knowledge (True/False)

1. Several criteria must be met in order to diagnose a personality disorder.

2. Everyone has a personality disorder to some degree.

3. Long-term rigidity and relational impairments are some of the key features of a personality disorder.

4. The person who has a personality disorder is not necessarily in distress.

5. Drug use must be ruled out before labeling someone with a personality disorder.

6. The *DSM-5* provides clear time frames in order to identify a personality disorder.

7. There is not a significant difference between schizotypal personality disorder and schizophrenia.

8. Bipolar personality disorder can be recognized by a pattern of extreme idealizing and devaluing of others.

9. Several personality disorders are similar to bipolar disorder.

10. Avoidant personality disorder often develops when there are overly involved caretakers.

Level 2: Comprehension

1. According to Millon et al., (2004), personality includes all of the following except
    a. temperament
    b. embedded characteristics
    c. habitual responses
    d. patterns

2. It is preferable to diagnose personality disorders in
    a. childhood
    b. A
    c. adolescence
    d. college age
    e. adulthood

3. According to Huff (2004), which of the following does not necessarily contribute to personality disorder development?
    a. Genetics
    b. Childhood trauma
    c. Sensitivity to stimuli
    d. Physical abuse

4. Which of the following is true about neural networks?

    a. They are permanent

    b. They fire randomly

    c. They are influenced by attachment experience

    d. They are irrelevant to the field of psychology

5. Bergmann makes a case for all of the following, except

    a. environment is a key factor in personality development

    b. biology is a key factor in personality development

    c. people can inherit trauma effects via hormones

    d. cortisol increases in traumatized individuals

6. According to Bettenhausen, personality disorders can best be understood by all of the following, except

    a. early relationships

    b. the amygdala

    c. current relationships

    d. the prefrontal cortex

7. Which of the following, according to Gawda and Kararzyna (2017), is not one of the most common personality disorders?

    a. Obsessive compulsive

    b. Borderline

    c. Narcissistic

    d. Schizotypal

8. Schizoid personality disorder can best be recognized by

    a. odd behavior

    b. avoidance of others

    c. dependence

    d. fear of abandonment

9. Which of the following would not be true of antisocial personality disorder?

    a. Dramatic

    b. Egocentric

    c. Selfish

    d. Impulsive

10. According to the *DSM-5*, OCPD is best described as

    a. fearful of people

    b. easily influenced

    c. love structure

    d. easily distracted

Level 3: Application

1. You are guest speaking in a marriage class. Pick three of the personality disorder types that you think would be difficult in a marriage. Define each and offer options for responding to each.

2. A church member comes to you seeking help because her college-age son does not seem to have any friends. She reports he seems content to be at home all the time, but she is concerned about his future. How can you tell if her son is just extremely shy or has avoidant personality disorder?

3. Describe the hallmarks of a personality disorder. How might you use these while meeting with a congregant to determine how to help them? How would you know when to refer them to a professional?

4. Some of your staff seems to be having difficulty getting along with each other. You suspect this may be partially due to personality issues. Create a short talk on how you would introduce the personality types to them with suggestions on how to appreciate their fellow staff members in place of being frustrated.

5. While meeting with a couple from your church, you suspect one of them may have BPD. How would you know this for sure, and how would you help them?

ANSWERS

LEVEL 1: KNOWLEDGE

1. T
2. F
3. T
4. F
5. T
6. F
7. F
8. T
9. T
10. F

LEVEL 2: COMPREHENSION

1. a
2. d
3. d
4. c
5. a
6. c
7. d
8. b
9. a
10. c

RESOURCES

Online Resources

- Right Now Media—https://www.rightnowmedia.org/
- Feeling wheel—https://edgeofmyknowledge.wordpress.com/2012/12/12/20-primary-and-secondary-emotions/
- Meet Your Master: Getting to Know Your Brain—Crash Course Psychology #4—https://www.youtube.com/watch?v=vHrmiy4W9C0&t=13s

Readings

- *Anatomy of the Soul*—Curt Thompson
- *Boundaries*—Henry Cloud and John Townsend
- *Changes That Heal*—Dr. Henry Cloud
- *Healing Trauma*—edited by Marion Solomon and Daniel Siegel
- *How We Love*—Milan and Kay Yerkovich
- *Recovery of Your Inner Child*—Lucia Capacchione
- *Shame and Grace, Healing the Shame We Don't Deserve*—Lewis Smedes
- *Stop Walking on Eggshells*—Paul Mason and Randi Kreger
- *The Dialectical Behavior Therapy Skills Workbook*—Matthew McKay, Jeffrey C. Wood, and Jeffrey Brantley
- *When Misery Is Company*—Anne Katherine Wood
- *When Love Is Not Enough*—Nancy Thomas
- *Who Is Pushing Your Buttons*—John Townsend

- *Highly Sensitive Person*—Elaine Aron
- *How People Grow: What the Bible Reveals About Personal Growth*—Henry Cloud and John Townsend
- *Enneagram: A Christian Perspective*—Rohr and Ebert
- National Collaborating Center for Mental Health (2009). *Antisocial Personality Disorder: The NICE Guidelines on Treatment, Management, and Prevention (National Clinical Practice Guideline)* 1st Edition, London, Royal College of Psychiatrists Publications
- *Mind Over Mood Workbook*—Greenberger, Pakesky, and Beck

CLASSROOM ACTIVITIES

1. Have a group discussion about when you may have encountered one of the personality disorders, how you handled it, and what you may do differently now.

2. Role-play expected interactions with personality disorder congregants.

REFERENCES

American Psychiatric Association. (2013). *Diagnostic and statistical manual of mental disorders* (5th ed.). Washington, DC: Author.

American Psychological Association. (2004). Can the clinically inflexible learn to be resilient. *Monitor on Psychology, 35*(3), 49.

Aron, E. (1996). *The highly sensitive person. How to thrive when the world overwhelms you.* New York, NY: Broadway Books.

Attanasio, P. (Producer). (2004–2012). *House* (Television Series). United States, NBC Universal Television.

Bergmann, U. (2012). *Neurological foundations for EMDR practice.* New York, NY: Springer Publishing Co.

Bettenhausen, R. (2017). *The relational brain: A path to heal broken relationships.* Lulu.com

Black, D. (2015). The natural history of antisocial personality disorder. *Canadian Journal of Psychiatry, 60*(7), 309–314.

Bornstein, R. (2007). Dependent personality disorder: Effective time limited therapy. *Current Psychiatry, 6*(1), 37–45.

Bressert, S. (2017a) Obsessive compulsive personality disorder treatment. Retrieved from https://psychcentral.com/disorders/obsessive-compulsive-personality-disorder/treatment/

Bressert, S. (2017b) Paranoid personality disorder treatment. Retrieved from https://psychcentral.com/disorders/paranoid-personality-disorder/treatment/

Eikenaes, I., Egeland, J., Hummelen, B., & Wilberg, T. (2015). Avoidant personality disorder versus social phobia: The significance of childhood neglect. Retrieved from *http://journals.plos.org/plosone/article?id=10.1371/journal.pone.0122846*

Gawda, B., & Kararzyna, C. (2017). Prevalence of personality disorders in a general population among men and women. *Sage Journals Psychological Reports, 120*(3) 503–519.

Huff, C. (2004). Where personality goes awry. *Monitor on Psychology, 35*(3) 42.

Lenzenweger, M. (2008) Epidemiology of personality disorders. *Science Direct, Psychiatric Clinics of North America, 31*(3), 395–403.

Li, D. (2018). Personality disorders. Retrieved from http://step1.medbullets.com/step1-psychiatry/114038/personality-disorders

Mason, P., & Kreger, R., (2010). *Stop walking on eggshells* (2nd ed.). Oakland, CA: New Harbinger Publications.

Millon, T., Grossman, S., Millon, C., Meagher, S., & Ramnath, R. (2004) *Personality disorders in modern life* (2nd ed.) Hoboken, NJ: Wiley.

National Institute for Mental Health. (2016). Borderline Personality Disorder. Retrieved from https://www.nimh.nih.gov/health/topics/borderline-personality-disorder/index.shtml

Samuels, J., Eaton, W., Bienvenu O., Brown, C., Costa, P., & Nestadt, G. (2002). Prevalence and correlates of personality disorder in a community sample. *The British Journal of Psychiatry, 180*(6), 536–542.

Shapiro, F. (2001) *Eye movement and desensitization and reprocessing.* New York, NY: Guilford Press.

Shore, A. (2000) Attachment and the regulation of the right brain, *Attachment and Human Development.* 2(1), 23–47.

Triebwasser, J., Chemerinski, E., Roussos, P., & Siever, L. (2012). Schizoid personality disorder. *Journal of Personality Disorders*, 26(6), 919–926.

Van Noppen, B. (2010). Obsessive compulsive personality disorder (OCPD). Retrieved from https://iocdf.org/wp-content/uploads/2014/10/OCPD-Fact-Sheet.pdf

Walsh, J. (2016). Schizotypal personality disorder: A clinical social work perspective. *Journal of Social Work Practice, 31*(1), 67–78.

IMAGE CREDITS

CHAPTER 14

Elders: Challenges and Growth in Later Life

Shirley Liao-Sanders, PhD

LEARNING OBJECTIVES

Upon completion of this chapter, readers will be able to

1. identify some common struggles and issues of later life;

2. identify and describe common cognitive impairments in older adults;

3. facilitate a pastoral response to the needs of elders in the congregation with dementia and of their families;

4. identify and define caregiving phases;

5. list risk factors for adverse caregiving outcomes;

6. list factors for healthy lifestyle/aging;

7. facilitate a pastoral response to the church's role in promoting successful aging; and

8. identify roles in the congregation that would be suited to elders.

I will be your God through all your lifetime, yes, even when your
hair is white with age. I made you and I will care for you.
I will carry you along and be your Savior.
(Isaiah 46:4, *The Living Bible*)

THE STORY OF PASTORS DAVE AND JENNY

Dave and Jenny met as undergraduate students at a Christian University. They got married before Dave graduated and started his seminary studies. It had been a long-time calling of Dave's to attend seminary and to become a church pastor. One year later, Jenny finished her undergraduate studies and got an administrative job at a large multicultural church that she and Dave were members of. During that time, both Dave and Jenny had been quite involved with various ministries at the church—his was teaching and hers was with the youth groups.

FIGURE 14.1   **Retrospection**

Shortly before Dave completed his seminary training, he was offered a job as an associate pastor at the church. Dave was elated and grateful while his responsibility expanded from primarily teaching to caring for the couples/family's ministry. Jenny began her own seminary training so that she would feel more equipped to work with "the kids" whom she had developed close relationships with, as well as with their families, many of whom were immigrants. They would refer to Jenny as "Pastor Jenny" out of respect.

While Dave and Jenny were settling into their new roles as ministers, it was brought to Dave's attention that one of the adult Sunday School teachers Jeff (a long-time, revered member of the church) tended to repeat himself in class and had trouble remembering conversations and dates while increasingly becoming irritable. Jeff was a beloved high school science teacher who had recently retired at age 60 and was happily married with two adult children. In the last few months, several church members and some from Jeff's Sunday School class had expressed their concerns to Dave.

Around the same time, one of the middle school kids whom Jenny had been working with over the past couple of years shared with Jenny about the tensions she was experiencing at home where four generations of family members lived together (including a great-grandmother who was 85 years old, grandparents who were in their 60s, the child's parents, and their three children). Jenny began to realize that in order for her to be able to help this child, who appeared sad and was isolating herself from the rest of the youth group, she would need to visit the family and try to help sort through the difficulties at home.

On a date night, as Dave and Jenny shared with each other about their week, both of them realized that they felt unfamiliar and inadequate in dealing with issues faced by older adults at the church and in shepherding them with their own unique needs and struggles in older adulthood. Dave and Jenny, who were in their late 20s at that time, and who both had parents and grandparents who were healthy and alive, for the first time unexpectedly needed to confront some of the more difficult issues of aging.

AN INTRODUCTION TO THE INCREASING OLDER ADULT POPULATION IN THE UNITED STATES

When I was a predoctoral intern in 2006, working at a community mental health agency that specifically provided services to older adults, there was a sense of urgency within the agency and among other similar organizations. We all felt the need to raise awareness of the emerging increase of the older adult population in the United States and the urgency to be prepared to meet older adults' unique needs. This historically large population of older adults is referred to as the Baby Boomer generation. Baby Boomers were born between the years 1946 and 1964 with the initial wave turning 65 in 2011. In the following decades, our society has and will continue to experience the significant impacts of this group socially and economically. According to a report called "An Aging Nation" (U.S. Census Bureau, 2014), the number of people older than 65 years is expected to be 83.7 million in 2050, double that in 2012. By 2030, all the Baby Boomers will be age 65 or over, thus more than 20% (1 in every 5 persons) of the population in the United States will be seniors at that time (p. 4). This number will be only slightly smaller than the percentage of the country's youths (under 18), which is 22%.

I remembered speaking on these numbers in workshops and seminars shortly after the beginning of the 21st century; now, here we are, living out those projected numbers. Furthermore, the increasing expected life span regardless of gender and race also contribute to this growing number of seniors. For instance, the population of the **old-old** (age 85 and above) in 2036 will double that of 2014 and triple by 2049 (p. 9). Globally, the United States has the largest group of the old-old among developed countries.

While aging is an inevitable process in life, so now also is the quickly growing rate of older adults around us, and in our own communities. In addition, this elderly population is extremely diverse in their ethnic, racial, cultural, religious, political, social, and economic makeup. Therefore, their needs can vary quite significantly within the group. As in the story of Dave and Jenny, today more and more clergy, regardless of their specific areas of ministry, find themselves in the positions of needing to respond to issues related to this large group of congregants who are now in their senior years. Therefore, as pastors and ministry leaders, it is imperative that we equip ourselves with knowledge, understanding, and awareness of aging and of issues unique to older adults so that we can continue to be effective in serving all of God's people.

Healthy Aging and Some Common Challenges in Later Life

The moment we were born, we began the aging process. As discussed earlier, Americans are now living longer than ever. It is important to note that aging can be a grace-filled and rewarding experience. The biblical patriarch Abraham is a good example of such (Gen. 25:7–8) who lived one hundred 75 years and died in "good old age."

The Centers for Disease Control and Prevention (2015), defines **healthy aging** as "the development and maintenance of optimal physical, mental (cognitive and emotional), spiritual, and social well-being and function in older adults" (p. 1). In other words, healthy/ successful aging is not simply to avoid disease but, a state of well-being. Research has shown that healthy aging is easiest to attain when an older adult's community provides a safe, supportive environment for them to maintain a sense of overall well-being while investing resources in preventing/minimizing the effects of diseases on those functions. There are a plethora of misconceptions, stereotypes, and myths revolving around aging/older adulthood. Sexuality is one of them. Sexuality and sexual intimacy are natural and healthy human experiences and desired even in old age. One's religiosity may have negative effects on one's view of sexuality and sexual intimacy (Bouman, Arcelus, & Benbow, 2006; Rheaume & Mitty, 2008). As church leaders, without a clear understanding of sexuality in older adulthood and our own biases, we could unintentionally place critical judgment on our elder church members, which may reduce our connectedness and ministry effectiveness with them.

Another stereotype about aging is that as an individual enters into older adulthood, he or she is no longer "useful" and retreats from social interactions. On the contrary, many elders take on multiple roles, such as being grandparents, volunteers, and pursuing new hobbies, even after they retire from a paid employment. They stay active and continue to contribute to their family and to society, especially as life expectancy increases, there is a "prolonged co-existence of several generations" (Hubatkova, 2018). Even though these "active agers" may experience more stress than their cohorts, their reported well-being is higher.

For most of our congregants, the church community is the primary community in which they identify and feel a sense of belonging. Thus churches hold a pivotal position in contributing to the congregants' meaningful experiences of aging, filled with vitality. Studies show that "the ability to forgive, feel grateful and experience joy" is one of the keys to healthy/successful aging, as well as church attendance and involvement in religious activities (Hartman-Stein & Potknowicz, 2003, p. 128). However, it is important to match an older adult's ideology and personality characteristics to their environment to obtain the benefits of community; otherwise, the stress involved in the incongruity may negatively affect the older adult's overall health. Specifically, it is the social and interpersonal aspect of a community that an older adult belongs to, for instance a church that has the most significant, direct, and positive effect on an older adult's sense of identity, meaning in life, and well-being (McDougle, Konrath, Walk, & Handy, 2016).

Although throughout our lives, we come to reflect on the meaning of life and the issue of death and dying, these existential questions are unavoidably heightened during the stage of late adulthood (65 and over). The famous human development model developed by Erik H. Erikson (1902–1994) proposed that in this stage, existential identity is *the* challenge. With the natural decay of the body and normal cognitive decline, the existential, anxiety-provoking question of life and death is lived for the older adults.

Even for those with a strong Christian faith, the experience and process of dying is difficult and can feel dreadfully alone. I recall visiting a healthy 95-year-old woman at her home; it was definitely a profoundly bittersweet moment for both of us when she showed me a stack of photo albums from the past years. As she flipped through the pages of her albums and fondly recalled the stories of each photo, she pointed to the people in them—schoolmates, friends, fellow churchgoers, etc.—and concluded each story with, "He's dead now, and she's dead … oh she died, too."

Grief and loss issues are complex for older adults. In fact, **complicated grief** is the most prevalent in the elderly population (Newson, Boelen, Hek, Hofman, & Tiemeier, 2011). They grieve and mourn over the time passed, dreams that were never realized and now will never be, the passing of loved ones and, the relational ruptures and regrets that cannot be mended if those involved have passed on. It is helpful and important for those who shepherd older adults to be familiar with grief work, as presented in Chapter 5 of this book, with the understanding that an older adult may experience a wide range of grief, simply due to the many years that he or she has lived. Some or many of these griefs and losses may never be worked through during their lifetime. Furthermore, for the old-olds, it is not uncommon to experience their own children's deaths. Newson et al., (2011) suggest that the loss of a child is the most noticeable predicator for complicated grief, followed by the loss of a spouse and the loss of several people, which sadly are familiar experiences for many older adults, especially the old-old. Being able to tolerate one's own existential anxiety and helplessness while listening to an older adult recounting his or her stories of grief, loss, and bereavement can be overwhelming and yet is essential in offering care and counseling for the older adult.

KEY TERMS

The old-old: those who are 85 years old and above

Healthy aging: the development and maintenance of optimal physical, mental, spiritual, and social well-being/functioning in older adults

Complicated grief: see Chapter 5

Discussion Questions

1   What comes to mind—for example, images—when you think of words like "aging," "old," and "older adult"? How might they influence your attitude/approach to elderly church members? What are some challenges for you in working with older adults or if you were Dave/Jenny in the vignette?

2   What is the importance of understanding issues relating to older adults? What are some biblical examples of aging that you can share with the congregants to promote healthy aging?

3   According to Erik Erikson, what is the developmental challenge for late adulthood? How might grief/loss issues complicate an older adult's ability to accomplish this developmental goal?

COGNITIVE IMPAIRMENTS IN OLDER ADULTS

Although some cognitive decline—for example, forgetfulness—is a part of the normal process of aging, and not all older adults experience cognitive impairments that interfere with their daily functioning or performance. When the cognitive deficits begin to impede an older adult's level of functioning and their ability to perform daily tasks, a clinical examination of possible diagnosis of dementia is necessary. If dementia is identified, it is necessary to provide the treatment needed to slow down the progression of the disease and/or to lessen the debilitating effects of dementia. The following section will discuss various types of dementia, relevant information, and some issues that are complicated by cognitive impairments in older adults.

Memory Loss and Dementia

The grief, loss, and bereavement issues older adults often experience are further and significantly complicated by dementia, which is termed and classified as major and minor neurocognitive disorders in the current *Diagnostic and Statistical Manual of Mental Disorders, 5th Edition* (*DSM–5*). **Dementia** is defined by McKhann et al., (1984) as "the decline of memory and other cognitive functions in comparison with the patient's previous level of function as determined by a history of decline in performance and by abnormalities noted from clinical examination and neuropsychological tests" (p. 940). A typical example of dementia manifests when a person's memory is progressively declining as they age, *and* the memory loss notably affects the way they are used to *functioning*, as Jeff was in the earlier story. Whenever any question/doubt arises regarding whether an individual is experiencing signs of dementia, a clinical examination of the probability of dementia is imperative.

"Dementia is not a specific disease; it is a term used to describe a wide range of symptoms" (Alzheimer's Association, n.d.). In other words, dementia is diagnosed based on observable behaviors. Therefore, members of the clergy do not need to hesitate to recommend an older adult who seems to experience some cognitive deficits or their family to work with a qualified clinician, or to obtain a second opinion, since the threshold for diagnosis may vary considerably among clinicians. A thorough examination from a professional who is an expert in the geriatric population is important for the patient and their family to obtain the "right" help. That said, the individual affected by memory issues or confused might not be open to seeing a physician for this purpose; it's very possible that he or she will be open to a routine physical, however. The physician can then make the determination as to whether the individual needs further evaluation.

A complete clinical assessment, including neuropsychological testing is able to identify the potential cause of the symptoms, leading to an accurate diagnosis, which would guide the professional to offer a proper and effective treatment plan for the patient. For instance, one of the symptoms of depression is memory difficulty (Chapter 2), which needs to be clearly differentiated from memory problems that are due to dementia. In addition, Anxiety can also interfere with cognitive functioning. Furthermore, in the early stages of dementia, patients are alert and without obvious symptoms that are associated with dementia as the disease progresses. In fact, often patients and those who are around them attribute some of the problems, such as forgetfulness, agitation, and sleep difficulty, to aging (McKhann et al., 1984).

Types of Dementia

Among the various types of dementia, **Alzheimer's disease** (AD) is the most common (60%–80% of the dementia cases). Currently, it is the sixth leading cause of death in the United States, accounting for 1 in 9 deaths of those who were 65 years and older (Centers for Disease Control and Prevention, 2018). Within the senior population, AD is the fifth most common health concern (Vann, 2016) with others being physical conditions such as, arthritis, heart disease, cancer, etc. So, while younger people can also be affected by early onset AD, it is still primarily associated with the elder population.

It is worth noting that among these top 10 most common health problems, the 10th is substance abuse. One in 5 older adults in the United States has abused alcohol or other substances, including prescription drugs, at some point. Therefore, compared to working with younger congregants at church, it would be even more essential and useful for Pastor Dave to actively inquire about Jeff's history with physical and psychological health, including substance abuse history, to have a fuller picture of what difficulties Jeff may experience and to provide and connect him to the appropriate services.

Symptoms of AD include difficulty remembering *recent* conversations, names, or events, and apathy and depression are also common. As AD progresses, the ability to communicate may be impaired. Other symptoms in the later stage are poor judgment, disorientation, confusion, behavior changes, and difficulty speaking, swallowing, and walking. To date, there is no cure for AD, and 99% of all clinical drug trials have failed (Dovey, 2018). However, there are common medications prescribed to patients with dementia to help lessen symptoms for a limited amount of time and/or slow down the worsening of degeneration. The typical category of medications for a patient with a dementia diagnosis at various stages/severity of symptoms is **cholinesterase inhibitors** (CHEIs)—Donepezil (Aricept, all stages), Rivastigmine (Exelon, mild-moderate), Galantamine (Razadyne, mild-moderate), or Memantine (Nameda, moderate-severe).

Presently, the most researched and known etiological hypothesis of AD is the Amyloid Hypothesis, which posits that the accumulation of the amyloid β-peptide (Aβ), a protein in the brain causes AD. This build-up creates **plaques and tangles**, which along with degeneration of brain nerve cells have been the best known, primary AD pathogenesis even though there are strengths and weakness to this theory (Hardy & Selkoe, 2002).

It is not uncommon for an older adult to take numerous medications for multiple health conditions and problems. However, they may not understand or even remember the purpose of each medicine. By knowing the names and the general uses of medications prescribed for AD/dementia, it could help those who care for the elderly individual know how to relate and support this older adult appropriately.

At the beginning of the current millennia, studies began to examine and define a transitional stage between normal aging and early dementia (mild AD), and now commonly known as **mild cognitive impairment** (MCI) in the hope that with early detection, pharmaceutical treatment may delay or prevent some patients with very early cognitive impairment from progressing to AD. The diagnosis of MCI is made by "1) evidence of memory impairment, 2) preservation of general cognitive and functional abilities, and 3) absence of diagnosed dementia" (Morris et al., 2001, p. 397).

The Mini Mental Status Exam (MMSE) is frequently used as the initial diagnostic tool and can be simply administered by a primary care physician. Researchers show that patients with 27/30 on the MMSE, and whose family and/or friends have already noticed some changes in cognitive functioning, are at greater risk to develop dementia and should be referred for a comprehensive evaluation and follow-ups for possible development of dementia (O'Bryant et al., 2008).

While AD is clearly the most common type of dementia, the second is controversial. A quick online search would readily demonstrate the differences in information on **vascular dementia** (VasD) and **dementia with Lewy bodies** (DLB) with each accounting for approximately 10%–15% of dementia cases. The diagnosis of VasD is a two-step approach (Bakchine & Blanchard, 2005): (1) the presence of dementia and (2) a finding of a vascular etiology, such as arterial hypertension that leads to strokes or bleeding in the brain. Symptoms of VasD are impaired judgment or ability to make decisions or plan or organize in the early stage. In fact, for many patients who suffer from VasD, memory is preserved, which is an essential differential evaluative characteristic from the memory loss that is often associated with the initial symptoms of AD, as stated in the earlier section of this chapter. The location, number and size of the brain blood vessel blockage or damage determine the degree of the VasD individual's cognitive and physical functioning impairment.

In DLB, abnormalities are found in areas of the brain that regulate behavior, cognition, and movement. Symptoms of DLB include memory loss and thinking problems common in AD, plus sleep disturbances, well-formed visual hallucinations, and slowness, gait imbalance, or other Parkinsonian movement features, such as tremor and rigid posture.

When compared to AD, DLB symptoms tend to respond better to CHEIs. Here again is another example why an accurate diagnosis is crucial—if the visual hallucinations experienced by individuals with DLB are mistakenly for a psychotic symptom, then treated with antipsychotic medications, worsening of the symptoms will occur due to the neuroleptic sensitivity in DLB. Clergy can empower the individual and their caregivers to proactively seek proper help to ensure the accurate treatment.

Other less common dementia are mixed dementia, Parkinson's disease, frontotemporal dementia, Creutzfeldt-Jakob disease, normal pressure hydrocephalus, Huntington's disease, and Wernicke-Kosakoff syndrome. Among them, Parkinson's disease is perhaps the better-known one by the public. As the disease progresses, patients frequently demonstrate symptoms that are similar to DLB or AD. It is worth noting that Lewy Body Dementia is an overall term for DLB *and* Parkinson's disease.

Grief and Loss/Bereavement Issues in Cognitive Impaired Older Adults

It is not difficult to imagine the overwhelming sense of loss an older adult may experience during the early stages of dementia. When I worked as a practicum student at the Alzheimer's research center at the University of California, Irvine (now "UCI MIND"), I administered neuropsychological testing to healthy older adults and those with dementia as part of the research data collection. It was heartbreaking to see the sadness in these respectable, silver-haired patients who were at the early stage of their diagnosis. Many were intelligent and had been successful in their respective professions. I recall one elderly woman in her 70s telling me how disoriented and frightened she felt one day when she was asked to sign a check by a bank teller, and she just could not "remember" how to do it. That incident prompted her to seek a comprehensive evaluation and follow-ups by professionals.

This deep sense of grief and loss experienced when watching one's inner self slip away daily can be more disturbing than losing one's physical capacity. To complicate this process, activities that are often helpful for an individual to work through grief and loss issues, such as talking with trusted others or writing down one's experiences, are *the* cognitive abilities that are progressively declining with dementia.

Therefore, it is important to remember that when planning a support or bereavement group for older adults, one must take into consideration that some may be experiencing undiagnosed cognitive impairments, and that tracking/remembering what is communicated in the group can be overwhelming and frustrating for them, which in turn exacerbates the stress/distress of these older adults. Thus, they may stop attending the group even when they need the support.

As dementia progresses, Grief and Myran (2006) discussed a frequently encountered ethical dilemma that those who closely work with older adults in the mid-late stage of dementia have. Should we remind these cognitively impaired older adults of their losses—for example, a spouse's death—and have them experience the grief repeatedly due to memory loss or simply let these memories fade with the disease? In their article, Grief and Myran (2006) provided several case studies of the tormenting effects on cognitively impaired older adults where the caregivers responded to their question about the whereabouts of their deceased spouse or adult child, by reminding them of these deaths. To these elders with substantial memory deficits, it was as if they heard the news for the first time, they experienced the loss all over again. Therefore, the study raised the pressing question: Should the caregivers tell the "truth"? It was proposed that by doing so it was an experience of re-traumatization to the cognitively impaired seniors. What then shall we do as a Christian community with the same question, and what advice shall we offer to an older adult's family members when they are facing this dilemma? In addition to being an ethical dilemma in geriatric care, it might also be a moral issue to us, as Christians: Shall we "lie" or advise the family to hide the "truth" from the memory-deficit older adult so to spare them from experiencing the gut-wrenching experience of mourning repeatedly?

In the same article, it was noted that when the caregivers were able to creatively find ways to distract the older adults in such situations, they eventually ceased to inquire, particularly when the dementia continued to unavoidably worsen. The observation was consistent with my own clinical experiences working with memory-impaired older adults, after sadly realizing that my honest answer only brought intense heartaches that were unable to be processed and worked through by these elders.

Each church community needs to prayerfully reflect and come to a stance that is the most beneficial and loving for the suffering older adults and their family/friends, in all aspects—spiritually, physically, and emotionally—while attending to the limitations and familial/cultural context that each older adult and their family are dealing with. This may require clergy to first hew out their own beliefs, questions, and potential biases on the topic of lying (when the purpose is to extend mercy and kindness) versus telling the truth so that we can wisely guide those we serve who are caring for a cognitively impaired older adult.

KEY TERMS

Dementia: the decline of memory and other cognitive functions in comparison with the individual's previous level of function as determined by a history of decline in performance and by abnormalities noted from clinical examination and neuropsychological tests

Alzheimer's disease: the most common type of dementia. Symptoms include difficulty remembering recent conversations, names, or events, as well as apathy and depression

Plaques and tangles: the build-up of the amyloid β-peptide (Aβ), a protein/amino acids in the brain causing AD

Cholinesterase inhibitors (CHEIs): the category of medication prescribed to patients with dementia; Donepezil (Aricept, all stages), Rivastigmine (Exelon, mild-moderate), Galantamine (Razadyne, mild-moderate), or Memantine (Nameda, moderate-severe)

Mild cognitive impairment: transitional stage between normal aging and early dementia (mild AD)

Vascular dementia: a type of dementia, accounts for 10%–15% of the cases and symptoms include impaired judgment/ability to make decisions or plan or organize in the early stage, and memory is often preserved

Dementia with Lewy bodies: a type of dementia with the following symptoms: memory loss/thinking problems, sleep disturbances, visual hallucinations, and slowness, gait imbalance or other Parkinsonian movement features, such as tremor/rigid posture

Discussion Questions

1   Do you know anyone who suffers from dementia? What is your experience with the individual? Do you notice any thoughts/feelings that you have toward the individual or the disease?

2   How would you approach Jeff and the complaint about him/his memory? Based on the symptoms presented in the story, what type of dementia might Jeff suffer from?

3   What are some ideas and important considerations you might want to remember while developing programs/activities for older adults at church?

4   Describe your thoughts/feelings about the ethical/moral dilemma of reminding an older adult with memory deficits of their loss of a loved one?

CAREGIVER'S NEEDS

As the senior population continues to climb as projected, increasing numbers of family members will be confronted with the pressing need to take on the caregiver role for their elderly parents, grandparents, etc. To complicate the situation, due to the rapidly-skewing ratio of older adults and those who are between ages 18 and 30, the pool of caregivers is dwindling. However, family caregivers have been mostly overlooked by society and research studies until quite recently. It seems very likely that church communities have overlooked ministering to the complex needs of caregivers as well.

Family Caregivers

In the consensus report (2016), initiated by the Committee on Family Caregiving for Older Adults of the National Academy of Sciences, Engineering and Medicine, Schulz and Eden began with the statistic that "[a]t least 17.7 million individuals in the United States are family caregivers of someone age 65 and older" (p. 1). The need for family caregivers is typically the result of some form of physical, mental, or cognitive condition that impairs the older adult's ability to function independently. In other words, 7.7% of Americans at age 20 or above are in a family caregiver role. Among these elderly care recipients, 71.4% experience probable dementia (p. 47).

In the earlier example of Jenny, we can reasonably posit that when she visits the home of the teen girl, what she would find is not only a multi-generational household but also a home of multigenerational family caregivers. We could also easily imagine that if Jenny were familiar with older adults' issues and demographics, she probably would not be as shocked or surprised to see the young girl sharing some of the family caregiving responsibilities and that she might be feeling the effect of it, in addition to perhaps vicariously feel the stress from her parents who are caregivers to the older family members.

It is important to keep in mind that *who* the family caregiver is for an older adult may be determined by relationship, this is complicated by the sociocultural definition and structure of family being significantly more complex than in previous generations. Furthermore, the care given widely varies in terms of the type as well as the frequency with which that care is offered. Nonetheless, the care received from the loved ones is often meaningful to the older adult regardless of type and frequency.

Due to the difference of life expectancy between genders, a common situation that I come across in clinical settings happens after an older adult loses her spouse. In the case, for example, the elderly widow did not want to move closer to her adult children because she was physically independent and cognitively intact. Besides, the community of church friends and neighbors she had made and fostered close relationship with over the years were extremely important to her and her husband, and then to her as a widow. Often, one of this new widow's close friends would be a younger woman who is in a close age range to the older woman. As the aging process proceeds, this younger female friend could naturally fall into a caregiver role and the friendship would develop a layer of meaningfulness to both. At times, the family members would offer some remuneration to this friend of the older adult. In a case where the older adult developed cognitive impairment, the role of this friend-caregiver might gradually expand

and become more intertwined with the older adult's life. Thus, the care ministry for the family caregivers may need to reconsider how a "family" caregiver is defined at the church and whom the ministry is called to reach out and extend the invitation to participate.

In some cases, the elder's adult children eventually had to intervene when dementia reached moderate-severe stages. If they have power of attorney, or if the elderly individual is declared incompetent, the family might consider either moving the cognitively impaired older adult to one of their homes, or to place them in a nursing facility near where they live.

The separation of an older adult from a friend-caregiver can have a deep impact on the caregiver, as well as the individual receiving care. As one woman in a similar relationship with her older adult friend put it to me, "When I said good-bye to her because her daughters moved her to be closer, I knew that was the last time I would see her. It's like she died already. I was so sad, but no one really understood."

"The diagnosis of dementia can be a crisis for a social unit … not just for an individual caregiver" (Gottlieb & Wolfe, 2002, p. 338). A good example of this type of crisis, as well as a common scenario among family caregivers, is illustrated by my friend who is in her late 50s. She tactfully and methodically coordinates with her two siblings living in two other states, because their elderly mother is at the mid-stage of AD and insists on living alone. When the mother, for instance, needs to pay her utility bills or go to a doctor's appointment, the siblings have agreed to divide the caregiver responsibilities. One schedules the appointment, another picks up the mother and drives her to the appointment, while the third transfers money to the mother's account to pay for her visit. The constant phone calls and electronic communication among the siblings are the external manifestation of the stress that the three of them internally experience as a unit and as individuals. Interestingly, "[r]egardless of language or cultural background, many family caregivers in the United States do not relate to the term 'caregiver' or describe the help they provide as 'caregiving,' instead they view their interactions as part of their familial roles and expectations justified by longstanding spousal or kin relations" (Schulz & Eden, 2016, p. 22). Another commonly used term among those in the eldercare community is "care partner."

Impacts on the Caregiver/Care Partner

Studies have consistently shown that caregivers are at a much higher risk to suffer from depression and anxiety, and general emotional distress, compared with their non-caregiver cohort (Gottlieb & Wolfe, 2002; Rhee et al., 2008; Schulz & Eden, 2016). Much of this emotional distress is related to the feelings of helplessness, powerlessness, and hopelessness involved in caregiving, especially for a person suffering from a chronic and degenerative disease, such as dementia. The caregivers themselves are vulnerable to health problems, largely predicated by the number, frequency, and severity of the older adult's dementia-related behavior problems. Caregivers are also prone to suffer financial difficulties resulting from the time they are absent from work, or withdrawing from the workforce altogether, when the care needed is demanding and constant. Of interest to clergy is that studies suggest that the caregiver's spiritual health can be negatively affected by the caregiving duty (Acton, 2002).

At the same time, there are benefits to being a caregiver, especially when the caregiver feels competent in providing the care needed and experiences the positive feedback from the care receiver. It adds to the caregiver's sense of confidence, self-esteem, and value as a person, while the relational bond deepens in spite of suffering. In the end stage of any disease, it might also provide a final opportunity to spend time with the loved ones. While dramatic resolutions of conflicts are rare, they can happen.

Another factor that influences the effect of caregiving on the individual is the quality of the relationship that the caregiver had with the care recipient prior to the onset of the disease and before care is required. It should not be assumed that the individual who takes on the caregiver's role has the best/closest relationship with the care receiver. It may be out of obligation, which may evoke unbearable shame and guilt inside the individual if they do not fulfill this strong sense of compulsory responsibility—for example, filial piety—which is deeply rooted and commonly embedded in more collectivistic cultures (e.g., Asian, Hispanic). The pressure from this sense of obligation mixed with unresolved relational strains can trigger a range of intense emotions such as anger and dread in the caregiver.

This dynamic is often seen between adult children and their parent(s). If they are referred for clinical intervention, the focus of such an intervention is on helping the adult child process/work through as much of the past hurt as possible while coping with the present stress as a caregiver. Forgiveness takes time and is a process that is correlated with an individual's attachment style (Liao, 2007).

It is essential for those who come alongside the caregiver in a similar situation to not take sides and to not rush them through this complex, multi-faceted experience. Pastoral care with this type of case requires the minister to have the capacity/ability to bear the caregiver's ambivalence without unintentionally exacerbating the shame and guilt that are already gnawing at the caregiver's heart. Furthermore, it is often an unsettling experience for children, regardless their age to see their parents as weak and fragile.

When offering support and help to the caregiver, their existing coping style—for example, rationalization or avoidance—must be considered. In addition, the most effective types of support for caregivers are those that aim to provide educational information to increase the caregiver's sense of competency and those that present opportunities for the caregivers to have a period of respite (Gottlieb & Wolfe, 2002; Shultz & Eden, 2016). Interventions and programs focused on health-promoting self-care, which Acton (2002) defined as "actions a person take to improve their health, maintain optimal functioning and increase general well-being" (p. 73) can be beneficial for the burdened caregivers.

On the other hand, there are those who choose not to, or are not able to, take on the caregiver's role for their family member(s). This choice frequently is based on the financial need to work, their geographic distance from the ill family member, or their roles in providing care for others, especially their children. Our empathic and non-judgmental posture toward them is crucial to not add to feelings of shame, guilt and sorrow that are already present. We do not have a full picture of what might have transpired in the past between the older adult and their family members at their younger ages—such as abuse and trauma, and the current limitations that the family members are struggling with—which make the caregiver role not a feasible option.

Caregiver's Roles

Caregivers take on multiple roles and go through typical **caregiving phases** over time: (1) Awareness, (2) Unfolding Responsibilities, (3) Increasing Care Demands, and (4) End of Life (Shultz & Eden, 2016, p. 78). In the **Awareness** phase, there is increasing realization in the older adult's interpersonal network of their need for a caregiver. The older adult at this phase may dismiss and minimize the need. A common example is the argument that happens between the older adult who recently receives a diagnosis of dementia and refuses to give up their independence, and their family members who worry about the older adult's ability to drive safely. Usually, a family member will emerge as primary caregiver or lead of the caregiver unit. During the **Unfolding Responsibilities** phase, primary/lead caregiver moves into their role as caregiver and assumes the associated boundaries and responsibilities. The role becomes increasingly clear to the family. Potential conflicts among family members occur at this stage when the familial dynamics begin to shift. As the older adult's condition progresses, caregiver enters into the phase of **Increasing Care Demands**—from monitoring symptoms and medication, communicating to healthcare providers and offering emotional support, to helping the older adult implement self-care tasks (e.g., bathing, feeding), and becoming surrogate decision maker for the older adult as they lose the ability to manage more of their activities of daily living (**ADL**). ADL "include[s] the fundamental skills typically needed to manage basic physical needs, comprised the following areas: grooming/ personal hygiene, dressing, toileting/continence, transferring/ambulating and eating" (Mlinac & Feng, 2016, p. 506). ADL is *the* tool used by health care professionals to assess an individual's ability to complete tasks, which needs to be distinguished from an elder's ability to recognize the need to complete the task. For instance, a person who is at the mid-stage of AD is able to recognize the need to go to the bathroom but cannot complete the task. In the movie, *Still Alice* (Brown, Koffler, & Lutzus and Glatzer & Westmoreland, 2014), there is a realistic scene when Alice painfully experiences the awkwardness, frustration, and embarrassment that an AD patient feels when she urinates on herself, even though her ability to recognize the need to go to the bathroom is intact. In the **End of Life** phase, the caregiver's burden and stress continue to increase while the decisions regarding nursing home, palliative care and repeated hospital visits take place and eventually the death of the care recipient occurs. Meanwhile, a greater meaning is reported and can be experienced by the caregiver. When developing a care ministry for caregivers, more effectiveness can be accomplished when leaders understand and strategically target these phases, depending on the church's resources. It might be helpful to involve professionals who specialize in working with older adults, such as geriatric/geropsychologists and social workers, hospice, and family care centers for dementia/AD to offer guidance and training for church staff.

KEY TERMS

Caregiving phases: four typical phases that caregiver goes through overtime

Awareness phase: the first caregiving phase. an emerging realization in the interpersonal network of the older adult's need for a caregiver; older adult may dismiss/minimize the need, a primary caregiver emerges

Unfolding Responsibilities phase: the second caregiving phase. Primary caregiver moves into the role and assumes the boundaries and responsibilities as he or she becomes defined and clear to the family

Increasing Care Demands phase: the third caregiving phase. Older adult loses the ability to manage increasingly more of their ADL, caregiver begins to help older adult implement self-care tasks and becomes a surrogate decision maker

End of Life phase: the last caregiving phase. Caregiver's burden and stress continue to increase while decisions regarding nursing home, palliative care, and repeated hospital visits take place and eventually the death of the care recipient occurs; the caregiver can experience a greater meaning

Activities of daily living: a commonly used assessment tool to determine an individual's ability to manage basic physical needs, includes the following areas: grooming/personal hygiene, dressing, toileting/continence, transferring/ambulating, eating

Discussion Questions

1   Is/was anyone in your family/extended family a caregiver for an older adult? What have you noticed about their experience regarding some of the points that were brought up in this chapter section?

2   What are some challenges for church leaders to come alongside an adult child considering whether to assume a caregiver role?

3   What are your thoughts/ideas regarding developing resources/programs for your church to reach out to caregivers of elderly family members?

MISTREATMENT OF ELDERS

Do not cast me away when I am old;
do not forsake me when my strength is gone.
—Ps. 71:9, NIV.

Risk Factors

Given the caregiver's distress and the isolating nature of the caregiver's role, particularly when the elderly care recipient's ADL decreases, mistreatment/neglect can happen to the elderly population. Shultz and Eden (2016) define mistreatment as a behavior that "has intentionally caused harm or create a serious risk of harm to a vulnerable older adult" (p. 106). According to California Welfare and Institutions Code Section 15630(b)(2)(C), a clergy member is not a mandated reporter of elder abuse, *unless* he or she is "regularly employed on either a full-time or part-time basis in a long-term care facility or [has] care or custody of an elder or dependent adult", *or* when the abuse is apparently present. I believe, however, that it is important for the church community to be equipped with the knowledge of the types of mistreatment that elders in the church may undergo. Consequently, the church is able to protect these defenseless older adults.

The various types of **elder mistreatment** include physical, emotional, or sexual abuse; neglect (e.g., intentionally withholding medication, food, and water); abandonment; and financial exploitation. The estimated occurrence of elder abuse is 7%–10% each year and in most cases, family members are the culprits (Shultz & Eden, 2016). Older adults with dementia or who need physical assistance are more likely to be abused. Researchers attempted to understand how the caregiving relationship evolves into such a detrimental state and identified the **six risk factors** for adverse caregiver outcomes: (1) **sociodemographic factors**—for example, lower income/education, 50 years or older, spouse, female; (2) **intensity and type of caregiving tasks**—for example, high behavioral/medical care demands, dementia care; (3) **caregivers' perceptions of the caregiving situation**—for example, lack of choice in being the caregiver; (4) **caregivers' own health and functioning**—for example, poor physical health, stress, sleep difficulty; (5) **caregivers' social and professional supports**—for example, no one to help with caregiving, no social interaction with others, and no access to professional services; and (6) **care recipients' physical home environment**—for example, clutter, lack of appropriate/necessary home modifications to meet the care recipient's need, such as easy access into the bathtub, and railing installment (Shultz & Eden, 2016, p. 108).

Among them, as mentioned earlier in this chapter, intensity and type of caregiving tasks is a strong predictor of a caregiver's stress/burden. In addition, Bonnie and Wallace's book (2002) pointed out that a caregiver's alcohol/drug abuse problems are involved in 44% of the elder abuse cases, as well as the level of depression/hostility in the caregiver. The abuser's dependency on the senior is another risk factor for mistreatment, as most perpetrators are found to be financially dependent on the victim.

Financial Abuse

Of the various types of elder abuse, financial abuse is the most difficult to determine and yet, is the fastest growing form of abuse (Bonnie & Wallace, 2002, p. 391). Elder financial exploitation and abuse leave a devastating impact on the victims when their savings are gone, and they are not able to recover the money by returning to the workforce. Financial abuse can also render the older adult homeless due to a lack of funding for their living expenses. However, it is often extremely difficult, especially during the initial stage of the exploitation, to assess whether abuse is happening. For instance, it is normative in many cultures for older adults to gift their money to their younger family members or try to help with their financial needs. It is hard to tell if the elder is deceived into a scheme or if they are cognitively capable of making the decision.

Adding to the layers of an older adult's vulnerability is their feelings of isolation or being alone. The movie, *Bernie* (Glotzer et al., 2011) based on the true story of Bernie Tiede and a wealthy elderly widow, highlighted the complex/complicated relationship between a caregiver and an older adult. The ambiguous abusive relationship between the two ultimately resulted in murder. Although this is an extreme story, when there is a suspicion that an elderly member in the congregation may be taken advantage of, for example when they start talking about an individual's involvement in their life that had not been mentioned before, it might be a red flag.

In such situations, depending on their training and the particulars of the relationship with the elder individual, clergy might consider inviting this "new family member/friend" for a church activity and/or to visit the older adult's home when the individual is reportedly present. In this way, the clergy would be able to assess the situation firsthand and to alert the potential abuser that the older adult is not completely isolated, thus easily manipulated. It is important to check in with the older adult periodically, especially if their church involvement and attendance begin to decrease.

Finally, the minister or pastor does not need to deal with the situation alone. Clergy can request a professional consultation with a social worker at Adult Protective Services (APS), refer the individual for family counseling, and/or connect the individual with a law enforcement agency, if fraudulent or illegal activity seems to have occurred.

KEY TERMS

Elder mistreatment: a behavior that intentionally causes harm or creates a serious risk of harm to a vulnerable older adult

Six risk factors for adverse caregiver outcome: sociodemographic factors, intensity/type of caregiving tasks, caregivers' perceptions of caregiving situation, caregivers' own health/functioning, caregivers' social/professional supports, and care recipients' physical home environment

Discussion Questions

1   What are your thoughts/feelings about making a report to APS in a situation where elder abuse may be present?

2   What are the challenges you may face in (a) deciding to make a report and (b) making the report?

SUCCESSFUL AGING

The glory of young men is their strength, gray hair the splendor of the old.
—Proverbs 20:29, NIV

FIGURE 14.2   **Community is a key component of successful aging**

Healthy Living

Although the aging process is an irreversible and continuous process of adaptation (Bohlmeijer, Roemer, Cuijpers, and Smit, 2007) due to the many age-related changes that happen in our body and mind along with the genetic disposition that we are endowed with, it does *not* mean that we are to resign to a poor quality of life as we age. **Healthy life** is defined by Drewnowski and Evans (2001) as "a full range of functional capacity at each life stage, from infancy to old age" (p. 89). By proactively engaging in a well-being centered approach to life, it is possible to live an abundant life even during the last stage of our physical existence. This certainly applies to older adults who are experiencing health concerns, including cognitive impairment.

Physical Exercise and Nutrition

As we age, our ability to live independently without relying on a caregiver's help typically brings satisfaction toward our sense of self and about life. Independent daily living skills begin with our physical capacity to provide ourselves with basic living needs. For example, being able to go to a grocery store and carry the grocery bags home, as well as other ADLs are basic and yet essential to our sense of independence. Adequate physical exercise that helps seniors focus on maintaining strength and mobility is a key to daily functioning. At least one hour per week of moderately intense physical exercise decreases the likelihood of all causes of mortality (Acree et al., 2006). Physical exercise for older adults with dementia is important to increase their muscle strength, which helps with balance, particularly when gait performance is affected by the disease (Telenius, Engedal, and Bergland, 2015). Because older adults tend to fall more easily, appropriate physical exercise can help prevent falls that could be fatal to an older adult. Furthermore, once a senior is injured in a bad fall, they could easily develop a fear of falling, which restricts the older adult's activity level. The more inactive an older individual is, the more likely they are to lose the physical strength to stay mobile. Consequently, their quality of life declines.

Physical exercises are also known to decrease depressive and anxious moods, which are often present in older adults with dementia. Telenius et al., (2015) reported that physical exercises are able to decrease dementia-related apathy. As a result of financial constraints, many older adults cannot afford to pay for gym memberships. Some church communities already offer exercise time as a way to promote fellowship among elders. Unless there are mobility concerns, walking is an inexpensive form of exercise available to almost anyone, and can also be a good time to socialize with a workout buddy. The exercise time can be enhanced by seeking experts in geriatric physical exercise to aid the church in developing an exercise program that meets the physical needs and limitations of older adults.

Along with physical exercise, optimal nutrition contributes to quality of life. There can be age-related loss of taste and changes of experiences of thirst, hunger, and satiety in late adulthood. Inadequate nutritional intake is a risk threatening an older individual's well-being. Therefore, nutritional intake and the necessary adjustments based on age-associated changes can crucially preserve quality of life. Noticing signs of malnutrition may be an unusual, but significant part of our ministry to older adults and represent a very practical way to be supportive of this community within our congregations.

Psychological Well-Being

Fry (2001) proposed that psychological well-being is "an umbrella construct of psychological health constituting an amalgam of various affective, experiential and cognitive components that act and interact with one another in complex ways and are influenced, in turn both directly and indirectly, by other variables of health, positive outlook, and social emotional resources" (p. 2). In other words, psychological health includes aspects of emotional, cognitive, and social functioning of an individual. These facets interact with each other while impacting one another. Meeting with a church lay counselor or a professional psychotherapist at times of greater emotional distress can facilitate psychological healing, which contribute positively to well-being.

Reminiscence and Life Review are psychotherapeutic interventions commonly used by counselors trained to work with older adults. Based upon the psychological theory that an individual's sense of living a meaningful life is the primary developmental need in older adulthood, psychotherapists use them to help older adults reflect and review life in the past and to come to a coherent and elaborate narrative about the meaning of one's life. Through this process of examining and reflecting on where and how God has led an individual in the years past, and the affirmation of the purpose of one's life, combined with the trust that He will be "faithful til the end," an older adult is able to use the opportunity to work through some of the past hurts and regrets while being able to develop a renewed motivation to live in the present moment.

Adequate and appropriate cognitive stimulation in the environment is important to maintain and enhance cognitive functioning. **Cognitive training** is helpful for healthy older adults and for older adults with MCI to preserve and improve cognitive abilities. Because our brain is malleable even in old age, various programs have been developed to systematically guide the participants to practice brain exercises that aim to improve memory, attention, information processing and other areas of cognitive functioning. In addition, Kueider, Bichay, and Rebok (2014) reported that cognitive training seems more effective when delivered in a group setting. Thus, churches can incorporate cognitive training in their ministries with older adults with help from trained professionals—for example, geriatric psychologists who offer and teach cognitive training. Some hospitals and many adult day care facilities schedule routine cognitive training into their programs.

Spiritual Renewal and Liveliness

Older adults have all "been there; done that," and thus, are in the golden years to learn, lead, and serve. Studies have consistently shown that religious involvement and spirituality, generally predict well-being (Fry, 2001; McDougle et al., 2016). Centuries ago, the psalmist called our attention to this truth: "The godly will flourish like palm trees, and grow strong like the cedars of Lebanon … Even in old age they will still produce fruits, they will remain vital and green" (Ps. 92:12–14, New Living Translation).

Youthfulness is praised and valued. Globally, billions per year are spent to prevent or delay the effects of aging. Aging is treated as a threatening and dreadful experience. Even with age-related problems, however, being old can be the last adventure that we take on our journey through life. How do we prepare for this adventure even when young? How do we make the best of it, given the age-associated limitations? How do we, as a church community equip, and come alongside one another as fellow travelers? Our own beliefs about aging, our past positive or negative experiences with older people, and our attitude toward change and the unknown significantly impact how we relate to older adults around us. In turn, they will affect how we age and how we walk through the last stage of earthly life that awaits us all.

KEY TERMS

Healthy life: maintaining a full range of functional capacity at each life stage (infancy to old age); a proactive attitude to engage with a well-being centered approach to life

Cognitive training: based on the theory that our brain continues to be malleable as we age, brain exercises are developed to maintain and improve targeted areas of cognitive functioning (memory, attention, etc.)

Discussion Questions

1   What existing programs at your church promote healthy living? What are your thoughts/ideas about creating a church ministry that focuses on physical, emotional, and spiritual well-being?

2   How does successful aging affect an individual's spiritual life?

3   How might the church community have unintentionally reinforced the misconceptions/myths/stereotypes of aging/older adults? What are the potentially negative impacts in the congregation?

REVIEWING THE CONCEPTS

Learning Objectives

- Identify some common struggles and issues of later life
  - Common and complicated grief and loss issues
  - Physical and mental declines
  - Dementia

- Identify and describe/differentiate among common cognitive impairments in older adults
  - Age-related memory loss
  - Dementia is a decline of memory and other cognitive functions as determined by a history of decline in performance and by clinically and neuropsychologically noted abnormalities.
  - MCI is a clinically identified impairment between age-associated memory loss and AD
  - Most common type of dementia is AD, caused by plaques and tangles.
  - VasD is caused by vascular disease with executive functioning impairments— for example, judgment, decision making, planning.
  - DLB includes symptoms of visual hallucination and Parkinsonian movements.

- Facilitate a pastoral response to the needs of older adults and their families in the congregation with dementia, and of their families
  - It is important for ministry leaders to have adequate knowledge about dementia.
  - Families are looking for education on how to better care for patients with dementia and need respite from caregiving responsibilities.
  - Approach some potential ethical/moral dilemmas resulting from the symptoms of dementia from the stance of love and kindness.

- Define and identify caregiving phases
  - Four typical phases that caregivers go through are Awareness, Unfolding Responsibilities, Increasing Care Demands, and End of Life.

- Identify and explain risk factors for adverse caregiving outcomes
  - Sociodemographic factors (e.g., female, lower income, and education, older, spouse, living with care recipient)
  - Intensity and type of caregiving tasks
  - Caregiver's perception of the caregiving situation (e.g., lack of choice to assume the role of caregiver)
  - Caregiver's mental/physical health, functioning
  - Caregiver's social/professional supports
  - Care recipient's physical home environment (e.g., cluttered, messy)
- Identify some factors for healthy lifestyle/aging and facilitate a pastoral response to the church's role in promoting successful aging
  - Physical exercises, age-conscious diet, psychological well-being, spiritual vitality
  - Use knowledge learned about aging/age-associated issues to create and develop programs/activities that (1) attend to older adults' struggles and (2) promote and maintain healthy lifestyle practices in all ages

Chapter Review Questions

Level 1: Knowledge (True/False)

1. Since we all age, we know how to age graciously and to care for older adults.

2. As we age, our cognitive function declines, such as memory, thus dementia is unavoidable in older adulthood.

3. Grief/loss issues can be quite complicated in older adults.

4. Since dementia is a degenerative disease, there is no method to detect it early.

5. AD is the most common type of dementia.

6. There is no cure for dementia. Therefore, patients with dementia are not prescribed medication.

7. A great number of people in the United States are in caregiver roles.

8. ADL is a frequently used tool to assess an individual's ability to carry out basic self-care tasks.

9. Mistreatment does not happen to older adults.

10. Since older adults often suffer from physical/health conditions, it is important to advise them not to engage in any physical exercise so as not to jeopardize their quality of life.

Level 2: Comprehension

1. Which of the following is *not* true about the current aging population in the United States?

    a.   Growing rapidly

    b.   The makeup of the elderly population is quite homogenous

    c.   Having a significant social and economic impact nationwide

    d.   Baby Boomers started turning 65 in 2011

2. Healthy aging is defined as the development and maintenance of optimal levels of well-being and functioning in the following area(s):

    a.   Physical

    b.   Mental

    c.   Spiritual

    d.   Social

    e.   All of the above

3. Which aspect of community is most important to an older adult's sense of identity, meaning in life, and well-being?

    a.   The community's size

    b.   The number of resources available

    c.   The social, interpersonal connectedness offered

    d.   The community's location

4. Which of the following issues is prevalent in older adults?

    a.   Complicated grief

    b.   Difficulties in intimate relationships

    c.   Competency

    d.   Trust

5. Which of the following is true about dementia?

    a.   It is a specific disease

    b.   All older adults will someday suffer from it

    c.   Should be differentiated from memory difficulty because of depression or anxiety

    d.   Thorough clinical examination or neuropsychological testing is not required for an accurate diagnosis

6. Which of the following medication is not prescribed for dementia?

   a. Aricept

   b. Exelon

   c. Nameda

   d. Ritalin

7. What are some psychological/emotional struggles that older adults with dementia may experience and need care for?

   a. Feeling helpless

   b. A deep sense of loss and sadness

   c. Agitation/shame

   d. Family's response

   e. All of the above

8. What are some important considerations for a church who is called to care for caregivers of older adults?

   a. Define and identify who the caregivers are

   b. Make sure the adult children take on the caregiver role

   c. Take on an empathic, non-judgmental approach

   d. a and c

   e. All of the above

9. Which of the following is *the* key predictor of a caregiver's stress level and adverse caregiving outcome?

   a. Intensity/type of caregiving tasks

   b. Caregiver's gender & ethnicity

   c. Caregiver's relationship with care recipient

   d. Care recipient's level of appreciation

10. Psychotherapeutic intervention(s) specifically useful for older adults:

    a. Cognitive-behavioral therapy

    b. Reminiscence therapy

    c. Emotional focused therapy

    d. Life review

    e. b and d

Level 3: Application

1. Write a 5-minute minisermon integrating what you have learned about aging with the wisdom of living an abundant life in the Bible.

2. A parishioner shares with you that her elderly mother has frequently been forgetting to turn off the stove recently. She says, "But mother's in her late 70s; we all forget things when we age." How might you talk to her about age-related memory loss versus probable dementia?

3. A parishioner in his 50s asks to meet you for pastoral counseling. He is concerned about his aging parents who live in another state. He feels conflicted that he has not been as involved in caring for them as his sibling. What questions might you ask to assess the situation? How might you help him sort through his ambivalence while offering information about the caregiver's role and the phases a caregiver typically goes through?

4. Describe a church-based caregiver ministry. What are some important aspects of the caregiver's role, needs, and risk factors for adverse caregiving outcome that should be included and addressed in the ministry?

5. An elderly widowed parishioner shares that her nephew helps her with chores. She has been giving him money to start his own business. What is your legal responsibility as clergy to report suspected elder mistreatment? What are the various types of elder mistreatment? How might you approach this situation with the woman to assess and monitor for possible financial exploitation by her nephew?

ANSWERS

LEVEL 1: KNOWLEDGE

1. F
2. F
3. T
4. F
5. T
6. F
7. T
8. T
9. F
10. F

LEVEL 2: COMPREHENSION

1. b
2. d
3. c
4. a
5. c
6. d
7. e
8. d
9. a
10. e

RESOURCES

Online Resources

- Alzheimer's Association—https://alz.org/
- National Institute on Aging—https://www.nia.nih.gov/
- APS, California (each state has its own website)—http://www.cdss.ca.gov/Adult-Protective-Services

Readings

- *Being Mortal: Medicine and What Matters in the End*—Atul Gawande
- *Ending Ageism, or How Not to Shoot Old People*—Margaret Morganroth Gullette
- *Baby Boomers and Beyond: Tapping the Ministry Talents and Passions of Adults over 50*—Amy Hanson
- *Aging with Grace: What the Nun Study Teaches Us About Leading Longer, Healthier, and More Meaningful Lives*—David Snowdon, PhD

Video Resources

- *The Brain-Changing Benefits of Exercise: TED Talks*—Ted.com https://www.ted.com/talks/wendy_suzuki_the_brain_changing_benefits_of_exercise
- *Share The Orange: Alzheimer's Research UK*—https://www.facebook.com/AlzheimersResearchUK/videos/1997871156897734/--

- *Experience 12 minutes in Alzheimer's Disease: abcNEWS.com*—https://youtu.be/LL_Gq7Shc-Y
- *Away from Her* (2006): Lions Gate, PG-13—A Canadian film about an older couple's struggles/experiences due to the wife's dementia.
- *Still Alice* (2014): Sony Pictures Classics—PG-13—A drama about the effects of early onset of AD on a highly educated woman and her family.
- *Bernie* (2011): Millennium Entertainment, PG-13—The true story of Bernie Tiede's caregiving relationship with/murder of a wealthy elderly woman.
- *The Best Exotic Marigold Hotel* (2011): 20th Century Fox, PG-13—In exotic India, various common issues/struggles in later life are portrayed.

CLASSROOM ACTIVITIES

1. Invite a panel of older adults and interview them about their experiences of aging and how they keep themselves physically, psychologically, and spiritually healthy.

2. Role-play a counseling session where a congregant is telling you about his or her frustration toward his or her elderly parent who has increasing problems with memory.

3. In small groups, share and discuss your feelings about your own aging and your experience of working with elders.

4. In small groups, share personal experiences (direct or observed) of being a caregiver for an elder.

REFERENCES

Alzheimer's Association (n.d.). Choosing a doctor to evaluate memory and thinking problems. Retrieved from https://www.alz.org/national/documents/topicsheet_choosingdoctor.pdf

American Psychiatric Association. (2013). *Diagnostic and statistical manual of mental disorders* (5th ed.). Washington, DC: Author.

Acree, L. S., Longfors, J. Fjeldstad, A. S., Fjeldstad, C., Schank, B., Nickel, K. J., Montgomery, P.S., &Gardner, A. W. (2006). Physical activity is related to quality of life in older adults. *Health and Quality of Life Outcomes, 4*(37), 1–6. doi: 10.186/1477-7525-4-37

Acton, G. J. (2002). Health-promoting self-care in family caregivers. *Western Journal of Nursing Research, 24*(1), 74–86.

Bakchine, S., &Blanchard, F. (2005). Diagnostic criteria for vascular dementia: a step towards new ones? *Psychogeriatrics, 4*(4), 127–129.

Bohlmeijer, E., Roemer, M., Cuijpers, P., &Smit, F. (2007). The effects of reminiscence of psychological well-being in older adults: A meta-analysis. *Aging & Mental Health, 11*(3), 291–300. doi: 10.1080/13607860600963547

Bonnie, R. J., & Wallace, R. B. (Eds.). (2002). *Elder mistreatment: Abuse, neglect, and exploitation in an aging America.* Washington, D.C.: The National Academies Press.

Bouman, W. P., Arcelus, J., & Benbow, S. M. (2006). Nottingham study of sexuality & ageing (No SSAl). Attitudes regarding sexuality and older people: A review of the literature. *Sexual and Relationship Therapy, 21(2),* 149–161.

Brown, J., Koffler, P., & Lutzus, L., (Producers) & Glatzer, R., & Westmoreland, W. (Directors). (2014). *Still Alice* [Motion Picture]. United States: Sony Pictures Classics.

Centers for Disease Control and Prevention. (2018). A Public Health Approach to Alzheimer's and Other Dementias. Retrieved from https://www.cdc.gov/aging/aginginfo/pdfs/Module2-Alzheimers-Other-Dementias-Basics.pdf

Centers for Disease Control and Prevention. (2015). At A Glance 2015. Retrieved from https://www.cdc.gov/chronicdisease/resources/publications/aag/healthy-aging.htm

Dovey, D. (2018, February 15). Alzheimer's disease is completely reversed by removing just one enzyme in new study. *Newsweek.* Retrieved from http://www.newsweek.com/alzheimers-disease-completely-reversed-removing-just-one-enzyme-new-study-807156

Drewnowski, A., & Evans, W. J. (2001). Nutrition, physical activity, and quality of life in older adults: Summary. *Journal of Gerontology, 56A* (11), 89–94.

Fry, P. S. (2001). The unique contribution of key existential factors to the prediction of psychological well-being of older adults following spousal loss. *The Gerontologist, 41(1),* 69–81.

Glotzer, L., Linklater, R., McFadezan, D., Mesvrve, D., Payne, J., Rattray, C., Shafer, M., Sledge, G., & Williams, M. (Producers). Linklater, R. (Director). (2011). *Bernie* [Motion Picture]. United States: Millennium Entertainment.

Gottlieb, B. H., & Wolfe, J. (2002). Coping with family caregiving to persons with dementia: A critical review. *Aging & Mental Health, 6(4),* 325–342. doi: 10.1080/1360786021000006947

Grief, C. J., & Myran, D. D. (2006). Bereavement in cognitively impaired older adults: Case series and clinical considerations. *Journal of Geriatric Psychiatry and Neurology, 19(4),* 209–215. doi: 10.1177/0891988706292753

Hardy, J., & Selkoe, D. (2002). The amyloid hypothesis of Alzheimer's disease: Progress and problems on the road to therapeutics. *Science, 297(5580),* 353–356. doi: 10.1126/science.1072994

Hartman-Stein, P. E., & Potkanowicz, E. S. (2003). Behavioral determinants of healthy aging: Good news for the baby boomer generation. *Online Journal of Issues in Nursing, 8(2),* 127–146.

Hubatkova, B. (2018). Number of roles and well-being among older adults in Czech Republic. *International Journal of Ageing and Later Life, 11(2),* 61–86. doi: 10.3384/ijal.1652-8670.16-323

Kueider, A., Bichay, K., & Rebok, G. (2014). Cognitive training for older adults: What is it and does it work? *Center on Aging, October 2014 Issue Brief,* 1-8.

Liao, S. (2007). The influences of attachment styles and religiousness/spirituality on forgiveness. (Unpublished doctoral dissertation). Biola University, La Mirada, CA.

McDougle, L., Konrath, S., Walk, M., & Handy, F. (2016). Religious and secular coping strategies and mortality risk among older adults. *Social Indicators Research, 125(2),* 677–694. doi: 10.1007/s11205-014-0852-y

McKhann, G., Drachman, D., Folstein, M., Katzman, R., Price, D., & Stadlan, E. M. (1984). Clinical diagnosis of Alzheimer's disease: Report of the NINCDS-ADRDA work group under the auspices of Department of Health and Human Services Task Force on Alzheimer's Disease. *Neurology, 34(7),* 939–944.

Mlinac, M. E., & Feng, M. C. (2016). Assessment of activities of daily living self-care, and independence. *Archives of Clinical Neuropsychology, 31(6),* 506–516. doi: 10.1093/arclin/acw049

Morris, J. C., Storandt, M., Miller, J. P., McKeel, D. W., Price, J. L., Rubin, E. H., & Berg, L. (2001). Mild cognitive impairment represents early-stage Alzheimer disease. *Archives of Neurology, 58(3),* 397–405.

Newson, R. S., Boelen, P. A., Hek, K., Hofman, A., & Tiemeier, H. (2011). The prevalence and characteristics of complicated grief in older adults. *Journal of Affective Disorders, 132(1-2),* 231–238. doi: 10.1015/jad2011.02.021

O'Bryant, S. E., Humphreys, J. D., Smith, G. E., Ivnik, R. J., Graff-Radford, N. R., Petersen, R. C., & Lucas, J. A. (2008). Detecting dementia with the mini-mental state examination (MMSE) in highly educated individuals. *Archives of Neurology, 65(7),* 963–967. doi: 10.1001/archneur65.7.963

Rheaume, C. and Mitty, E. (2008). Sexuality and intimacy in older adults. *Geriatric Nursing, 29(5),* 342–349.

Rhee, Y. S., Yun, Y. H., Park, S., Shin, D. O., Lee, K. M., Yoo, H. J. ... Kim, N. S. (2008). Depression in family caregivers of cancer patients: The feeling of burden as a predictor of depression. *Journal of Clinical Oncology, 26(36),* 5890–5895. doi: 10.1200/JCD.2007.15.3957

Schulz, R., & Eden, J. (Eds.) (2016). *Families caring for an aging America.* Washington, DC: The National Academies Press.

Telenius, E. W., Engedal, K., and Berglan, A. (2015). Effects of a high-intensity exercise program on physical function and mental health in nursing home residents with dementia: An assessor blinded randomized controlled trial. *PLoS ONE, 10(5),* 1–18. doi: 10.137/journal.pone.0126102

U. S. Census Bureau. (2014, May). *An Aging Nation: The Older Population in the United States* (Report No. P25-1140). Washington, DC: U.S. Government Printing Office.

Vann, M. R. (2016, August 1). The 15 most common health concerns for seniors. *Everyday Health.* Retrieved from https://www.everydayhealth.com/news/most-common-health-concerns-seniors/

IMAGE CREDITS

Fig. 14.1: Source: https://stocksnap.io/photo/KH9F6O9IH9.

Fig. 14.2: Copyright © 2013 Depositphotos/Londondeposit.

Pastoral Health and Responding to the Emotional Demands of Ministry

Robert Fisher, MS, LMFT

LEARNING OBJECTIVES

Upon completion of this chapter, readers will be able to

1. understand the complex nature of the role of pastor;

2. identify common motivations, expectations, and perceptions of pastors, and their impact;

3. define flourishing and the healthy habits associated with it; and

4. advocate for the creation of a network of care and support, collaborative leadership, resourcing, and engagement.

Being a pastor is a tough, demanding job, one that is not always very well understood or appreciated.
(Jackson Carroll, *God's Potters*, 2006, p. 2)

The life of ministry, by its very nature, cannot be stress free.
To believe otherwise is naïve at best, unbiblical at worst. Nor should it be stress free, for without challenge there can be no growth.
(Cameron Lee and Kurt Fredrickson, *That Their Work Will Be a Joy*, 2012, p. 25)

THE STORY OF PASTOR SAM

Sam is in his early 40s. He is married, and he and his wife have two teenaged children. When asked about his job as a pastor, he initially comments, "I love it! Can't imagine doing anything else. I mean, seriously, how lucky am I? I have the privilege of sharing God's love with a world in need each and every day." As our conversation deepens, however, Sam begins to paint a slightly different picture. "The hours can be long. I tend to be a bit of a perfectionist in my preparation, wanting to communicate as effectively and efficiently as

FIGURE 15.1   **Leading and living well**

possible. People today seem to have a short attention span. It seems as though, if you're not engaging them, they either tune you out or look elsewhere." I inquire a bit more, wondering about the effect this has on Sam. "It can be challenging. On the one hand, I know God is pleased with me. Yet, I can't help but compare myself, to other pastors as well as the heroes of our faith." In asking him who he is referring to, he mentions, "I don't know. Any of them, I guess. Abraham. Elijah. David. The apostles. The early church leaders. They had such a tremendous impact! No matter how hard I try, I feel like I'm falling short of their example. I'm either not creative enough, not faithful enough, not engaging enough, or all of the above." Acknowledging Sam's feelings of inadequacy, I inquire about his support system. "It's okay, I guess. My wife is supportive. The elders seem to care about me. And, I have a few close friends I can share with." Sam's countenance speaks of a broader experience, so I decide to press in a little further, asking him about the balance between ministry and family life. "It could be better. I try to be present and engaged when I'm home, but it's not easy. There's always more I could be doing. At church and at home."

Sam's story is not uncommon. Like many pastors, he is hard-working, kind, compassionate and faithful to the call God has placed on his life. He cares deeply for his church, the surrounding community, and God. He's a committed husband and father, loving and intentional. And he's sacrificial and generous with his time, giving wherever, and whenever, he is able. For these reasons and more, Sam is someone others gravitate toward. He is often invited to celebrate, mourn, and sit with others in their most tender of moments—experiences that lead Sam to describe himself as lucky, fortunate, or blessed.

At the same time, Sam is feeling overwhelmed, insecure, and exhausted. He does his best to attend to the myriad responsibilities he bears, but inevitably falls short. In the midst of these feelings and experiences, Sam questions his worth, value, and effectiveness. Why can't he manage all of this? How come others don't seem to be struggling? Is he doing something wrong? Has he somehow lost God's favor?

Sam's questions and experiences highlight the complex nature of vocational ministry.

The Complex Nature of Vocational Ministry

Pastors are called upon to serve a multitude of functions within the body of Christ, an experience Dr. Dan Allender describes as "diverse, disparate, and maddening" (Allender, February 2018). Expectations abound. They must be expert preachers, dynamic and engaging in their presentation of God's Word. Their lives and presence ought to draw others to Jesus, transforming congregations and communities in the process. They are to be warm, inviting, attentive, responsive, and available, ready to meet the spiritual, emotional, relational, and physical needs of those around them. Their staffs and churches should operate efficiently and effectively, free of conflict and abounding in grace. Their budgets are balanced; their church buildings are artistic and technologically advanced, and their meetings are productive, inspiring, and marked by God's presence. These expectations are inflated and unrealistic. However, they seem to capture the experience of many within ministry, that pastoring a local church is no small task. It "requires the knowledge of a social scientist and the insight and imagination of a poet, the executive talents of a business [leader] and the mental discipline of a philosopher" (Niebuhr, 1929, p. 173–174).

What Is the Pastor and What Do They Do?

In his work on The Flourishing in Ministry Project at the University of Notre Dame, Dr. Matt Bloom (2017b) notes, "pastoral work seems to require an **expert-generalist**, someone who is highly skilled at performing an extraordinarily wide range of tasks and activities" (p. 2). The problem, though, is that "most individuals, in fact, are **expert specialists**, highly skilled to perform some of these tasks, less skilled to perform others, and insufficiently skilled to perform others still" (Bloom, 2017b, p. 2). As a result of this tension between what seems to be required and what is possible, Bloom states that "forty percent of pastors report stress related to significant work demands" (Bloom, 2017b, p. 2).

Bloom (2017b) goes on to describe "six characteristics of pastoral work that may create potential challenges for the wellbeing of clergy" (p. 2–7).

1. Ministry is high-stakes work

2. Ministry work is complex, continuous, and diverse

3. Ministry work is punctuated by unexpected events

4. There is little structure or guidance for prioritizing ministry work

5. The downside of the turn toward more digital and less in-person communication

6. External change is rapid

By definition, pastoring implies engagement with others. And the earlier characteristics highlight the relational nature of leading a church—a church made up of people. Further examination of these characteristics seems to lead to another conclusion; people, and the lives they lead, are unpredictable. Plans change. Life happens. Unexpected, and often unwanted, circumstances arise. When they do, it seems those within the church, and sometimes those outside of it, turn to their pastor for help.

What they find, most often, is a person who desires to come alongside. For though there are many motivations among those who pursue the pastorate, somewhere among them is likely an affinity for God's children. It may manifest differently in each, but most pastors care about people, seemingly out of an awareness of our beauty as God's creation, or of our brokenness and God's longing to redeem and restore. This intersection between need and caring response is both beautiful and complex. When navigated well, with realistic and healthy expectations, gratitude and appreciation can result. When expectations and demands are high, however, and disappointment experienced, well-being can become compromised.

Sam seemed to find himself as this crossroad. He loved being a pastor and felt grateful for the opportunity to care for others. Most days, he felt successful. On occasion, though, he struggled to shake the feeling that he could be doing more, often triggered by disappointment. Time was not on his side. There weren't enough hours in the day to accomplish the tasks he had in mind when his day began **and** respond to the unanticipated needs of the congregation. By the time Sam found himself in my office, he was weary. The demands he placed upon himself, as well as those placed upon him by others, were more than he could bear, physically, emotionally, spiritually, and relationally. As a result, Sam was wondering whether he was cut out to be a pastor. His concern triggered a curiosity within me, prompting an examination of scripture regarding the role of a pastor within the local church.

In Ephesians 4:12, the apostle Paul lists pastors, along with apostles, prophets, evangelists, and teachers, as serving to "equip [Christ's] people for works of service, so that the body of Christ may be built up." The context of this passage, along with others in Romans 12 and 1 Corinthians 12, seems to suggest that pastors serve *certain* functions within a local church body, not all, and that each member of the body of Christ is unique and distinct in what they contribute to the health and well-being of the body as a whole. If that is true, how have we arrived at the conclusion that pastors ought to be *expert generalists*?

The Developing Role of the Pastor

An examination of scripture seems to turn up certain roles or responsibilities associated with the title of pastor. Beginning in the Old Testament and carrying through the New Testament, scripture presents the image of a shepherd, one who offers care, protection, and oversight (Stitzinger, 1995). In addition, various New Testament texts refer to pastoring as providing guidance, leadership, and teaching (Acts 15; Acts 20:28–31; 1 Cor. 12; Eph. 4; Phil. 1; 1 Tim. 2, 3, and 5; 2 Tim. 1:1–14; Titus 1; James 5; 1 Pet. 5). Scripture also highlights the importance of the heart (Prov. 4:23; Phil. 4:17) as well as the influence of the Spirit, manifesting in qualities such as love, comfort, compassion, wisdom, and boldness (Col. 3:12–15).

In the centuries that have followed, different emphases have surfaced. In the 1500s, Reformers highlighted preaching. In the 1600s, Puritans attended to the importance of healing the soul. In the 1700s, Methodists focused upon the value of community in nurturing spiritual health. In the 20 century, organizational health was a common pursuit. And, the 21 century has brought with it a renewed awareness of the need for evangelism and social justice (Shelley, 2016).

As the local church has directed its efforts to various causes, the role of pastor has become more complex *and* more specialized, depending upon the context within which one serves. In smaller churches, pastors are often expected to take on most, or all, of the roles listed previously. It is not uncommon for these smaller church pastors to preach, lead worship, facilitate small groups, offer pastoral care, and handle most of the administrative responsibilities associated with leading a church. Bivocationality, though not limited to pastors of smaller churches, can add another layer of complexity, increasing responsibilities in an effort to survive financially (Lee & Fredrickson, 2012).

Sam fell into this category, simultaneously juggling a number of responsibilities. As he shared about the impact of this multifaceted approach to ministry life, it became clearer as to why Sam was so exhausted. Throughout the course of a day or worship service, Sam was constantly shifting gears. By nature of his circumstances, he was required to continually adjust his mindset in preparation for the next task. The pressure to do them all well, and resulting anxiety associated with inevitably missing the mark, were becoming unsustainable.

Pastors within larger churches can have a different experience. Whereas smaller churches might expect their pastors to be expert generalists, larger churches seem inclined to adopt a specialized approach, staffed by a team of "experts," each with a unique area of focus (teaching, worship, youth, children, outreach, etc.). Though there appear to be substantial benefits to this approach, including the opportunity to lead out of one's strength and gifting, there may also be a number of drawbacks. Unlike smaller churches, where pastors seem to be "in touch" with their congregation members' needs, pastors within larger congregations may find themselves less familiar with the concerns of certain people within the church as their roles may be somewhat insulating. Other potential drawbacks could include feeling "stuck" in one's role, and facing the challenges associated with leading within the context of a team (prioritizing, casting vision, making decisions, and communicating collaboratively).

The shifting landscape of culture further complicates matters, forcing pastors into choppy, unfamiliar waters. They must learn how to engage a society that is highly technological, responding to rises in online church attendance and digitized communication. They must navigate the beliefs associated with consumerism, where value is determined by personal preference, entertainment, and comfort. Most significantly, they must do so in an age that is progressively post-Christian, where their opinions are often viewed as insignificant, irrelevant, antiquated, bigoted, insensitive, or extreme. Culturally, pastors are losing their influence, less often seen as beneficial members of local communities (Barna, 2017).

It is no wonder, then, that, like Sam, many pastors feel uncertain of their impact or unappreciated for their contributions to their communities. As we will see in the sections that follow, this uncertainty can lead to a variety of consequences. In Sam's case, it led him to work harder, putting in extra hours in an effort to accomplish more and prove his worth. When this proved unsuccessful in alleviating his anxiety, he felt discouraged and began to question God's call on his life, an experience that ultimately resulted in Sam reflecting on what it was that drew him to ministry years ago.

KEY TERMS

Expert-generalist: someone highly skilled at performing an extraordinarily wide range of tasks and activities

Expert-specialist: someone highly skilled to perform certain tasks, less skilled to perform others, and insufficiently skilled to perform others still

Discussion Questions

1   How would you define the role of pastor? How does this definition align with, or differ from, the responsibilities set forth in scripture?

2   What might be some of the dangers associated with the belief that pastors are to be expert generalists?

3   Why might vocational ministry be considered "high-stakes" work?

4   List some changes you have seen within culture that may affect the responsibilities, or experience, of a local pastor?

MOTIVATIONS, EXPECTATIONS, PERCEPTIONS, AND THEIR IMPACT

Sam grew up in the church. His parents were small group leaders and their home was a common meeting place for gatherings. Sam was relatively social and enjoyed the buzz around the house during these meetings. As he grew older, Sam became more curious about his own beliefs. Eventually, his curiosity morphed into questions and he found himself engaging in conversations with his youth leaders, friends, and a pastor at his church. Most aspects of the Christian faith made sense to him, but Sam had some nagging questions regarding God's character. Was God truly loving? Or dangerous? Could God be trusted? Was He reliable? Sam left home, attending college in a neighboring state. He visited a number of churches, one of which was deeply committed to local missions. Sam decided to volunteer one weekend and, in his own words, "Everything changed. I saw God at work, loving the needy through relationships. They appreciated the food and clothing that we brought, but it was the simple things that made the greatest difference. A smile or hug. Engaging in conversation. Taking an interest in their stories. Seeing them as people. That's what kept me coming back. That's what drew me in. A year later, it was clear. I wanted to be a pastor."

The "Call" to Vocational Ministry

Each pastor's journey into ministry is unique, impacted by a variety of influences, motivations, and experiences. While each path is distinct, there appear to be some common threads that "make answering God's call more likely" (Barna, 2017, p. 57).

One thread is the influence of God himself. Throughout scripture, God speaks to a number of individuals, calling them to follow him into lands and circumstances both known and unknown (Gen. 12, Exod. 3, 1 Kings 19, Judg. 6, Luke 1). In similar, yet different ways, many pastors have felt a **calling** from God. Whether audibly or experientially, directly or indirectly, they have experienced God leading, directing, and guiding them toward the pastorate. It might be described as the work of the Holy Spirit, a "gut" feeling, or an undeniable set of circumstances or an unanticipated chain of events, evidences of God's hand opening doors and removing obstacles previously thought of as immovable.

For many, the church has also played a role in their call to vocational ministry as attendance and involvement appear to set the stage for a likely greater influence: relationships. The pastors, youth leaders, volunteers and mentors that give of their time and energy, taking an interest in the lives of children and teens, leave a significant mark. The encouragement, intentionality, and relational presence offered through these experiences, coupled with their occurrence during the formative years of childhood and adolescence, likely contribute to the experience most pastors have of sensing their call to ministry between the ages of 14 and 21 (Barna, 2017).

In addition to the movement of God and the effect of the church, there also appear to be intrapersonal influences at work in one's pursuit of vocational ministry: factors such as temperament, personality, relational history, and attachment style. We may think of **temperament** and **personality** as hard-wired, part of our genetic makeup. **Relational history**, in contrast, is dynamic, a collection of our interactions with caregivers, friends and significant others. As discussed in earlier chapters, we integrate our relational experiences, examining how our emotional, physical, and relational needs were engaged with and responded to, our **attachment style** takes shape. The result is a tendency to operate out of a place of security, trust, and confidence, or insecurity, fear, and suspicion. In the former, the allure of ministry life may be an opportunity to give to others out of a place of fullness, an altruistic motivation. In the latter, there could be a desire to meet a previously unmet need, to repair a wound, or overcome a perceived deficiency, attempting to prove one's value, worth or significance. In these cases, ministry becomes more self-serving and, often, disappointing, and burdensome.

A number of factors contribute to one's decision to pursue God's call into vocational ministry. Regardless of the influences, what seems most important is an awareness of one's own process (what led *me* here) and the impact that has on one's experience of, and performance in, the role of pastor.

Expectations

"I came away from my childhood with a pretty accurate slogan for church ministry: *Where you control nothing and are responsible for everything*" (Kinnaman, in Barna, 2017). David Kinnaman's father was a pastor. He witnessed the joys and challenges of church ministry. In the process, it seems he arrived at the following conclusion: there are few roles that carry with them such lofty expectations as that of a pastor. Whether those expectations are fair or not, self-, other- or God-imposed, rooted in truth or misperception, pastors are seemingly forced to confront them or struggle under their immense weight.

When operating from a healthy core, pastors are able to acknowledge their limitations and humanness. They are able to differentiate between influence and control, recognizing their need for a Savior. When functioning from a place of unhealth, some pastors can lose sight of their finiteness. Rather than pointing others toward God, there is a misguided attempt to become like God, a process culminating in "doing *for* God" rather than "being *with* God" (Scazzero, 2015, p. 25).

When congregations struggle to differentiate between pastor and God, they, too, may begin to hurl unrealistic demands upon the pastor (Tripp, 2015). Rather than seeking care, support, or guidance, the expectation becomes, "heal me," "remove my burden," "fulfill my need," or "validate my worth." In essence, the pastor is thrust into the role of Savior, setting pastor and parishioner up for disappointment and disillusionment.

Sam knew these dynamics all too well. He understood that ministry brought with it certain complications. Sam was aware of the moral standards he was to embody and the biblical truths he was tasked with expounding upon. His love and passion for God, combined with his heart for people, inspired him to give, sacrifice and serve in hopes of revealing God to others. Initially, Sam felt successful. His ministry grew, and people were affirming of his efforts. Over time, Sam was faced with additional responsibilities, as well as a greater diversity of opinions and expectations among congregation members. Sam gradually realized he could no longer meet them all. He felt terrible. The weight of unmet expectations was influencing his view of himself, others, and God—a topic we'll explore in the next section.

Perceptions

Perceptions are our mental understandings, the result of experiences acting upon our beliefs. One might think of them as expressions of what we *believe* to be true, whether accurate or misguided. As pastors, it is important to examine one's own perceptions of God, self, and others, as well as the perceptions held by colleagues, congregations, board members and denominational leaders. Successfully navigating these perceptions results in one being grounded and self-aware. A lack of success in this area can lead to unending striving and feelings of guilt, shame, depression, and despair (Scazzero, 2015).

When unrealistic expectations become the standard, pastors are often left feeling as though they are not enough. The resulting self-criticism and contempt can lead to an inner dialogue filled with comments such as, "I could have done more," "I should have seen that coming," "I'm never going to get it right," or "I'm no longer fit to be a pastor." These self-defeating beliefs wreak havoc on a pastor's sense of identity and purpose, influencing their mood, decision-making, and relationships (Tripp, 2015).

At times, rather than blaming themselves, pastors may direct their judgments toward God or others. In regard to God, one might think, "God demands too much of me," or "God doesn't care … about me, this church, my congregation, the world." The result is a belief about God as distant, uncaring, or inaccessible. When the criticism is placed upon others, pastors may think, "They want me to fail," or "I wish they were someone else's problem." Thus, congregation members can become sources of frustration, leading some pastors to withdrawal and isolate amidst their contempt and bitterness.

Self-perceptions can also be overly positive. For instance, pastors might think too highly of themselves, taking too much credit for what went "right." In so doing, they may diminish the work of God and/or others, viewing themselves as responsible for the positive outcome. Congregations can be prone to feeding into this false belief, holding pastors in such high regard that they are placed on a pedestal, viewed as some form of superhuman (Lee & Fredrickson, 2012). This belief causes significant dangers for pastors and parishioners in that it separates the pastor from the body of Christ, no longer viewed as *a* member (like all others), but as *distinct*, other than, different from. The result is often a loss of community and an unspoken message that a pastor's life must somehow embody a level of sanctification and perfection that is unrealistic and unattainable. Sadly, this prohibits pastors from receiving the gift of being known and admonished, a gift the church was "designed to deliver" (Tripp, 2015, p. 88).

In those cases where a pastor is married and/or has a family, perceptions can extend beyond the pastor, to his or her family. Spouses and children may be viewed as an extension of the pastor and, therefore, held to a higher standard when it comes to lifestyle choices, behavior, and character. For some family members, it may seem as though their lives are to be free of the common struggles or challenges that others face. For others, there could be the sense that congregation members are watching their behaviors, as if they are living "in a glass house," their choices on display, prone to evaluation and interpretation by others. These experiences may culminate in pastors, or their family members, performing or pretending, fearful that their struggles, the struggles of a family member, or circumstances within their family or marriage may somehow threaten that pastors standing, and even job security, within the congregation.

This intense pressure, resulting from the heightened attention placed upon the life and choices of the pastor, or family member, stands in stark contrast to picture of dependence upon God painted in the Scriptures. Jesus describes himself as the vine, inviting his followers to abide in him. In the Old Testament, God often characterizes himself as a shepherd, a narrative Jesus also uses in John 10. Further, In Matthew 11, Jesus describes his yoke as "easy" and his burden as "light," the offer of rest standing as a stark contrast to the work that is involved in maintaining the perceptions described earlier. Throughout scripture, the narrative is clearly one in which God is at the center. Therefore, a healthy vision, as well as a healthy perception of a pastor by a congregation, is that of a man, or woman, in pursuit of God's best, seeking to be transformed while inviting others to join him or her in that process. Pastors are branches, connected to the vine. They are among God's sheep: reliant and dependent upon *God* to act.

Sam began to realize how much energy he had been putting into being not only above reproach, but near perfect. He acknowledged a constant striving—an effort to prove his worthiness to God, himself, and others. In the process, ministry had become a burden greater than he could bear. He saw God as disappointed, himself as a failure, and people to be avoided; the unconscious result of feeling overwhelmed and incapable of more. Sam was stressed, unsure of what to do or how to act. Somewhere along the way, he felt as though he had lost his identity and his joy. His tank was empty, and his reserves were spent; his well-being had become compromised.

Negative Impacts/Effects

Recent literature has pointed to some alarming trends related to pastoral health. When a pastor is unable to successfully navigate the complexities of ministry life, their experience of the pastorate often deteriorates, resulting in at least one of the following.

Performance and Perfectionism

Those pastors who align with the false belief that they must continually be doing more in an effort to satisfy the needs of every member of their congregation and/or prove their own value or worth often become performance oriented. They begin to measure success in ministry by how much they accomplish, or external factors such as church attendance, number of conversions, the size of their volunteer force, and giving (Scazzero, 2015). A number of challenges result, including a constant striving to be better, do more, or out-perform previous "successes." They begin to measure their own performance against that of other pastors and churches—a process complicated by the digitization of our society. Thus pastors who fall into the trap of comparing themselves to others not only have their neighboring pastors to contend with, but also the gifted preachers, teachers, and thinkers from around the globe.

Perfectionism raises performance to an entirely different level. It is no longer good enough to do more; rather, the requirement is to be without fault, a standard that no human being can live up to. In an attempt to validate one's worth to one's self, another, or God, these pastors seek to meet seemingly every need. They appear incapable of saying, "No," and, in so doing, require more of themselves than Jesus did during his time on Earth. Sadly, this striving can create a ripple effect, extending beyond the life of the pastor and into the lives of family members, fellow staff, leadership, and the congregation.

Compassion Fatigue and Vicarious Traumatization

Pastors are caregivers. Some more gifted than others, but all are expected to give of their time, energy, and resources to those who are in need. Pastors are sought out to pray for the sick, discouraged, and troubled; they are invited into deeply intimate moments such as weddings and funerals; they are pursued as wise counselors, and they are asked to serve as a triage and trauma experts in the midst of crises. Further, of the people in the United States seeking help for a serious mental illness, one-fourth approach their clergy person before anyone else (Wang, Berglund, & Kessler, 2003). Thus, not only are pastors invited into the suffering of others, they are often among the first ones called.

In addition to these personal hardships, pastors are also looked upon to respond to local, national, and global events—a request most view as a tremendous honor, not to mention a core component of their calling. As such, they willingly give of their time and resources, often making themselves, their staff, and their facilities available to those in need. Rarely, if ever, do they pause to examine the costs.

Over time, however, these experiences can pile up. When they do, the meaning and joy derived by offering care are slowly replaced by feelings of stress and exhaustion. Willful participation deteriorates into obligation and demand. It is precisely in these moments when, according to Matt Bloom (2013), pastors' transition from **positive sacrifice** to **negative sacrifice**. Positive sacrifice "is part of the experience of thriving, in part, because it confirms that we are giving our best to something profoundly important" (p. 16). Contrastingly, negative sacrifice "erodes well-being" as the individual "experiences too much stress, too much fatigue, and too many resource expenditures" (Bloom, 2013, p. 16). In other words, the individual is overcome by **compassion fatigue**, weary, and overwhelmed from the care and concern they have offered others.

Vicarious traumatization is the result of repeated exposure to the trauma of another. Pastors, although often unaware, experience this phenomenon frequently. As they respond to a death within their congregation, care for someone recounting abuse, enter the halls of a hospital, or intervene in a domestically violent situation, pastors find themselves staring into the face of human depravity. These encounters leave a mark. Commonly, pastors carry these trauma stories within their bodies, manifest as tension, lethargy, or reactivity. It seems as though, due to the powerful effect of mirror neurons, a pastor's brain may also be affected. These neurons blur the lines between what we see and what we do. "When we see someone else suffering or in pain, mirror neurons help us to read his or her facial expression and actually feel the suffering of the pain of the other person" (Iacoboni, 2009, p. 5). Thus, although the effect is not as great as it is for the individual who experienced the trauma firsthand, this secondary exposure appears to become encoded within the brain of the responder.

Isolation and Withdrawal

When left unattended, compassion fatigue and vicarious traumatization can trigger a decision to isolate and withdrawal. Parishioners, as well as family members, become objects to be avoided, either because of the demands for care that they may impose, or the lack of empathy and understanding they may display. In certain cases, pastors might turn their attention to God by way of prayer, meditation, and study. In more severe circumstances, they may be inclined to isolate completely, seeking comfort and distraction in other forms. The most common forms of escape seem to be television, social media, food, and work, although pornography and alcohol seem to be growing in prevalence. According to the self-reported figures in *The State of Pastors*, 1 in 5 pastors admits to struggling with an addiction, most commonly to pornography (Barna, 2017, p. 11). The decision to isolate and withdrawal has far-reaching consequences, and in those cases where addiction ensues, it may also lead to a growing sense of guilt and shame.

Depression and Burnout

Unfortunately, the downward spiral of exhaustion does not culminate in isolation and withdrawal. Rather, those experiences can devolve into a sense of despair and the belief that one's circumstances will never improve. The disappointments resulting from perfectionism, the exhaustion experienced in compassion fatigue, and the shame and guilt manifest in addiction can all give way to a feeling of depression and, worse still, **burnout**.

Though incidences of burnout vary, recent research has found that 33% of pastors report high to severe levels (Bloom, 2017c) and that 76% of pastors know at least one pastor who has burned out of ministry (Barna, 2017, p. 49). Even more alarming, there appears to be "some evidence of higher levels of burnout among pastors over 40, female clergy, and clergy of color" (Bloom, 2017c, p. 4).

Christina Maslach described burnout as "a psychological syndrome of emotional exhaustion, depersonalization, and reduced personal accomplishment that can occur among individuals who work with other people in some capacity" (Maslach, 1993, p. 19). According to Maslach and her colleagues, burnout is the result of "a gradual process of loss in which the mismatch between the needs of the person and the demands of the job grows ever greater" (Maslach and Leiter, 1997, p. 24). In regard to pastors, Lee and Fredrickson (2012) identify six potential mismatches related to pastors' workloads, their level of control, the rewards they receive for the work they do, the health of their congregations, potential conflicts in values, and issues of fairness.

Burnout results in a number of effects, its impact felt on emotional, relational, physical, spiritual, and financial levels (Adams, Hough, Proeschold-Bell, Yao, & Kolkin, 2016). In the midst of these challenging circumstance, pastors tend to attribute blame to themselves, overlooking the conditions that also contributed. This blame, it seems, breeds discouragement, discouragement breeds inadequacy, and inadequacy breeds uncertainty regarding their call to ministry (Lee & Fredrickson, 2014).

Physical Effects

In addition to the relational, emotional, and spiritual pitfalls common in vocational ministry, it appears some pastors also experience physical complications. Whether it is the sedentary nature of pastoring, the number of meetings involving a meal, a disregard for one's body, or simply poor lifestyle choices related to diet, exercise, and sleep, it seems as though vocational ministry can create a dangerous breeding ground for a number of health risks. Common among these are increased incidences of obesity, hypertension, and elevated cholesterol levels—circumstances that can place pastors at greater risk of heart disease, stroke, diabetes, arthritis, asthma, and other chronic diseases (Grey Matter Research and Consulting, 2003; Halaas, 2004; Lee & Fredrickson, 2014; Proeschold-Bell & LeGrand, 2012; Proeschold-Bell, et al., 2017).

Sam was ready for a change, unwilling to become yet another casualty of burnout, depression, or moral failure. The warning signs had captured his attention and ignoring them was no longer an option. Sam knew he had to become a better steward of the body God had given him and that he must adopt healthier rhythms or risk losing his life, and his family, and his ministry. Compelled by circumstances and motivated by hope, Sam's posture was now that of a humble pupil, aware of his limitations, open to direction, and ready to learn.

KEY TERMS

Calling: the experience one has of God leading, directing, and guiding toward a particular vocation or decision

Temperament and personality: hard-wired aspects of our being

Relationship history: the collective whole of our past interactions with others

Attachment style: the manner in which we interact with others that is influenced by our relationship history and the ability (or inability) of others to meet our relational needs

Perceptions: our mental understandings and expressions of what we *believe* to be true

Positive sacrifice: enhances well-being, giving our best to something profoundly important

Negative sacrifice: erodes well-being, giving more than we are able, experienced through stress fatigue and burnout

Compassion fatigue: weariness or exhaustion as a result of extended care and concern for others

Vicarious traumatization: the result of repeated exposure to the trauma of another

Burnout: "a psychological syndrome of emotional exhaustion, depersonalization, and reduced personal accomplishment" (Maslach, 1993, p. 19)

Discussion Questions

1   In what ways have you felt "called" by God in your pursuit of vocational ministry?

2   Describe how the following factors have influenced your decision to pursue a career as a pastor: experiences within a local church, temperament and personality, relational history, and attachment style.

3   What needs might you be seeking to meet through your role as a pastor?

4   Name some of the expectations you might place upon yourself as a pastor. Add to that list those expectations that a congregation member might impose. How might you differentiate between those expectations that are healthy and those that are not?

5   A number of pitfalls, or potential dangers, of ministry were covered in this section. What signs or symptoms might you need to look for in an effort to avoid them? If others were to point out some of these symptoms in your own life, how do you imagine you would respond? What factors might influence you to avoid or ignore their feedback? What factors would allow you to receive it?

TURNING THE TIDE

Although the dangers in the previous section are not experienced by *all* pastors and ministry leaders, their prevalence is great enough to motivate institutions such as Duke University and the University of Notre Dame to embark upon the Clergy Health Initiative and Flourishing in Ministry Project, respectively (Bloom, 2017a; Flourishing in Ministry Project, 2013; Proeschold-Bell & LeGrand, 2010). The goal of these endeavors, and others like them, is to draw attention to healthy lifestyle choices and patterns in an effort to enhance wellness and well-being among clergy.

Flourishing and Well-Being

According to researcher Matt Bloom (2017a), "flourishing happens when ministry is a life-enriching rather than life-depleting experience" (p. 3). Bloom goes on to differentiate between wellness (physical health) and **well-being** (psychological, social, and spiritual health). "Wellbeing is about a flourishing life," the product of what Bloom defines as **everyday happiness**, **resilience**, **self-integrity**, and **thriving**; "the building blocks of wellbeing" (Bloom, 2017a, p. 5–7). Everyday happiness, according to Bloom, is our subjective evaluation of our experiences, a system devised to aid in monitoring our well-being. Resilience encompasses our response system, the ability to integrate and adapt to our surroundings. Self-integrity is made up our identity, or self-concept—the result of knowing and accepting who we are and living authentically. The fourth component, thriving, emerges out of an ability to find meaning, purpose, and connectedness in life (Bloom, 2017a).

Insight and Self-Awareness

In our rapid-moving, technologically advanced society, productivity is highly valued. One of the many flaws of constant movement, however, is the inability, or unwillingness, to slow down and evaluate. Inherent in Bloom's concept of flourishing is knowledge of self, a characteristic deeply rooted in one's capacity to pause, reflect, and ponder—activities aimed at gaining insight into one's behavior and awareness of one's motivations. Healthy leaders demonstrate these qualities, structuring their lives in such a way as to ensure they remain a priority (Scazzero, 2015). They take the words of Proverbs 4:23 and 1 Timothy 4:16 seriously, recognizing that "the heart is the inescapable X-factor in ministry" (Tripp, 2015, 68).

As pastors grow in self-awareness, they begin to acknowledge their strengths and limitations, the good and bad parts of themselves. Their ability to own these qualities, incorporating them into a cohesive sense of self, fosters authenticity, humility, and compassion. Their reliance upon God is deepened—mindful that He alone is sovereign. Their emotional intelligence is heightened as they embrace the sensory nature of their existence. This gives rise to empathy, breathing new life into relationships, the workplace, and the pulpit. Self-awareness, one quickly realizes, is a gift that extends beyond the individual, making way for a more robust understanding of God, others, and life itself (see 2 Cor. 12:8–10).

Creating Healthy Habits

As pastors acknowledge their limitations, admitting their need for both God and others, they begin the process of establishing healthier rhythms and routines in life. This journey toward health looks different for each person. Inevitably, however, it involves struggle. Change, though necessary for growth, is difficult. It involves letting go of that which is familiar, known, and comfortable. There is pain, sacrifice, and setback. As such, it is important to acknowledge the significance of commitment, perseverance, grace, perspective, and the support of trusted others (Num. 11:16–17; John 14:26; John 16:33; Acts 4:32–36; Eph. 2:8–9).

Trusting God

In *Emotionally Healthy Leadership*, Peter Scazzero highlights the importance of slowing down to allow for "loving union" with God (Scazzero, 2015, p. 116). Using Jesus's life as the model, Scazzero reminds us that "Jesus spent ninety percent of his life—thirty of his thirty-three years—in obscurity," arguing that at least part of the greatness of Jesus's ministry was the result of time spent with God (Scazzero, 2015, p. 120–131). The implications of these words are twofold. First, healthy ministry life requires a relationship with God. Second, one must become comfortable with obscurity—a departure from a culture that currently values fame, popularity, and status.

Adopting New Rhythms

Relationship with God takes form in prayer: time alone with God, where a pastor's heart is gradually reshaped by God's presence. Relationship also draws the pastor into God's Word, for the purpose of transformation, not exegesis. The result is a renewed identity and an awareness of the value of attending to one's needs. Contemplative practices such as **lectio divina** and the **prayer of indifference** create space for pastors to listen for God's leading, fostering trust and reliance upon God's activity, not one's own (see Ruth Haley Barton's *Sacred Rhythms* for more on these practices). This process of letting go of control, becoming more self-reflective, and trusting in God's power and plans takes practice; and is tremendously freeing. Anxieties are lessened, pressures removed, and burdens lifted as pastors are reminded of God's authority and their limitations. As they successfully adopt this approach to life, they are able to hear, as Paul did, "My grace is sufficient for you, for my power is made perfect in weakness" (2 Cor. 12:9). Numbers 20:7–12 offers a bit of a contrast; while God is faithful, Moses' deviation from God's plan results in a missed opportunity. In both examples, we are reminded that the best outcomes result when leaders rely upon God's strength, not their own.

As a pastor's relationship with God is placed in its proper place, priorities begin to shift. The pastor realizes the importance of Sabbath rest, intended to restore, and revitalize. As they tend to their souls, they become more aware of their bodies and the value of exercise, nutrition, and sleep. Thus they begin to adopt healthier rhythms, more conscious of their diet, activity levels and work-life balance. Within this process, they become more aware of their relational needs and the value of both knowing and being known by others. For some, this may take shape within the context of a Soul

Care group, a facilitated gathering of fellow pastors wherein the goal is transparency, encouragement and mutual submission to God's purposes and plans. Regardless, as a pastor begins to engage, experience, and explore their own needs, the needs of significant others come into focus, improving the quality of relationship with spouses, children, friends, and congregations (Bloom, 2017d; Bloom, 2017e; Lee & Fredrickson, 2012; Scazzero, 2015).

Patience in the Process

It bears repeating, these habits take time to cultivate. They require determination, commitment, and sacrifice. There will be setbacks and disappointments, during which the temptation to fall back into old ways of being will be great. Past hurts will surface, and doubts will be raised—invitations to believe that this process is simply too hard. Pastors who are able to navigate these choppy waters come to realize this: these are the realities of being human. Life brings joy and struggle, heartache and healing. Therefore, they rest in the same gospel and saving grace they so often preach, finding comfort in the words of John 16:33 and Romans 5:1–5, aware that God is good and ever-faithful (Tripp, 2015).

1 Kings 19 provides a beautiful example of this dynamic, transformative process. As Elijah flees into the wilderness, fearful as his life is in danger, God attends to his physical, spiritual, and relational needs. First, he provides bread and water, highlighting the importance of Elijah's body, the vessel he has been given in order to do the work to which God has called him. Second, through a gentle whisper, God reminds Elijah that he is neither forgotten nor alone. Third, God provides a companion, Elisha, with whom Elijah can share his joys and sorrows, accomplishments, and defeats—one whom he can teach and, ultimately, relinquish his responsibilities to. Pastors would be wise to structure their lives similarly, taking time to care for their bodies (diet, exercise, rest), souls (nurturing their relationship with God), and relationships (sharing in the ups and downs experienced in life).

KEY TERMS

Well-being: referring to one's psychological, social, and spiritual health—influenced by everyday happiness, resilience, self-integrity, and thriving

Lectio divina: scripture reading and meditation for greater understanding of and closeness to God

Prayer of indifference: "Not my will, but thy will be done," Mary's "Fiat," or other prayers and scripture passages designed to increase reliance upon God

1   How might the diversity of experiences associated with pastoring affect pastors' everyday happiness? What might they do to foster a more positive experience of their day?

2   Self-awareness was presented as a vital component of becoming healthy. Why might that be? What are some characteristics of someone who is self-aware and why might they be beneficial in vocational ministry?

3   Describe potential experiential differences between approaching scripture in order to listen for God, rather than learn about God.

4   Why must one be patient in this process of becoming healthy?

STRONGER TOGETHER

As pastors embrace their identity in Christ, they begin to recognize the immense value of leading alongside others: leading in the context of community. An awareness of their finiteness seems to pave the way for the creation of healthy **boundaries**—structures intended to assist pastors in living out of the realities of time, gifting, and resources. As these boundaries take shape, pastors become aware that others may be better suited to navigate, speak into, or lead conversations regarding particular circumstances, scenarios, or topics. They are able to realize that they are, in fact, expert specialist and that the body of Christ is filled with other expert specialists. Paul's words in Romans 12 and 1Corinthians 12 take flight, recognizing that we are meant to complement, not compete with, one another.

Collaboration and Partnership

Healthy pastors collaborate. They partner with others, recognizing the value of a team approach (Barna, 2017; Bloom, 2017d; Bloom, 2017e). Jesus offers the greatest example. Jesus was reliant and dependent upon the Father. He surrounded himself with a core group of twelve, along with many others. He embraced his role, his purpose, his mission. And, he affirmed the value, goodness, and influence of those around him, bearing witness to the unique calling placed upon each. Jesus was not threatened by the success of others. Rather, he embraced and encouraged it, delighting in the expansion of the Kingdom— aware of the impact his followers, through the power of the Holy Spirit, were capable of having. Jesus's disciples bought in. They worked together in pursuit of that which Jesus had modeled, confident in what they had seen and experienced. Today's pastors are invited to do the same, joining together in a common pursuit, serving one another—conscious that they are stronger together than they are alone.

Collaboration takes many forms. Within each local church, education and empowerment are key. Given a consumer culture where individuals are conditioned to be served, this may require gentleness, time, and intentionality. Some church members may need to be reminded that they, too, are called to serve. Others may need encouragement, followed by an invitation to share their gifts with others. Training programs may need to be developed; leadership teams assembled. Over time, this will result in the *church* being the church, actively participating together to meet the needs of the community. In addition, it "will lighten [the] pastor's burden in ways that will benefit the health of the whole congregation" (Lee & Fredrickson, 2012, p. 20).

Collaboration extends beyond the walls of the church as pastors reach out for wisdom and guidance, drawing upon the experience and expertise of others. This may involve a phone consultation with a local therapist in an effort to process a difficult situation. Or, it could be represented in a pastor teaming up with local churches in an effort to provide a needed resource to the community. Whatever the form, partnering is a reminder of our interdependence, an antidote to isolation and competition.

Resourcing

The needs of our communities are greater than any one pastor, or church, can meet. One benefit to collaboration is the identification, and creation, of a network of support. Pastors need partners to serve *with*; however, they also need individuals, organizations, and resources to *refer to*. As parishioners present their needs, pastors must evaluate which ones they are well-positioned to meet, and which are beyond the scope of their training, experience availability, passion, or expertise. (According to Barna's [2017] research, pastors feel least equipped in the areas of counseling, administration and conflict and are less satisfied with their jobs when called upon to respond in these areas.) In such cases, both pastor and parishioner are better served through a referral to a trusted other, whether that be a fellow pastor, mental health provider, physician, community clinic, recovery program, shelter, website, or print material. Creating a system of referral sources requires time, energy and intentionality as pastors care deeply for their congregation members and, as such, must be convinced that the care offered by the referring party aligns with their values, beliefs, and church culture. Once established, however, these resources allow for greater care while also assisting pastors in operating out of their strengths, alleviating many of the pressures they experience when attempting to resolve issues they may feel ill-equipped to handle.

KEY TERMS

Boundaries: structures intended to assist pastors in living out of the realities of time, gifting, and resources

Collaboration: partnering with others in meeting the needs of a local church; it stems from an understanding of the diversity of giftedness represented in the body of Christ

Discussion Questions

1   Discuss the potential benefits and challenges of leading in a collaborative manner.

2   As a group, identify ten needs congregation members may present to their pastor(s). Which of these needs may be better met by someone other than the pastor? Who might that pastor partner with? How might this partnership be communicated to the congregation member? What would the role of the pastor be in this process?

LEADING AND LIVING WELL

In his article "The Stages of Ministry," researcher Matt Bloom (2017d) draws upon the image of a theatre as a metaphor for the role social support plays in a pastor's well-being. In describing the dynamics of the front, back, and off stages, Bloom creatively advocates for the presence of unique and specific others in an effort to promote flourishing. In so doing, Bloom invites pastors to cease pretending and, rather, lead a life characterized by **authenticity**. This invitation extends to the congregation as well, a call to look upon one's pastor as a person, rather than an actor, performer, or miracle worker.

Relationships

Pastors need friends, people they can open up to and be real with (Barna, 2017). They need spaces where they can explore and express the joys and frustrations of ministry, free from expectation, judgment, or shame. They need people who understand them, who have walked in their shoes, experienced the complex nature of their profession, and are able to offer empathy in response. Bloom (2017d), describes these individuals as "wise guides," "similar others who can empathize," a pastor's most significant source of support (Bloom, 2017d, p. 5–6). Finally, pastors need to have fun. They need to laugh, play, and explore their surroundings, free from the pressures of leading, caring, teaching, and serving others. If they are able to do so, they experience joy, longevity, and rest. They become **resilient**—a far cry from the burnout, exhaustion, and discouragement they encounter when isolated.

Pastors must also feel cared for by their congregation. Though the pastor serves a unique function within the local church, he or she remains a member of that church body. Therefore, it is imperative that the pastor experience a sense of connection, of being known, and is afforded the same grace, forgiveness, and understanding that is embodied among other congregation members. Few relationships have a greater influence on a pastors' ability to flourish than the relationship between a pastor and his or her local church (Barna, 2017; Bloom, 2017e; Lee & Fredrickson, 2012). Fostering this relationship requires two primary ingredients: a healthy congregation and a self-aware pastor. Congregations would do well to view their pastor as a person, offering them grace, loving them with compassion, and pursuing them with kindness. Pastors must be willing to acknowledge their humanity, needs, and limitations. As pastors identify safe people (individuals whom they trust) within a relationally healthy congregational climate, they are afforded the opportunity to ask for support and encouragement in times of need, freed from the fears that previously drove them into isolation.

Awareness and Engagement

Pastors benefit from an awareness of, and engagement with, the world around them. As leaders within their local communities, involvement in their neighborhoods and cities affords them opportunities to embody Christ's love to a world in need. Many pastors serve as chaplains for their local fire or police department. Some serve on city councils. And others invest in the lives of children and families as coaches, tutors, or mentors. In each and every circumstance, these pastors are demonstrating that their care extends beyond the walls of the churches they lead and into the public arena (fulfilling the great commission). As they do so, demonstrating compassion, kindness, and humility, they may be invited to speak into various cultural issues. Thus it is essential that pastors study and engage culture so that, when called upon to address a topic, they are able to offer an informed perspective. In living and leading in this manner, pastors are teaching their congregations how to meaningfully converse in a world desperately in need of hope and wisdom.

KEY TERMS

Authenticity: being true to one's self and no longer pretending or performing

Resilient: able to integrate and adapt to one's surroundings

Engagement: involvement in local neighborhoods and cities, affording pastors opportunities to embody Christ's love to a world in need

Discussion Questions

1   In your own words, define resiliency. What factors might contribute to a pastor's resiliency?

2   Discuss the interconnectedness between pastor and congregation. Why must both be healthy in order for a church, and pastor, to flourish?

3   Is it necessary for a pastor to engage the world around them? Why or why not? What might be some of the benefits, or joys? What might be some of the drawbacks, or struggles?

SUMMARY

We are relational beings, made in the image of God. As such, that which affects us is also likely to have an impact on those around us. Applied to pastors, this means that their well-being impacts, influences, and effects the well-being of those around them. If a pastor is struggling, there is likely a ripple effect upon their staff, congregation, family, and community. If a pastor is flourishing, this too seeps into the milieu of their spheres of influence. In this chapter, we have linked a pastor's well-being to a number of factors, primarily their physical, emotional, spiritual, and relational health. In order to flourish, pastors must pay attention to the condition of their heart, for their calling brings with it great responsibility.

Imagine, for a moment, a well, fed by an underground stream, full of fresh, pure, clean water. When functioning as intended, the well gives life to those who drink from it, becoming a source of strength, security, and longevity. If, however, the well is cut off from the stream, it becomes stagnant, susceptible to impurities or contamination.

Pastors are a well, of sorts. If they become isolated and disconnected from God, their well can become poisoned. Inevitably, their churches suffer as people become disillusioned, malcontent, and malnourished. Some may wither away. Others may revolt, breeding dissension. Many will leave. Those that are healthy and connected to *the* source of life will find a new well. Those who are not, sadly, will either give up their search or carry their disease to the next well, jeopardizing its health and vitality.

When pastors and their churches are fed by God, their communities thrive, full of purpose, hope, and meaning.

> May our pastors remain deeply connected to God. May He fill them to overflowing, pouring out his presence on their friends, families, congregations, and communities. May He structure their lives in a manner that fosters health, complete with healthy rhythms and trusted relationships. And may He affirm their identity and the value of authenticity, collaboration, and interdependence. Amen.

REVIEWING THE CONCEPTS

Learning Objectives

- Understand the complex nature of the role of pastor
  - Pastors are expert specialists who are often expected to be expert generalists, able to exceed at performing a wide variety of tasks.
  - The role of pastor has developed over time, influenced by the shifting landscape of culture.
  - The complexity of the role can leave some pastors feeling uncertain and insecure.

- Identify common motivations, expectations and perceptions of pastors, and their impact
  - Common motivations include God (a sense of "calling"), participation in a local church as a child, innate qualities such as temperament and personality, and intrapersonal experiences forming one's relational history and attachment style.
  - Expectations abound and, left unchecked, can suffocate or imprison a pastor.
  - Self-perceptions related to worth or value, combined with the perceptions of others to be more than human, can result in an independence that stand in contrast to the dependence upon God, and others, represented in scripture.
  - When left unattended, unhealthy motivations, expectations, and perceptions can result in negative impacts, including performance and perfectionism, compassion fatigue and vicarious traumatization, isolation and withdrawal, depression and burnout, and physical health concerns

- Define flourishing and the healthy habits associated with it
  - Flourishing results when ministry is life-enriching, determined by one's everyday happiness, resilience, self-integrity, and thriving.
  - Insight and self-awareness allow a pastor to acknowledge their strengths and limitations, fostering reliance upon God and others.
  - The healthy habits of flourishing pastors include trusting God through prayer, scripture meditation, and Sabbath, and identifying and prioritizing one's needs.
  - This process requires time and patience, determination and sacrifice.

- Advocate for the creation of a network of care and support, collaborative leadership, resourcing, and engagement
  - Congregational needs are greater than any one person can meet; healthy pastors lead within the context of community.
  - Collaboration involves empowering congregation members to serve, seeking guidance from local professionals, and partnering with other pastors.
  - Pastors need friends: "wise guides" have the greatest impact.
  - As pastors engage the needs of their communities, they are better positioned to offer hope, wisdom, and care when it is needed most.

Chapter Review Questions

Level 1: Knowledge (True/False)

1. Forty percent of pastors report stress related to significant work demands.

2. The role of a pastor is unchanging, the same today as in the past, unaffected by church size, geographic location, and cultural context.

3. According to Barna research, the majority of pastors attended church as children, were involved in their youth ministry as teens, and experienced a call to ministry between the ages of 14 and 21.

4. Performance-oriented pastors are less likely to measure success in ministry based on accomplishments, church attendance, giving, and volunteer force.

5. It is not uncommon for pastors to be among the first responders in circumstances involving loss, tragedy, or mental illness.

6. Positive sacrifice erodes well-being as stress builds, fatigue sets in, and resources are depleted.

7. Pastors can experience vicarious traumatization in their care-giving efforts, in part because of to the powerful effect of mirror neurons.

8. Most pastors feel well equipped in the areas of counseling, administration, and congregational conflicts.

9. The support of family members has the greatest effect on a pastor's well-being.

10. Pastors and the churches they serve are deeply interconnected: the health of one greatly affects the health of the other.

Level 2: Comprehension

1. According to researcher Matt Bloom, ministry work is:

   a. unpredictable

   b. complex

   c. high-stakes

   d. all of the above

2. The 21st-century church has experienced a renewed awareness of the need for

   a. healthy organizational structure, systems, and policies

   b. dynamic preaching and collaborative leadership

   c. evangelism and social justice

   d. spiritual health and healing the soul

3. Which of the following is **not** among the cultural changes pastors must navigate?

   a. Consumerism

   b. Loss of influence

   c. Accusations of insensitivity and irrelevance

   d. Increased requests for face-to-face meetings

4. _____ and _____ are innate qualities, whereas _____ and _____ are the result of experiences.

   a. temperament, personality; relational history, attachment style

   b. relational history, attachment style; temperament, personality

   c. performance, perfectionism; isolation, withdrawal

   d. depression, anxiety; burnout, compassion fatigue

5. According to self-reported figures in *The State of Pastors*, 1 in 5 pastors admit to struggling with an addiction, most commonly to

    a. their work

    b. pornography

    c. alcohol

    d. food

6. According to Christina Malasch, burnout involves all of the following, **except**

    a. emotional exhaustion

    b. depersonalization

    c. reduced personal accomplishment

    d. depression

7. Based on research conducted as part of Duke University's Clergy Health Initiative, pastors experience higher than normal levels of

    a. loneliness and isolation

    b. guilt and despair

    c. heart disease and cancer

    d. obesity and chronic diseases

8. Among the four building blocks of well-being are

    a. insight and self-awareness

    b. collaboration and partnership

    c. resilience and thriving

    d. everyday happiness and authenticity

9. A facilitated group experience, aimed at fostering transparency, encouragement, and reliance upon God among pastors is called

    a. Soul Care

    b. Prayer of indifference

    c. Mentoring

    d. Collaboration

10. According to researcher Matt Bloom, and research conducted by Barna, the following have the greatest influence on a pastors' ability to flourish:

    a. Family members and denominational leaders

    b. Similar others and the relationship between pastor and congregation

    c. Contemplative practices and boundaries

    d. Sabbath rest and fun

Level 3: Application

1. Describe the similarities and differences between pastoring a small and large church. Be sure to include the challenges inherent in each as well as potential benefits.

2. According to Barna research, 76% of pastors know at least one pastor who has burned out of ministry. In your own words, discuss why this number so high? What are the main predictors of burnout? And, how can it be combated?

3. How are technology and consumerism changing the way pastors, and churches, function? List and describe three approaches you would view as a healthy response to their influence.

4. Pastors need friends. Primary among them are "wise guides" or similar others. Why are these individuals such a valuable resource for pastors and clergy? What do they offer that is unique and distinctive? Use two examples from scripture to support your argument.

5. Collaboration and partnership are essential for health in vocational ministry. Yet many pastors feel overwhelmed by the weight of expectations and demands. What factors might prevent a pastor from asking for help when they need it? How might a pastor overcome these factors? Incorporate the imagery of the body of Christ (1 Cor. 12) into your response.

ANSWERS

LEVEL 1: KNOWLEDGE

1. T
2. F
3. T
4. F
5. T
6. F
7. T
8. F
9. F
10. T

LEVEL 2: COMPREHENSION

1. d
2. c
3. d
4. a
5. b
6. d
7. d
8. c
9. a
10. b

RESOURCES

Online Resources

- University of Notre Dame's Flourishing in Ministry—http://wellbeing.nd.edu/flourishing-in-ministry/
- Duke University's Clergy Health Initiative—https://divinity.duke.edu/initiatives/clergy-health-initiative
- Rick Warren—http://pastors.com
- Soul Shepherding—https://www.soulshepherding.org
- Barna—https://www.barna.com
- Life.church—https://open.life.church
- The Allender Center—https://theallendercenter.org
- Center for Vocational Ministry, Azusa Pacific University—https://www.apu.edu/vocational-ministry/

Readings

- *That Their Work Will Be A Joy: Understanding and Coping With The Challenges of Pastoral Ministry*—Cameron Lee and Kurt Fredrickson
- *The Emotionally Healthy Leader*—Peter Scazzero
- *Leading With A Limp*—Dan Allender
- *Strengthening The Soul of Your Leadership*—Ruth Haley Barton

Video Resources

- Q Conferences—http://qideas.org/videos/r/
- Right Now Media—https://www.rightnowmedia.org

CLASSROOM ACTIVITIES

1. Brainstorm current perceptions of pastors (and the church). Identify potential motivations for these perceptions (based on historical events) and helpful ways to engage those who hold these perceptions.

2. Compare and contrast the church as it was in the 1st century to the church now. Is there a tendency to romanticize the early church? If so, why? In what ways might the early church have struggled? Why might we overlook these struggles?

3. Compose a list of the factors that might contribute to a pastor's resiliency.

4. Write a letter to your pastor, thanking him or her for the ways in which he or she has had a positive effect on you and/or have led the church well in the midst of difficult circumstances.

5. We are prone to perceive others' jobs as easier than they are. How might this apply to pastors? What might their congregation members perceive as simple that, in actuality, might be more complex?

6. Compare and contrast different biblical leaders (Moses, Joseph, David, Ruth, Esther, Mary, Jesus, Peter, Paul). What do they have in common? What is unique about them? What can you learn from their experiences?

7. Bivocationality is on the rise. Why might this be? How might this impact pastors?

8. Discuss the pros and cons of collaboration.

REFERENCES

Adams, C; Hough, H; Proeschold-Bell, R.; Yao, J.; & Kolkin, M. (2016, July). Clergy burnout: A comparison study with other helping professions. *Pastoral Psychology*. DOI: 10.1007/s11089-016-0722-4

Allender, D. (2018). "Vicarious Traumatization" as presented at CIFT Counseling Pastors' Forum. http://ciftcounseling.com/wp-content/uploads/2018/02/Dan-Allender.mp3

Barna (2017). *The state of pastors*. Ventura, CA: Author.

Barton, R. (2006). *Sacred rhythms: Arranging our lives for spiritual transformation*. Downers Grove, IL: Inter-Varsity Press.

Bloom, M. (2013). "Flourishing in Ministry: Emerging Research Insights on the Well-Being of Pastors." https://workwellresearch.com/media/images/Emerging%20Insights.pdf

Bloom, M. (2017a). "Flourishing in Ministry: Clergy, Ministry Life and Wellbeing." https://workwellresearch.com/media/images/FIM%20Flourishing%20in%20Ministry_8JZszRH.pdf

Bloom, M. (2017b). *A burden too heavy?* Retrieved from https://workwellresearch.com/media/images/FIM%20Report%20Workload.pdf

Bloom, M. (2017c). Burning out in ministry: Research insights from the flourishing in ministry project. Retrieved from https://workwellresearch.com/media/images/FIM%20Report%20Burnout.pdf

Bloom, M. (2017d). The stages of ministry: Research insights from the flourishing in ministry project. Retrieved from https://workwellresearch.com/media/images/FIM%20Report%20Stages%20of%20Ministry_YusOEKp.pdf

Bloom, M. (2017e). Never alone: Social support and flourishing in ministry: Research insights from the flourishing in ministry project. Retrieved from https://workwellresearch.com/media/images/FIM%20Social%20Support_rtj181y.pdf

Carroll, J. (2006). *God's potters: Pastoral leadership and the shaping of congregations.* Grand Rapids, MI; Eerdmans Publishing.

Flourishing in Ministry Project (2013). *Emerging research insights on the well-being of pastors.* South Bend, IN: Creative Commons through the University of Notre Dame. https://workwellresearch.com/media/images/Emerging%20Insights.pdf

Grey Matter Research (2003, August 1). Just how healthy is the typical pastor? Retrieved from http://www.greymatterresearch.com/index_files/Pastor_Health.htm

Halaas, G. (2004). *The right road: Life choices for clergy.* Minneapolis, MN: Augsburg Fortress Publishers.

Iacoboni, M. (2008). *Mirroring People: The Science of Empathy and How We Connect with Others.* New York, NY: Picador.

Lee, C., & Fredrickson, K. (2012). *That their work will be a joy: Understanding and coping with the challenges of pastoral ministry.* Eugene, OR: Wipf & Stock Publishers.

Maslach, C. (1993). Burnout: A multidimensional perspective. In W.B. Schaufeli, C. Maslach, & T. Marek (Eds.), *Professional burnout: recent developments in theory and research* (pp. 19–32). Philadelphia: Taylor & Francis.

Maslach, C. and Leiter, M. (1997). *The Truth About Burnout: How Organizations Cause Personal Stress and What to Do About It.* San Francisco, CA: Jossey-Bass.

Niehbuhr, R. (1929). *Leaves from the Notebook of a Tamed Cynic.* Reinhold Niebuhr.

Proeschold-Bell, RJ, & LeGrand, S. (2010). High rates of obesity and chronic disease among United Methodist clergy. *Journal of the Obesity Society.* https://onlinelibrary.wiley.com/doi/abs/10.1038/oby.2010.102

Proeschold-Bell, R. J., Turner, E.L., Bennett, G.G., Yao, J., Li, X., Eagle, D.E., ... and Toole, D.C. (2017). A 2-Year holistic health and stress intervention: Results of an RCT in clergy. *American Journal of Preventative Medicine,* 53(3), 290–299. Retrieved from http://www.ajpmonline.org/article/S0749-3797(17)30244-1/fulltext

Scazzero, P. (2015). *The emotionally healthy leader.* Grand Rapids, MI: Zondervan Publishing Company.

Shelley, M. (May 2016). The ever-broadening role of the pastor. *Christianity Today.* Retrieved from http://www.christianitytoday.com/pastors/2016/may-web-exclusives/ever-broadening-role-of-pastor-.html

Stitzinger, J. (Fall 1995). Pastoral ministry in history. *The Master's Seminary Journal,* 6(2(, 143–180l. https://www.tms.edu/m/tmsj6f.pdf

Tripp, P. (2015). *Dangerous calling.* Wheaton, IL: Crossway Publishing.

Wang, P.S., Berglund, P.A., & Kessler, R.C. (2003). Patterns and correlates of contacting clergy for mental health disorders in the United States. *Health Services Research* 38(2), 647–673.

IMAGE CREDITS

Index

CPSIA information can be obtained
at www.ICGtesting.com
Printed in the USA
BVHW012209060922
646391BV00011B/303